BEYOND THE SITE

Regional Studies in the Aegean Area

Edited by
P. Nick Kardulias
Kenyon College

UNIVERSITY
PRESS OF
AMERICA

Lanham • New York • London

Copyright © 1994 by
University Press of America® Inc.
4720 Boston Way
Lanham, Maryland 20706

3 Henrietta Street
London WC2E 8LU England

Library of Congress Cataloging-in-Publication Data

Beyond the site : regional studies in the Aegean area /
edited by P. Nick Kardulias.
p.   cm.
Papers presented at an invited session sponsored by the Society for the
Anthropology of Europe at the 90th annual meeting of the American
Anthropological Association held in Chicago, Nov. 24, 1991.
Includes bibliographical references and index.
1. Aegean Sea Region—Antiquities—Congresses.
2. Ethnoarchaeology—Aegean Sea Region—Congresses.
I. Kardulias, P. Nick.   II. Society for the Anthropology of
Europe (U.S.)
DF261.A177B49   1994   939'.1—dc20   94–19443 CIP

ISBN 0–8191–9632–0 (cloth : alk. paper)
ISBN 0–8191–9633–9 (pbk. : alk. paper)

Αφιερωμένο στούς γονείς μού, Δρόσο καί
Θεωδοσία, μέ άπειρη αγάπη καί εκτίμηση

List of Contributors

Sytze Bottema
Biologisch-Archaeologisch
  Instituut
Rijksuniversiteit Groningen
Faculteit der Letteren, Postraat 6
9712 ER Groningen, Netherlands

Claudia Chang
Department of Anthropology and
  Sociology
Sweet Briar College
Sweet Briar, Virginia 24595

John F. Cherry
Department of Classical Studies
University of Michigan
Ann Arbor, Michigan 48109-1360

Mark A. Dann
1038 Parkway Drive
Columbus, Ohio 43212

Jack L. Davis
Department of Classics
University of Cincinnati
Cincinnati, Ohio 45221-0226

Myra J. Giesen
1034 Hilltop Drive
Lawrence, Kansas 66044

Timothy E. Gregory
Department of History
365 Dulles Hall
The Ohio State University
Columbus, Ohio 43210

Julie M. Hansen
Department of Archaeology
Boston University
Boston, Massachusetts 02215

P. Nick Kardulias
Department of
  Anthropology/Sociology
Kenyon College
Gambier, Ohio 43022-9623

John C. Kraft
Department of Geology
University of Delaware
Newark, Delaware 19716-2544

Daniel J. Pullen
Department of Classics
Florida State University
Tallahassee, Florida 32306-4031

George (Rip) Rapp, Jr.
Archaeometry Laboratory
University of Minnesota
Duluth, Minnesota 55812-2496

David S. Reese
Department of Anthropology
Field Museum of Natural History
Chicago, Illinois 60605

Joseph L. Rife
Department of Classical Studies
University of Michigan
Ann Arbor, Michigan 48109-1360

Curtis N. Runnels
Department of Archaeology
Boston University
Boston, Massachusetts 02215

Mark T. Shutes
Department of
  Sociology/Anthropology
Youngstown State University
Youngstown, Ohio 44555

Michael G. Stys
7171 First Street
West Bloomfield, Michigan 48324

Susan B. Sutton
Department of Anthropology
Indiana University-Purdue
  University
425 University Boulevard
Indianapolis, Indiana 46202

Tjeerd H. van Andel
Department of Earth Sciences
The University of Cambridge
Downing Street, Cambridge
CB2 3EQ
United Kingdom

Richard W. Yerkes
Department of Anthropology
Lord Hall
The Ohio State University
Columbus, Ohio 43210-1364

Contents

III. Archaeological Investigations: The Use of Regional Scale Data

IV. Specialized Studies: Flora, Fauna, and Population Structure

V. Computer Modelling

List of Figures

List of Tables

Acknowledgments

Although each of the authors has individual debts to mention, there are a number of people who have made important contributions to the preparation of the book as a whole. Although their names do not appear in the formal references, I owe a great debt to John R. White and Gary F. Fry, both of Youngstown State University, who provided me with a sound, broad-based foundation in archaeology as mentors, and then demonstrated its application as colleagues over a period of 22 years. Their insistence on competent field work, constant questioning of the archaeological record, and the ability to move smoothly among the basic subdisciplines in anthropology impressed me from the outset of my career with the need for archaeology to be interdisciplinary and to incorporate information from more than just one isolated site. I have also benefitted over the years from conversations with Curtis Runnels, Mark Shutes, Michael Toumazou, Timothy Gregory, and Priscilla Murray on the interpretation of material evidence in a regional context. George McCarthy, Kenyon College, provided many valuable insights into the publishing process; his guidance was critical in pointing out the important details that lead to a polished final product. Sharon Duchesne carefully prepared the manuscript and assisted in editing the various papers; her aid was truly indispensable. Jack L. Davis and an anonymous reviewer provided important critical comments that forced the authors to hone their individual papers. Timothy Allen, Adrienne Conlan, Eric Eggers, Andrew Kindon, Matthew Koehler, Holly Mortensen, Cynthia Sheldon, J. Kenneth Smail, and David Suggs read a number of the chapters with care and patience. The College of Wooster and Kenyon College both provided funds to type the several drafts of the manuscript. Oxford University Press kindly granted permission to reprint a portion of Byron's poem *Childe Harold's Pilgrimage* from *Lord Byron: The Complete Poetical Works*, edited by Jerome J. McGann (1980).

Finally, I wish to acknowledge a long-standing debt to my parents, who, despite their limited formal education, instilled in me a respect for the value of intellectual pursuits and an appreciation of the Greek countryside. For all their support over the years, I gratefully dedicate this book to them.

Preface

This volume developed out of an Invited Session sponsored by the Society for the Anthropology of Europe at the 90th Annual Meeting of the American Anthropological Association held in Chicago on November 24, 1991. The papers of two members of the original panel, M. Fotiadis and S. Papamarinopoulos, are not included, but articles by T.H. van Andel, G. Rapp and J. Kraft, S. Bottema, J. Hansen, C. Runnels, D. Pullen, J. Cherry, and D. Reese have significantly augmented the collection and make it representative of the range of scholarly research that characterizes modern regional studies. The purpose of both the symposium and this volume is to demonstrate the manner in which various disciplinary specialties can assist the process of reconstructing the complex cultural mosaic in an area. While archaeologists initiated many of the long-term studies that fall under the rubric of regional studies, they quickly recognized the need for the input of many others to accomplish the goal of understanding ancient social dynamics. It soon became clear that an understanding of the past was incomplete without comprehension of the present. The study of contemporary economy, social organization, migration, etc. became the basis for analogies about the past, but also demonstrated the vitality of modern Aegean society. Thus, cultural anthropologists and ethno-archaeologists have become crucial team members. Because humans have an interactive relationship with the landscape, earth scientists, biologists, and others joined interdisciplinary teams to illuminate the intricacies of the natural environment. The combined efforts of scholars involved in such collaboration provided a balanced view of how culture, past and present, has acted as the human adaptive mechanism. The various studies are not always fully integrated, but the level of information is much more complete, and hypotheses to guide future research can be based on a broad array of variables. It is important to explore the emergence of regional studies in archaeology generally and the roots of such work in the Aegean before the reader turns to the specific studies.

The systematic study of regions has become a mainstay of archaeology in many parts of the world. One can trace the trend all the way back to the origins of American archaeology. Squier and Davis (1848) provided an early comprehensive report on earthworks in the Ohio and Mississippi Valleys. Similarly, Aegean scholars documented site locations and performed selective excavations to determine regional sequences (e.g., Wace and Thompson 1912). As archaeology matured, settlement pattern studies, combining survey and excavation in a comprehensive research plan, gained great analytical rigor in the New World with Willey's (1953) work in Peru, and with the River Basin Surveys of the 1940s and 1950s in the U.S. The complementary development in the Aegean was the Minnesota Messenia Expedition, which sprang from the work of William McDonald.

In an attempt to make clearer the parameters of their studies, scholars have recently defined regions more explicitly. Marquardt and Crumley describe a region as "a spatial configuration at a scale at which certain phenomena exhibit recognizable areal distribution" (1987:12). Regions, they argue, exhibit spatial and temporal elements within which researchers can discern patterns. In addition, they suggest regions contain boundaries (social, political, physiographic, etc.) that vary according to the scale of the analysis (Marquardt and Crumley 1987:13). Gamble (1986:40) echoes these concerns with an approach that considers the spatial, demographic, and social factors that define a region and provide the basis for variation in human adaptive behavior. Gamble breaks down Europe into three provinces, each of which contains three regions. He places the southern Balkans in the Eastern Region of the Mediterranean province based on relief, drainage patterns, and summer droughts (Gamble 1986:72-74).

The physiographic features Gamble uses can be combined with Marquardt and Crumley's socio-politico-economic factors to describe the Aegean as a series of regions. Ancient and modern political boundaries, and natural features (mountains, rivers, coastlines, etc.) dissect Greece, the western coast of Turkey, and the Aegean islands into units of analysis, including Lakonia, Messenia, Elis, Arkadia, the Korinthia, and the Argolid (all in the Peloponnesos); Boeotia, Thessaly, Akarnania, Attika, and the Pindos Range (Epiros) in central Greece; and Macedonia and Thrace (including European Turkey) in the north. The western coast of Turkey separates roughly into three zones, the Troad, Ionia, and Caria, that correspond with ancient subdivisions. The Aegean islands present unique insular settings, which one can examine as distinct regions. A few large islands, such as Crete, can be divided into several regions. Typically, the studies portray diachronic profiles; surface surveys record sites of all past periods, and ethnographic and ethnoarchaeological work fills in the modern settlement context.

Archaeological investigation in the circum-Aegean region has had a long and distinguished history. Such research was at the cutting edge of the new discipline of archaeology in the 19th century. Most of this work focused on individual sites or major art monuments. There was, however, also from the outset a concern with entire regions. Various classical authors provided information about ancient topography. Using these data, modern scholars attempted to reconstruct the ancient landscape across which the giant figures of the Hellenic past strode. But this interest did not evolve into the examination of man/land interaction which has characterized prehistoric studies elsewhere around the world. By the early 20th century, Greek archaeology had gone off on its own trajectory, a route that took it further from the work done in Western Europe and North America. The standard routine received a significant jolt and stimulus in the late 1940s and early 1950s when prehistorians in Greece brought new techniques and an integrated regional perspective to their work in the Aegean. The effects of this introduction were revolutionary--a variety of scholars contributed to truly interdisciplinary research, an integrated program that has become the norm, for prehistoric studies at least. A variety of fields now contribute to examination of the Aegean past and present. The nature of such research programs is the subject of this collection of essays. Specialists outline their individual work, how it fits into the general research plan, and evaluate that role, with a statement of prospects for the future.

The introductory paper by Nick Kardulias discusses the emergence of such regional studies in the Aegean as a Kuhnian paradigm shift, which engendered a new perspective on the evolution of Greek society. He outlines the major developments in regional studies, beginning with the work of the Minnesota Messenia Project, and discusses more recent developments in Melos, the southern Argolid, and the Nemea Valley. What all of these studies share, and what the papers in this volume demonstrate, is a focus on the landscape as a dynamic, integrated phenomenon, the understanding of which requires consideration of the interplay between natural and cultural forces through time. As a result, regional studies are interdisciplinary, and tend to have an explicit theoretical orientation. There are several threads which run through the papers in this volume: (1) The natural environment provides the backdrop against which all human behavior must be assessed, so earth sciences have become a critical component of regional studies. (2) Thus, expanding the range of methods brought to bear on archaeological questions is necessary. (3) While specialists provide new insights into past and present ecological dynamics, regional syntheses also require theoretical perspectives capable of melding the various studies into a coherent explanation; general systems theory, world systems theory, efficiency models based on microeconomic theory, and cultural ecology are some of the major approaches researchers use. (4)

The wealth of new evidence that the various scholars have generated often provides the basis for challenging standard interpretations of both the Aegean past and present. (5) Many Aegean archaeologists are fully conversant with developments in the discipline (e.g., surface survey, computer applications for archaeological analysis, sampling procedures) and can contribute to the broader archaeological discourse on these topics.

An important feature, some might argue the essential base, of regional studies is the examination of the physical surroundings. Such fields as geomorphology and palynology are concerned with the evolution of the natural landscape, and the effect of human action on this process. Such studies allow us to move beyond the overly simplistic models of the relationship between humans and the environment that once held sway; no one universal pattern of geomorphological activity can explain conditions in all regions, as Vita-Finzi once suggested. The studies in this section demonstrate the need to examine variation in such processes in various regions. Tjeerd van Andel presents an overview of the problems earth scientists face in communicating effectively with their colleagues in archaeology. The paper by George Rapp and John Kraft discusses changes in shorelines in general, followed by examples of their work over a period of 20 years. They explore the impact of such changes on settlement location and the connection to certain historical problems, such as the Bronze Age setting of Troy. Sytze Bottema reviews the role of palynology in environmental reconstruction, then provides a case study of some cores from Zileria in the Almiros plain near Volos in east central Greece; he places this work in the context of landscape evolution. These studies are all based in the natural sciences and employ techniques (e.g., analysis of sediments and petrology, identification of ancient pollen, sophisticated computer simulations) generally outside the archaeologist's expertise.

Perhaps the most innovative development in Aegean archaeology in the past three decades has been the introduction of systematic surface survey. While it is true that archaeologists had, from the beginning, attempted to locate sites mentioned in the ancient texts, the goals of such investigations were often limited to urban settlements or large rural religious sanctuaries. The search for these sites was often haphazard or biased in the selection of study areas. Systematic survey, introduced by the Minnesota Messenia Project and refined by other research in Kythera, Melos, Kea, the Argolid, Boeotia, and elsewhere, introduced a much more rigorous framework. Archaeologists began to discuss settlement distribution and patterns in a more systematic manner. In this section, John Cherry assesses the role of archaeological survey as a technique for investigating total human use of the landscape; he examines the contributions of survey work over the past two decades, and evaluates its current status. Other papers demonstrate the ways in which regional survey and excavation data can be used to investigate particular problems. Daniel Pullen's paper on Early Bronze Age mortuary practices, Timothy Gregory's discussion of the "fall" of the Roman Empire, and Curtis Runnels' statement on lithics in their regional context synthesize various levels of evidence to provide models for understanding interactions at the supra-site level.

Special methods also define another category of investigation that is site-specific and relates to the reconstruction of past lifeways, which include subsistence patterns, demographic profile of a population (age structure, level of trauma and disease, genetic relations to other groups), and settlement structure. Julie Hansen provides an overview of palaeoethnobotanical research based on her work at sites that span the Upper Palaeolithic to Roman periods; she documents shift in diet as one element in human exploitation of various flora. David Reese updates Payne's bibliographic review of faunal studies at a number of Aegean sites; despite the increased awareness of the value of such material, Reese's summary makes it clear that much still needs to be done before we can develop synthetic statements about regional diet. Joseph Rife and Myra Giesen present an osteological analysis of human skeletons from Isthmia, where graves date from the Archaic through the Late Byzantine periods, and offer the opportunity to relate biological diversity to historical transition.

The innovations in remote sensing and computer-aided drafting and design of the past decade have had a major impact on both the planning of research projects and the rigor of analysis. At the site-specific level, a suite of methods now assist archaeologists in planning excavations and in locating features by non-intrusive techniques. Michael Stys presents a study of the utility of AutoCAD in providing rapidly a reconstruction of a complex ancient building, the Roman Bath at Isthmia. Based on a precise laser theodolite survey of the structure, Stys demonstrates the flexibility of AutoCAD, which stores all drawings in a mathematical database, in providing a series of reconstruction scenarios, which serve as hypotheses to be tested against the archaeological evidence. The refined level of data obtained at individual sites can be built into a regional model. Using data obtained from Landsat images and topographic and geological maps, Mark Dann and Richard Yerkes construct a Geographic Information Systems (GIS) model of the Korinthia. Using several known sites, they isolate a characteristic signature (based on key features such as aspect, elevation, local hydrology, and soils) of Late Medieval sites and predict the location of other sites from the same period. Such models can be expanded into multiple layers to deal with other time periods and enhance our ability to deal with a variety of factors that influence settlement distribution. In addition, GIS models and AutoCAD-generated maps can be of great utility to other researchers, such as geomorphologists and cultural anthropologists who share interests in soil type distribution.

The active participation of ethnographers in regional studies is another important development. Most archaeologists see the value of having detailed descriptions and explanations of contemporary cultural patterns, both to serve as sources for inferences about the past, and to bring our discussion of the cultural landscape up to the present. As Herzfeld has noted, anthropology has much to learn from the study of contemporary Greek society. In this section, Susan Sutton reevaluates the Greek village as a cultural phenomenon. Through her recent work in three regions, Sutton demonstrates that villages gain and lose population as families negotiate "their positions in regional systems of political economy." Mark Shutes examines changes in agricultural production strategies in Ancient Korinth and the impact of these alterations on organized social life in the region. He also considers the impact of the elimination of EEC trade barriers on local farmers. Both of these studies present data and approaches which allow us to challenge anthropological models of "traditional peasant" societies. Materialist and cultural ecological perspectives view these societies as adaptations to particular environmental, social, and political circumstances. Claudia Chang's paper presents a challenge of another sort, i.e., to incorporate ethnoarchaeology into regional studies at the planning stage so that deductive hypotheses can be formulated and tested. Chang's particular concern is with contemporary pastoralism and what it can reveal about animal husbandry in the past--the insights we gain can be highly instructive, especially when ethnoarchaeologists help frame the questions that guide the research program.

The seventh section considers some practical aspects of doing archaeology in Greece. We do not operate in a social or political vacuum and it is important to comprehend the effect our work has on local groups. In addition, we operate within and must understand the bureaucratic structure of the Greek state. Nick Kardulias discusses the political framework of archaeology in Greece and argues that the serious impediments to the conduct of research by foreigners are tied directly to this system.

In the concluding section, Jack L. Davis evaluates the accomplishments, shortcomings, and prospects of regional studies in the Aegean area. A major gulf separates archaeologists who work in Greece into two camps; typically, we draw the line between those who study historic and prehistoric periods. The regional approach has made great inroads, and its accomplishments are often noted, but differences do exist between the camps. The New or Processual Archaeology, with its emphasis on a hypothetico-deductive framework, middle-range theory, covering laws, and formation processes, has made significant headway in prehistoric studies, but less in traditional classical archaeology. Prehistoric archaeologists and those historic archaeologists with an explicit theoretical orientation are generally more receptive to the use of a variety of theoretical models (e.g., world systems theory, models of economic behavior, cultural ecology) and the papers in this volume clearly reflect this tendency. Regional studies, in their effort to crosscut time periods and disciplines, can bridge the gap between historians and prehistorians, and seem to offer the best opportunity for an integrated, comprehensive study of the Aegean past.

Gambier, Ohio
April, 1994

References Cited

Gamble, C.
    1986 *The Palaeolithic Settlement of Europe*. Cambridge University Press, Cambridge.
Marquardt, W., and C. Crumley
    1987 Theoretical Issues in the Analysis of Spatial Patterning. In *Regional Dynamics: Burgundian Landscapes in Historical Perspective*, edited by W.H. Marquardt and C.L. Crumley, pp. 1-18. Academic Press, Orlando.
Squier, E.G., and E. Davis
    1848 *Ancient Monuments of the Mississippi Valley*. Smithsonian Institution Contributions to Knowledge No. 1, Washington, D.C.
Wace, A.B., and M.S. Thompson
    1912 *Prehistoric Thessaly*. Cambridge University Press, Cambridge.

Willey, G.R.

　1953　*Prehistoric Settlement Patterns in the Virú Valley, Peru.*
　Bureau of American Ethnology Bulletin 155. Smithsonian
　Institution, Washington, D.C.

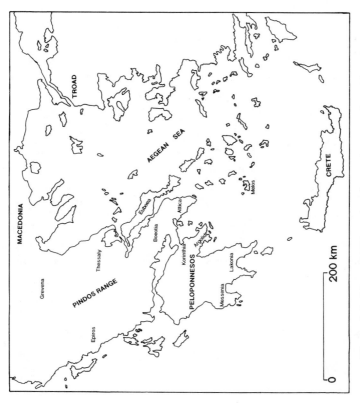

Figure 1.1. Map of Greece showing regions mentioned in text.

I.
INTRODUCTION

Chapter 1

Paradigms of the Past in Greek Archaeology

P. Nick Kardulias

Introduction

The past 30 years have witnessed significant changes in the conduct of
Aegean archaeology. Steeped in the classical tradition, archaeological
research in Greece (Figure 1.1) through the early 1950s had developed
its own unique chronological measures and approaches to excavation.
Scholarship in this area exhibited an insularity fostered by the
conventions of anchoring field research to classical texts. While no one
can deny the many contributions such text-aided archaeology produced,
the other side of the coin was a reluctance to adopt many of the new
methods and theoretical frameworks then current in North America and
Europe (Dyson 1993). This complacency in the face of drastic scholarly
changes going on in other countries began to erode in the 1950s, but by
no means did it completely succumb to the enticements of the New
Archaeology of the next decade. Binford, Flannery, and others offered
archaeologists the prestigious label of "scientist"--many became true
believers and converted, others proceeded cautiously and withheld
allegiance until concrete results were in hand, and still others spurned
the offer outright. On the whole, archaeologists working in Greece
belong to the last group. As Jacobsen has noted: "Until quite recently,
archaeology in Greece has been dominated by concerns with description
and classification, and creative approaches to the interpretation of the

archaeological remains in human terms have been notably limited or lacking" (1985:93). But the perspective represented by the New Archaeology and its intellectual predecessors did make significant inroads in certain areas.

Perhaps the clearest example of this new spirit is the introduction of systematic regional survey to Greek archaeology. While it is true that there has been an interest in regional scale studies in Greece since the 19th century, the techniques developed since World War II provide a more rigorous framework and incorporate a host of methods not available or not used by archaeologists in the first half of the present century. Most often, such extensive examinations developed out of the need to learn more about the zone around major excavations; in some cases survey was viewed as supplemental, perhaps even subordinate, to the excavation. The Minnesota Messenia Survey originated as an attempt to place the Pylos excavations into a broader environmental context (McDonald and Rapp 1972). Similarly, the Southern Argolid Survey (Jameson et al. 1994) derived its initial impetus from the excavation of prehistoric Franchthi Cave and classical Halieis. The initial work, however, rapidly developed into multi-pronged investigations into a vast array of elements that comprise the complex mosaic upon which humans play out their lives. As many of the researchers realized, to understand the past one needs, in addition to data from historical texts and excavation, a comprehension of the interrelationships among the various natural factors which define the parameters of human existence and of current cultural conditions. Thus, a variety of disciplines came to the aid of archaeology in the attempt to delineate more precisely the complex processes of interaction between humans and their environment. For many of these researchers environment was defined broadly as both the physical, natural surroundings, and the cultural context. The concern often was and is the mutual impact between humans and the total context. To cover all of the different areas of potential interest in such an extensive program, archaeologists called on skilled specialists, such as geologists, geomorphologists, palynologists, botanists, faunal experts, ethnographers, and osteologists to provide detailed studies of specific phenomena. Through the study of minutiae scholars gained a greater appreciation for the subtlety of human interaction with the landscape and the dynamic relationship between the two.

Other projects that studied areas previously not the subject of intense investigation have been designed explicitly from the outset as interdisciplinary. Examples of such projects include the Cambridge and

Bradford Boeotia Archaeological and Geological Expedition (Bintliff and Snodgrass 1985) and the Grevena Project (Savina et al. 1991). It has become commonplace now to invoke a regional focus and to assemble teams of specialists to unravel the complex interconnections between people and the environment.

Paradigms and Scientific Revolutions

Below I will discuss the significance of this transition in terms of a model developed by Thomas Kuhn to explain major changes in scientific perspectives (1970). Kuhn concludes the postscript to his book, *The Structure of Scientific Revolutions*, by stressing the need to study the community structure of various disciplines. Key questions include the following: "How does one elect and how is one elected to membership in a particular community, scientific or not? What is the process and what are the stages of socialization to the group? What does the group collectively see as its goals: what deviations, individual or collective, will it tolerate; and how does it control the impermissible aberration?" (1970:209). Kuhn's analysis of development in science deals with such questions in light of a powerful explanatory framework which other disciplines have borrowed, on occasion, in the attempt to understand their respective evolution and the current status of the field. Sterud (1973) used a Kuhnian model to describe developments in prehistoric archaeology. Greek historical archaeology has failed to produce such a reflexive examination of the status of scholarship in the Aegean world. Indeed, classical archaeology has proved to be unusually resistant to the incursions of theoretical examination. By no means does this statement imply that classical archaeologists operate in a theoretical vacuum; rather, it is meant to suggest that, with some notable exceptions, many represented by the contributors to this volume, archaeology and indeed cultural studies at a broader level (history, anthropology), have not been explicit in laying out the basic assumptions from which interpretations derive and by which they are colored.

Kuhn argues that specific paradigms characterize science, or any discipline, at various points in time. He defines paradigms as "...universally recognized scientific achievements that for a time provide model problems and solutions to a community of practitioners" (1970:viii).

Kuhn identifies several stages in the development of a discipline, the pre-paradigm, normal science or first paradigm, and revolution or new paradigm phases. In the pre-paradigm period there are contending views concerning the proper methods, problems, and standards of solution. When a community reaches a consensus on these issues, a discipline enters the normal science stage, in which scientists follow certain conventions that prove successful in solving key problems (Kuhn 1970:7). A critical point Kuhn makes is that researchers cannot divorce facts from theory, i.e., identification of problems and methods pursued to solve the problems derive in large part from the reigning paradigm--one may not even consider an alternative because it is not part of the framework teachers impart to their students. Textbooks incorporate and help disseminate the rules which derive from the paradigms. Because the paradigm, and the theories and rules drawn from it, has proven effective, members of the community do not question the basic assumptions; these are simply taken for granted, as articles of indisputable fact or, at least, faith.

Recognition of an anomaly, i.e., a problem the current paradigm is unable to solve, initiates a scientific revolution. Because normal science is not innovative, it fails to provide insights necessary to resolve problems beyond the pale of its standard approach. There is turmoil as certain individuals not fully indoctrinated in or persuaded by the reigning paradigm offer alternative approaches, what Kuhn calls novel theories (1970:74). Many researchers persist in applying the old approach; if the attempt fails, the road is opened to a new approach--a shift in paradigms or revolution.

Kuhn stresses that science does not change by the accumulation of knowledge or theories. Rather, individuals must often reject an approach in its entirety and construct another based on new fundamentals: "...scientific revolutions are here taken to be those non-cumulative developmental episodes in which an older paradigm is replaced in whole or part by an incompatible new one" (1970:92). Paradigms are not isolated intellectual phenomena. They are closely tied to the prevailing trends in thought, so that a shift in paradigms is symptomatic of a change in worldview. Because such a shift requires a dramatic overhaul of perspective, the change is often abrupt and requires the advocacy of a new generation of scientists who have little to lose.

In his application of a Kuhnian model to the development of prehistory, Sterud places the pre-paradigm period prior to 1859 (1973:8-10). The competing approaches of the day included the Three-Age System (Fagan 1989:34) and the Biblical account of creation. The contending perspectives generated a model (paradigm) with ample time depth and an evolutionary view of change. Specific approaches developed to deal with early prehistoric, palaeolithic humans on the one hand, and Neolithic and later cultures on the other hand. Palaeolithic prehistoric archaeologists employed the methods of palaeontology and geology, while students of the Neolithic and Bronze Age focused on historical approaches in this normal science phase in the discipline. Sterud provides an illuminating glance at paradigm development in prehistoric archaeology, but here I wish to focus on the historic aspect, especially as it is reflected in Classical Archaeology.

A Paradigmatic Shift in Greek Archaeology

The normal science phase in classical archaeology incorporated techniques developed originally by, among others, Winckelmann (1880 [1767]) for art history, philologists for the study of ancient texts, and architects for the examination of large monuments. Reliance on texts is a critical component of this approach. In a forthcoming book, Ian Morris (1994) provides a detailed discussion of the development of classical archaeology and its resultant differences from the anthropological form of the discipline. Classical archaeology falls under what some call the Great Tradition (Renfrew 1980), a composite of humanistic studies in which classical texts (histories, drama, philosophy, science, medicine) formed the core of a proper education. In the late 18th and early 19th centuries, German scholars gave a specific form to this tradition with their rigorous attention to details of texts and emphasis on philological abilities. The foremost classical scholars were Germans because of their attention to method. The new discipline, called *Altertumswissenschaft*, developed a strong following: "The new professionals were initiated through the experience of the Seminar, where the Professor inculcated in his students the method of source criticism... The overarching model which controlled research was the concept of the *Zeitgeist*, or spirit of the age. Paradoxically, through the use of critical skills the Greeks were enshrined as being beyond historical criticism. History consisted of identifying the *Zeitgeist* which belonged to each *Volk*... In the case of the Greeks, all references to impurities and weaknesses were purged in the fires of source criticism to leave a race beyond comparison" (Morris 1994).

Hierarchy and Romanticism were two key elements of this perspective. These notions became the core of Hellenism, defined by Morris as: "the idealization of ancient Greece as the birthplace of a European spirit" (1994). He argues that Greek archaeology was subsumed under classics--archaeology commonly served to illustrate or augment the classical texts, which became the authority. Perhaps the best example of the text-aided nature of classical archaeology in Greece is the extensive use of Pausanias as a guide to excavation. Descriptions by the second century A.D. peregrinator not only provide the foundation for site interpretation but also define the basic problems for the discipline. For example, Pausanias is concerned with public architecture in cities, towns, and sanctuaries. As a result, for the longest time classical archaeologists focused on urban centers and large rural religious complexes. In addition, Pausanias provides great detail about foundation stories and other myths, tales, and histories of the places he visits. Similarly, because of the quantity of literary sources that refer to specific locations, classical archaeologists often attempt to apply specific labels to particular parts of the archaeological landscape. I do not deny both the success and utility of this exercise. Classical archaeologists often have an enviable degree of reliability in their assigning of specific names and functions to particular monuments. Their prehistoric counterparts rarely have the opportunity to deal with their information with such precision; certainly, the prehistorian is severely limited in identifying the presence of a particular named individual in his/her data. Classical archaeologists can populate their accounts with real, known people. The point is, however, that the texts often define the problem, the methods, and the standards of proof. This situation fits precisely the condition Kuhn calls normal science: "Normal science means research firmly based upon one or more past scientific achievements, achievements that some particular scientific community acknowledges for a time as supplying the foundation for its further practice" (1970:10). Textbooks encapsulate and help to disseminate the key ideas of normal science. In many ways, normal science is formulaic: "...an attempt to force nature into the preformed and relatively inflexible box that the paradigm supplies. No part of the aim of normal science is to call forth new sorts of phenomena; indeed those that will not fit the box are often not seen at all. Nor do scientists normally aim to invent new theories, and they are often intolerant of those invented by others. Instead, normal-scientific research is directed to the articulation of those phenomena and theories that the paradigm already supplies" (Kuhn 1970:24).

For classical archaeology, the paradigm involves several levels. First, is the notion that ancient Greek (and Roman) authors explored, perhaps for the first time, universal themes of human existence in a manner that transcends time. Classical literature, history, philosophy and to a lesser extent medicine and science, are commonly viewed as forming the core of the western tradition, and thus are crucial elements in formal education. Acceptance of these tenets is essential to the recruitment of scholars that Kuhn discusses in the postscript. Second, since the ancients had such a feel for human life, if we can discover more about them through archaeology and textual analysis, we can perhaps make more informed decisions about our lives. Third, texts, as products of the human mind, provide a cultural reality and reflect the values of ancient society. Fourth, those values were the stimuli for human behavior and are thus the key things we should try to comprehend about the past. Fifth, the archaeological record reflects technology, behavior, and values and can serve as a supplement in the effort to understand the ancient mentality.

The specific method for accomplishing this unification of past and present involves careful textual analysis, which in turn requires strong language skills. Since most of the texts referred to conditions in cities, it is not surprising that early classical archaeologists conducted excavations in those urban places that loomed large in the ancient writings. An outgrowth of this emphasis was the notion that many elements of the archaeological record then have a literary referent--one can label specific events, individuals, or monuments. Think, for example, of the Vergina tomb assigned to Philip II of Macedon. Another example is Broneer's (1971) attribution of the wheel ruts in the altar foundation at Isthmia to the period of supposed abandonment of the Sanctuary of Poseidon after the destruction of Korinth, which sponsored the games, by Mummius in 146 B.C. Examples of such efforts to tie the archaeological findings to literary sources abound in the scholarship. Another tenet that is implicit in at least early classical archaeology is that if a site, person, or event is mentioned in a classical text, the subject is important; if no such reference exists, or if it is minimal, the subject is seen as somewhat marginal. Thus, for many years, classical archaeology revealed a great deal about monumental public architecture but precious little about domestic architecture; we know much about the lives of elites, but little about the existence of ordinary citizens. Finally, one must consider the classical archaeologist's image of where his/her discipline fits into academe. I think it is safe to say that most classical archaeologists, past and present, find their niche in the humanities rather than the social sciences. This perception has consequences for how the discipline operates, for its theoretical underpinnings. As part of the humanities, classical archaeology has placed greater emphasis on subjective, rather than objective interpretations--the search concentrates on the explication of the unique features of Greek antiquity rather than on recurrent patterns which crosscut time and space, except in the most general way. The commonalities that are discussed deal more with elements of the ethereal human spirit, rather than materialist concerns. There is a sense that Greek antiquity gains little from analysis based on, for example, Darwinian evolutionism or cultural materialism.

Classical archaeology is closely tied to art history and as a result practitioners have been accused of "going for the goodies" in the form of fine pottery, metal votives, temple architecture, etc. The field is maligned by outsiders as the search for aesthetically pleasing museum-quality pieces. While some of this does occur, it is not an isolated phenomenon. Archaeologists who work in the Near East, Egypt, China, Mesoamerica, South America, and the American Midwest also have concentrated on spectacular artifacts and structures at the expense of locating and understanding the mundane elements of life which had such a great impact on social life.

I do not want to leave the impression that archaeological work in Greece and the Aegean was a fully integrated whole between 1831, when the modern Greek state was formed and archaeological work began in the country, and the 1950s. From the outset researchers made a distinction between prehistoric (Bronze Age, Neolithic, and earlier) and historic periods. The text-aided archaeology described above obviously not only applies to the latter, but also to the former in that people like Schliemann used literary sources as a guide to excavation, with some spectacular results. However, the written sources provided much less assistance for the prehistoric than the historic period, and so prehistorians developed a series of techniques, assumptions, and perspectives different from their classical counterparts. Each area, in its own way, developed a set of operative principles under which a great deal of fieldwork was conducted--the normal science phase.

According to Kuhn, anomalies, or inconsistencies between data and the ability of the paradigm to explain them, arise from time to time. The first reaction is to attempt a solution using the old paradigm. Often the crisis cannot be resolved by the standard methods because the problem must be addressed in a totally different manner. New paradigms, with new concepts and views on how the parts interact, may be presented by people who have little stake in the old perspective and thus offer valuable insights which provide a better understanding of the phenomenon. Entirely new perspectives (or paradigms) may emerge from such reevaluation. For example, the conventional wisdom held that the transition to agriculture involved the willful abandonment of a hunting and gathering lifestyle, with its tenuous daily food quest, for the security of food production. Various studies (Lee and DeVore 1968; Sahlins 1972) have proved that modern hunters and gatherers enjoy rather leisurely lives despite the severity of the environments in which they find themselves. In addition, foraging societies can develop very complex sociopolitical structures (Price and Brown 1985). Prehistorians have made sweeping changes in their approach to studying hunter-gatherers as a result of the new paradigm (Binford 1978, 1980; Jochim 1976; Keeley 1988); the concept of the uni-dimensional hunter-gatherer is an analytical anachronism. Much of the change in the study of foraging societies is directly attributable to a shift away from the old structural-functional models to a perspective informed by evolutionary thought and ecology. Snodgrass (1985) identifies such a change in Greek archaeology with his discussion of changes in the study of the Aegean Bronze Age. The old model emphasized events, especially military episodes, but failed to explain many key developments. The new approach studies processes in order to comprehend change in its larger cultural context. One of the best examples of the new perspective is Renfrew's classic *The Emergence of Civilisation* (1972). Snodgrass makes the point that Aegean Bronze Age archaeology has experienced an important shift, which I identify with a scientific revolution, but classical archaeology proper, which deals with the historic periods, has not yielded to the new perspective.

In the new emphasis on process, prehistoric archaeology in Greece turned to regional scale studies in which a variety of disciplines presented a coordinated picture of past human adaptation and interaction with the environment. What we have witnessed in the past three decades is the establishment of a holistic approach to the examination of the Greek past.

There are several ways to think about this change. I will first discuss some of the general points involved with this transition and then focus on particular studies. Although archaeologists have understood for some time the need to conduct regional scale analyses (see, for example, Fowler and Stilwell [1932] for a description of sites in the Korinthia) with the aid of specialists, it was not until Willey's (1953) work that systematic survey and settlement pattern studies became an established part of research designs in the Americas and elsewhere (see, however, the work of the River Basin Surveys in the 1940s). Many scholars realized the constraints of a site-specific focus and broadened their research horizons. Perhaps it is best to place these studies in the most basic framework archaeologists recognize. We often present three basic goals for the discipline (Fagan 1989:33): (1) The delineation of a region's culture history in which we describe the sequence of events and cultures, (2) the reconstruction of past lifeways, to provide details concerning the routines of daily life (diet, subsistence patterns, tool production, etc.), and (3) the study of culture process, or the effort to explain why and how culture change occurred. Regional studies to some degree attempt to answer questions in all three of these areas and can thus be viewed as an expression of the holistic character of anthropological archaeology, which attempts to deal with the interactive biological and cultural aspects of human existence within an environmental context. The need for specialists becomes apparent when one considers the myriad forms of evidence available for investigation. The mere fact of incorporating researchers from the physical sciences in archaeological projects could not help but affect our views of the human past. In his introductory text on Greek archaeology, Biers (1987:17) acknowledges the importance in Greece of such studies which attempt "... to discover the total ancient environment...", even though the book is entirely traditional in its layout and coverage.

From a theoretical perspective, the focus on regions is expressed in the concept of landscape archaeology. Marquardt and Crumley (1987:1) provide an excellent statement of the nature of regional study when they define landscape as: "the spatial manifestation of the relations between humans and their environment. Included in the study of landscapes are population agglomerations of all sizes, from isolated farmsteads to metropoleis, as well as the roads that link them. Also included are unoccupied or infrequently occupied places...that societies use and imbue with meaning" (Marquardt and Crumley 1987:1). Their study in southern Burgundy, based on a "holistic concept of culture" (1987:2), attempted to discern regional patterns of human behavior by means of multidisciplinary studies that crosscut many time periods and different scales of analysis (i.e., local community, regional, national). They argue persuasively that an integrated approach to regional analysis transcends the typical focus and methods of economic studies, and incorporates both social and ecological factors into an explanatory framework. Greece is an ideal place to carry out their agenda, i.e., the effort to integrate natural sciences, social sciences, and the humanities. In this, and in their emphasis on a dynamic concept of region in which investigators identify landscape signatures (the material residues of human activity reflected in the cultural remains and alterations of the physical environment), Marquardt and Crumley lay out a program which gives explicit form to many of the operative principles of similar work in the Aegean (1987:3-4). They point out the need to identify a region contextually, to discuss the issues of boundaries and cultural perceptions of space, and to view the defined region as an open system (Marquardt and Crumley 1987:16). Many of these particular points received treatment in the various regional studies in the Aegean, and form the backdrop to the papers in this volume. For example, researchers understand the ecological context to include not just the natural forces of erosion, sedimentation, etc., but also the manner in which humans trigger certain events and are affected by the, in many cases, unexpected consequences (e.g., see van Andel et al. 1986). The dynamic nature of regions stressed by Marquardt and Crumley (1987) underlies the thinking of all the contributors to this volume.

The Minnesota Messenia Expedition (MME) was the first truly interdisciplinary project in Greece. Its purpose was to document "...the interaction among humans, other biota, and the physical environment" (McDonald 1972:6). The investigation focused on ecological interactions to reconstruct the Bronze Age, and especially the Late Bronze Age (LBA), environment in southwestern Greece. The impressive range of studies in the MME included excavation, regional survey, analysis of documents, studies of materials, cultural and economic studies, and environmental research. The archeological survey located 332 prehistoric sites and 286 historic sites. The selection of survey zones was made on the basis of the principals' intimate knowledge of the contemporary countryside and ancient sources that deal with topography. Factors which structured the choice of areas to investigate included location of best agricultural land, copious water, defensibility, good drainage, and good possibilities for communication. This somewhat subjective selection process was bolstered by the first systematic use of aerial photography for site discovery in Greece (McDonald and Hope Simpson 1972:121-122). But the aim of the project went beyond merely identifying site locations. There is great consideration given to the reasons people opted to inhabit particular locations. In treating these reasons, the various environmental, geographic, and anthropological studies lent a degree of sophistication not previously seen in Aegean archaeology. Perhaps the most prominent thread that runs through the book is the value of science and technology to the archaeologist. The 17 specialized studies had a common goal: to figure out "... the environment in which the Messenians of the Late Bronze Age found themselves and how they seem to have affected and adapted to it" (McDonald and Rapp 1972:240). Important results included determination of: (1) the configuration of the ancient coastline and location of harbors; (2) the Bronze Age road network within Messenia and routes linking the area to its neighbors; (3) land use patterns; e.g., around Pylos in the LBA there was extensive land clearing to open space for grain and olive cultivation. Despite such sporadic intensive exploitation, most areas revealed only moderate use in the LBA (McDonald and Rapp 1972:247); (4) Climate is essentially unchanged and evidence for irrigation agriculture is scanty; (5) metals were imported into Messenia where craftsmen reworked the ingots into various artifacts; (6) local village craftsmen used Messenian materials to produce pottery for local consumption; (7) trade links with other parts of Greece clearly existed; agricultural products may have been exchanged for metal, some pottery, amber, obsidian, and other luxury goods; (8) settlement distribution was densest and most widespread in the LBA (168 sites); (9) demographic profile; through ethnographic analogy and archaeological survey, the authors set the number of LBA villages at a minimum of 250 with a population of at least 50,000 for the whole area. The MME was certainly a pioneering effort in Greece and demonstrated the robust results available to those who drew on many disciplines to determine profiles. The regional interdisciplinary focus, and systems orientation implied in the analysis, are key elements of the new paradigm. The work was revolutionary in its impact as many scholars turned to regional studies. A few further examples will demonstrate how such projects built on the MME foundation.

The Melos project of the British School was explicitly processual in its perspective and carried on the regional focus of the MME. The basic goal was to document the processes of culture change that led to the emergence of complex society on Melos in the MBA and then again in the eighth century B.C. The authors framed the investigation around a "Concrete ecological approach within a systemic frame" (Renfrew and Wagstaff 1982:1). They rejected an inductive approach because it fails to yield broad generalizations and stressed instead the deductive approach espoused by Binford (1962). This was a clear departure from traditional archaeology in Greece. A sophisticated multi-layered systems approach examined the key interactions on the island, and then successively in the region (Cyclades), the area (Aegean), and the relevant world system (Eastern Mediterranean). The ecological focus was made clear through the initial discussions of island geology, geomorphology, local resources, and traditional land use. Syntheses, guided by the theoretical framework, then discussed the island's intra-systemic relations, with a focus on subsistence strategies and population change, inter-systemic relations, i.e., trade from prehistoric to medieval times, and two overviews of the whole system. Renfrew elaborated on the concepts of interaction, intensification, and exploitation to explain the trajectory of sociopolitical evolution on Melos; his peer polity interaction model did not merely describe early states, it offered a coherent explanation for their emergence. Renfrew suggested that the interests of traditional archaeology (art style, religious belief, ideational system) can be incorporated into integrated regional work, but the new paradigm is clearly different in its systemic, nomothetic approach (Renfrew 1982:289). Another major innovation in this project was the initial use in Greece of a formal probabilistic sampling strategy in the archaeological survey (Cherry 1982:6). The concept of sampling was, and to a considerable degree still is, foreign to most classical archaeologists. The appropriate use of sampling methods can enhance the reliability of generalizations, and has become a central concern in the new paradigm. Yet another critical component of this new perspective is a concentration on indigenous social dynamics, rather than foreign intrusions, as the source of important social change. The ecological focus of many regional studies often acts as a bulwark against diffusionist ideas--the more one understands the intricate relationships between humans and their total environment, the less likely one may be to attribute change to exotic sources. Renfrew and his colleagues have taken a strong anti-diffusionist stand; the same is true for some members of the MME (McDonald and Thomas 1990:414-416). For example, the notion of a Dorian invasion is largely an unsatisfactory answer to questions about the Mycenaean decline.

The Stanford University Southern Argolid Archaeological and Environmental Survey (Jameson et al. 1994) deserves mention as a project which has expanded the range of innovative techniques brought to regional scale analysis. An offshoot of excavations at Halieis (Jameson 1969) and Franchthi Cave (Jacobsen 1976), the project encompassed a broad range of individual studies all geared to understanding man-land interaction over the past 20,000 years; this is a much greater time depth than either of the two previous projects. In addition to excavation and survey, the project featured detailed geomorphological analysis which documented eustatic fluctuation and sedimentation rates; researchers considered how past humans were affected by such environmental changes (e.g., the impact on Upper Palaeolithic hunters of reduction in the size of coastal plains due to marine ingression) and determined other conditions (e.g., the effect of constructing, maintaining, and abandoning agricultural terraces and retaining walls). Because no excavation was possible at sites found during the survey, there was a reliance on survey data as an independent body of information. Some scholars feel survey data are too limited to permit adequate discussion of the past cultures they represent (Hope Simpson 1985:xvii), but the members of this and other projects disagreed with such an assessment. The survey data do not simply supplement excavation information, but rather form the core of regional statements. Under the aegis of the Argolid Exploration Project, work in the southern Argolid included investigations conducted by the University of Pennsylvania, Indiana University, and Stanford University. In addition to the excavations and archaeological survey, the research included a wide range of ethnographic research (see many of the articles in Dimen and Friedl 1976, and *Expedition* 1978 volume 21), ethnoarchaeology (Murray and Chang 1981; Murray and Kardulias 1986), geomorphology (Pope and van Andel 1984; van Andel and Shackleton 1982; van Andel and Lianos 1983, 1984; van Andel et al. 1980), lithic analysis (Jacobsen and Van Horn 1974; Kardulias 1992; Runnels 1975, 1982, 1985, 1988), innovative dating methods (Pope et al. 1984), and articles that integrate several levels of research (Runnels and van Andel 1987; van Andel et al. 1986). The final reports on Franchthi Cave (Hansen 1991; Jacobsen and Farrand 1987; Perlès 1987, 1991; Schackleton 1988; van Andel and Sutton 1987; Wilkinson and Duhon 1991) and the Stanford survey (Jameson et al. 1994; Runnels et al. 1994; Sutton 1994; van Andel and Runnels 1987) make the Argolid project one of the most thoroughly documented regional studies in Greece. Many of these studies would have been completely foreign to traditional classical archaeology only one or two generations ago. The recruitment for prehistoric archaeologists under the new paradigm requires at least a passing familiarity with many scientific areas which contribute to archaeological synthesis.

One of the largest and most recent regional projects in Greece is the Nemea Valley Archaeological Project (NVAP; Wright et al. 1990). Nemea was the location of a secondary Bronze Age settlement and a major Panhellenic sanctuary in historic times. It is interesting to note that the regional analysis emerged out of the concerns of the prehistoric component at the site. Although an extensive program of excavation revealed the ancient sanctuary (Miller 1990), little effort was made to define the nature of the broader context (physical and social) within which the site operated. The excavation of Bronze Age Tsoungiza provides a wealth of data about a rural satellite of the key center at Mycenae. The archaeological survey (Cherry et al. 1988) was linked to the Tsoungiza excavation, but was not limited in chronological scope; sites range in date from Middle Palaeolithic to Late Byzantine. A sophisticated sampling procedure based on the work in Melos (Cherry 1982) and Kea (Cherry et al. 1991) provided ample coverage of the various environmental zones within the project area. Geomorphology, ethnography, and pollen analysis complete the range of studies NVAP personnel conducted. The major contribution of this project is that all the various analytical facets were fully integrated from the outset. This is particularly true for the excavation and archaeological survey; in most earlier projects the former preceded the latter, but at Nemea these two facets operated in concert, and so could deal with similar questions from the outset. In terms of field techniques, the excavation maintained very tight control of context by digging 1 x 1 meter units and screening all soil. The use of a flotation system enhanced the retrieval of floral and micro-faunal remains and facilitated explanation of dietary selection as part of a strategy of past adaptation. Another methodological innovation was the extensive use of computerized forms to record survey and excavation information and to assist in rapid data retrieval and analysis. The survey employed the non-site approach (Dunnell and Dancey 1983) which the survey directors used elsewhere to great benefit.

Conclusion

There have been many other regional studies in Greece over the past 30 years which have made major contributions and demonstrated the shift in orientation. Various groups have conducted such work on Kythera (Huxley and Coldstream 1973), Crete (Hayden and Moody 1991; Watrous 1975), in Boeotia (Bintliff and Snodgrass 1985; Gregory 1980), Macedonia (Savina et al. 1991), Thessaly (Milojčić et al. 1966), and Lakonia (Hope Simpson and Waterhouse 1961). The work of Higgs and his colleagues (Dakaris et al. 1964; Higgs and Vita-Finzi 1966) in Epiros focused on the Palaeolithic period, but involved excavation, surface survey, and the use of ethnographic analogy, and so qualifies as regional study. Current projects include the Grevena Survey, and the Korinthia Regional Research Consortium (Gregory and Kardulias 1989; Kardulias and Shutes 1992). Most proposals for archeological research in Greece now include a variety of integrated studies, e.g., excavation, surface survey, geophysical prospecting, geomorphological analysis, material sourcing, absolute dating, and examination of floral and faunal remains. The scope in many projects has moved from the single site to the total landscape. While not universal, the stress on regional study in many projects has created a new central focus for investigations. The new paradigm that forms the foundation of regional studies, and which reflects the fundamental shift that has occurred in Greek archaeology, exhibits a number of important traits:

(1) It tends to be anti-diffusionist. Causation is not viewed as a simple external stimulus, but as a complex phenomenon that involves internal social dynamics. Researchers explore the potential for indigenous change.

(2) General systems theory. Ecological relationships lend themselves well to discussion in terms of homeostatic and change-inducing mechanisms.

(3) The work is coherently interdisciplinary. Various specialists contribute from the beginning to the planning of a project and can thus structure their research with specific questions in mind. In early projects, such specialists served an ancillary role.

(4) The focus is not on individual artifacts or even sites, but on the region as a unit of interaction.

(5) Surface survey data are treated as an independent source of information about a region. While such data certainly aid in interpreting a site, they form a body of information that can stand independently and shed light on a wide range of regional traits.

(6) Regional studies often introduce new analytical methods and tools. In Greece, it is largely through regional analysis that remote sensing, geological/geomorphological studies, and other techniques have made their way into the research repertoire.

Regional study contrasts with the traditional approach which tended to be particularistic rather than generalizing, with an emphasis on artifacts and features (especially stone architecture) within individual sites as objects of study in their own right rather than as reflecting human adaptation to the environment. The use of earth and social sciences is a major addition by regional studies--various disciplines are not just supplemental but integral to regional research. The work of regional projects over the past three decades has indeed revolutionized our understanding of the Greek past and, in fact, our definition of archaeology. No longer can classical archaeology view its topics in splendid isolation--we must consider a broad spectrum of past human behaviors; studies of contemporary communities provide the inferential base for interpretation. The recruitment of individuals to fill future scholarly ranks requires serious consideration of skills in addition to the traditional training in history, language, and art history. Although the revolution is by no means complete, the emergence of regional studies signalled a realignment whose repercussions are still being felt. In addition, it is unfortunate that many of the exciting innovations in Aegean archaeology go unnoticed by Americanist archaeologists. The two communities have much to discuss to their mutual benefit.

References Cited

Biers, W.R.
  1987 *The Archaeology of Greece. An Introduction*. Revised ed.
  Cornell University Press, Ithaca.
Binford, L.
  1962 Archaeology as Anthropology. *American Antiquity* 28:217-225.
  1978 *Nunamiut Ethnoarchaeology*. Academic Press, New York.
  1980 Willow Smoke and Dogs' Tails: Hunter-Gatherer Settlement Systems and Archaeological Site Formation. *American Antiquity* 45:4-20.
Bintliff, J., and A.M. Snodgrass
  1985 The Cambridge/Bradford Boeotian Expedition: the First Four Years. *Journal of Field Archaeology* 12:123-161.
Broneer, O.
  1971 *Isthmia. Volume I. Temple of Poseidon*. American School of Classical Studies at Athens, Princeton.
Cherry, J.F.
  1982 A Preliminary Definition of Site Distribution on Melos. In *An Island Polity: The Archaeology of Exploitation in Melos*, edited by C. Renfrew and M. Wagstaff, pp. 10-23. Cambridge University Press, Cambridge.
Cherry, J.F., J.L. Davis, A. Demitrack, E. Mantzourani, T.F. Strasser, and L.E. Talalay
  1988 Archaeological Survey in an Artifact-Rich Landscape: A Middle Neolithic Example from Nemea, Greece. *American Journal of Archaeology* 92:159-176.
Cherry, J.F., J.L. Davis, and E. Mantzourani (editors)
  1991 *Landscape Archaeology as Long-Term History: Northern Keos in the Cycladic Islands*. UCLA Monumenta Archaeologica 16, UCLA Institute of Archaeology, Los Angeles.
Dakaris, S.I., E.S. Higgs, and R. Hey
  1964 The Climate, Environment and Industries of Stone Age Greece: Part I. *Proceedings of the Prehistoric Society* 30:199-245.

Dimen, M., and E. Friedl (editors)

    1976 *Regional Variation in Modern Greece and Cyprus: Toward a Perspective on the Ethnography of Greece.* Annals of the New York Academy of Sciences, No. 268. New York.

Dunnell, R.C., and W.S. Dancey

    1983 The Siteless Survey: A Regional Scale Data Collection Strategy. In *Advances in Archaeological Method and Theory*, vol. 6, edited by M.B. Schiffer, pp. 267-287. Academic Press, New York.

Dyson, S.

    1993 From New To New Age Archaeology: Archaeological Theory and Classical Archaeology--A 1990s Perspective. *American Journal of Archaeology* 97:195-206.

Fagan, B.

    1989 *People of the Earth.* 6th edition. Scott, Foresman, Boston.

Fowler, H.N., and R. Stilwell

    1932 *Corinth. I.1. Introduction. Topography. Architecture.* Harvard University Press, Cambridge.

Gregory, T.E.

    1980 Ohio Boeotia Expedition: Field Seasons 1979-1980, Preliminary Report. *Teiresias Archaeologica* 31-41.

    1990 Intensive Archaeological Survey and its Place in Byzantine Studies. *Byzantine Studies* 13(2):155-175.

Gregory, T.E., and P.N. Kardulias

    1989 An Island Survey in the Saronic Gulf. *Old World Archaeology Newsletter* 13(2):21-22.

Hansen, J.M.

    1991 *The Palaeoethnobotany of Franchthi Cave, Greece.* Excavations at Franchthi Cave, Greece, Fascicle 7. Indiana University Press, Bloomington.

Hayden, B.J., and J.A. Moody

    1991 The Vrokastro Survey Project, 1986-1990. *American Journal of Archaeology* 95:292 (abstract).

Higgs, E.S., and C. Vita-Finzi

    1966 The Climate, Environment and Industries of Stone Age Greece: Part II. *Proceedings of the Prehistoric Society* 32:1-29.

Hope Simpson, R.

    1985 Preface. In *Contributions to Aegean Archaeology: Studies in Honor of William A. McDonald*, edited by N.C. Wilkie and W.D.E. Coulson, pp. xviii-xx. Center for Ancient Studies Publications in Ancient Studies Number 1, University of

Minnesota, Minneapolis.

Hope Simpson, R., and H. Waterhouse
  1961 Prehistoric Laconia: Part II. *Annual of the British School at Athens* 56:114-175.

Huxley, G., and N. Coldstream (editors)
  1973 *Kythera: Excavations and Studies Conducted by the University of Pennsylvania Museum and the British School at Athens.* Noyes Press, Park Ridge, New Jersey.

Jacobsen, T.W.
  1976 17,000 Years of Greek Prehistory. *Scientific American* 234(6):76-87.

  1985 Another Modest Proposal: Ethnoarchaeology in Greece. In *Contributions to Aegean Archaeology: Studies in Honor of William A. McDonald*, edited by N.C. Wilkie and W.D.E. Coulson, pp. 91-107. Center for Ancient Studies Publications in Ancient Studies Number 1, University of Minnesota, Minneapolis.

Jacobsen, T.W., and W.R. Farrand
  1988 *Franchthi Cave and Paralia. Maps, Plans, Sections.* Excavations at Franchthi Cave, Greece, Fascicle 1. Indiana University Press, Bloomington.

Jacobsen, T.W., and D. Van Horn
  1974 The Franchthi Cave Flint Survey: Some Preliminary Results (1974). *Journal of Field Archaeology* 1:305-308.

Jameson, M.H.
  1969 Excavations at Porto Cheli and Vicinity, Preliminary Report I: Halieis, 1962-1968. *Hesperia* 38:311-42.

Jameson, M.H., T.H. van Andel, and C.N. Runnels
  1994 *A Greek Countryside: The Southern Argolid from Prehistory to the Present Day.* Stanford University Press, Stanford, in press.

Jochim, M.
  1976 *Hunter-Gatherer Subsistence and Settlement: A Predictive Model.* Academic Press, New York.

Kardulias, P.N.
  1992 The Ecology of Bronze Age Flaked Stone Tool Production in Southern Greece: The Evidence from Agios Stephanos and the Southern Argolid. *American Journal of Archaeology* 96:421-442.

Kardulias, P.N., and M.T. Shutes
  1992 Regional Study in the Korinthia-The Korinthia Exploration Project 1991. *Old World Archaeology Newsletter* 15(2):20-26.

Keeley, L.
  1988 Hunter-Gatherer Economic Complexity and "Population

Pressure": A Cross-Cultural Analysis. *Journal of Anthropological Archaeology* 7:373-411.

Kuhn, T.S.
  1970 *The Structure of Scientific Revolutions*. 2nd edition. University of Chicago Press, Chicago.

Lee, R., and I. Devore (editors)
  1968 *Man the Hunter*. Aldine, Chicago.

Marquardt, W., and C. Crumley
  1987 Theoretical Issues in the Analysis of Spatial Patterning. In *Regional Dynamics: Burgundian Landscapes in Historical Perspective*, edited by W.H. Marquardt and C.L. Crumley, pp. 1-18. Academic Press, Orlando.

McDonald, W.A.
  1972 The Problems and the Program. In *The Minnesota Messenia Expedition. Reconstructing a Bronze Age Regional Environment*, edited by G.R. Rapp and W.A. McDonald, pp. 3-17.. University of Minnesota Press, Minneapolis.

McDonald, W.A., and R. Hope Simpson
  1972 Archaeological Exploration. In *The Minnesota Messenia Expedition. Reconstructing a Bronze Age Regional Environment*, edited by G.R. Rapp and W.A. McDonald, pp. 117-147. University of Minnesota Press, Minneapolis.

McDonald, W.A., and G.R. Rapp (editors)
  1972 *The Minnesota Messenia Expedition. Reconstructing a Bronze Age Regional Environment*. University of Minnesota Press, Minneapolis.
  1972 Perspectives. In McDonald and Rapp, pp. 240-261.

McDonald, W.A., and C.G. Thomas
  1990 *Progress into the Past. The Rediscovery of Mycenaean Civilization*. 2nd edition. Indiana University Press, Bloomington.

Miller, S.G.
  1990 *Nemea. A Guide to the Site and Museum*. University of California Press, Berkeley.

Milojčić, V., J. Boessneck, D. Jung, and H. Schneider
  1965 *Paläolithikum um Larissa in Thessalien*. Habelt, Bonn.

Morris, I.
  1994 Archaeologies of Greece. In *Classical Greece: Ancient Histories and Modern Archaeologies*, edited by I. Morris. Cambridge University Press, Cambridge, in press.

Murray, P., and C. Chang
  1981 An Ethnoarchaeological Study of a Contemporary Herder's

Site. *Journal of Field Archaeology* 8:490-502.

Murray, P., and P.N. Kardulias
1986 A Modern Site Survey in the Southern Argolid, Greece. *Journal of Field Archaeology* 13:21-41.

Perlès, C.
1989 *Les Industries Lithiques Taillees de Franchthi (Argolide, Grèce), Tome I: Présentation Générale et Industries Paléolithiques.* Excavations at Franchthi Cave, Greece, Fascicle 3. Indiana University Press, Bloomington.
1991 *Les Industries Lithiques Taillees de Franchthi (Argolide, Grèce), Tome II: Les Industries du Mesolithique et du Néolithique Initial.* Excavations at Franchthi Cave, Greece, Fascicle 5. Indiana University Press, Bloomington.

Pope, K., and T.H. van Andel
1984 Late Quaternary Alluviation and Soil Formation in the Southern Argolid: Its History, Causes and Archaeological Implications. *Journal of Archaeological Science* 11:281-306.

Pope, K., C.N. Runnels, and T.-L. Ku
1984 Dating Middle Palaeolithic Red Beds in Southern Greece. *Nature* 312:264-266.

Price, T.D., and J. Brown (editors)
1985 *Prehistoric Hunter-Gatherers: The Emergence of Cultural Complexity.* Academic Press, San Diego.

Renfrew, C.
1972 *The Emergence of Civilisation: The Cyclades and the Aegean in the Third Millennium B.C.* Methuen, London.
1980 The Great Tradition versus the Great Divide: Archaeology as Anthropology? *American Journal of Archaeology* 84:287-298.
1982 Polity and Power: Interaction, Intensification and Exploitation. In Renfrew and Wagstaff, pp. 264-290.

Renfrew, C., and M. Wagstaff (editors)
1982 *An Island Polity: The Archaeology of Exploitation in Melos.* Cambridge University Press, Cambridge.

Runnels, C.N.
1975 A Note on Glass Implements from Greece. *Newsletter of Lithic Technology* 4(3):29-30.
1982 Flaked-Stone Artifacts in Greece during the Historical Period. *Journal of Field Archaeology* 9:363-373.
1985 Trade and Demand for Millstones in Southern Greece in the Neolithic and the Early Bronze Age. In *Prehistoric Production and Exchange: The Aegean and Eastern Mediterranean*, edited by B.

Knapp and T. Stech, pp. 30-43. UCLA Monographs in Archaeology No. 25, Los Angeles.

1988 Early Bronze-Age Stone Mortars from the Southern Argolid. *Hesperia* 57:257-272.

Runnels, C.N., D. Pullen, and S. Langdon (editors)

1994 *Artifact and Assemblage: Finds from a Greek Countryside, Volume I: The Prehistoric Pottery and the Lithic Artifacts.* Stanford University Press, Stanford, in press.

Runnels, C.N., and T.H. van Andel

1987 The Evolution of Settlement in the Southern Argolid, Greece: An Economic Explanation. *Hesperia* 56:303-34.

Sahlins, M.

1972 *Stone Age Economics.* Aldine, Chicago.

Savina, M., S.E. Aschenbrenner, and N. Wilkie

1991 *Terra Incognita* no Longer: Archaeological Survey in Grevena. *American Journal of Archaeology* 95:328 (abstract).

Shackleton, J.C.

1989 *Marine Molluscan Remains from Franchthi Cave.* Excavations at Franchthi Cave, Greece, Fascicle 4. Indiana University Press, Bloomington.

Snodgrass, A.M.

1985 The New Archaeology and the Classical Archaeologist. *American Journal of Archaeology* 89:31-37.

Sterud, G.

1973 A Paradigmatic View of Prehistory. In *The Explanation of Culture Change: Models in Prehistory*, edited by C. Renfrew, pp. 3-17. University of Pittsburgh Press, Pittsburgh.

Sutton, S.B. (editor)

1994 *Shepherds, Farmers, and Sailors: The Regional Ethnohistory of the Southern Argolid Peninsula.* Stanford University Press, Stanford, in press.

van Andel, T.H., T.W. Jacobsen, J.B. Jolly, and N. Lianos

1980 Late Quaternary History of the Coastal Zone Near Franchthi Cave, Southern Argolid, Greece. *Journal of Field Archaeology* 7:389-402.

van Andel, T.H., and N. Lianos

1983 Prehistoric and Historic Shorelines of the Southern Argolid Peninsula: A Subbottom Profiler Study. *International Journal of Nautical Archaeology and Underwater Exploration* 12:303-324.

1984 High-Resolution Seismic Reflection Profiles for the Reconstruction of Postglacial Transgression Shorelines: An

Example from Greece. *Quaternary Research* 22:31-35.

van Andel, T.H., and J.C. Shackleton
  1982 Late Paleolithic and Mesolithic Coastlines of Greece and the
  Aegean. *Journal of Field Archaeology* 9:445-454.

van Andel, T.H., and S.B. Sutton
  1987 *Landscape and People of the Franchthi Region*. Excavations
  at Franchthi Cave, Greece, Fascicle 2. Indiana University Press,
  Bloomington.

van Andel, T.H., and C.N. Runnels
  1987 *Beyond the Acropolis: A Rural Greek Past*. Stanford
  University Press, Stanford.

van Andel, T.H., C.N. Runnels, and K. Pope
  1986 Five Thousand Years of Land Use and Abuse in the Southern
  Argolid, Greece. *Hesperia* 55:103-128.

Waterhouse, H., and R. Hope Simpson
  1960 Prehistoric Laconia. Part I. *Annual of the British School at
  Athens* 55:67-107.

Watrous, L.V.
  1975 Explorations on the Plain of Lasithi in Crete. *Athens Annals
  of Archaeology* 8:206.

Wilkinson, T.J., and S.T. Duhon
  1991 *Franchthi Paralia: The Sediments, Stratigraphy, and Offshore
  Investigations*. Excavations at Franchthi Cave, Greece, Fascicle 6.
  Indiana University Press, Bloomington.

Willey, G.R.
  1953 *Prehistoric Settlement Patterns in the Virú Valley, Peru*.
  Bureau of American Ethnology Bulletin 155. Smithsonian
  Institution, Washington, D.C.

Winckelmann, J. J.
  1880[1767] *The History of Ancient Art*. J.R. Osgood, Boston.

Wright, J.C., J.F. Cherry, J.L. Davis, E. Mantzourani, S.B. Sutton,
and R.F. Sutton
  1990 The Nemea Valley Archaeological Project: A Preliminary
  Report. *Hesperia* 59:579-659.

II.
ENVIRONMENTAL STUDIES

Chapter 2

Geo-archaeology and Archaeological Science—A Personal View

Tjeerd H. van Andel

Introduction: A Matter of Thoughtful Conversation

Those archaeological surveys that have made use of Quaternary geology and other environmental sciences in recent years have shown how much this interdisciplinary analysis of landscape history is able to contribute to our understanding of the parameters of prehistoric as well as historic human settlement.

The relationship, however, between archaeology and the sciences it enlists in its endeavors tends to be uneasy. This discomfort, so evident in the reminiscences of Butzer (1975, 1980), Gladfelter (1977) or Hassan (1985), is to be expected, because it derives from major differences in concept and method of research. I shall be brief here because the issue is not new, but a few things may be fruitfully said. Being a geologist, I shall concentrate on geology as an example of archaeological science.

What is archaeological science, as distinct from scientific archaeology? Does it consist of: (1) scientists providing data archaeologists believe they need; (2) scientists collaborating with archaeologists on problems chosen by the latter; (3) archaeologists experienced in the use of science and skilled in collaborating with scientists; or (4) interdisciplinary activity by scientists and archaeologists focussed on archaeological issues? Ideally it should be the last, initiated and managed by a member of (3), but in practice (1), and less so (2), are more common. I do not wish to deny the utility of having one's bones identified or bronzes analyzed, but why so often is so little use made of the data later?

Clearly, this practice gains either partner very little. So why is it so common? A recent file of applicants for a major post in archaeological science shows that their publications, mostly entitled something like "The bones of..", were almost all found in appendices to excavation reports, without clear evidence that they had mattered a great deal to the excavator. Is this because physical, biological or geological scientists are seen as status symbols rather than employed for real needs?

There are many explanations. The geologist may have failed to recognize that the practice of geology in an archaeological context is quite markedly different from that in the mainstream. Or perhaps neither geologist nor archaeologist perceived that a geological proposition or archaeological question, although quite clear to the poser, may seem irrelevant, impractical, or even unintelligible to the other side. Also, the specialist's final report may, in the end, fail to address the topics that were closest to the archaeologist's heart.

At issue here is communication. Successful collaboration depends on correct answers to such fundamental questions of archaeological strategy as:

(1) What are, conceptually and operationally, the questions I should like some scientist to help answer?

(2) Which discipline or subdiscipline is best equipped to deal with these matters?

(3) How should my problem be phrased so that collaboration may be maximized?

(4) What do I need to learn so that I may understand the scientist's answers and make maximum use of them?

(5) Can I afford this financially?

Scientists, widely regarded as mighty grant-getters, are often supposed to pay for their collaboration themselves, but helping archaeologists ranks low among the funding priorities of chemistry, physics or earth science.

These questions (an analogous set exists for volunteer scientists) are difficult because of one's ignorance of the content and capability of the other discipline, and even more because of language problems so subtle that communication is often more apparent than real. As a result, the finer points and pitfalls of the interpretations proffered from each side are seldom fully appreciated. An example is the casualness with which many archaeologists deal with the impact of changing sea levels (van Andel 1989a).

It takes much time and very good intentions to overcome this barrier of ignorance and language confusion because we face here fundamental differences in the philosophy and practice of our respective disciplines. In its day-by-day reality science relies above all on a deep respect for evidence. It demands that any evidence, to be accepted, should be verifiable, and insists that all assumptions, error margins, or confidence limits (whether statistical or not) should be explicit and explicitly taken into account. If at all possible, alternate explanatory hypotheses must be considered, all hypotheses must be testable, and a full list (including rejected ones) should be presented. One expects theory to spring from evidence, generating the need for new evidence which spawns revised theory, and so forth. The reverse has sometimes been claimed in the literature of archaeological theory. Scientists also accept that the objective of research is to raise new questions as much as to attempt to answer old ones.

Most archaeologists subscribe consciously or subconsciously to the same precepts, although a widespread belief exists that the TRUTH can be more closely approximated the longer one delays writing the report. But the advent of modern archaeology (a term I use here to cover all descriptors beginning with post-) has brought new gurus from philosophy and the philosophy of science, such as Carl Hempel, who are not all regarded by scientists as having any notion of what science is about. Sometimes, in fact, the new spiritual leaders seem downright perverse, for example when they preach that theory takes precedence over evidence, or that evidence should not be obtained unless guided by theory. There is also a current vogue among social scientists to insist that the progression of scientific paradigms and laws is no more than a progression of social contracts, a view so patently absurd that discussion seems futile. And we part company entirely when the main objective of archaeological study is stated to be the acquisition of arguments for socio-economic and political reform (e.g., Shanks and Tilley 1987, passim). This easily leads to the political use of archaeology, something we have seen enough of in recent history to regard with great wariness even the mere chance of it happening again. These are serious barriers to the deployment of archaeological science.

It is clear that badly done geo-archaeology is as disastrous as the odd geological views held by some archaeologists. This raises the question of how one may insure that one's geologist is any good. Although many practitioners of archaeological geology are outstanding, the subject is not in the main-stream of the earth sciences and offers little credit. Also, it has at times provided a refuge to some geologists who found it difficult to hold their own in the center. There is no clear solution to this problem of selection but to strive for meaningful communication, to offer real integration, and to guarantee a fair share in the excitement of the interpretation. If not, science collaborators are, as is sometimes the case, degraded to technicians, and that does not encourage bright young scholars to enter the field.

Multidisciplinary or Interdisciplinary Approach

Members of different disciplines collaborate in two modes, an interdisciplinary and a multidisciplinary one. Although often regarded as equivalent, the two are in reality very different, as W.A. McDonald (McDonald and Rapp 1972) has pointed out, and they deliver different benefits. Interdisciplinary collaboration assumes intensive exchange of information, ideas and procedures from the planning stage through to final publication. It is true teamwork and all partners derive maximum benefit from a detailed and specific mutual understanding of each others' capacities, operations, and results. Integration comes naturally this way. Multidisciplinary projects lack these advantages. Their results are no better than the fragmentary understanding the scientists have of the archaeological objectives and the archaeologists of the scientific results. Here science and archaeology do not go hand-in-hand into the sunset, and much archaeological science is never fully used.

A fully integrated interdisciplinary study can be quite a strain on its participants, with potential points of friction arising at every turn. Daily communication between archaeologists and other scientists is the key to the reconciliation of problem definitions and data acquisition, and both are key prerequisites for the deep integration of hypotheses and interpretation that so sharply distinguishes an interdisciplinary approach from a merely multidisciplinary one.

Return to Reality

Would it not be simpler, and serve almost as well, to assume, at least geologically, that the landscape we need to understand has changed so little in the last 50,000 or 5,000 years that one can evaluate the past by simple backward extrapolation from the present, making suitable but modest allowances? This assumption underpinned the early use of site catchment analysis (Higgs and Vita-Finzi 1972; Jarman et al. 1972), a cherished concept later found to be quite insecure in its applications (Dennell 1980; Findlow and Ericson 1980; Gilman and Thornes 1985:35-41; Roper 1979). The same assumption, although implicit more often than explicit, is made in other contexts. A simple but dramatic case in point is the post-glacial change of sea level which removed, in a few thousand years, the resources of vast coastal plains now submerged off what are today rocky Mediterranean shores (e.g., Jameson et al. 1994; van Andel and Shackleton 1982).

Doing better is not always easy, however. For example, to meet the archaeologists' expectations we must understand the changing landscape on human scales of time and space, and that implies a resolving power measured in centuries or decades. Such time scales are taken for granted by historians, but geologists find them difficult to accommodate. Because the demand for precision in time and space diminishes as we go deeper into the past, the collaboration tends to be much happier for the Palaeolithic than for historical times.

Aspects of Archaeological Geology

What do we geologists do (and do well, we hope) when we take part in the study of archaeological problems? Many diverse things, of course. Some of us elucidate cave sediments, at times by rather old-fashioned, yet useful methods (something that is not always true of our attempts to apply the latest technology). Others who examine site formation processes find that an entire industry (for example Groenman-van Waateringe and Robinson 1988, passim; Schiffer 1987) has been re-inventing the basic knowledge that has long been familiar to sedimentologists. This suggests that we might train at least some archaeologists in appropriate branches of science to a level where they know the state of the art and can communicate, but how do we keep them in touch with the rapid progress of most fields?

Stratigraphy and geochronology and their interpretation are as critical in geology as they are in archaeology and we ought to be comfortable with each other in these endeavors. Yet it is here that we sometimes see the differences in philosophy and method I have alluded to above most clearly. When dealing with a complex stratigraphy and sparse geochronology of variable quality, it is essential to create, within the confidence limits of the data, chronological scenarios that range from those most pleasing to one's preconceptions to the one most perversely irritating (e.g., van Andel 1989b). It is perfectly legitimate to express a preference for one specific scenario on other grounds than chronology, but the complete range of possibilities should be clear to the author and made explicit to the reader. Unfortunately, the debate on the origin of anatomically modern human beings (see the discussions at a Royal Society Conference on "The Origin of Modern Humans and the Impact of Science-Based Dating" in 1992: Philosophical Transactions: Biological Sciences, Issue 1280, London, 1992) is not as reassuring on this point as one might wish.

Coincidence in time remains popular as "evidence" for causal relations, but to be entertained even as a mere possibility, such coincidence should be close in human terms, that is, on a scale of only years. Alas, all geochronological data have uncertainty limits and geochronological synchroneity is therefore a relative thing. The confidence limits of dates often permit us to say no more than that two events took place within the same century or millennium which is akin to regarding the American revolution as simultaneous with the election of Ronald Reagan. The debate over the proposal that the demise of the Minoan civilization resulted from an eruption of Santorini volcano nicely illustrates the mess arising from such inappropriate views of synchroneity, a condition only recently alleviated by Sturt Manning's brilliant analysis of the radiocarbon data (e.g., Manning and Weniger 1992).

Of course, the same problems plague geologists in equal measure; if one is convinced that the dinosaurs were wiped out by the impact of a large asteroid, one had better be prepared to demonstrate that impact and demise coincided within no more than a few years and that the extinction followed rather than preceded the impact. Because this has so far been impossible to do, this particular idea, so popular with the press, remains an unproven hypothesis. Obviously, the farther one goes back in time, the more difficult the question of synchroneity becomes, and many an archaeologist has been deeply troubled by her or his geologist's inability to say exactly when some natural event or catastrophe took place.

Fixing events in a relative or absolute time-frame is not the only use to which stratigraphy can be put, although it is by far the most common one. Stratigraphic mapping of deposits of a given age, for instance, is of great value in limiting the area that needs to be examined in the search for sites of that age. Terrain covered by young alluvium can be excluded in a survey concerned only with older sites (see, for example, Bintliff and Snodgrass 1985; Jameson et al. 1994), with major benefit to the budget. Occasionally maps of this kind are used to draw attention to areas where magnificent sites might be concealed by alluvium (e.g. Zangger 1991, 1992:201-213), although the sediment cover may render their excavation formidably difficult.

Geological maps based on a detailed Holocene stratigraphy are powerful tools in the interpretation of site patterns. Wells (1988, 1992), for example, has shown that many coastal prehistoric sites of northern Peru are distributed mainly as a function of an intermittent accretion of coastal alluvium that greatly increased the area of arable land.

Alternate interpretations need to be considered here: is a certain area free of sites of a given period because it was not suitable for settlement at that time, or was the land so useful that only its margins were sacrificed for housing? Or is the area covered by later deposits that conceal any sites that might have been there? An instructive example here is Bintliff's view (1976) that in the Bronze Age the Argive plain in Greece was a vast and useless swamp later covered with thick post-Bronze Age alluvium. This view was demolished when Finke (1988) demonstrated that the surface of the plain today is an Early Bronze Age soil, covered only here and there with thin younger deposits. Not surprisingly, Bronze Age and later sites have been increasingly turning up in the plain, once attention had been drawn to its real surface age.

Ancient soils have interested Old World archaeologists mainly for their agricultural usefulness, but have proved very unwilling to yield up the desired information. The same paleosols (Holliday 1989), however, are key elements in the stratigraphy required for detailed late Quaternary mapping, being especially valuable in correlating strata of highly variable lithology, a common situation in complex landscapes. The stratigraphic use of paleosols rests on the fact that, in many regions such as the Mediterranean, they form chronosequences of increasing maturity with time-dependent characteristics which, once calibrated for a given region, identify their ages within broad but useful limits. The members of a chronosequence depend primarily on the regional climate and only secondarily on local climate and substrate and so are quite uniform over large areas. An example of the utility of palaeosol stratigraphy is the sequence developed for the Peloponnesos by Pope and van Andel (1984; Pope et al. 1984) and for northern Greece by Demitrack (1986) and van Andel (Runnels and van Andel 1993a, 1993b). This use of stratigraphy has proved highly economical in the search for Middle Palaeolithic sites in these regions, and has led to the discovery of a hitherto unsuspected Early Palaeolithic in Thessaly (Runnels 1988; Runnels and van Andel 1993b) and serendipitously in

Epiros (Runnels and van Andel 1993a).

Analogous is Wells' (1988) use of paleosols and desert varnish to map deflation surfaces of various ages in northern coastal Peru which in this vast, empty landscape have facilitated the search for early paleo-Indian sites. Similar geomorphological methods have been applied by Goldberg (1986; Goldberg and Bar-Yosef 1990; Goldberg and Brimer 1984) in the Negev in Israel and, with modifications that show the subtlety and flexibility of the method, by Hoffecker (1988) in his search for Pleistocene human sites in Alaska.

The Evolving Landscape and Its Human Users

Notwithstanding this rich bouquet of applications, I agree with Karl Butzer (1982:1-7) that what archaeological geology does best (and possibly most enthusiastically) is the analysis of landscapes in terms of the changing options they present to their human occupants. As the intensity of occupation increases, the human beings themselves become major environmental, and hence, geological agents affecting these options. While valuing the many other things geologists can do in an archaeological context, I believe the study of the co-evolution of landscape and human culture to be our most exciting challenge and, fraught as it is with difficulties, thus far our most successful undertaking (see, for example, Mooers and Dobbs 1993; Rossignol and Wandsnider 1992).

The examination of a landscape as it evolves in tune (or out of tune) with human occupation and exploitation benefits the study of nature and of human behavior alike. Much can be learned from even a long-inhabited landscape regarding such important processes as river system dynamics (see, for example, Bell 1982; Bork 1989; Macklin et al. 1992; Patton and Schumm 1981; Schumm 1981; Schumm et al. 1984) or the evolution of shorelines (e.g., Beets et al. 1992; Kraft et al. 1985; Kraft and Rapp 1988; Mason and Jordan 1993). Inversely, the changing opportunities and constraints that are the consequence of the evolving landscape are critically important to our understanding of human history.

Our current concern about the global destruction wrought by human exploitation, for example, can draw on a vast literature on landscape changes resulting from human use (see, for example, Berglund 1986, 1992; Limbrey and Evans 1978; Limbrey et al. 1975). Initiated long ago by Iversen (1941), this field of study has flourished especially in western Europe where it strongly emphasizes the Middle Ages and later times (e.g., Roberts and Glasscock 1983; see also the journal *Landscape History*), and deserves to be known better in North America.

Surprisingly, the impact of changing landscapes on human history has attracted much less interest than its inverse, the impact of human beings on the landscape, notwithstanding a promise of rich results. A superb demonstration of what can be achieved comes from decades of collaboration between archaeologists and the soil survey in Holland (Edelman 1950). Their results vividly document the problems, successes and failures associated with six thousand years of living by a rising sea. The old ways of coping with the ever-present threat of floods there seem well-suited to application even today in less prosperous coastal areas of the world. Unfortunately, access to this work is hampered by publication in Dutch (e.g., Bierma et al. 1988), but others, for example the synthesis of van Es et al. (1988), at least display their results in striking and easily understood chronological map sequences.

The co-evolution of human settlement and landscape has too many facets to explore here, but one of the more revealing must surely be the selection of sites by the earliest farmers. The subject has received much attention, although mostly with a view to settlement siting rather than to the suitability of the land for cultivation, two related but not identical issues. Obviously, the subject must be difficult; almost everywhere thousands of years have so altered soils and hydrology that the study of their condition in the remote past holds little promise. And indeed, in Greece, for example, the growing number of archaeological surveys has yielded little that suggests clear preferences for certain types of soils. The question of water is more promising, although the difficulties encountered in inferring its past supply from present conditions are legion. Neolithic farmers at Franchthi Cave in Greece, for example, appear to have exploited marshes watered by springs that are now submerged by the sea (van Andel and Runnels 1987:70-71). In Thessaly, their contemporaries left behind swarms of settlement mounds on vast late Quaternary river terraces now elevated 5-15 m above the present river. Today these lands are watered only by winter rains, but a detailed geological analysis has shown that many Early and Middle Neolithic settlers farmed the land when it was still under construction by the Peneios River then flowing at a much higher level and therefore the cause of frequent winter and spring floods. Flood-water cropping in the spring makes sense in a Neolithic context, but the consequence is that the concept of early sedentism needs modification because the sites could not have been occupied throughout the year (van Andel et al. 1994). Intermittent site occupation on the Ulua River plain in Honduras (Pope 1985) has been observed also for Maya farmers of the last millennium B.C.

Land use, whether it be for settlement or agriculture, will produce soil erosion, an issue viewed with concern in modern times and now gaining interest in archaeology (Bell and Boardman 1992). However, not only humans cause soil erosion; climate changes, the evolution of river systems, and the rise or fall of sea or land are also capable of doing so. The potentially complex nature of these situations has been insufficiently recognized in many early studies, such as the well-known alluvial model for Mediterranean rivers of Vita-Finzi (1969; Bintliff 1977; Davidson and Theocharopoulos 1992; Pope and van Andel 1984; van Andel et al. 1990; Wagstaff 1981). Great advances in our understanding of stream dynamics and modern soil erosion have clarified many of the complexities during the last 25 years. A growing number of local and regional diachronic studies of ancient soil erosion in the Mediterranean region (e.g., Runnels and van Andel 1987; van Andel et al. 1986) and elsewhere (Bell 1992; Van Vliet-Lanoë et al. 1992) shows the importance of this phenomenon for an understanding of early agricultural economics, but it is still too early to construct useful generalizations.

Similar complexity, also widely underestimated, afflicts the subject of Pleistocene and Holocene sea level changes and their impact on coastal land use and human migrations. Having addressed this subject in some detail recently (van Andel 1989a), I only note here that suitable general recipes, easy to apply by the excavators of coastal sites and surveyors of coastal regions, do not exist. Numerous are the cases where the consequences of post-glacial sea level change have been seriously misunderstood, and it is clear that the answers needed by the archaeologist must come from highly experienced collaborators.

Challenges

Obviously, the garden of archaeological geology has not yet been exhaustively cultivated and wider application of the geologist's skill may open new territories to archaeological exploration. So far, the course of archaeological geology has been determined largely by whatever cries for help issued from the archaeological community as they pursued their own research agenda. I suggest that it is time for archaeological geologists to establish their own long-term priorities for the systematic exploration of the less known reaches of their subject, then persuade archaeologists to join them.

Underexploited areas are not difficult to find. I think here above all of the study of major alluvial plains (Gladfelter 1985). Pioneered successfully in the Netherlands (see Louwe Kooymans 1972 for a superb example), the methods available today face a major challenge in the early settlements and cities of the great river plains of China. Covered as those are by a thick alluvium, geophysical and drilling techniques require further development before they can be employed there, and generous funding will be needed, but the potential rewards are great. Like the Dutch did, we might best learn first in simpler river valleys, perhaps those of the middle Nile.

Randomly looking around for other openings, there is the matter of the human impact, mainly by burning I suppose, on the pre-agricultural landscape as far back as the discovery of the use of fire (Bush 1988; James 1989). This is a subject of vast speculation, unreasonable application of modern anthropological observations, and very little hard data. It is not easy to see what might improve this situation, but I do sometimes hear that there are no limits to what geochemistry can do.

It is also obvious that the continental shelves, which emerged in the last glacial period and especially during its recent maximum, were exploited by human beings (Shackleton et al. 1984; van Andel 1989b), but their archaeological exploration presents enormous difficulties, not the least of which is the high cost of work at sea. Small-scale investigations such as the study of the shelf exposed while Franchthi Cave in Greece was occupied (Shackleton and van Andel 1986) have been encouraging, and Stright (1986a, 1986b) is optimistic about the application of high-resolution seismic reflection in the Gulf of Mexico. Although a lifetime spent in seafloor exploration by such methods and others renders me a bit skeptical about the practicality of archaeology at sea, one cannot deny that the subject has appeal and that relatively simple geophysical methods might be suitably adapted by clever hands. On the other hand, when presented with the suggestion that manned submersibles are the answer, it is best to turn away; much as I have enjoyed working with those in the deep ocean, the experience has firmly suggested that we should first solve the problem of locating the targets with high precision (probably under some overburden) before we consider spending vast kilobucks on a gadget that covers less terrain in a day than the smallest human survey team does in an hour.

Touched upon earlier, site formation processes are a subject that seems to be ripe for the attention of sedimentologists with more sophisticated approaches than have hitherto been used. The fine work of Paul Goldberg (Goldberg 1989; Goldberg and Laville 1985) is an example of what can be achieved. Many also have high expectations of soil micromorphology (Bullock et al. 1985; Courty et al. 1989; Fedoroff et al. 1987). If this method is suitably combined with allied skills from sedimentary petrology and geochemistry, we may really begin to understand how sites form. I, for one, would very much like to know how a Romano-British city on the Welsh Border, deserted in the 5th century and well away from any early medieval towns, managed to convert itself into the gently rolling, grassy plain of today.

On the other hand, let us not be too enthusiastic about the role of natural catastrophes in human prehistory and history. The often surmised seismic destruction of ancient sites is rarely solidly documented (Rapp 1986), and to the best of my knowledge there are no known cases of civilizations destroyed by volcanic eruptions, sudden sinking of the land, or vast floods.

Still, there seems to be plenty to do for capable hands and scientific minds, especially if these minds can get around the communication problems that have bedeviled many previous efforts. Without real integration of science and archaeology not much will happen. If the archaeologists are not careful about picking their collaborators in science, much chaff will continue to adulterate the grain, and if excavation directors continue to insist on preparing their final reports single-handedly, much scientific output will remain unused. On the other side, more senior scientists, their futures assured, might consider taking a part-time interest in archaeological science, a subject where full-time employment is rare.

Numerous regional archaeological surveys, well integrated with paleoenvironmental research, have demonstrated the importance of the co-evolution of landscape and human culture from earliest prehistory to the present time. In doing so these studies have greatly enriched archaeology itself, while bringing a rich harvest for paleobotany, paleozoology, paleolimnology, and Quaternary geology. Their importance for such new subjects in the earth sciences as neotectonics is only beginning to be appreciated. The effort needed to bring such multi-disciplinary programs to a full interdisciplinary conclusion is small compared to the importance of the results.

References Cited

Beets, D.J., L. van der Valk, and M.S.F. Stive
  1992 Holocene Evolution of the Coast of Holland. *Marine Geology* 103:423-442.
Bell, M.
  1982 The Effects of Land-use and Climate on Valley Sedimentation. In *Climatic Change in Later Prehistory*, edited by A. Harding, pp. 127-142. Edinburgh University Press, Edinburgh.
  1992 The Prehistory of Soil Erosion. In *Past and Present Soil Erosion*, edited by M. Bell and J. Boardman, pp. 21-36. Oxbow Monograph 22, Oxford.
Bell, M., and J. Boardman (editors)
  1992 *Past and Present Soil Erosion*. Oxbow Monograph 22, Oxford.
Berglund, B.E.
  1986 The Cultural Landscape in a Long-term Perspective: Methods and Theories behind the Research on Land-use and Landscape Dynamic. *Striae* 24:79-87.
Berglund, B.E. (editor)
  1992 *The Cultural Landscape during 6000 Years in Southern Sweden: The Ystad Project*. Ecological Bulletin Vol. 41. Munksgaard, Copenhagen.
Bierma, M., O.H. Harsema, and W. van Zeist
  1988 *Archeologie en Landschap*. Meulenhoff, Amsterdam.
Bintliff, J.L.
  1976 Sediments and Settlement in Southern Greece. In *Geoarchaeology*, edited by D.A. Davidson and M.L. Shackley, pp. 267-275. Duckworth, London.
  1977 *Natural Environment and Human Settlement in Prehistoric Greece*. BAR International Series 28. British Archaeological Reports, Oxford.
Bintliff, J.L., and A.M. Snodgrass
  1985 The Cambridge/Bradford Boeotian Expedition. *Journal of Field Archaeology* 12:123-163.
Bork, H.-R.
  1989 Soil Erosion During the Past Millennium in Central Europe and its Significance in the Geomorphodynamics of the Holocene. *Catena* supplement 15:121-131.

Bullock, P., N. Fedoroff, A. Jongerius, G. Stoops, T. Tursina, and U. Babel
    1985 *Handbook for Soil Thin Section Description.* Waine Research, Wolverhampton.
Bush, M.B.
    1988 Early Mesolithic Disturbance: A Force on the Landscape. *Journal of Archaeological Science* 15:453-462.
Butzer, K.W.
    1975 The Ecological Approach to Archaeology: Are we Really Trying? *American Antiquity* 40:106-111.
    1980 Context in Archaeology: An Alternative Perspective. *Journal of Field Archaeology* 7:417-422.
    1982 *Archaeology as Human Ecology.* Cambridge University Press, Cambridge.
Courty, M.A., P. Goldberg, and R. Macphail
    1989 *Soils and Micromorphology in Archaeology.* Cambridge University Press, Cambridge.
Davidson, D.A., and S.P. Theocharopoulos
    1992 A Survey of Soil Erosion in Viotia, Greece. In *Past and Present Soil Erosion*, edited by M. Bell and J. Boardman, pp. 149-154. Oxbow Monograph 22, Oxford.
Demitrack, A.
    1986 *The Late Quaternary History of the Larissa Plain, Thessaly, Greece: Tectonic, Climatic and Human Impact on the Landscape.* Ph.D. dissertation, Stanford University, Stanford. University Microfilms, Ann Arbor.
Dennell, R.
    1980 The Use, Abuse and Potential of Site Catchment Analysis. In *Catchment Analysis: Essays on Prehistoric Resource Space*, edited by F. J. Findlow and J. E. Ericson, pp. 1-2. Anthropology Department, University of California, Los Angeles, Report 10.
Edelman, C.H.
    1950, *Soils of the Netherlands.* North Holland Publishing Company, Amsterdam.
Fedoroff, N., L.M. Bresson, and M.A. Courty (editors)
    1982 *Soil Micromorphology.* Association Française pour l'Étude du Sol, Paris.
Findlow, F.J., and J.E. Ericson (editors)
    1980 *Catchment Analysis: Essays on Prehistoric Resource Space.* Anthropology Department, University of California, Los Angeles, Report 10.

Finke, A.E.W.

1988 *Landscape Evolution of the Argive Plain, Greece: Paleoecology, Holocene Depositional History and Coastline Changes*. Ph.D. dissertation. Stanford University. Stanford. University Microfilms, Ann Arbor.

Gilman, A., and Thornes, J.B.

1985 *Land-use and Prehistory in South-east Spain*. Allen and Unwin, London.

Gladfelter, B.G.

1977 Geo-archaeology: The Geomorphologist and Archaeology. *American Antiquity* 42:519-538.

1985 On the Interpretation of Archaeological Sites in Alluvial Settings. In *Archaeological Sediments in Context*, edited by J.K. Stein and W.R. Farrand, pp. 41-52. University of Maine Press, Orono.

Goldberg, P.

1986 Late Quaternary Environmental History of the Southern Levant. *Geoarchaeology* 1:225-244.

1989 Soils, Sediments and Acheulian Artefacts at Berekhat Ram, Golan Heights. In *Soil Micromorphology*, edited by M. Fedoroff, L.M. Bresson, and M.A. Courty, pp. 583-590. Association Française pour l'Étude du Sol, Paris.

Goldberg, P., and O. Bar-Yosef

1990 The Effect of Man on Geomorphological Processes upon Evidence from the Levant and Adjacent Areas. In *Man's Role in the Shaping of the Eastern Mediterranean Landscape*, edited by S. Bottema, G. Entjes-Nieborg and W. van Zeist, pp. 71-86. Balkema, Rotterdam.

Goldberg, P., and B. Brimer

1984 Late Pleistocene Geomorphic Surfaces and Environmental History of the Avdat Area. In *Prehistory and Palaeoenvironments in the Central Negev, Israel*, vol. 3, edited by A.E. Marks, pp. 1-13. Southern Methodist University Press, Dallas.

Goldberg, P., and H. Laville

1985 Les dépots du gisement Natoufien et Khamien de Hatoula (Israel): Charactéristiques, origine et signification. In *Le site Natoufien-Khamien de Hatoula, près de Latroun, Israel*, edited by M. Lechevallier and A. Ronen, pp. 59-70. Les Cahiers du CRFJ Vol. 1, Jerusalem.

Groenman-van Waateringe, W., and M. Robinson (editors)

1988 *Man-made Soils*. BAR International Series 410. British

Archaeological Reports, Oxford.

Hassan, F.A.
1985 Paleoenvironment and Contemporary Archaeology: A Geoarchaeological Approach. In *Archaeological Geology*, edited by G. Rapp Jr. and J.A. Gifford, pp. 85-102. Yale University Press, New Haven, Connecticut.

Higgs, E.S., and C. Vita-Finzi
1972 Prehistoric Economies: A Territorial Approach. In *Papers in Economic Prehistory*, edited by E.S. Higgs, pp. 27-36. Cambridge University Press, Cambridge.

Hoffecker, J.J.
1988 Applied Geomorphology and Archaeological Survey Strategy for Sites of Pleistocene Age: An Example from Central Alaska. *Journal of Archaeological Science* 15:683-713.

Holliday, V.T.
1989 Paleopedology in Archeology. *Catena* supplement 16:187-206.

Iversen, J.
1941 Landnam i Danmarks Stenaldern. *Danmarks Geologiske Undersögelse* 2:1-68.

James, S.R.
1989 Hominid Use of Fire in the Lower and Middle Pleistocene: A Review of the Evidence. *Current Anthropology* 30:1-26.

Jameson, M.H., C.N. Runnels, and T.H. van Andel
1994 *A Greek Countryside: The Southern Argolid from Prehistory to the Present Day*. Stanford University Press, Stanford, in press.

Jarman, M.R., C. Vita-Finzi, and E.S. Higgs
1972 Site Catchment Analysis in Archaeology. In *Man, Settlement and Urbanism*, edited by P.J. Ucko, G.W. Dimbleby, and R. Tringham, pp. 61-66. Duckworth, London.

Kraft, J.C., İ. Kayan, and S.E. Aschenbrenner
1985 Geological Studies of Coastal Change Applied to Archaeological Settings. In *Archaeological Geology*, edited by G.R. Rapp Jr. and J.A. Gifford, pp. 17-26. Yale University Press, New Haven, Connecticut.

Kraft, J.C., and G.R. Rapp Jr.
1988 Geological Reconstruction of Ancient Coastal Landforms in Greece with Predictions of Future Coastal Changes. In *The Engineering Geology of Ancient Works*, Monuments and Historical Sites, edited by P.G. Marinos and G.C. Koukis, pp. 1545-1556. Balkema, Rotterdam.

Limbrey, S., J.G. Evans, and H. Cleere (editors)

1975 *The Effect of Man on the Landscape: The Highland Zone.*
Council for British Archaeology, Research Report 11. London.
Limbrey, S., and J.G. Evans (editors)
1978 *The Effect of Man on the Landscape: The Lowland Zone.*
Council for British Archaeology, Research Report 21. London.
Louwe Kooijmans, L.P.
1974 *The Rhine/Meuse Delta: Four Studies on its Prehistoric Occupation and Holocene Geology.* Analecta Praehistorica Leidensia VII. E.J. Brill, Leiden.
Macklin, M.G., B.T. Rumsby, and T. Heap
1992 Flood Alluviation and Entrenchment: Holocene Valley-Floor Development and Transformation in the British Uplands. *Bulletin of the Geological Society of America* 104:631-643.
Manning, S.W., and B. Weninger
1992 A Light in the Dark: Archaeological Wiggle Matching and the Absolute Chronology of the Close of the Aegean Late Bronze Age. *Antiquity* 66:636-664.
Mason, O.K., and J.W. Jordan
1993 Heightened North Pacific Storminess during Synchronous Late Holocene Erosion of Northwest Alaska Beach Ridges. *Quaternary Research* 40:55-69.
McDonald, W.A., and G.R. Rapp, Jr.
1972 *The Minnesota Messenia Expedition: Reconstructing a Bronze Age Regional Environment.* University of Minnesota Press, Minneapolis.
Mooers, H.D., and C.A. Dobbs
1993 Holocene Landscape Evolution and the Development of Models for Human Interaction with the Environment: An Example from the Mississippi Headwaters Region. *Geoarchaeology--An International Journal* 8:475-492.
Patton, P.C., and S.A. Schumm
1981 Ephemeral Stream Processes: Implications for Studies of Quaternary Valley Fills. *Quaternary Research* 15:24-43.
Pope, K.O.
1985 *Paleoecology of the Ulua Valley, Honduras: An Archaeological Perspective.* Ph.D. dissertation, Stanford University, Stanford. University Microfilms, Ann Arbor.
Pope, K.O., C.N. Runnels, and T.-L. Ku
1984 Dating Middle Palaeolithic Red Beds in Southern Greece. *Nature* 312:264-266.

Pope, K.O., and T.H. van Andel
   1984 Late Quaternary Alluviation and Soil Formation in the
         Southern Argolid: Its History, Causes and Archaeological
         Implications. *Journal of Archaeological Science* 11:281-306.
Rapp Jr., G.
   1986 Assessing Archaeological Evidence for Seismic Catastrophes.
         Geoarchaeology 1:365-380.
Roberts, B.K., and R.E. Glasscock (editors)
   1983 *Villages, Fields and Frontiers. Studies in European Rural
         Settlement in the Medieval and Early Modern Periods.* BAR
         International Series 185. British Archaeological Reports, Oxford.
Roper, D.C.
   1979 The Method and Theory of Site Catchment Analysis: A
         Review. *Advances in Archaeological Method and Theory* 2:119-
         140.
Rossignol, J., and L. Wandsnider (editors)
   1992 *Space, Time and Archaeological Landscapes.* Plenum Press,
         New York.
Runnels, C.N.
   1987 The Evolution of Settlement in the Southern Argolid, Greece:
         An Economic Explanation. *Hesperia* 56:303-334.
   1988 A Prehistoric Survey of Thessaly: New Light on the Greek
         Middle Palaeolithic. *Journal of Field Archaeology* 15:277-290.
Runnels, C.N., and T.H. van Andel
   1993a A Hand Axe from Kokkinopilos, Epirus, and its Implications
          for the Paleolithic of Greece. *Journal of Field Archaeology*
          20:191-203.
   1993b The Lower and Middle Paleolithic of Thessaly, Greece.
          Journal of Field Archaeology 20:299-318.
Schiffer, M.B.
   1987 *Formation Processes of the Archaeological Record.*
         University of New Mexico Press, Albuquerque.
Schumm, S.A.
   1981 Evolution and Response of the Fluvial System:
         Sedimentological Implications. *Society of Economic Paleontologists
         and Mineralogists*, Special Publication 31:19-29.
Schumm, S.A., M.D. Harvey, and C.C. Watson
   1984 *Incised Channels: Morphology, Dynamics and Control.* Water
         Resources Publications, Littleton, Colorado.
Shackleton, J.C., T.H. van Andel, and C.N. Runnels
   1984 Coastal Paleogeography of the Central and Western

Mediterranean during the Last 125,000 Years and Its Archaeological Implications. *Journal of Field Archaeology* 11:307-314.

Shackleton, J.C., and T.H. van Andel
  1986 Prehistoric Shore Environments, Shellfish Availability and Shellfish Gathering at Franchthi, Greece. *Geoarchaeology* 1:127-143.

Shanks, M., and C. Tilley
  1987 *Reconstructing Archaeology*. Cambridge University Press, Cambridge.

Stright, M.J.
  1986a Human Occupation of the Continental Shelf during the Late Pleistocene/Early Holocene: Methods for Site Location. *Geoarchaeology* 1:347-364.
  1986b Evaluation of Archaeological Site Potential on the Gulf of Mexico Continental Shelf Using High Resolution Seismic Data. *Geophysics* 51:605-622.

van Andel, T.H.
  1989a Late Quaternary Sea Level Changes and Archaeology. *Antiquity* 63:733-745.
  1989b Late Pleistocene Changing Sealevel and the Human Exploitation of the Shore and Shelf of Southern South Africa. *Journal of Field Archaeology* 16:133-155.

van Andel, T.H., K. Gallis, and G. Toufexis
  1994 Early Neolithic Farming in a River Landscape: A Test Case from Thessaly, Greece. In *Mediterranean Quaternary River Environments*, edited by J. Woodward, in press.

van Andel, T.H., and N. Lianos
  1983 Prehistoric and Historic Shorelines of the Argolid Peninsula, Greece: A Subbottom Profiler Study. *International Journal for Nautical Archaeology and Underwater Exploration* 24:303-324.

van Andel, T.H., C.N. Runnels, and K.O. Pope
  1986 Five Thousand Years of Land Use and Abuse in the Southern Argolid. *Hesperia* 55:103-138.

van Andel, T.H., and C.N. Runnels
  1987 *Beyond the Acropolis: A Rural Greek Past*. Stanford University Press, Stanford, California.

van Andel, T.H., and J.C. Shackleton
  1982 Late Paleolithic and Mesolithic Coast Lines of Greece and the Aegean. *Journal of Field Archaeology* 9:445-454.

van Andel, T.H., E. Zangger, and A. Demitrack
  1990 Land Use and Soil Erosion in Prehistoric and Historic
    Greece. *Journal of Field Archaeology* 17:379-396.
van Es, W.A., H. Sarfatij, and P.J. Woltering
  1988 *Archeologie in Nederland*. Meulenhoff, Amsterdam.
Van Vliet-Lanoë, B., M. Helluin, J. Pellerin, and B. Valadas
  1992 Soil Erosion in Western Europe from the Last Interglacial to
    the Present. In *Past and Present Soil Erosion*, edited by M. Bell
    and J. Boardman, pp. 101-114. Oxbow Monograph 22, Oxford.
Vita-Finzi, C.
  1969 *The Mediterranean Valleys: Geological Changes in Historical
    Times*. Cambridge University Press, Cambridge.
Wagstaff, J.M.
  1981 Buried Assumptions: Some Problems in the Interpretation of
    the "Younger Fill" Raised by Recent Data from Greece. *Journal
    of Archaeological Science* 8:247-264.
Wells, L.E.
  1988 *Holocene Fluvial and Shoreline History as a Function of
    Human and Geologic Factors in Arid Northern Peru*. Ph.D.
    dissertation, Stanford University, Stanford. University Microfilms,
    Ann Arbor.
  1992 Holocene Landscape Change on the Santa Delta, Peru: Impact
    of Archaeological Site Distribution. *The Holocene* 2:193-204.
Zangger, E.
  1991 Tiryns Unterstadt. *Archaeometry* 90:831-840.
  1992 *The Flood from Heaven--Deciphering the Atlantis Legend*.
    Sidgwick and Jackson, London.

Chapter 3

The Prehistoric Environment of Greece: A Review of the Palynological Record

Sytze Bottema

Introduction

During the past thirty years ample evidence on the evolution of vegetation in Greece has appeared, generally in the form of pollen diagrams and to a lesser extent in macrofossil studies. Many of the pollen analyses were undertaken in conjunction with archaeological projects to reconstruct the botanical environment of prehistoric people and to explain past climate.

We now have enough pollen records for an orientation in this field of research. As palynological research continues, it should focus directly on the relation between the natural evolution of vegetation and human impact on plant regimes. Thorough surveys have to be made to evaluate this connection.

In addition to the traditional explication of pollen diagrams, new mathematical and statistical methods are being developed. They are not so much meant to analyze the present evidence botanically, but to focus on the potential for discerning past climatic conditions in pollen data.

In this contribution the information on the Greek pollen record from the last 15,000 years will be briefly reviewed. I attempt to give a general picture of the landscape during successive periods. The model is based on the subfossil pollen precipitation contained in sediment archives. This subfossil pollen precipitation has to be translated in terms of vegetation, a problematic task. Supportive evidence is derived from studies of modern pollen precipitation.

Modern plant associations formed by a combination of species in a characteristic way can be recent developments, with no subfossil counterparts indicated by the record. It is likely that our interpretation of the palynological information will improve in the future; it may even change fundamentally.

Reconstructing the Environment of Prehistoric Humans in Greece

Palynological research in Greece during the last 30 years has supplied us with a substantial body of data. General information on the subject has appeared in Van Zeist and Bottema (1982) and Marks (1986). Additionally, a study of Late Quaternary vegetation by Willis (1992a, 1992b, 1992c) and another by Atherden et al. (1993) of younger deposits in Greece were reported at the 8th International Palynological Congress at Aix-en-Provence in September, 1992.

The value of the information, presented as pollen diagrams obtained from the coring sites shown on the map (Figure 3.1), varies from location to location. A map with the distribution of human habitation for the various past periods differs very much from the evidence of the pollen record. Local geomorphology has great influence on the development of suitable pollen records, which do not necessarily coincide exactly with the surroundings of prehistoric people. The quality of pollen-bearing sediment cannot always be predicted, since higher elevations have a climatic regime that is more favorable for the preservation of organic remains than lower elevations, especially under pronounced Mediterranean climatic conditions. To avoid secondary deposition, sediments from small catchment basins are preferred. In practice such situations are rare, especially in lowlands where large alluvial plains are present.

Early Neolithic settlements have been found on the Thessalian and Macedonian plains and it is obvious that palynological research focusses upon such areas (Wijnen 1982). Sedimentation in those plains is common but that does not always guarantee the presence of reliable pollen records. Accumulation can be very irregular. Local erosion may

Figure 3.1. Location of pollen records from Greece up to 1992: 1. Gravouna (Turner and Greig 1975); 2. Tenagi Philippon (Wijmstra 1969); 3. Volvi (Bottema 1982(1985)); 4. Giannitsa (Bottema 1974); 5. Edessa (Bottema 1974); 6. Vegoritis (Bottema 1982 (1985)); 7. Khimaditis (Bottema 1974); 8. Kastoria (Bottema 1974); 9. Litochoro (Athanasiadis 1975); 10. Ioannina (Bottema 1974); 11. Pertouli (Athanasiadis 1975); 12. Viviis (Bottema 1979); 13. Xinias (Bottema 1979); 14. Voulkaria (Wright 1972); 15. Trikhonis (Bottema 1982(1985)); 16. Boeotia (Turner and Greig 1975); 17. Kaiafa (Wright 1972); 18. Osmanaga (Wright 1972); 19. Aghia Gallini (Bottema 1980); 20. Zileria (Reinders and Bottema 1983); 21. Halos (Reinders 1988); 22. Lerna (Jahns 1990); 23. Kiladha (Bottema 1990); 24. Thermisia (Sheehan 1979); 25. Paikon (Athanasiadis and Gerasimidis 1987); 26. Lailas (Athanasiadis and Gerasimidis 1984/1985); 27. Kokkini Br./Flampouro (Athanasiadis and Gerasimidis 1986).

destroy parts that have been deposited shortly before. Sedimentation may be very rapid for short periods, even depositing coarse material that not only lacks pollen but that cannot be sampled nor penetrated with simple coring techniques. During some periods sediment was not deposited at all, resulting in hiatuses in the record. When sediments dry up during the summer, pollen can be corroded, and partly or completely destroyed.

The formation of suitable pollen archives is hindered by the effect of the hot Mediterranean summer, especially in the southern part of Greece. Annual summer drought, or at least periodic drying up of basins or swamps, made organic remains disappear from the sediment. The most predictable source of water is the sea, but one has to realize that the Holocene sea-level rise invaded the lower elevations in Greece. Younger sediments are thus found close to the present coast line (Van Andel and Sutton 1987), whereas Early Holocene and Late Pleistocene sediments are lying in water deeper than 80 m. Such depths can, of course, not be sampled with simple hand-coring equipment.

As a result, there is an uneven spatial distribution of pollen records (Figure 3.1); coverage is unequal throughout the peninsula. There is also a variation in the time period represented by the records (Figure 3.2), some covering 50,000 years or more (Ioannina, Tenagi Philippon, Xinias), while others inform us about the pollen rain of the last millennium only (Athanasiadis 1975).

Another factor is the elevation at which the pollen samples are drawn. The cores are collected either from elevations below 100 m or above 400 m. In between there is a gap where the formation of suitable sediments is less frequent or the area has been insufficiently surveyed. The availability of pollen records connected with the presence of archaeological sites does not differ fundamentally from that in other countries. Direct evidence, mainly pollen sites present within a few hundred meters of prehistoric settlements, is very scarce.

One may wonder if it is not more profitable to apply pollen analysis to samples obtained directly from archaeological excavations. Such research has been done in many places around the world with dubious results. Especially in climates with a hot dry summer, the conditions for the preservation of pollen are very poor. Turner (1985) has written an extensive essay on this subject that is of interest to archaeologists.

The analysis of subfossil sediments demonstrates that the subfossil pollen precipitation occurred under certain conditions in a catchment. This information has to be translated into actual vegetation. Information on the modern pollen rain from samples collected in a known vegeta-

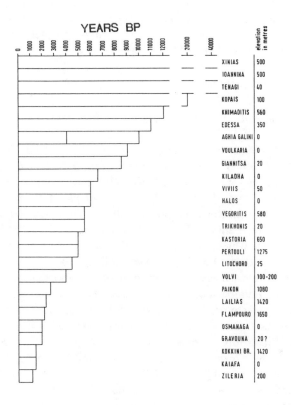

Figure 3.2. Time covered by the various pollen diagrams from Greece.

tional regime may serve as a reference point. Of course the modern plant cover is often not a natural undisturbed vegetation. In this context, undisturbed means not influenced by human activity. Sheehan (1979) and Bottema (1974, 1979) have performed studies in which they measured the present-day pollen precipitation in Greece and used the data to explain the modern vegetation. The correlation of modern pollen profiles to contemporary vegetation is used as an inferential base to interpret the value of the subfossil pollen rain.

The Pollen Sequence

The Late Glacial: 15,000-10,000 B.P.

Pollen diagrams that inform us about the older period, from about 15,000 to 10,000 B.P., originate mostly from the mainland mountain area at elevations of ca. 400 to 600 masl (Ioannina, Xinias, Khimaditis, and Edessa). From Thrace, evidence is available at 40 m (Wijmstra 1969). A core from Kopais in Boeotia, although not radiocarbon dated, very likely covers this period, also (Turner and Greig 1975).

This period, which coincides with the Late Glacial as it is known from northwestern Europe, shows pollen assemblages that are characterized by *Artemisia* (Wormwood) and Chenopodiaceae (Goosefoot family), Plumbaginaceae (sea lavender, thrift) and *Ephedra*. These herbs are characteristic for steppe vegetation growing under rather harsh conditions characterized by little precipitation. Pollen of trees in this period is mainly confined to that of *Pinus* (pine) and some *Betula* (birch), although many other types can be found in very low numbers. It is concluded from this evidence that a narrow tree belt was found in the mountains where it was not yet too cold for hardy species and where enough moisture formed because of the low temperature prevailing at such elevations. Many other tree species occurred elsewhere in Greece, maybe at low elevations on the southern coasts, but these are, unfortunately, not covered by pollen records of that time. In the interior, many species that could not form forests in the given conditions, could maintain themselves as individuals in edaphically favorable situations, for instance in pockets on south exposures where run-off water gathered, or on shadowy north slopes.

It is questionable to what extent Late Glacial temperatures in Greece can be compared with the ones reconstructed for that period in Northwestern Europe. In the latter area the average annual temperature was an estimated 2-4° C lower than at present, at least for the middle part of the Late Glacial. Such a lowering in temperature will not have prevented tree growth in Greece, although the species composition of the forest will have been different. The very open vegetation can only have been present if precipitation was much lower than at present. The Late Glacial landscape of Greece must have been far from monotonous. The diverse substratum, the diversity in slope exposures, the elevation, and the latitude all resulted in a varied pattern.

Because the sea level rose after the Ice Age, the coastline moved inland. We have no Late Glacial or Early Holocene pollen records originating from land that was later covered by water, but one must postulate that the plant, shrub, and tree species that now form the typical man-induced Mediterranean evergreen vegetation occurred somewhere in that zone. For the olive, later an important economic oil producer, introduction from somewhere else during the later Holocene is possible. Its pollen is not encountered in older deposits whereas today such pollen, produced by the enormous acreage devoted to olive orchards around the Mediterranean, even reaches The Netherlands by long-distance transport. The most distinctive plant association of the Mediterranean, described by plant geographers as Oleo-Ceratonion, is characterized by two possible imports, the olive and the carob (*Ceratonia siliqua*). Presence of the latter tree, which gave its name to the gold standard (carat), is difficult to prove before the Roman Period.

Before 10,000 B.P. fauna with a steppic character existed in Greece and the subsistence of Palaeolithic people will have depended upon the given ecological conditions that must have been fundamentally different from those of the next period.

The Holocene: 10,000 B.P.-Present

A considerable change in conditions occurred around 10,300 B.P. The pollen precipitation of the central Pindos range changed from assemblages dominated by steppic types to assemblages characterized by deciduous oak, grasses, and other herbs (Bottema 1974, 1979).

The shift from minimal to maximal oak-pollen percentages is measured roughly by radiocarbon dating and the estimated sedimentation rate. Oak forest did not expand in the same way, at the same time, all over the Greek mountains. Vegetation patterns, and, subsequently, vegetation changes, in a mountainous area like Greece cannot be compared easily with those, for instance, postulated for relatively flat northwestern Europe at a higher latitude. If we try to follow the changes in characteristic plant or tree species in Greece, plants not only could increase or decrease in zones but could also move along the slopes. Thus, species disappeared from the Lower Rhine Basin during the Ice Age, whereas at the same time certain species maintained themselves on the Pindos, simply by shifting their position. The large number of plant and tree species in the Balkans compared to northern Europe points to a long tradition without catastrophic events in the first area, compared to the effect of the glacial events at higher latitudes. The quantities, shape, and exact location of the plant types are very difficult to estimate. The present-day vegetation may not be of much use as a reference for the early Holocene because modern analogues are not abundant.

Conclusions about the nature of the spread of deciduous-oak forest over mainland Greece are drawn from three pollen diagrams. Around the basin of Ioannina (Figure 3.1), on the west side of the Pindos mountains, at an elevation above 500 m, oak pollen increased at about 11,000 B.P. Maximum values developed about 2,500 years later, assuming a constant sedimentation rate. Maximum values for the tree-pollen ratio, a kind of measure for the density of forest, occurred considerably later. A core from former Lake Xinias (ca. 500 m), north of Lamia (Figure 3.1) has produced a pollen diagram that closely resembles that from Ioannina. Even today, sunny, open oak forest is found where the Thessalian plain merges with the Pindos chain. The east and west side of the Pindos differ from each other, for instance, in the composition of the higher mountain-belt forest. The west side has more fir and beech forest.

Further to the north, pollen diagrams from Lake Khimaditis, situated between the Vermion and Vernon ranges, at an elevation of 570 m, and Edessa between the Vermion and Voras mountains at 350 m, inform us about the Early Holocene development of the oak forest. Near Edessa, oak pollen values increased somewhat before 10,645 ± 200 B.P. (GrN-6189) and climaxed (reached a maximum) at about 9420 ± 80 B.P. (GrN-6187). The Khimaditis area, which lies a few hundred meters higher to the westward interior, witnesses a maximum of deciduous-oak forest at 9345 ± 85 B.P. (GrN-6598). It is not possible to date the beginning of the expansion of oak pollen in the Khimaditis area because the sediment below the radiocarbon date on peat, is formed by clay. This clay, which is older than 9400 B.P., may have had a completely different sedimentation rate than the overlying strata.

The behavior of oak pollen and the fact that steppe elements are still present up to about 9400 B.P., together with the presence of a clay deposit, indicate that the discharge of water towards Lake Khimaditis was not controlled by a dense vegetation. After 9400 B.P. the optimal tree growth seems to have retained the water, thus causing the basin to turn from a lake into a swamp.

In the Pindos Mountains, just as in the northern ranges, open oak forest with some juniper and grasses dominated the zone above 400 m. At higher elevations where moister conditions prevailed, more demanding deciduous tree species, such as elm (*Ulmus*) and lime (*Tilia*), started to spread.

During the Late Glacial the most important tree belt was formed by pine (*Pinus*) and fir (*Abies*). Their pollen numbers decrease during the early Holocene. The reason for such a decrease can be relative, simply caused by the increase in oak pollen. The lower coniferous values may also point to a shift of these trees to higher elevations, further from the pollen-catchment basin. A lowering in absolute numbers of needle-leaved evergreens in the Greek mountains is also possible.

We are familiar with an important climatic shift at the end of the Pleistocene. It is more difficult to indicate the exact conditions that prevailed at the beginning of the Holocene in mainland Greece. Was the spread of oak forest caused by an increase in precipitation, by an increase in temperature, or was it caused by both? What was the distribution of temperature and precipitation over the seasons?

These questions are valid not only for the first millennium after the Pleistocene, but also for much of the Holocene. The influence of climate upon human economy, for instance resulting in crop failure that would have attacked the basis of human habitation, is often emphasized by archaeologists. If we are dealing with the environmental conditions of Greece during the Holocene it is clear that, whatever the exact influence of climate may have been, the general conditions permitted the presence of forest in the whole country. This is in sharp contrast to the glacial period when steppe vegetation prevailed. Crop failures will have occurred from time to time due to various reasons, but there is no solid evidence that the fall and rise of empires was caused by changes in climate.

At about 9300 B.P., an open deciduous-oak forest covered the Greek mainland from 400-800 m elevation, and from that time on a more diverse vegetation developed. As concluded from the presence of *Pistacia* pollen, terebinth quite probably formed part of the open oak forest. Among the herbs and grasses that grew in the woodland, burnet (*Sanguisorba minor*) was very characteristic. *Poterium spinosum*, a thorny relative of *Sanguisorba* and well known from Mediterranean vegetation degraded to maquis or phrygana, has the same pollen type but cannot stand cold winters. It is not likely that winters were much warmer at that time than at present because the pollen of the *Sanguisorba minor*-type is not accompanied by types normally found together with *Poterium*. At higher elevations more moisture-demanding species such as elm, lime, and hazel were found and in the upper zone was a narrow section of conifers together with some birch.

Overall, the period lasted from about 9300-8200 B.P. Both the previous period and this one must have had some form of human habitation which relied upon hunting and gathering, a way of life that cannot be characterized in greater detail from the pollen record.

The upper part of a very long diagram prepared from a three-hundred-meter deep core, taken in Tenagi Philippon, a part of the plain of Drama at 40 m above sea level, provides evidence for developments in the lowland of Thrace (Wijmstra 1969). The pollen record shows the same characteristics as those from northwestern Greece, but the date of the initial expansion of deciduous oak in Tenagi is 14,600 ± 200 B.P. (GrN-4183). From that time onward, a diverse vegetation dominated by oak with an admixture of *Pistacia, Sanguisorba minor, Tilia, Ulmus*, and *Fraxinus excelsior* developed on the slopes around the marshy plain.

Wijmstra defines the beginning of the Holocene with the second and definite increase of oak pollen over that of herbs, a level dated to 7850 ± 50 B.P. A chronostratigraphy of the Tenagi record and a close correlation with the northwestern Greek pollen diagrams are difficult to establish, but the palynological sequences resemble those of the northwestern mountains. Many plant and tree species typified as Mediterranean and nowadays growing on the flanks of the hills around the plain of Drama are, however, not identified in the subfossil pollen precipitation. This is one of the restrictions of a discipline based upon an abundance of microfossils; this measure does not represent all categories in an efficient manner. The study of macroscopic remains, such as charred wood and seeds, can greatly expand our information base. Data on the occurrence of species that may have escaped attention in the pollen record can be obtained, for instance, from Hansen's (1991) work with floral remains. In her study in the southeastern Peloponnesos, she provides information on the presence of species seldom or never found in the pollen record, such as apple and pear. These Rosaceous trees are not indicated in pollen diagrams because they are insect-pollinated, and, in addition, are very difficult to identify beyond the family level.

A change in the pollen record, dated to ca. 8200 B.P., has led to the conclusion that the forest composition changed. It is not much later that the first farming activity is indicated by archaeological investigations in the Thessalian and Macedonian plains (Theocharis 1973). At first, the effect of prehistoric farmers upon the surrounding vegetation was limited. Still, from this time onward we confront changes in the vegetation which are no longer of a purely natural order. Anthropogenic factors increase rapidly in importance and eventually become the dominant elements affecting vegetation.

The exploitation of the vegetation must have influenced the pollen record. In the forest, lumbering caused a decrease in trees. On clearings, animals can graze and, especially in later periods, the subalpine meadow became an attractive natural pasture ground. Farm land produced pollen from crops and weeds, as we see in the palynological record.

Evidence of changes in the tree-pollen assemblage for this period is available from Tenagi, Xinias, Ioannina, Khimaditis, Edessa, Giannitsa, Kopais, and from the island of Crete. It is not likely that at that time the interior was changed very much by early herdsmen, who probably did not move out of the lowland plains until later.

The palynological changes are most clearly seen in the north in the area of the Vernon, Voras, and Vermion ranges. Deciduous-oak pollen values decreased in those areas while pollen of hazel (*Corylus*), fir (*Abies*), and pine (*Pinus*) increased (Bottema 1974). In the Thracian lowland of the Drama area, the Tenagi diagram indicates little change (Wijmstra 1969).

The southwestern side of the Pindos, in the Ioannina area, demonstrates a vegetation that was not much different from the millennium before. Open oak forest prevailed at lower elevations from about 300 - 700 m but was already dense enough to outshade Burnet (*Sanguisorba minor*). At higher elevations, a diverse belt of oak, lime, elm, and hazel developed. Above that zone, conifers and a few beech were found.

Thessaly does not seem to have changed much by 8000 B.P. and the vegetation around the basin of Xinias, as well as on the mountains, largely was the same open oak forest that became denser and more diverse at higher elevations. From coastal Thessaly we have evidence from a core taken near the ruins of Halos where the plain of Almiros meets the Pagasitic Gulf (Bottema 1988). The sediment in this core started to increase at about 7000 B.P. Tree pollen was outnumbered by that of grasses, which may have been of local origin. Trees would not have grown in the wet and partly salty marsh, but would have been found on the higher soils outside the delta. Oak pollen dominates over that of pine, hazel, elm, fir, lime, and eastern hornbeam. The species composition resembles that of inland Thessaly.

To the southeast, Kopais (Turner and Greig 1975) is the recording locality for Boeotia. Situated at about 100 m elevation, the basin of Kopais is surrounded by mountains that reach 1700 m. The pollen diagram from Kopais lacks absolute dates, so the correlation with other diagrams is problematic. Kopais' zone 5 is correlated with the first part of the Holocene and probably dates from 8000 B.P. and later. Marshes existed at the foot of mountains that were covered by open oak forest mixed with *Pistacia* and *Juniperus*. Although an elevation of 100 m is in reach of typical xerophytic evergreen Mediterranean vegetation (Turner and Greig 1975:172-173), the subfossil record supplies little evidence for such scrub. The oak pollen is found in combination with *Pistacia, Sanguisorba (Sarcopoterium)*, and especially large numbers of *Juniperus*. Compared with the evidence of other records, the combination of these types points to dry open woodland. Tree species, such as beech, hazel or hornbeam, which demand more moisture, were absent and there are no trace of olives. This suggests that wild olive did not grow in the area. The olive has a good pollen dispersal and would not easily escape detection. The Kopais area has a typical Mediterranean climate at present (Turner and Greig 1975) with an annual precipitation range of 400-800 mm. At the beginning of the Holocene the precipitation must have been lower. It is possible that after 8000 B.P. (K5-K6) precipitation increased and that forest became denser, resulting in a decrease in the number of Juniper.

Around 6500 B.P., the Greek landscape developed further. All over the mainland the deciduous-tree belt witnessed the spread of the hop hornbeam (*Ostrya carpinifolia*) and the eastern hornbeam (*Carpinus orientalis*). Other changes in pollen precipitation and related vegetation had a regional character. In part of the Vernon, Voras, and Vermion ranges above ca. 400 m, but also in the Macedonian lowland and in the Thracian record with evidence from the Pangaion, Menikion, and Rhodope mountains, a further spread of the coniferous forest occurred. For the first time beech (*Fagus*) appeared, probably in the coniferous belt.

On the Epiros side (west) of the Pindos, the quantities of beech and needle-leaved tree pollen remain unchanged. The same can be said for Thessaly. Everywhere the penetration of the sun into the forest or woodland is diminished, as is concluded from the disappearance of light-demanding types such as burnet (*Sanguisorba minor*).

On the island of Crete the conifers behaved quite differently. *Pinus* had reasonable values before 8000 B.P. It is not clear how the vegetation changed because the record shows a hiatus in pollen after ca. 7400 B.P. Halos, on the Pagasitic Gulf, shows a prolongation of the forest pattern that existed already before 6500 B.P. In Boeotia, in the Kopais record, this phase must be found somewhere in zone K6, but palynological correlation is difficult. The types characteristic of the changes between 8200-6500 B.P. and afterwards in the northern and central part of Greece are not found in the Kopais record. The Kopais region has a much more pronounced Mediterranean climate at present than northern Greece and displayed comparable differences during the period in question.

The evidence from Crete does not extend beyond ca. 5000 B.P., assuming a constant sedimentation rate in the Agia Galini record (Bottema 1980; see also Moody 1987). Above this level no pollen was found in the sediment. The late 6th millennium evidence contains low amounts of tree pollen, mostly of deciduous oak. The Early Prepottery Neolithic of Knossos dates back to the beginning of the 8th millennium. Thus, prehistoric humans had already been influencing the environment for one and a half millennia prior to 6500 B.P., the time for which we tried to reconstruct the landscape. Not surprisingly, the record of south-central coastal Crete at about 5000 B.P. indicates significant deforestation.

The interval between 6500 and 4000 B.P. can be called the period of eastern and hop hornbeam (*Carpinus orientalis* and *C. carpinifolia*). Because the pollen of both tree species cannot be separated by using a light microscope, the proportion in which their pollen occurred and the numbers of the respective tree species are not known. At present, both species are found in one context, i.e., on calcareous soil at higher Mediterranean elevations (Quézel and Barbéro 1985). According to Davis (1982:684) *Ostrya* is found in Turkey on somewhat higher and stonier slopes (50-1700 m) than *Carpinus orientalis* (sea level up to 1300 m). *Ostrya* grows especially on the edge of clearings or comparable locations with sufficient light. *Carpinus orientalis* can stand grazing relatively well and may even profit from it (Turrill 1929). Still, such indications are not enough evidence to suggest an anthropogenic cause for the expansion during the 7th millennium B.P. Other causes may have been responsible for the development of a different forest composition.

Clear proof for the impact of prehistoric people upon the surrounding vegetation indicated by pollen types dates from about 4000 B.P. At this time a series of herb-pollen types known as primary indicator types appear; these include *Cerealia* pollen and secondary indicator types, weeds like plantain and sorrel (Behre 1981, 1990; Bottema 1982 (1985); Bottema and Woldring 1990).

Apart from pollen of plants that are the direct result of farming, we may trace secondary changes that may have been triggered by human activity. In this respect, the sudden increase in beech (*Fagus*) in the mountain belt requires attention. It is apparent that the initial appearance or increase of beech all over Europe is always connected with human activity (Bottema 1988). In fact, the species demonstrates a weedy behavior; it profits from the appearance of abandoned, impoverished land, and clearings resulting from lumbering or from meadows that are no longer grazed.

As usual, the various parts of Greece reacted in their own unique ways. The mountain ranges in the north and the Epirotic part of the Pindos reacted in the way described above. At higher elevations in Thessaly it was not beech that increased, but pine that replaced juniper and decreased the amount of light that could penetrate the canopy. Leaching of the soil may have taken place through increased precipitation, as concluded from the appearance of Ericaceae.

At lower elevations, cores have been taken in swamps in the alluvial plains. Prehistoric settlers will certainly not have favored the wetter parts to build their houses, and so the pollen record may not give information about a landscape chosen by prehistoric people. In the plain of Macedonia, a core from the lake of Giannitsa informs us about the extensive marshes and also about the large part of the bordering mountain slopes that saw its pollen blown or washed into the plain. Thus, this catchment collected pollen from local as well as from distant sources; it is not easy to unravel the various origins. In this case pollen will also have been washed in by rivers and floods. Anthropogenic indicators are present in the pollen diagram, but the scientific efforts are more directed towards tracing them than using them for a solid reconstruction of prehistoric environment.

On the east coast, south of Volos, where the Almirotic plain meets the Pagasitic Gulf, the settlement site of Halos was not far away from the core location (Reinders 1988). The pollen record for this area does not show sharp demarcation lines between the anthropogenic pollen assemblages and those of more natural periods. Gradually, the effects of people living in the area became more and more pronounced in the pollen diagram. For Boeotia it is difficult to characterize this period because of the lack of dates and questionable pollen correlation.

The Kiladha core, prepared from sediment collected from the sea in front of Franchthi Cave in Argolis on the Peloponnesos, leads to the conclusion that a dry open deciduous-oak forest dominated the area inhabited by Neolithic people. In this respect the landscape may have resembled the lower part of Crete. The xerophytic, scrubby evergreens, so typical for the lower Mediterranean zone at present, were still to come. Jahns (1990, 1991) and Moody (1987) have provided additional information for southern Greece and Crete, respectively.

Information from near sea level at Lake Trikhonis, in Akarnania, is also available. There is, however, a controversy about the chronology of the sediment which is dated by paleomagnetism, radiocarbon, and pollen types (Creer et al. 1981). The paleomagnetism and the pollen dating differ by about thirty per cent. Despite uncertainty about the age of characteristic events, we can postulate that a zone of Mediterranean types, such as *Quercus coccifera, Pistacia lentiscus, Phillyrea*, and Ericaceae (*Erica arborea*) grew up to about 300 m, although the pollen cannot be identified to the species level. Higher up the slopes, deciduous trees became increasingly important. A mountain belt with conifers or beech must, however, be sought in the northern part of the Pindos range, as can be concluded from the low pollen values of such trees around Trikhonis.

Indeed puzzling in connection with the dates is the continuous curve for *Olea* pollen in the Trikhonis core. Olive pollen is not encountered during the first part of the Holocene in the majority of the Greek records. The Trikhonis record may be young on the basis of the continuous *Olea*-curve, but this notion is difficult to bring into line with other indicative types. The origin of olive culture is thought to lie in northern Palestine and southern Syria where the tree occurred naturally in tabor-oak forest or in lower evergreen-oak forest (Neef 1990).

At about 3200 B.P. (^{14}C years), a series of peculiar events took place (Bottema and Woldring 1984[1986], 1990). In the pollen diagrams, a set of highly indicative types, mainly fruit-bearing trees exploited by humans, appear together with an increase or appearance of primary and secondary types indicative of farming. In the stratigraphic record this palynological event directly follows a Santorini volcanic event that can be identified by tephra (Sullivan 1988). Furthermore, there are indications of a change in sedimentation. It can be concluded from the pollen record that a change to wetter conditions may have lasted from ca. 3200-1500 B.P. This event and the period it covers is discussed extensively in several publications (Bottema and Woldring 1984[1986], 1990; Bottema 1992) and will be summarized here.

The pollen record in the younger Holocene of northern Greece and western Turkey indicates that towards the end of the fourth millennium, walnut (*Juglans regia*), sweet chestnut (*Castanea sativa*), manna ash (*Fraxinus ornus*), and plane tree (*Platanus orientalis*) appeared simultaneously. At the same time, pollen of olive, grape, and hemp either appeared or increased. The types indicative of cultivation and grazing increase and make one conclude that the agricultural and fruticultural activity suddenly bloomed. The date of this agro-economic event can be obtained if sufficient organic material is present. This was the case in the cores of Khimaditis I and III and Edessa (Bottema 1974), and in a series of Turkish sites (Bottema and Woldring 1990). The wave of fruticulture very likely came from Turkey and spread rapidly to northern Greece.

The origin of this phase centers around 3100-3200 B.P., but in some diagrams, such as Khimaditis I or Edessa, dates deviate and have to be explained. Sullivan (1988) defined volcanic ash layers in Gölcük and Köyçeğiz Gölü as produced by the Santorini eruption. The tephra deposit directly antedated the peculiar pollen assemblage described above. Based on dendrochronology Baillie and Munro (1988) date the Santorini eruption to 1629 B.C., equivalent to 3300 B.P. in uncalibrated radiocarbon years.

At the same time that the agro-fruticultural pollen assemblage appears, there is a change in pollen depositional character, especially of Turkish sites in the Anatolian steppe. The originally high values of certain Compositae, especially Liguliflorae (*Dandelion*-type plants), *Matricaria*-type or *Centaurea solstitialis*-type suddenly declined in the diagrams. The question is, why were they present before? The pollen of such composites is normally not found in large numbers. They are pronouncedly insect-pollinated and do not disperse much pollen into the air, even if they are abundant in the environment. If they are found in quantities higher than a few per cent of the total, there is something behind it. One possibility is that the special sample may have been subjected to corrosion and the very corrosion-resistant yellow composite pollen has remained and is subsequently over-represented (Havinga 1984; Bottema 1975). If the quality of the pollen is good, one must seek other explanations. My explanation of certain situations where unexpectedly high values for certain composites are identified took form when coring the small lakes of Zileria in the summer of 1979. At about one o'clock in the afternoon while the sun was burning on the Thessalian plain, a combine harvester was working about one kilometer away from me. Chaff was rising, lifted by the hot air over the heated plain. In the middle of the lake where we were coring from a boat, a constant rain of fine dust and clearly visible chaff was settling on the water. The back flow of dust and chaff seemed to be concentrated in spots, e.g. the lake of Zileria, that had a lower temperature than the surrounding plain. This phenomenon must also have developed over hot plains during the summer where farming had destroyed all natural vegetation or where there was a natural steppic vegetation. In the Zileria sediment, Liguliflorae, including typical summer flowering species, had high values because of concentration, something that did not happen to spring-flowering trees or plants.

Under steppe conditions, whether the steppe was natural or man-made, such a system persisted, causing the high percentages of special pollen types. Then at 3200 B.P. something happened that did not necessarily change the numbers of such yellow flowering composites very much, but did change the depositional system. The result was a cooler, moister or even cloudier climate, that influenced the eastern Mediterranean economy from 3200 B.P. onward, also illustrated by the typical agro-fruticultural pollen assemblage. The cause of this shift is still mainly a matter of hypothesis and is discussed by Bottema and Woldring (1990).

Palynological Information from Mikro Zileria

The palynological information on the Greek paleo-environment, as in other areas, has a relatively low resolution, that is to say, we are only informed on slices of time representing often less than one measuring point every 400 years. In some favorable situations we have obtained average palynological evidence on the past environment once in 100 years. Only on very short projects where specific problems were more intensively studied, do we find a higher resolution. If we want a high resolution, we need a fairly high sedimentation rate. In addition, a sample is about 1 cm thick and thus it covers a certain number of years. The latter can be calculated from isotope dates or can be counted if laminated sediments are found, a rare phenomenon.

A very rapid sedimentation was found in Mikro Zileria. A pollen diagram of this small lake in the plain of Almiros, in Thessaly (Figure 3.1), will be discussed here. The sedimentation rate, calculated in two radiocarbon dated cores, amounts to 3.5 mm near the edge to ca. 7 mm per year in the center of the lake.

The site of the two small lakes of Makro and Mikro Zileria is west of Almiros, not far from the ruins of Halos, at an elevation of 1.50

masl. The origin of the lakes is still debated. One explanation is that they are of volcanic origin, created by gas explosions like the '*Maar*'-type kraters from the Eiffel. They may also have been formed by karstic action and represent some form of 'Doline'. Cores have been taken in Mikro Zileria where the water was ca. 5 m deep at the edge and 10 m in the center. In both cores, the lower part is dated about 1400 B.P.

The preservation of the pollen in the Zileria sediment is very good; the concentration varies and this may point to different sedimentation rates within one core. A selection of characteristic pollen types from a core, collected about 15 m from the southern edge of the lake in water 4.90 m deep, is shown in Figure 3.3. The lowest part of the core has been dated to 1440 ± 90 B.P. (ca. A.D. 500; GrN-12051). The upper part of the core from 4.90 m down to 6.60 m is formed by gray clay, that turns to gyttja in the lower part.

From spectrum 1 (Figure 3.3) at the bottom of the sediment up to spectrum 20, the Zileria diagram is characterized by fluctuating values of deciduous oak pollen, from a maximum of 60% to a minimum of 10-20% of the total count. The herbaceous counterpart of the oak pollen is that of the Gramineae (grasses) and to a lesser extent that of *Plantago lanceolata* (ribwort plantain). A large variety of tree pollen other than oak is present in low percentages.

From about A.D. 500 to 1500 we can detect four periods dominated by deciduous oak pollen, separated by periods of grass pollen dominance. Calculation of the time period is based on the assumption that sedimentation was constant. The percentages of tree types, other than those of the deciduous oak, do not change. Because of their low values, one may postulate that they existed at a considerable distance, perhaps somewhere in the mountains. It is likely that the deciduous oaks in the Almiros plain were suffering from human activity. When human pressure dwindled, oaks started to spread again. The length of the periods, 200 years on average, does not really surpass the life expectancy of deciduous oaks. During the strong depression of oak pollen, one can imagine that grazing sheep prevented regeneration of oaks. The presence of relatively high values for *Sanguisorba minor*-type (burnet) during the open phases suggests that no intensive cultivation of crops took place.

From spectrum 20 upward, the environment of Zileria must have shifted fundamentally. The sediment changed to clay, and oak pollen

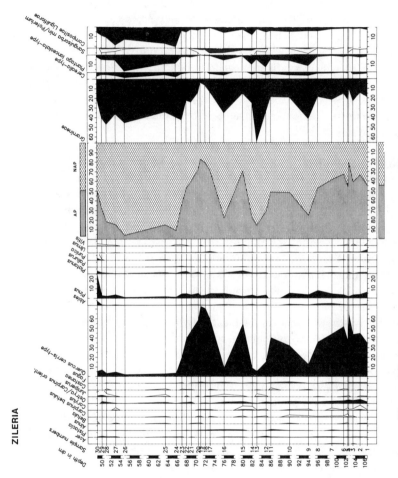

Figure 3.3. Selection of pollen curves from Mikro Zileria (Almiros).

almost vanishes from the spectra. The plain was changed into a steppe that lacked protective vegetation cover. Thus, the soil surface was heated intensely during the summer, and it is concluded from the high Liguliflorae values that this type was concentrated in the way described in the preceding section. Grasses measure more than 40%, and plantain up to 17%, whereas burnet disappeared from the pollen precipitation. The upper part of the core, spectra 29 and 30, presents a different picture. There is some increase not only in tree pollen, including the traditional deciduous oaks, but also in several other types. *Pinus* (pine) and *Abies* (fir) very likely regenerated somewhere on the Othrys, maybe by planting. *Olea* (olive), and *Punica* (pomegranate) were cultivated, partly on the edge of the lake. *Platanus* (plane tree) and *Juniperus* (juniper/cypress) may have been planted in the nearby town of Almiros.

In the analysis of the pollen diagram we have assumed that the sedimentation rate for the Zileria core has been constant. Of course, this assumption is of crucial importance for a correlation with historical events in the southern part of the Thessalian plain. For the lowest part of the core, the ^{14}C date of 1440 B.P. after calibration, suggests an age at the beginning of the Migration period. Three periods of more intensive occupation of the Almiros plain made the deciduous-oak woodland disappear, but did not visibly change the sediment.

The most important change at about spectrum 20 would have occurred ca. A.D. 1500. Spectrum 20 may be younger because the upper sediment may be looser than the lower deposits. A correlation with a historical event can be made only if we have better dates and a clearer sense of the agricultural history of the area. The same can be said for the upper 20 cm where we see some regeneration of the mountain forest that may be due to the return of Greeks to the lowland after the Turkish occupation (19th century).

The importance of the preceding analysis is that the pollen record is based upon thirty spectra, demonstrating many details. Shifts in population, connected to the northward retraction of Turkish occupation, do not seem likely according to research in the Peloponnesos (Frangakis and Wagstaff 1992).

References Cited

Athanasiadis, N.
  1975 Zur Postglazialen Vegetationsentwicklung von Litochoro
        Katerinis und Pertouli Trikalon (Griechenland). *Flora* 164:99-132.

Athanasiadis, N., and A. Gerasimidis

1986 *Zur postglazialen Vegetationsentwicklung von Boras-Gebirge (Almopia-Griechenland).* Aristotelian University of Thessaloniki, Scientific Annals of the Department of Forestry and Natural Environment 4:213-249.

1984/1985 *Standortkundliche Verhältnisse und postglaziale Vegetationsentwicklung der Wälder Lailas, Bez. Serres und Katafygi im Pieria-Gebirge (Nordgriechenland).* Aristotelian University of Thessaloniki, Scientific Annals of the Department of Forestry and Natural Environment.

1987 *Zur postglazialen Vegetationsentwicklung von Paikon-Gebirge (Nordgriechenland).* Aristotelian University of Thessaloniki, Scientific Annals of the Department of Forestry and Natural Environment 11:405-445.

Atherden, M., J. Hall, and J.C. Wright

1993 A Pollen Diagram from the Northeast Peloponnese, Greece: Implications for Vegetation History and Archaeology. *The Holocene* 3(4):351-356.

Baillie, M.G.L., and M.A.R. Munro

1988 Irish Tree Rings, Santorini and Volcanic Dust Veils. *Nature* 332:344-346.

Behre, K.-E.

1981 The Interpretation of Anthropogenic Indicators in Pollen Diagrams. *Pollen et Spores* 23:225-245.

1990 Some Reflections on Anthropogenic Indicators and the Record of Prehistoric Occupation Phases in Pollen Diagrams from the Near East. In *Man's Role in the Shaping of the Eastern Mediterranean Landscape* edited by S. Bottema, G. Entjes-Nieborg, and W. van Zeist, pp. 219-230. Balkema, Rotterdam.

Bottema, S.

1974 *Late Quaternary Vegetation History of Northwestern Greece.* Unpublished Ph.D. dissertation, University of Groningen, Groningen.

1975 The Interpretation of Pollen Spectra from Prehistoric Settlements (with Special Attention to Liguliflorae). *Palaeohistoria* 17:17-35.

1979 Pollen Analytical Investigation in Thessaly (Greece). *Palaeohistoria* 21:19-40.

1980 Palynological Investigations on Crete. *Review of Palaeobotany and Palynology* 31:193-217.

1982 (1985) Palynological Investigations in Greece with Special

Reference to Pollen as an Indicator of Human Activity. *Palaeohistoria* 24:257-289.

1988 A Reconstruction of the Halos Environment on the Basis of Palynological Information. In *New Halos, a Hellenistic Town in Thessalia, Greece*, by H.R. Reinders, pp. 216-226. Unpublished Ph.D. dissertation, University of Groningen, Groningen.

1992 *Forest, Forest Clearance and Open Land at the Time of the Roman Empire in Greece: The Palynological Record*. Proceedings of the 6th EPC Workshop on 'Evaluation of Land Surfaces Cleared from Forests in the Mediterranean Region during the Time of the Roman Empire', Mainz, Germany, 14-16 June 1991.

Bottema, S., and H. Woldring
1984(1986) Late Quaternary Vegetation and Climate of Southwestern Turkey. Part II. *Palaeohistoria* 26:123-149.

1990 Anthropogenic Indicators in the Pollen Record of the Eastern Mediterranean. In *Man's Role in the Shaping of the Eastern Mediterranean Landscape* edited by S. Bottema, G. Entjes-Nieborg and W. van Zeist, pp. 231-264. Balkema, Rotterdam/Brookfield.

Creer, K.M., P.W. Readman, and S. Papamarinopoulos
1981 Geomagnetic Secular Variations in Greece through the Last 6000 Years Obtained from Lake Sediment Studies. *Geophysical Journal of the Royal Astronomical Society* 66:193-219.

Davis, P.H. (editor)
1982 *Flora of Turkey and the East Aegean Islands*. Volume 7. Edinburgh University Press, Edinburgh.

Frangakis, E., and J.M. Wagstaff
1992 The Height of Zonation of Population in the Morea c. 1830. *Annual of the British School in Athens* 87:439-446.

Hansen, J.M.
1991 *The Palaeoethnobotany of Franchthi Cave*. Excavations at Franchthi Cave, Greece, Fascicle 7. Indiana University Press, Bloomington.

Havinga, A.J.
1984 A 20-year Experimental Investigation into the Differential Corrosion Susceptibility of Pollen and Spores in Various Soil Types. *Pollen et Spores* 26:541-558.

Jahns, S.
1990 Preliminary Notes on Human Influence and the History of Vegetation in Southern Dalmatia and Southern Greece. In *Man's Role in the Shaping of the Eastern Mediterranean Landscape*

edited by S. Bottema, G. Entjes-Nieborg, and W. Van Zeist, pp. 333-340. Balkema, Rotterdam.

1991 *Untersuchungen über die holozäne Vegetationsgeschichte von Süddalmatien und Südgriechenland.* Unpublished Ph.D. dissertation, Universität Göttingen, Göttingen.

Marks, A.

1986 *Umweltgeschichtliche Aspekte des Neolithikums in Thessalien.* Magisterarbeit im Fach Ur und Frühgeschichte. Universität Köln.

Moody, J.A.

1987 *The Environmental and Cultural Prehistory of the Khania Region of West Crete: Neolithic through Late Minoan III.* Ph.d. dissertation, University of Minnesota, Minneapolis. University Microfilms, Ann Arbor.

Neef, R.

1990 Introduction, Development and Environmental Implications of Olive Culture: The Evidence from Jordan. In *Man's Role in the Shaping of the Eastern Mediterranean Landscape* edited by S. Bottema, G. Entjes-Nieborg, and W. van Zeist, pp. 283-294. Balkema, Rotterdam.

Quézel, P., and M. Barbéro

1985 *Carte de la Végétation Potentielle de la Région Méditerranéenne.* Feuille no. 1: Méditerranée orientale. Editions du Centre National de la Recherche Scientifique, Paris.

Reinders, H.R.

1988 *New Halos, a Hellenistic Town in Thessalia, Greece.* Unpublished Ph.d. dissertation, University of Utrecht, Utrecht.

Reinders, H.R., and S. Bottema

1983 Investigations at Halos and Zileria. Preliminary report 1982. *Bulletin Antieke Beschaving* 58:91-100.

Sheehan, M.C.

1979 *The Postglacial Vegetational History of the Argolid Peninsula, Greece.* Unpublished Ph.D. dissertation, Department of Biology, Indiana University, Bloomington.

Sullivan, D.G.

1988 The Discovery of Santorini Minoan Tephra in Western Turkey. *Nature* 333:552-554.

Theocharis, D.

1973 *Neolithic Greece.* National Bank of Greece, Athens.

Turrill, W.B.

1929 *The Plantlife of the Balkan Peninsula. A Phytogeographic Study.* Clarendon Press, Oxford.

Turner, C.
    1985 Problems and Pitfalls in the Application of Palynology to
        Pleistocene Archaeological Sites in Western Europe. In
        Palynologie Archéologique, edited by J. Renault-Miskowsky, M.
        Bui-Thi-Mai, and M. Girard, pp. 347-373. CNRS Notes et
        Monographies Techniques 17, Paris.
Turner J., and J.R.A. Greig
    1975 Some Holocene Pollen Diagrams from Greece. *Review of
        Palaeobotany and Palynology* 20:171-204.
van Andel, T.H., and S.B. Sutton
    1987 *Landscape and People of the Franchthi Region.* Excavations
        at Franchthi Cave, Greece, Fascicle 2. Indiana University Press,
        Bloomington.
Van Zeist, W., and S. Bottema
    1982 Vegetational History of the Eastern Mediterranean and the
        Near East during the last 20,000 Years. In *Palaeoclimates,
        Palaeoenvironments and Human Communities in the Eastern
        Mediterranean Region during Later Prehistory* edited by J.L.
        Bintliff and W. Van Zeist, pp. 277-321. Bar International Series
        133. British Archaeological Reports, Oxford.
Willis, K.
    1992a. The Late Quaternary Vegetational History of Northwest
        Greece. I. Gramousti Lake. *New Phytologist* 120:107-117.
    1992b. The Late Quaternary Vegetational History of Northwest
        Greece. II. Rezina Marsh. *New Phytologist* 120:119-138.
    1992c. The Late Quaternary Vegetational History of Northwest
        Greece. III. A Comparative Study of Two Contrasting Sites. *New
        Phytologist* 120:139-155.
Wijmstra, T.A.
    1969 Palynology of the First 30 Metres of a 120-Metre-Deep
        Section in Northern Greece. *Acta Botanica Neerlandica* 18:511-
        528.
Wijnen, M.-H.J.M.N.
    1982 *The Early Neolithic Settlement at Sesklo: An Early Farming
        Community in Thessaly, Greece.* Unpublished Ph.D. dissertation,
        Universitaire Pers Leiden, Leiden.
Wright Jr., H.E.
    1972. Vegetation History. In *The Minnesota Messenia Expedition:
        Reconstructing a Bronze Age Environment,* edited by W.A.
        McDonald and G. Rapp, Jr., pp. 188-199. University of
        Minnesota Press, Minneapolis.

Chapter 4

Holocene Coastal Change in Greece and Aegean Turkey

George (Rip) Rapp, Jr. and John C. Kraft

Introduction

In this paper we argue our position for the need for three-dimensional geologic data in making paleogeomorphic reconstructions of coastal change. At the outset we want to pay tribute to someone who had the observational and analytical powers to "get it right" two millennia ago: "The learned Lady Hestiaea of Alexander Troas had the prescience to posit a much more deeply recessed bay at the time of the Trojan War" as noted by Strabo (Luce 1984:33-34).

The reconstruction of geological and ecological environments has provided an increasingly clear picture of the landscapes and habitats that have sustained human development. In reconstructing ancient environments, both the geologist and the archaeologist depend on incomplete stratigraphic records and on evidence that is frequently insufficient for an absolute chronology. Few areas of the earth's land surface have witnessed long and continuous periods of deposition; on the contrary, erosion is the terrestrial norm.

In coastal areas three geologic processes combine to drive geomorphic change. Eustatic and relative sea level changes have an immediate impact on the coastal zone. Vertical (up or down) tectonic movements offset or augment eustatic sea level rise or fall. Finally, erosion or deposition may drive the transgressional or regressional migration of the shoreline.

Since 1970, initially associated with the Minnesota Messenia Expedition and the Nichoria Excavation (Rapp et al. 1978), we have been regularly engaged in the study of Holocene coastal change in Greece and the Aegean coast of Turkey. Figure 4.1 shows the areas of Quaternary sedimentation in the region and the names of some of the sites where we have worked. The bibliography lists not only the references from this article but also our other publications concerning coastal change in this region.

Herodotus, Plato, Strabo, Pausanius, Livy, and others noted shoreline changes, but they had no context for analyzing them. Today we use a number of geologic concepts and methodologies to investigate evolution and geomorphic change along active coasts. The initial phase of a paleogeomorphic reconstruction relies on detailed field geomorphology to ascertain the broad scheme of landscape evolution. This may be aided by knowledge of the vertical position of dated archaeological structures or horizons and first-hand reports from ancient texts. However, in our two decades of work we have found that intensive core drilling with detailed analysis of the sedimentary record is absolutely necessary to provide an adequate picture of the sequence of coastal environments and the associated chronologies.

Coastal areas host a large percentage of the world's population. Such zones where land and water meet often contain large amounts and varieties of nutrients that in turn supply diverse assemblages of fauna and flora--all in a complex of geologic environments such as bays, estuaries, beaches, deltas, dunes, marshes, and adjacent floodplains. Add to this the high energy available from wind-driven waves and it is easy to see why constant change is the rule.

Methods for the Study of Coastal Change

Our approach to investigating Holocene coastal change has been to depict the landscape in terms of the morphology of sedimentary bodies and erosional features and the vertical and lateral sequences of environments (sedimentary environmental lithosomes) that were created by the forces and processes operating in the coastal environment. These processes include: local tectonism; eustatic sea level change; climatic change; ocean currents and wave regimes; the nature and frequency of

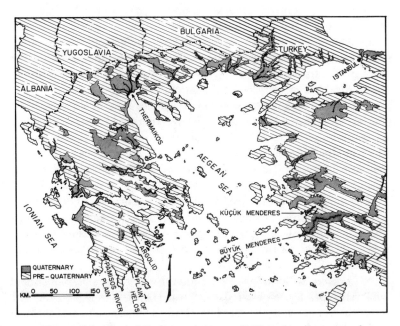

Figure 4.1. Map of Greece and Aegean Turkey showing areas of
Quaternary (including Holocene) deposition.

catastrophic events; sources, types, and quantities of sediments available and the resultant aggradation and progradation of deltaic floodplains into erosional and tectonically derived embayments; and the nature and intensity of human activity. All such processes leave a record in the local sediments of past physiographic change; hence our research methodology leans heavily on geologic core drilling and extensive analysis of the core sediments. Microfaunal and microfloral remains in the sediments record environmental parameters such as salinity, water depth, and even pollution. Essentially we are following one of the fundamental dictates of geology--uniformitarianism (or the modern variant called actualism).

Geologists have a well-developed concept of sedimentary environmental lithosomes, or facies. The word facies is used by geologists to mean the characteristics of a rock unit that reflect the conditions of its origin as differentiating it from adjacent units. A lithosome is a sedimentary deposit of essentially uniform character frequently having intertonguing relationships in all directions with adjacent deposits of different lithologic character. These depositional bodies delineate the shape and distribution of individual sedimentary environmental units in space and time. When coastal lithosomes are considered in terms of their lateral and vertical relationships to each other they provide a relatively complete historic/geologic record of the events that describe coastal change. For example, the details of the history of a transgression or regression of the sea will be reflected in the vertical sedimentary facies deposited.

Our work also draws heavily on Walther's Law of Correlation of Facies, which provides a means of interpreting environmental changes. According to Walther's Law, only those sedimentary facies that occur in laterally adjacent environments of deposition can occur in conformable vertical sequence. Thus we have a powerful tool that enables us to use three-dimensional stratigraphic sequences in the reconstruction of ancient (sedimentary) landscapes through time and space. This concept is frequently used in shoreline studies. Although these fundamental geologic concepts must be applied using common sense, when backed by surficial and drill core analyses these hard data (evidence) are exceedingly firm.

We proceed with two notes of caution. First, the wealth of important and reliable archaeological data at some sites is well known. The problem lies not with the data but with poor interpretation of the data and a lack of understanding of the associated geologic principles. Examples are common in the literature on "seismic destruction" and other geologic phenomena. Second, the problems associated with the use of generalized eustatic sea-level rise curves are not often realized. World or regional eustatic sea-level rise curves represent a broad synthesis and often are not applicable to local situations. Only local relative sea-level data can be treated as "factual" in paleo-geographic reconstruction. Indeed, most geologists have now abandoned the search for a single world sea-level curve because sea levels vary around the earth in response to earth rheology and variations in the shape of the geoid.

Although questions remain as to the accuracy of sea-level curves, as well as to the methodologies by which they were derived, the construction of sea-level curves and their use in paleo-geomorphic reconstruction are critical. In our research we have emphasized that most sea-level curves for the Holocene are either local relative sea-level curves for a single region or are composite or synthetic curves developed from data obtained by various methods from regions around the world. Our studies of the embayments in Greece and Aegean Turkey have shown that each embayment has its own local relative sea-level curve. This can be expected from the fact that these embayments are frequently down-dropping grabens controlled by local tectonics, and ranging from large grabens such as the gulfs of Korinth, Messenia, and Lakonia to smaller tectonic basins such as those at Navarino and the Aegean coast of Turkey. Belknap and Kraft (1985) demonstrated the influence of the antecedent geology on the stratigraphic preservation potential of Holocene marine transgression as well as the later infill of the embayments by alluvial and deltaic sedimentation.

Sea-level studies have become a "two-edged sword." One needs to use local relative sea-level positions to project paleogeographies of coastal settings and related historic and archaeologic events. On the other hand, composite curves drawn in from "nearby" areas most often lead to errors in interpretation. The problem is frequently compounded by the misuse of radiocarbon data. For instance, some scientists and archaeologists are still using the original Libby half-life for radiocarbon dates and some also ignore the corrections for atmospheric variation in ^{14}C, leading to significant errors in the time frame of interpretations.

Case Studies

We turn now to a few brief examples of the archaeological significance of our reconstructions. These are neither detailed nor represent a significant percentage of our published work. For details and for information on the other sites and areas in this region that we have studied please refer to the bibliography.

Messenia

Following our work in direct association with the Nichoria Excavation in the southwest Peloponnesos, we first expanded our coastal change studies to other important archaeological areas in that region. The modern Bay of Navarino was thought by most scholars of Helladic times to be Nestor's sandy Pylos. The long arcuate sandy barriers at the head of Navarino Bay, Osmanaga Lagoon, Voidokolia Bay, and the alluvial plain to the north provided us with an ideal setting to apply sedimentary sequence analysis in the interpretation of changes and descriptions of ancient landscapes (Kraft, Rapp, and Aschenbrenner 1980).

Briefly, in the early Holocene Epoch a marine transgression entered the deeply incised valley. By 9000 B.P. fluvial deposits had begun to infill the head of the embayment. The marine regression finally culminated in the formation of the present long arcuate sandy strand that cuts across the midpoint of the ancient embayment. The subsurface sedimentary record includes a number of buried shoreline sandy beach deposits. Figure 4.2 shows a sequence of shorelines from the peak Mesolithic transgression of approximately 9000 B.P. through the end of the Neolithic about 5000 B.P., and the end of the Bronze Age 3000 B.P. to the present shoreline that continues to prograde seaward.

Large quantities of sand were transported along the strandline of the Ionian Sea, forming a long sandy beach that would account for the Iliad's term "sandy Pylos." Major questions remain. Although we know the position of the shoreline at the end of the Bronze Age we do not know the details of the coastal environments for periods within the Bronze Age.

The Troad

Our most ambitious study has been in the Troad. It began in 1977 with Kraft's professional association with Turkish colleagues (Kraft et al. 1980, 1982) at the same time Rapp undertook a study of archaeological sediments from prehistoric Troy (Troia) (Rapp and Gifford 1982). These coastal studies continue today.

The debate concerning the geography of Homeric Troy has involved scholars for over two millennia. As far back as the early 1800s, Mac-

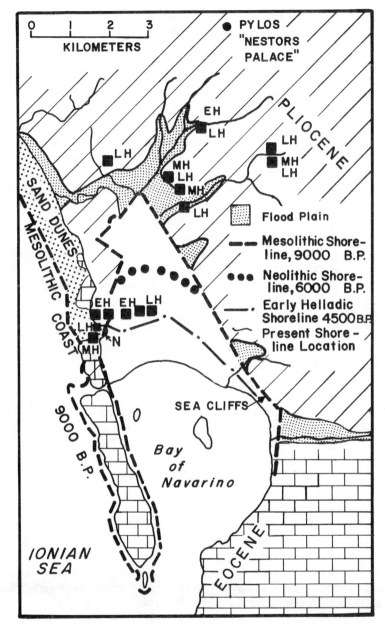

Figure 4.2. The Bay of Navarino area showing shoreline migration since the Mesolithic.

laren (1822) realized that in Homeric times the coast at the mouth of the Scamander and Simois rivers was well inland of its present position. Frazer (1937) credits Bruckner, an associate of Dörpfeld, with the suggestion that since the mouth of the Scamander would have presented an unfavorable topography for the Greek camp, the simplest solution lay in transferring the camp's position to Beşika Bay.

The floodplain of the two rivers adjacent to Troia provided another excellent opportunity to use core drilling to reconstruct the movement of the ancient shoreline of the marine embayment as sediment infill forced marine regression. This in turn necessitated a reassessment of views of the Homeric topography. Figure 4.3 illustrates in cross section the nature of transgression and regression of the sea along the axis of the Scamander River. A more complete discussion of the paleogeography and the Beşika hypothesis are presented below.

Our reconstructions have not gone without challenge so we use this opportunity to respond to our critics. Bintliff (1991) has taken exception to our interpretation of the paleogeography of the Scamander and Simois Valley systems adjoining ancient Troy (Troia). In a lengthy and tortuous analysis of our data and reconstruction of the late Holocene Trojan Plain (Kraft et al. 1982) he has attempted to reinterpret our work in the light of the writings of Strabo, Pseudo-Skylax, Herodotus, Homer, and others. He suggests that many of our conclusions were incorrect, but that our core drilling data and radiocarbon dates help provide him with the wherewithal to present a "new geography" of the Troad.

First, we should note that Bintliff rejects the Beşika hypothesis of Mey (1926) and Schede (1930) among others, and more recently Korfmann (1986, 1989), concerning the location of the Greek ships and camp in the Homeric epic. In doing so he is either unaware of or unwilling to utilize the critical studies of Kayan (1988, 1991) who analyzed 70 cores taken from the Beşika Plain. Kayan clearly identified lateral and vertical sequences of sedimentary strata and barrier-lagoon environmental settings covering the last 8,000 years. Kayan's results have excellent radiocarbon control at 2000, 3500, and 4000 years B.P. Lagoons extending 1-1.5 km landward were there in the Bronze Age. At Beşika relative sea stands were at or slightly above present levels 5000 to 6000 years B.P. Kayan's work certainly proves that Beşika was an excellent anchorage/defense area. With these hard geologic data at hand we cannot fathom Bintliff's categorical rejection of the Beşika hypothesis.

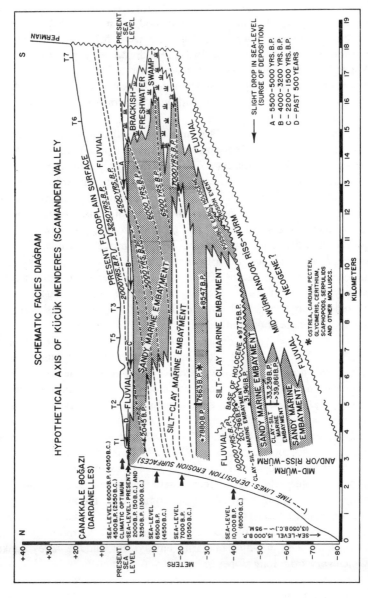

Figure 4.3. Schematic diagram showing facies correlations along the hypothetical axis of the Scamander River Valley.

In our work on the plains of the Scamander and Simois delta floodplains (Kraft et al. 1980, 1982) we used a synthetic sea-level curve derived from various points along the Anatolian coast. To our dismay many scholars have not understood this nor understood that all of our paleogeographic reconstructions were based strictly on our surficial geologic studies, our drill core sedimentological evidence, and Spratt's map (1839), the best extant map of the channels of the Scamander delta-floodplain before major human interference. In short, the sea-level curve was merely additional "supportive" information, not the basis of our interpretation.

Unfortunately, Bintliff's 1991 article shows that in venturing outside his expertise in physical geography he displays a lack of comprehension of several geologic concepts. He goes through a carefully reasoned reinterpretation of our data, cross sections, and map interpretations. In doing so he changed our 1980 and 1982 diagrams to conform with his views. He then converts our fluvial-deltaic sedimentary environmental lithosomes to the word "land" and proceeds to interpret new sea-level positions under the "land" strata. Thus he misunderstands the basic concepts of delta-floodplains, their tributaries and related environmental lithosomes and the nature of fluvial-deltaic progradation into marine embayments so typical of all embayments in the Aegean coastal system or indeed anywhere in the world. In order to propose his preferred interpretation he abused our data.

Bintliff has always made much of Vita-Finzi's "older and younger fills", much more so than Vita-Finzi himself (personal communication 1992). We doubt that there was even a single year in the last 6,000 in which a minimal sediment load was not carried onto the Scamander floodplain. Although the river sediments may ultimately be shown to indicate a period of greater volume of transport or surge of sedimentation, the "younger fill" in the Scamander floodplain is most likely a continuous record from 6000 B.P. to the present.

On a more positive note, Luce (1984) carefully analyzed our geologic interpretations as they relate to Homer and Strabo (and Strabo's correspondents). We highly commend to the reader this most lucid account of the Homeric textual implications related to the past 5,000 years of pervasive geologic changes in the morphology of the Scamander plain, its adjacent marine embayment, and the valley flanks, which vary from long slopes to ancient wave-cut cliffs at the Rhoeteum promontory and most importantly along the west end and northern cliffs of the Hissarlik cuesta. Luce adds, "Unfortunately, Strabo's main authority, Demitrios of Skepsis, espoused a 'false Troy' theory [Troy located some five km east of Hissarlik] and thus greatly diminishes the value for the present study of the interpretation of the Homeric data in the *Geography.*"

Luce (1984:) also had it right when he said, "It seems strange that scholars could accept the reality of extensive aggradation over the past two to three millennia in other Anatolian river valleys like those of the Hermus and Maeander while rejecting it for the Scamander valley. Such is the inertia of received opinion!"

Small changes in the sea-level curve we used could lead to widely divergent paleogeographies, hence we did not use the synthetic sea-level curve in our interpretation. We included the sea-level curve to show that our drill core results were entirely compatible with the generalized sea-level curve for the Anatolian coasts. Our data show that the Holocene embayment extended up to 15 km south of the present delta shoreline on the Dardanelles. The overwhelming mass of sedimentary infill in the paleovalleys is comprised of marine sands and silts with ages ranging from 9775 years B.P. (corrected) to the modern shoreline. The Scamander floodplain has prograded seaward to the Dardanelles during this time period while aggrading 25 m upward in the south to 2-3 m in the north. Our control points were too limited to engage in the speculation on valley paths presented by Bintliff (1991). We can suggest 3-7 m of floodplain aggradation since the end of the Bronze Age in the immediate vicinity of ancient Troia. Our evidence for specified paleoenvironments, including sedimentation and micropaleontological analyses, is absolute. There is room for some divergent opinion concerning shoreline elements because of the small number of drill holes used in our publications. Our current study with our colleague İlhan Kayan contains a vastly increased number of cores.

In the late 1970s we clearly did not pursue the writings of antiquity in the degree of detail undertaken by Luce (1984) and others. We noted Strabo's works and, lacking further expertise, located the shoreline as a smooth curving arc at 2000 B.P. Here our critics have a valid point. Consistent with our drill core data and the flanking hills of the lowest Scamander-Simois floodplain, more than one paleogeographic picture can be drawn, e.g., the position of the Scamander River on the floodplain. Our point is simply that when hard geologic data are available from coring, any reconstruction must be consistent with these data. As to Homer, his detailed descriptions are frequently quite specific but refer to local areas the locations of which remain unknown.

Major modifications in the reconstruction of Troia will result from the current Korfmann Expedition. The Troia geologic team (Kayan,

Kraft, and Rapp) have more than 70 new cores from the Trojan Plain, spanning the areas northwest and south of the Hissarlik cuesta. The analyses of these cores reveal a great deal more about the marine embayment that surrounded much of the Bronze Age Troia. It is interesting to speculate that with accelerator (AMS) dating and a large number of cores it may be possible eventually to delineate meander loops, point bars, levees, backswamps, etc. in the subsurface fluvial deposits of the plain with considerable precision.

Thermopylae

In some cases truly fundamental disagreements arise among historians, classicists, archaeologists, geographers, and natural scientists. This occurs despite a major adoption of scientific methodologies by most archaeologists. For our work in Greece, starting several decades ago, we formed an interdisciplinary team with S.E. Aschenbrenner, an anthropologist/archaeologist (see McDonald 1991).

Conflicts among historians over the 480 B.C. battle at Thermopylae, centering around the inconsistencies between ancient sources and the modern topography, gave us another opportunity to reconstruct the relevant paleogeography following a core drilling program. With the core recovery and analysis from seven holes we were able to delineate the considerable variation over time in the coastal physiography at Thermopylae (Kraft et al. 1987).

Figure 4.4 illustrates the broad picture of coastal change of the Gulf of Malia-Spherchios River floodplain. Concerning the details of the "pass" at Thermopylae, we were able to determine that in 480 B.C. a coastal pass of perhaps 100 m existed, with waves possibly lapping at the foot of the East Gate, Kolonos Hill, and of course at the West Gate, but it is critical to understand that *the land surface of that time is currently buried under up to 20 m of terrigenous clastic sediment and hot springs travertine deposits*. This points up the extreme difficulty encountered by those who use only observations of the current landscape to attempt a detailed reconstruction of earlier landscapes in depositional areas. Without core drilling to determine the location, elevation, and nature of the earlier coastal features, physiographic reconstructions will remain interesting guesses.

Unfortunately, some scholars still resist the "intrusion" of science into their turf, maintaining that archaeological data and ancient writings are sufficient to interpret historic events. For example, Pritchett (1985, and in other communications) has taken great exception to our work at

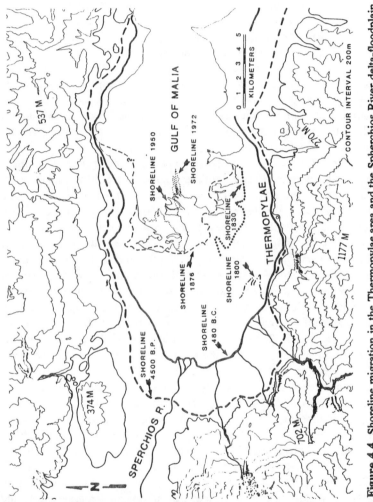

Figure 4.4. Shoreline migration in the Thermopylae area and the Spherchios River delta-floodplain.

the pass at Thermopylae. His (1985:209) summary of our interpretations of the sedimentary sequences (from drill core data) at Thermopylae states, "In short, the drill-hole evidence, taken 300 m west (of the 480 B.C. final defense hill, Kolonos) and 250 m north of the mountainside, sheds no light on the contours of the mountain or of course the road, and the claims made therefrom are specious."

Whatever merit one may see in such comments, the geologic data from the drill cores cannot be ignored. In this case we had interpreted (Kraft et al. 1987) the subsurface data as indicating in 480 B.C. a long narrow beach of about 100 m wide. As indicated above, our drill core data show that more than 20 m of hot spring deposits and sediments overlie the battlefield of 480 B.C. These sediments are underlain by marine sands dating to at least 4535 B.P. At the West Gate we drilled a hole that supports the statement of Herodotus that the pass was only one wagon track wide.

Pritchett (1993:322-325) again derides the use of geologic techniques in precise determination of topography since ancient times and suggests that our geologic evidence precludes a battle at Thermopylae in 480 B.C. Actually, we have carefully defined the shoreline terrain immediately west of Kolonos at the Middle Gate and showed the reconstructed topography to be quite compatible with the accounts of Herodotus and others in antiquity. To quote our work directly (Kraft 1991:6), " History is not equivocal regarding the middle gate at Thermopylae, particularly when the historical record can be augmented by and correlated with paleogeographic reconstructions of ancient landscapes of past millennia. Clearly the area west of the middle gate was 'wide enough' for the many recorded martial events that occurred here. And yet it was the constriction between the cliffs of Mt. Kallidromos and the waters of the Gulf of Malia that led to strategies of both defense and offense into and out of the pass at Thermopylae (cf. Kraft, Rapp, Szemler, Tziavos, and Kase 1987)".

Our sedimentary sequences and paleogeographic reconstructions at Thermopylae provide information for interpretations of later battles: Greeks vs. Gauls in 279 B.C., Romans vs. Antiochus the Syrian in 191 B.C., and others. We realize that with additional coring more details of ancient topographies would emerge. However, the basic subsurface geologic data, which indicate and date the major delta system to the west as well as the sequence of changing environments, cannot be ignored. It is perhaps understandable that Pritchett feels compelled to defend his long-held views (based on ancient writings and observation of *modern topography*) of the ancient battlefield topographies but we insist that a whole new class of data from subsurface geology *relating directly to the ancient surfaces and landscapes* provides an opportunity for a more accurate interpretation rather than an intrusion.

Discussion

Since we began our coastal change studies in 1970, by using core drilling to give us the third dimension--the time-dependent vertical sequence of geologic environments--combined with any available historic and archaeological data, others have also found these methods of great utility. Although it is not our purpose here to review the field we would call your attention to a few of the studies that have been particularly fruitful. Using closely-spaced coring and archaeological data Zangger (1991a) has provided an incredibly detailed reconstruction of the paleogeography at ancient Tiryns. He has also revealed two completely vanished environments in Greece, a shallow coastal bay at Dimini near Volos and a large freshwater lake near Lerna south of Argos, using data from over 200 cores (Zangger 1991b). In the search for ancient Helice, Schwartz and Tziavos (1979) used onshore coring as well as historic data to reconstruct the ancient coastal environment where the city of Helice was reported to have sunk into the Korinthian Gulf after the earthquake of 373 B.C.

In a seminal study backed by over 70 drill cores, our colleague Kayan (1991) developed a highly detailed and precisely delineated set of paleogeographic maps and geologic cross-sections showing the evolution of a mid-Holocene deeply-indented marine embayment at Beşika Bay near Troia. Kayan's precise paleogeographic research has lent renewed support to the concept that the Beşika plain, lying across the narrow strait from Tenedos Island, would have been the anchorage for the Greek fleet in the Trojan War.

Our work has depended on onshore core drilling where the relevant shorelines or sites have been buried by Holocene sediment. In some instances the relevant features are not buried beneath recent deposits but lie offshore. T. H. van Andel and his colleagues (van Andel et al. 1980) have reconstructed the Late Quaternary history of the coastal zone near Franchthi Cave in the southern Argolid using shallow marine seismic reflection studies.

From our perspective most American physical geographers have studied the evolution of landscapes using surficial evidence whereas geologists and European physical geographers have closely interrelated surficial processes with the resultant sedimentary/stratigraphic sequences. Using sediment grain size and composition, sedimentary structures, state of oxidation or reduction, and fossil flora and fauna obtained from core samples, geologists can reconstruct the sequence of depositional environments and, with ^{14}C or other dating, provide a chronology of events in the development of coastal landscapes. From the sedimentary record it is possible to differentiate the various sedimentary environments (e.g. floodplains, swamps, lagoons, barriers, beaches, deltas, near shore marine, etc.) that made up the coastal zone during the various periods of landscape development.

The study of microfossils has been of major importance in our work. The identification of near-shore marine versus deltaic floodplain and backswamp environments is necessary to allow us to delineate past coastal configurations with care. Freshwater ostracods and charophytes are easily differentiated from marine foraminifera and ostracods and their zonation in some cases, such as at Troia (Yang 1982) and at the Gulf of Malia (Tziavos 1977), have been critical to our interpretation.

Geologists who study coastline evolution have to unscramble the effects of three active phenomena that determine the coastal sedimentary record. These are the volume and nature of the sediments provided by rivers, eustatic (world wide) sea level change, and vertical tectonic movements. During the Holocene all three have been exceptionally dynamic in Greece and Aegean Turkey. Deforestation and other results of more intensive land use have increased sediment loads, glacial melting has caused sea level to rise approximately 130 m since the beginning of the Holocene (possibly stabilizing about 5000 B.P.), and tectonic forces have continued to alter elevations (both up and down) throughout the region.

Perhaps the most important geologic contribution to reconstructing past coastal landscapes is in the application of Walther's Law of Correlation of Facies. Facies represent distinct rock types that correspond broadly to environments of deposition (e.g. lagoon, beach, etc.). Walther's Law states that facies occurring in a conformable vertical sequence were formed in laterally adjacent environments and that facies in vertical contact must be the product of geographically neighboring environments. Hence, by noting the vertical sequences one can reconstruct the changes in shoreline environments over time.

Raphael (1969), a physical geographer, presented one of the pioneering works in Greek coastal paleogeography, as applied to history and archaeology, in his work in Elis. However, by not having any information on the three-dimensional stratigraphic record his work remains only a beginning. From the point of view of earth movements (tectonics), Kelletat (1978) demonstrated vertical uplift of more than 100 m along some of the flanks of the Peloponnesos during the Quaternary period. Without factoring in such data, no geomorphic assessment can provide a detailed picture of landscape change. Of particular note are his subsidence rates for grabens (down thrown blocks of the earth's crust bounded by faults on their long sides) which are hosts to many of the important rivers, deltas, and human habitats in the region.

Geologists have reasonably good data of world eustacy during the Holocene (Fairbridge 1961, 1981), with most agreeing on sea-level rise to approximately present levels by 5000 B.P. Of much greater importance to paleogeographic reconstruction are *local relative sea level rise curves* based on data from the area under study. In our work in Greece and Aegean Turkey such curves often were important in interpreting coastal landscape change (Kraft and Rapp 1988; Kraft et al. 1975, 1978, 1980). An excellent summation of the study of world sea levels with the hundreds of local variants is presented by Pirazzoli (1991). Kayan (1988, 1991) has delineated very similar relative sea-level curves in the Troad (based on more than 70 cores) and along the southwest coast of Anatolia, suggesting that a regional approximation of Aegean sea levels may be possible in future studies. However, currently one must depend on relative sea-level curves derived from geologic data on the local setting.

Many of our paleogeographic reconstructions have been based on a relatively small number of cores supplemented by a study of the surficial geology and geomorphology. Nevertheless, the geologic techniques and concepts have worked well. Clearly, more intensive coring will result in a more detailed picture. This is well demonstrated by our work in the Argolid (Kraft et al. 1977) which was based on only a few drill cores. Our determination of the ancient shoreline just west of the lower town of Tiryns in Helladic times has proved to be correct. However, the much more intensive study by Zangger (1991a), based on a large number of drill cores, has provided a detailed picture of the environment and land use by Helladic peoples well beyond our previous work.

A final aspect of our research methodology that should be noted is our effort to identify the major impacts of human land use. The major progradation and aggradation of the delta floodplains of many rivers in the region apparently began about five thousand years ago. This may reflect a major deforestation event with the coming of intensive agriculture in the uplands. In some cases we can record the direct human impact on cycles of coastal erosion and deposition, for example at Methoni in the southwest Peloponnesos (Kraft and Aschenbrenner 1977), or in the altered harbor works from the Bronze Age to the Medieval at ancient Ephesos on the Aegean coast of Turkey where we (Kayan, Kraft, Rapp) are working currently.

In all regional studies an understanding of landscape change over time is essential, particularly when the change has been so dramatic that the modern landscape does not correspond to that of the period under consideration. Our efforts have gone toward drawing paleogeographic maps so that archaeologists and historians may plot places and events on maps that accurately reflect the geomorphology of the time. Coastal change has been dramatic in the Aegean region. This change has controlled much of human exploitation of the coastal zone, particularly with respect to habitation sites, food resources, and transportation.

We end with a plea for more understanding of these dynamic phenomena and how they influenced human/environment interaction over time and how they now affect our interpretations of archaeological and textual material.

References Cited

Belknap, D.F., and J.C. Kraft
    1985 Influence of Antecedent Geology on Stratigraphic Preservation Potential and Evolution of Delaware's Barrier Systems. *Marine Geology* 63:235-262.
Bilgin, T.
    1969 Biga *Yarimadasi Guneybati Kisminin Jeomorfolojisi.* Universitesi Cografya Enstitusu, Yayin.
Bintliff, J.
    1991 Troja und Seine Palaolandschaften. In *Stuttgarter Kolloquim zur Historischen Geographie des Alterums,* edited by E. Olshausen, and H. Sonnabend, pp. 83-131. Bonn.
Fairbridge, R.W.
    1961 Eustatic Change in Sea Level. *Physics and Chemistry of the Earth* 4:99-185.
    1981 Holocene Sea-Level Oscillations. *Striae* 14:131-139.
Frazer, A.D.
    1937 *The Patomic System of the Trojan Plain.* Jameson Bookstore, Charlottesville, Va.
Kayan, İ.
    1988 Late-Holocene Sea-Level Changes on the Western Anatolian

Coast. *Palaeogeography, Palaeoclimatology, Palaeoecology* 68:205-218

1991 Holocene Geomorphic Evolution of the Beşik Plain and Changing Environment of Ancient Man. *Studia Troica* 1:79-93.

Kayan, İ., J.C. Kraft, and O. Erol.

1980 Truva Dogal Ceresinin Son 15000 Yiloaki Degismeleri. *Bilim ve Teknik,Sayi* 155-Ekim:8-13. TUBITAK Yay, Ankara.

Kelletat, D., Kowalczyk, D., Schroeder, B., and Winter, K.-P.

1978 Neotectonics in the Peloponnesian Coastal Regions. In H. Closs, D. Roeder and K. Schmidt, editors. *Alps, Appennines, Hellenides. Inter-Union Commission on Geodynamics. Scientific Report* 38:512-518. Stuttgart.

Korfmann, M.

1986 Beşik Tepe: New Evidence for the Period of the Trojan Sixth and Seventh Settlements. In *Troy and the Trojan War*, edited by M. Mellink, pp.17-28. Bryn Mawr College, Bryn Mawr, Pa.

1989 Beşik-Tepe. *Archaeologische Anzeiger*: 473-481.

Kraft, J.C.

1971 Sedimentary Facies Patterns and Geological History of a Holocene Marine Transgression. *Geological Society of America, Bulletin* 82:2131-2158.

1972 *A Reconnaissance of the Geology of the Sandy Coastal Areas of Eastern Greece and the Peloponnese.* College of Marine Studies, University of Delaware.

1991 Geology of the Great Isthmus Corridor. In *The Great Isthmus Corridor Route, Explorations of the Phokis-Doris Expedition*, vol. 1, edited by E.W. Kase, G.J. Szemler, N.C. Wilkie, and P.W. Wallace, pp. 1-16. Kendall/Hunt, Dubuque.

Kraft, J.C., and S.E. Aschenbrenner

1977 Paleogeographic Projections in the Methoni Embayment in Greece". *Journal of Field Archaeology* 4:19-44.

Kraft, J.C., S.E. Aschenbrenner, and İ. Kayan

1980 Late Holocene Coastal Changes and Resultant Destruction or Burial of Archaeological Sites in Greece and Turkey. In *Proceedings of the Commission on The Coastal Environment, 24th International Geographical Congress*, edited by M.L. Schwartz, pp. 13-31. Western Washington University Press, Bellingham.

1981 Gec Holosen Kiyi Degismelertinin Yunanistan ve Turkiye'de Archaeolojik Yerlesme Yerleri Uzerine Etkileri. *Ankara University Cografya Arastirmalari Dergisi*: 105-121.

1985 Geological Studies Applied to Archaeological Settings. In *Archaeological Geology*, edited by G. Rapp Jr. and J. Gifford, pp. 57-84. Yale University Press, New Haven.

Kraft, J.C., S.E. Aschenbrenner, and G. Rapp, Jr.

1977 Paleo-geography of Pre-Historic Archaeological Settings in Bronze Age to Neolithic Greece. *Science* 195:941-947.

Kraft, J.C., İ. Kayan, and O. Erol

1980 Geomorphic Reconstructions in the Environs of Ancient Troy. *Science* 209:776-782.

1982 Geology and Paleogeographic Reconstructions in the Vicinity of Ancient Troy. In *Troy: The Archaeological Geology*, edited by G. Rapp, Jr. and J.Gifford, pp. 11-42. Princeton University Press, Princeton.

Kraft, J.C., and G. Rapp Jr.

1988 Geological Reconstruction of Ancient Coastal Landforms in Greece with Predictions of Future Coastal Changes. In *The Engineering Geology of Ancient Works, Monuments and Historical Sites*, edited by P. Marinos, and G. Koukis, pp. 1545-1556. Balkema, Rotterdam.

Kraft, J.C., G. Rapp, Jr., and S.E. Aschenbrenner

1975 Late Holocene Paleogeography of the Coastal Plain of the Gulf of Messenia, Greece, and its Relationships to Archaeological Settings and Coastal Change. *Geological Society of America Bulletin* 86:1191-1208.

1980 Late Holocene Paleogeographic Reconstruction in the Area of the Bay of Navarino: Sandy Pylos. *Journal of Archaeological Science* 7:187-210.

Kraft, J.C., G. Rapp, Jr., G.J. Szemler, C. Tziavos, and E.W. Kase

1987 The Pass at Thermopylae. *Journal of Field Archaeology* 14:181-198.

Luce, J.V.

1984 The Homeric Topography of the Trojan Plain Reconsidered. *Oxford Journal of Archaeology* 3:31-43.

Maclaren, C.

1822 *Dissertation on the Topography of the Plain of Troy*. A. Constable, Edinburgh.

McDonald, W.A.

1991 Archaeology in the 21st Century: Six Modest Recommendations. *Antiquity* 65:829-839.

Mey, O.

1926 *Das Schlachtfeld bei Troja, Eine Untersuchung*. Walter de

Gruyter, Berlin.
Pirazzoli, P.A.
1991 *World Atlas of Holocene Sea-Level Changes.* Elsevier
Oceanographic Series 58. Elsevier, Amsterdam, New York.
Pritchett, W.K.
1985 In Defense of Thermopylae Pass. In *Studies in Ancient Greek Topography*, Part V, pp. 190-216. Classical Studies, vol. 31, University of California.
1993 *The Liar School of Herodotus.* J.C. Grieber, Amsterdam.
Raphael, C.N.
1969 The Plain of Elis, Greece--An Archaeological Approach. *Michigan Academician* 1:73-74.
Rapp, G. Jr., S.E. Aschenbrenner, and J.C. Kraft
1978 The Holocene Environmental History of the Nichoria Region. In *Excavations at Nichoria in Southwestern Greece, vol. 1, Site Environs and Techniques*, edited by G. Rapp, Jr., and S.E. Aschenbrenner, pp. 13-25. University of Minnesota Press, Minneapolis.
Rapp, G. Jr., and J.C. Kraft
1979 Aegean Sea Level Changes in the Bronze Age. In *Thera and The Aegean World*, edited by C. Doumas, pp. 183-194. Thera Foundation, London.
1990 Environmental Geology and the Paleogeography of Ancient Sites. In *The Engineering Geology of Ancient Works, Monuments and Historical Sites* vol. IV, edited by P. Marinos, and G. Koukis, pp. 1945-1948. Balkema, Rotterdam.
Rapp, G. Jr., and J. Gifford (editors)
1985 *Troy: The Archaeological Geology.* Princeton University Press, Princeton.
Schwartz, M., and C. Tziavos
1979 Geology in the Search for Ancient Helice. *Journal of Field Archaeology* 6:243-252.
Schede, M.
1930 Anatolia (Beşika). In *Archaeologischer Anzeiger, 1929: Jahr buch des Deutschen Archaeologischen Institutes*, vol. 44. Berlin and Leipzig.
Spratt, T.
1839 *The Plain of Troy.* H.M.S.N. Beacon, British Admiralty Chart.
Tziavos, C.
1977 *Sedimentology, Ecology and Paleogeography of the*

Spherchios Valley and Maliachos Gulf, Greece. M.S. thesis, Department of Geology, University of Delaware, Newark, Delaware.

Tziavos, C., and J.C. Kraft
  1985 Greece. In *The World's Coastline*, edited by E. Bird and M.L. Schwartz Van Nostrand, pp. 445-453. Reinhold, New York.

van Andel, T., T. Jacobsen, J. Joly, and N. Lianos
  1980 Late Quaternary History of the Coastal Zone near Franchthi Cave, Southern Argolid, Greece. *Journal of Field Archaeology* 7:389-402.

Vita-Finzi, C.
  1969 *The Mediterranean Valleys: Geological Changes in Historical Times.* Cambridge University Press, Cambridge.

Yang, L.-C.
  1982 *The Distribution and Taxonomy of Ostracods and Benthic Foraminifera in Late Pleistocene and Holocene Sediments of the Troad, Biga Peninsula, Turkey.* M.S. thesis, Department of Geology, University of Delaware, Newark, Delaware.

Zangger, E.
  1991a Tiryns Unterstadt. *Archaeometry* 90:831-840.
  1991b Prehistoric Coastal Environments in Greece: The Vanished Landscapes of Dimini Bay and Lake Lerna. *Journal of Field Archaeology* 18:1-15.

III.
ARCHAEOLOGICAL INVESTIGATIONS: THE USE OF REGIONAL SCALE DATA

Chapter 5

Regional Survey in the Aegean: The "New Wave" (and After)

John F. Cherry

Introduction: The "New Wave" of Greek Survey

Comparing the current scene in Aegean archaeology with that of twenty years ago, even a complete outsider could, I imagine, detect some major changes. Of these, the most far-reaching in its impact has been the explosion of multi-period, regional surface survey projects. As Snodgrass (1990:119) recently put it, "a wave of activity in intensive survey has swept across the scene of Greek archaeology." Of course, topographic exploration and landscape reconnaissance have intellectual roots in Greece reaching back several centuries (Constantine 1984; Tsigakou 1981). Almost exactly 100 years have now passed since there was initiated on the Cycladic island of Melos a strikingly modern project (Atkinson et al. 1904; Mackenzie 1897), in which many currently important regional issues and concerns played a central role (Cherry 1982:11-12). And it was as long ago as the period immediately after World War II that there emerged interdisciplinary collaboration on problems of regional scope, mainly at the instigation of prehistorians, and most notably in the work begun in the southwestern Peloponnesos during the 1950s and leading eventually to the highly influential publication of the University of Minnesota Messenia Expedition (McDonald and Rapp 1972). But it cannot be denied that it was only in the 1980s that survey moved to a front-stage position in Greece. Indeed, the growth of interest in this type of work has proliferated so much that the Greek Archaeological Service found it necessary, a few years ago, to impose restrictions for the first time on the number of permits issued to each of the foreign schools and institutes in Athens for survey-related activities by their members.

It is my contention that, in general, the regional research projects conducted within the past fifteen years or so in Greece differ very substantially in methodology and research goals from almost all previous work--so much so, in fact, that I suggested a few years ago (Cherry 1986) that they could be considered a "new wave" in Greek archaeology, and the phrase seems to have stuck (Bintliff 1992; Osborne 1989). Greece's climate, landscape, and natural environment provide extremely favorable conditions for effective survey in general, and for systematic, intensive survey in particular. The conjunction of generally moderate terrain and landforms, frequent shallow plowing in at least parts of most survey territories, winter rains, and an archaeological record that is both highly visible and (for most periods) readily dateable by reference to material from literally thousands of excavations conducted over the years in nearby zones, make the Aegean a nearly ideal setting for survey activity. So it is hardly surprising that, over the years, a very great deal of field survey has taken place-- everything from one man (and his bicycle) in the mountains of Arkadia, to multi-year endeavors involving dozens of scholars and literally hundreds of student participants. Appropriate methods have been in process of continual refinement for decades: indeed, innovations in method developed in recent years put Greece at the forefront of this type of research, to an extent not yet widely recognized. One message of this paper (perhaps of this volume as a whole) is that those who use the surface archaeological record to tackle regional problems in Greece should have more of an "attitude" (as one might say in the USA today)--that is, be aggressively positive in pointing to the massive *achievements* of survey to date, rather than adopting the cultural cringe in deference to excavators, historians, processual archaeologists in North America, or whoever else is thought to have greener grass on the other side.

Is it not telling, for instance, that one of the most recent books (also one of the oddest) devoted to regional archaeology and survey fails to mention Greece at all (Fish and Kowalewski 1990)? In fact, it not only provides no coverage whatsoever of any Mediterranean or European country, but includes just one Old World case study--almost as though methodologically sophisticated survey were thought to be the exclusive preserve of New World archaeologists. Yet even at the outset of the 1980s, as several surveys of Mediterranean surveys revealed (e.g., Cherry 1983; Dyson 1982; Keller and Rupp 1983; Snodgrass 1982), the sheer quantity and variety of regionally-based research under way in the Mediterranean was already very impressive; moreover, archaeologists working in Greece were arguably leading the way, in terms both of innovations in method and of the enthusiasm with which they embraced the richness of the surface record and the exciting possibilities it can afford for interdisciplinary research. The intervening years have only served to maintain and strengthen these trends.

As illustration of the point, I need mention only the fact that an attempt in 1993 to organize a newsletter, in which survey projects presently active in Greek lands might quickly report their results and progress towards publication, in short order elicited no less than 32 contributions (cf., Alcock et al. 1994:Figure 8.1). Current and recent projects in Greece describing themselves as "surveys" do, of course, also include work that is not properly of regional scope (e.g., detailed topographic and artifactual reconnaissances of individual urban settlements); work that focuses only on the locational, architectural and artifactual attributes of a single class of site within a region (e.g., isolated ancient towers); work that is targeted narrowly on one specific period in the long-term history of the region, or whose overall research design is largely dictated by the problems emerging from the archaeology of just one chronological era (e.g., the Mycenaean Late Bronze Age); surveys that have grown out of an excavation and are intended mainly to "put the site in its context;" prospection that has tried to tackle either too much, or too little, territory to allow conclusions that are well grounded in a spatially satisfactory sample of empirical data; and so on. Perhaps this is a statement of the obvious: work is being undertaken in various styles and under differing paradigms, some of it well executed, some ill-conceived. But could the same not be said of excavations in Greece, or indeed of regionally-based archaeological research in almost any country?

My point, however, is simply this: *survey has finally found a secure place as an accepted and valuable technique for investigating the Greek past and challenging traditional interpretations stemming from a narrower database.* No one now feels moved to write an *apologia* for doing survey, and it is generally acknowledged, even by the most conventional of scholars, that survey can be a legitimate form of research in its own right, and not simply the prelude to the allegedly more important and exciting task of excavation. We need to remember that Greece is a country of very modest size, yet its archaeology is now--and has been for decades--the central concern not just of its own Archaeological Service, but of hundreds (even thousands) of professional archaeologists working in Greece under the auspices of the numerous foreign schools and institutes in Athens. I venture to suggest that the ratio of research effort spent each year per square kilometer of territory is higher in Greece than almost anywhere else in the world (with such countries as Israel, Italy, and Britain as close competitors). The fact that a substantial proportion of this effort, which hitherto has been devoted primarily to excavation and its related activities, is now being expended on surveys--surveys, moreover, which in many cases have been conceptualized *ab initio* as addressing unashamedly regional questions from a genuinely interdisciplinary standpoint, and which have introduced methodological innovations that should be of interest well beyond the confines of Greece alone--this fact seems to me to offer ample justification for regarding the introduction of systematic surface survey as a genuinely "new wave." Anthony Snodgrass and I (1988:13) intended to be only slightly provocative when we wrote "... 'Digging up the past' will remain a primary activity of archaeologists in the field, in a variety of contexts and for a variety of purposes. But never again will this be their *only* field activity, and the day may even come when it is no longer their main one."

The present is surely an important time of transition and evaluation with respect to this "new wave", since the 1990s should see the definitive publication of a number of intensive regional survey projects initiated in the 1970s and 1980s. In fact in one instance, Anthony Snodgrass and John Bintliff's Boeotia Project (Bintliff and Snodgrass 1985, 1988a, 1988b; Bintliff 1985, 1991; Snodgrass 1987:93-131, 1990), a team has been hammering away at a single chunk of landscape almost every year *since the 1970s*, with a devotion more characteristic of the "big dig" at such sites as Korinth or Sardis, than of the "quick-and-dirty" two- or three-year survey; it will be instructive to judge from the eagerly anticipated final monograph what difference this longitudinal approach has made. When more of these projects reach final publication, as some soon will, we will have the opportunity to compare, and perhaps combine, the results of several survey projects carried out by different teams within a single large region. In my overview of the state of Mediterranean survey, written more than a dozen years ago, I anticipated the approach of a "stage when synthesis and comparison at a geographical scale considerably larger than that of the individual survey would be worthwhile" (Cherry 1983:403). In Greece, it has taken rather longer than I expected to reach this stage, but it does actually now seem to be on the verge of arriving. Thus, in the northeastern Peloponnesos, for instance, we can set side-by-side the data from surveys in half a dozen closely adjacent areas: the Nemea Valley (Cherry et al. 1988; Wright et al. 1990), the Berbati-Limnes area (Wells et al. 1990), the immediate hinterlands of Mycenae (French 1993:18) and of Tiryns and the Argive Plain (Zangger 1994), the Southern Argolid (Jameson 1976; Runnels and van Andel 1987), and the Methana peninsula (Mee et al. 1991). Furthermore, an ambitious attempt at using data from a wide range of surveys, as well as from more traditional archaeological and historical sources, in order to re-evaluate the landscapes of Roman Greece (Alcock 1993), provides an example that "should silence the skeptics who have questioned the comparability of field survey data and the feasibility of writing detailed historical reconstructions from them" (Mattingly 1994:162). We have even got to the point where re-survey seems worthwhile--for example, the intensive study by the Pylos Regional Archaeological Project of parts of the huge area covered by the Minnesota Messenia Expedition in the 1960s, or the re-examination by a team from the British School at Athens of many of the sites located in the Melos Survey in the 1970s. The publications stemming from all these various initiatives will begin to provide answers to some important questions that will assuredly have a major impact on future directions.

After the "New Wave": Some Current Directions

If this "new wave" has broken on the shores of Aegean archaeology, however, what comes next (Osborne 1989)? For instance, what precisely has been gained by the general adoption of far more labor-intensive modes of data collection than hitherto (for discussion and references, see Alcock et al. 1994)? How have our pictures of the past been modified by the discovery that seemingly disparate areas of inquiry--archaeology, historical ecology, geomorphology, cultural anthropology, ancient and medieval history, and so on--in fact share mutually overlapping areas of interest? What sorts of epistemological frameworks offer the most productive context for project integration that is truly interdisciplinary, and not merely a *farrago* of pieces of knowledge, albeit from different perspectives, about a single area--a sort of regional version of the infamous "tell-all-you-know" school of ancient history, of which Moses Finley (1985:61) was rightly so scornful? Will the veritable flood of new data emerging from recent regional studies force a change in the disciplinary relationships between, for instance, ancient historians and classical archaeologists (e.g., Barker 1991; Cherry et al. 1991; Foxhall 1990; Jameson 1976; Morris 1994; Osborne 1985, 1987; Wells 1993)? Is there a danger that the comparative approach, which the availability of high-quality data from numerous projects is now beginning to encourage, will in fact be still-born as a result of lack of agreed descriptive standards and non-conformity over definitional issues (e.g. how to define a "site"--or indeed whether the very notion of a site is an artificial and interpretative construct imposed upon the data)? Already some significant changes of direction and emphasis can be detected in the most recent work, and it may be useful to mention a few of these in a little more detail.

Some developments build on new technological opportunities drawn from various branches of archaeological science, especially the use of geophysics, geoprospection, and geochemical survey. The Boeotia Survey, mentioned above, has been notably innovative in these aspects of survey in Greece--not surprisingly, in light of the co-sponsorship of the project by the School of Archaeological Sciences at the University of Bradford, which has been able to supply ideas, expertise, equipment, and trained personnel. One good example of this work is to be seen in their study focused on a Boeotian late Hellenistic and early Roman site (Site PP17 in the Boeotia Survey's numbering system), at which it has been possible to compare the shape and extent of surface scatters of pottery and tile with features detected by resistivity survey (Gaffney and Gaffney 1986:Figures 32-33), as well as with the pattern of trace metal residues which have accumulated as a result of occupation (Davies et al. 1988:Figure 3). Although excavation would be a desirable next step, it is already possible to say (at far lower cost and trouble than any excavation would entail) that this short-lived site represents a small structure with an attached yard (for a composite distributional plan, see Alcock et al. 1994:Figure 8.10), and to say something about its patterns of use. This example also points up the fact that built structures, pottery scatters, and tile distributions do not overlap precisely, nor do they coincide with the patterns of inorganic residues that have accumulated over time from human and animal waste products--in other words, even on a site represented by structural remains, site extent and shape are characteristics dependent partly on the means by which one measures such variables. On the other hand, such data can play a very important role in helping assess crucial arguments about site function (Osborne 1985), and the nature of rural residence and agricultural practice in Classical Greece (Alcock et al. 1994), and no doubt in other periods also (Davis 1991).

Another productive example comes from the Lakonia Survey, in which a picture of small, well-dated, rural sites has been built up from examining quantified artifactual distributions, topography, and geophysical data, in conjunction with sophisticated statistical treatment of data on levels of soil phosphate (Buck et al. 1988a, 1988b, 1992; Cavanagh et al. 1988). One significant conclusion to emerge from this work is that "on-site" levels of soil phosphates often extend well beyond the "site", as minimally defined by its surface artifactual scatter alone. A fresh program of study, developed out of the Lakonia Survey and entitled the "Lakonia Rural Sites Project," commenced in 1992, with the intention of extending this approach in a systematic manner to a diachronic range of twenty single-period rural sites located in earlier work. Aside from careful, spatially-controlled artifactual collections and geophysical investigations on each site, this study involves substantial soil sampling, both on- and off-site. "The aim is to test soil chemical and mineral magnetic characteristics as indicators of past human activity. Soil properties to be analyzed include phosphorus, a range of metallic elements, and magnetic susceptibility. Particle size, percent [sic] organic carbon, calcium carbonate and iron oxides will also be determined" (Cavanagh and Mee 1993:30). Admirably multi-stage and flexible in conception, this program (which might well, at some sites, lead to excavation) has the virtue not only of contributing to the difficult topic of surface-subsurface relationships, but also of tackling head-on, by interdisciplinary means, the problems of understanding the very class of site encountered most frequently in field surveys--the small rural site, of which there are still so few excavated instances in Greece to serve as a guide.

I have focused on these examples from Boeotia and Lakonia because they seem to me to provide a pointer to the sorts of research that now need to be done if we are to advance beyond the stage of filling period-maps with dots, without having much idea of what those dots actually represent in terms of the material remains of human practice. There are a number of other technological applications and aids whose usefulness in the Greek context is still frankly experimental, but also full of promise. Devices such as laser theodolites and "total stations", with automatic data capture and interfaces to appropriate computer software, are already in very widespread use, and they make formerly tedious procedures, such as site mapping and the laying-out of grids for controlled artifact collection, both faster and more accurate. Hand-held global positioning systems (GPS), which spread into the archaeological world like wildfire in the immediate aftermath of the Gulf War, can now provide very precise positioning and relocation of sites and other features. They are likely to be especially effective when used in conjunction with new forms of remote sensing, including photography in the non-visible wavebands and digitized satellite imagery, as recent work in Messenia by University of Minnesota archaeologists and remote sensing experts has shown (summary in Joyce 1992:44-46). Thus, for instance, known features on the ground (such as ancient quarries) can be located by GPS and related to individual pixels in multi-spectral and other images from Landsat and the space shuttle; these pixels can be used as the basis for a computer classification and search for other locations with comparable spectral emission characteristics; and the GPS can be employed, once again, in locating these places during "ground-truthing." The Minnesota team claim that such procedures are aiding in the discovery not only of sites (including fortifications and a Classical temple) totally hidden by dense brush, but of such features as ancient clay beds and abandoned water channels. Similar methods have given the Nikopolis Project some success in isolating exposed Plio-Pleistocene sediments often associated in Greece with Palaeolithic and Mesolithic cultural material (French 1993:43-46; Stein and Cullen 1994). Finally, one must mention the rapid proliferation of Geographic Information Systems (GIS) applications (Kvamme 1989; Lock and Harris 1992). So far, there exist virtually no completed GIS-based case-studies from Greece from which one might judge the potential this technology holds for combining very different categories of information, for visualizing spatial data from surveys at different scales from regional to intra-site, and for associated management tasks (but see Dann and Yerkes, this volume). GIS has, inevitably, become a bandwagon; some of those rushing to jump aboard are doing so without thinking very clearly either about the questions GIS might help answer, or about the steep costs associated with establishing a whole series of digital map layers for areas where even accurate traditional maps at suitable scales are hard to come by. The early signs, nonetheless, are promising (e.g., Davis et al. 1993; Wiseman and Dousougli-Zachos 1994).

Another trend which represents an important change of emphasis is the expansion of survey beyond its former concentration on lowland rural landscapes. One aspect of this is the incorporation of careful reconnaissance of urban centers. It is possible, of course, only where conditions allow (e.g., the site must be largely free of modern construction, undisturbed by excavation over most of its extent, and, ideally, well cultivated), and it requires significant modifications of standard sampling procedures for rural survey to take account of the staggering densities of artifacts typically encountered. Where these conditions are met, it has already been demonstrated in a number of detailed case-studies that survey can be considerably more efficient and effective than excavation in producing "a better statistical sample of the physical traces of a city's past" (Snodgrass and Bintliff 1991:93; cf. Bintliff and Snodgrass 1988b). Significant advantages include not only the opportunity to reconstruct long-term urban history in a relatively unbiased fashion on the basis of large, spatially-extensive samples, but also the possibility of relating such information *directly* to the results of rural survey in the city's immediate hinterland and even further afield. The range of large sites on which intensive survey has been carried out in the last several years includes the Boeotian cities of Haliartos and Thespiai, and Hesiod's home town of Askra, the city of Phlius in the northeastern Peloponnesos (Alcock 1991), and the Classical port-town of Koressos and the prehistoric sites at Kephala and Paoura, all on the island of Keos (Cherry et al. 1991:199-216, 265-284). This is a development now widely paralleled elsewhere in the Mediterranean; recent examples come to mind from Spain, Italy, Turkey, and Tunisia.

Greek surveys are also beginning to deal more seriously and effectively than hitherto with regions or zones that were occupied only seasonally, or that were politically and economically peripheral throughout much of their histories. This applies in particular to the highland areas of Greece. It has taken all together too long for historians and archaeologists to heed Braudel's (1972:29) criticism that they "keep to the plain, the scene of the activities of the princes and powers of the day, and do not seem at all interested in going to the lofty mountains which lie nearby." In some countries such as Britain, of course, the lowland/highland distinction constitutes a fundamental structuring principle of both archaeological field research and of cultural heritage management (e.g., Darvill 1986). Recent work in Italian field survey suggests a similar development: for instance, the inclusion in Barker and Lloyd's *Roman Landscapes* (1991) of separate sections devoted to papers on agrarian structures on the lowlands and in the uplands and margins; or the inception of projects combining data from survey, documentary sources, and ethnography to study the long-term history of the exploitation of mountainous regions (e.g. Barker 1989; Barker and Grant 1991). One cannot yet point to anything of comparable sophistication from Greece. But whereas formerly there was a tendency to devote little attention to the more mountainous parts of study areas (on the grounds that they were too heavily vegetated, too steep, too sparsely settled in the past, or simply too unrewarding in terms of finds), all types of terrain are now being examined on the more equal footing they require, if we are to be able to document and understand the variety of settlement patterns that have existed at various times in response to differential exploitation of different zones. Some projects of recent years, indeed, have deliberately concentrated on upland or mountainous landscapes in their own right--from the surveys of Lasithi (Watrous 1982) and Sphakia (Nixon et al. 1989) in Crete, to those of the Methana peninsula (Mee et al. 1991), Aetolia (Bommeljé and Doorn 1987), southern Epiros (Wiseman and Dousougli-Zachos 1994), or the νομός (*nomos*) of Grevena (French 1990:49-50) on the mainland.

It is still too early to say how far the volumes of data now coming in from work of this kind will indicate radically different settlement histories. There are problems, of course--"the history of the mountains is chequered and difficult to trace" (Braudel 1972:44)--such as finding ways to recognize and deal with distinctive types of upland sites (e.g., villages and special-purpose loci), or to distinguish clearly between demographic change and readjustments in regional settlement structure. Yet there are also real benefits that have already begun to show. One is the likely effects that more all-embracing forms of survey will have on our understanding of the structure of sacred landscapes (Alcock 1993:172-214). An ancient source such as Pausanias may on occasion be frustratingly delphic (Snodgrass 1987:67-92), and is certainly more complex than the flawed *Blue Guide* for which he has all too often been taken (Elsner 1994); but he is unambiguous enough about the pervasiveness of ritual activity in the countryside, including mountain-top shrines, upland sanctuaries, cave cults, and the like. Survey has been effective in putting ancient peoples back into the countryside they once inhabited, but less attentive to matters concerning the placing of the gods. This systematic neglect seems now to be coming to an end (e.g., most recently, Alcock and Osborne 1994).

In a rather different way, increased attention paid to upland and marginal zones has encouraged more careful evaluation of the archaeology of pastoralism, and of the economic interpenetration of mountains, plateaux, and plains. Here, there have emerged two roadblocks. One is an ahistorical and decontextualized insistence on seasonal transhumance as an unchanging and ever-present factor in the long-term history of human settlement in the Mediterranean (e.g., Jacobsen 1984; for references and critique, see Cherry 1988). The other is the almost total lack of unambiguous criteria for distinguishing the material remains of specialized pastoralism in the archaeological record. It has come to be recognized that the relationship between pastoralism as a specific socioeconomic adaptation and the material culture resulting from it is one best investigated, initially, in a contemporary setting (Chang and Koster 1986); and that, in turn, has encouraged a variety of ethnographic and ethnoarchaeological studies, not only in Greece, but quite widely throughout the countries bordering the Mediterranean (see Cherry 1988:17-20). In Greece, most such fieldwork has in fact been carried out in the context of existing regional survey projects--for instance, in the southern Argolid of the Peloponnesos (Chang 1984; Koster and Koster 1976; Murray and Chang 1981), or Grevena in northern Greece (Chang 1992; Chang and Tourtellotte 1993).

In reality, these studies focusing on pastoralism are merely one thread in a much larger fabric which is coming together from the intertwining of a large number of strands of collaborative, regionally-based research under way in Greece these days: historical ecology, cultural ecology, historical geography, cultural anthropology, ethnohistory, ethnoarchaeology, systematic analysis of archival documents and of travelers' accounts, and, of course, archaeological field survey itself. Nearly all of the larger Greek survey projects in the last few years have been very multi-disciplinary indeed--a most encouraging development, though one that has also already revealed just how difficult it is to meld an unwieldy mixture of disparate sets of information into some sort of coherent picture. At any rate, basic data from survey, in conjunction with insights from ethnoarchaeology and cultural anthropology, and in interplay with new approaches within ancient history, seem set to play an ever larger role in understanding (for instance) the complex relationships of family economics, land tenure, and the farmed landscape in different regions of the Aegean at different times in the past (cf. Foxhall 1990). The 1992 Corfu conference on "Rural Structures and Ancient Societies" likewise gives a good snapshot of the temporal range and variety of approaches currently in play (Mendoni and Doukellis 1994).

"Temporal range" provides a *segue* to my final topic: the astonishing recent growth of regional studies of Late Antiquity, and of the medieval and post-medieval periods in Greece. A personal example serves to illustrate the point. In my survey on Melos in the mid-1970s (Cherry 1982), we were effectively forced to abandon archaeological analysis after the end of antiquity, because we knew so little about diagnostic pottery or other artifacts of the Frankish, Venetian, and Ottoman periods, nor did there appear to be other experts upon whom we could call; there is thus an awkward transition from archaeological survey data to historical and documentary information as the primary sources. That now seems another age. There have now been great improvements in our knowledge of the Byzantine and later ceramic sequences in different parts of the Greek world, as well as a fuller appreciation by survey archaeologists of the evidence offered by vernacular architecture. It has been a gratifying experience to see a fresh team return to Melos and do justice to the medieval sites and standing monuments so poorly served in earlier surveys there. A number of survey projects have come to realize that "the diachronic approach" really does involve coming to grips with the evidence of the past millennium or more. Ideally, this should mean continuing investigation right into the present to include the oft-mentioned "yesterday's discarded sardine can", and, while there have certainly been interesting specialized studies in the Greek context of "the archaeology of us" (e.g., Murray and Kardulias 1986), most projects familiar to me have not yet developed effective methods for the collection and analysis of modern material culture. On the other hand, a number of surveys have taken serious steps to exploit the richness of surviving historical archives, very few of them published and thus requiring fieldwork in Istanbul, Athens, or Venice by historians with specialized skills as well as an interest in the larger issues that motivate regional survey. Some of these archives offer an astonishing wealth of information on matters such as demography, subsistence, land-tenure, and taxation, and at a level of detail that allows these data to be related to identifiable on-the-ground settlements reaching back in some cases to the 14th or 15th centuries and *identifiable by survey*. Local archives, too, are proving to be an untapped resource, as Davis (1991) recently demonstrated in the case of several islands of the Cyclades under Ottoman rule. Since other papers in this volume deal explicitly with medieval and later Greece, no more need be said here about the impact this major growth area is already having.

Beyond the "New Wave"

It should be apparent by now from this admittedly very partial and limited discussion that I am enthusiastic about the real achievements of regional surveys in Greece, and excited about the possibilities for continued developments in the future. Survey has taken its rightful place, both institutionally and intellectually, on the Greek archaeological scene--and none too soon. At the same time, the breaking of this "new wave" has also washed up some difficult problems, whose resolution may be a prerequisite for further advances. Space allows mention here of only a couple of examples.

To find and date sites, at one time the central issue in methodological and procedural discussion in Greek survey, now seems rather easy, at least for most periods and parts of Greece; but that is not itself enough to advance our understanding of them. Regional and temporal variation in site distributions has always been a major goal of survey, yet tools for discriminating *types* of sites still remain at a frustratingly crude level. Thus, for instance, a classification by size has often been the primary basis for plotting sites on period-distribution maps. But it takes only a little reflection to make it obvious that this risks lumping together such things as local shrines, cemeteries, grave groups, small farms, seasonal shelters, and other functionally disparate entities whose surface expression may be of similar extent. Equally, the idea that independent small Classical farmsteads can be differentiated from such sites as rural cemeteries by the presence/absence of a "halo" of finds around the densest nucleus and by the preponderance of fine wares (e.g., Snodgrass 1987:113, 117) must confront the facts that such haloes are not a feature of the surface record everywhere in Greece, and that not all cemeteries produce quality grave goods.

How then can we turn our now more sensitive and sophisticated archaeological data from survey into a historical interpretation? Excavation may help, and--notwithstanding unfortunate misreadings, such as Popham's (1990) over-reaction to Snodgrass' (1987) muscular advocacy of survey--there is probably widespread understanding and agreement about the necessarily complementary roles of survey and excavation, ideally as part of a multi-stage research design. In principle, it is hard to argue against the notion that regional surveys should include excavation as an integral and essential part of their strategy. There is no question that even a few careful excavations at the sorts of small rural sites which form the most prominent feature of the surface record, in the Aegean as almost everywhere else in the

Mediterranean, would be enormously helpful; compared to what we know of villas and rural establishments in, say, Roman Italy or Britain, the mere handful of excavated farm sites in Greece constitutes a pathetic sample for wider inference. But in Greece--unlike several other Mediterranean countries, such as Italy--digging is more often than not expressly *excluded* by the conditions of the survey permit. Besides, I cannot resist noting that, during the time that survey has gone through the throes of achieving a measure of critical self-consciousness as regards methodological and interpretive issues, excavation has for the most part proceeded with "business as usual." At any rate, excavated sites also pose problems of their own in terms of site formation and functional interpretation, and the ambiguous evidence they provide often falls far short of the answers that ancient historians sometimes require of them (e.g., Snodgrass 1987:36-66). Perhaps we would do well to remind ourselves that *all* sites begin life as *surface* sites, and their burial in one sense only adds to problems of interpretation, rather than providing some easy-to-read record lying tantalizingly just beneath the surface. These issues, of course, have been at the center of the long-running debate in the New Archaeology about the so-called "Pompeii premise."

Another set of interpretive problems has arisen from the very fact that the new-style surveys have been spectacularly successful in recording and drawing attention to the importance of "off-site" artifact distributions (see Alcock et al. 1994 for references). Most survey projects now pay attention (albeit sometimes grudgingly) to the substantial proportion of the surviving archaeological record on the surface which does not occur at sites, but responses to that realization have been so divergent that there is the danger of a proliferation of survey datasets which are difficult or impossible to compare directly. In some instances, artifact concentrations have been labeled with some more neutral term such as "places of special interest;" in others, virtually every spot with artifacts or other cultural features has been numbered separately as a "site," so that ostensibly enormous site-densities are the result; yet other projects have abandoned all attempt to work with entities above the level of the artifact. These are all attempts to grapple with the observed facts that artifacts occur widely across the landscape, with varying degrees of density and clustering. Yet surprisingly little progress has been made towards a consensus about the taphonomic processes that produce such distributions, or towards an understanding of why in some regions artifacts are to be found everywhere, while in others they are relatively rare outside "sites": studies by Bintliff and Snodgrass (1988c) or Alcock et al. (1994) are about as far as we have got thus far in the Aegean.

Conclusion

There are many other such problem areas which one might discuss if space allowed. To some, these obstacles (and the sometimes abstruse discussion of them that has arisen in the literature) are merely proof that survey is hampered by crippling limitations, and that earlier claims of its potential were willfully exaggerated. To the present author, the very fact that such difficulties are being tackled squarely is evidence that survey has moved forward into a new and encouraging phase of critical self-awareness. The use of distributional data from the surface is bound to have limitations; but it is more useful to work at minimizing them, than merely lamenting them. In any case, survey stands as the chief means of acquiring data about the past at the regional scale. And since so many of the theoretical perspectives currently proving useful in the Aegean (e.g., structural history; the *annaliste* school; core-periphery, peer-polity, and world systems models; cultural ecology, etc.) presuppose the regional view, the innovations introduced by the "new wave" of surveys can be regarded as having had nothing but an invigorating influence on studies of change and adaptation in Greece, past and present.

References Cited

Alcock, S.E.
   1991 Urban Survey and the Polis of Phlius. *Hesperia* 60:421-463.
   1993 *Graecia Capta: The Landscapes of Roman Greece.* Cambridge University Press, Cambridge.
Alcock, S.E., J.F. Cherry, and J.L. Davis
   1994 Intensive Survey, Agricultural Practice, and the Classical Landscape of Greece. In *Classical Greece: Ancient Histories and Modern Archaeologies,* edited by I. Morris, pp. 135-168. Cambridge University Press, Cambridge.
Alcock, S.E., and R. Osborne (editors)
   1994 *Placing the Gods.* Clarendon Press, Oxford.
Atkinson, T.D., R.C. Bosanquet, C.C. Edgar, A.J. Evans, D.G. Hogarth, D. Mackenzie, C. Smith, and F.B. Welch
   1904 *Excavations at Phylakopi in Melos.* Society for the Promotion

of Hellenic Studies, Supplementary Paper No.4. Macmillan, London.

Barker, G.W.
   1989 The Archaeology of the Italian Shepherd. *Proceedings of the Cambridge Philological Society* 215:1-19.
   1991 Approaches to Field Survey. In *Roman Landscapes: Archaeological Survey in the Mediterranean Region*, edited by G.W. Barker and J. Lloyd, pp. 1-9. Archaeological Monographs of the British School at Rome 2. British School at Rome, London.

Barker, G., and A. Grant (editors)
   1991 Ancient and Modern Pastoralism in Central Italy: An Interdisciplinary Study in the Cicolano Mountains. *Papers of the British School at Rome* 59:15-88.

Barker, G., and J. Lloyd (editors)
   1991 *Roman Landscapes: Archaeological Survey in the Mediterranean Region*. Archaeological Monographs of the British School at Rome 2. British School at Rome, London.

Bintliff, J.
   1985 Greece: The Boeotia Survey. In *Archaeological Field Survey in Britain and Abroad*, edited by S. Macready and F. Thompson, pp. 196-216. Society of Antiquaries, London.
   1991 The Roman Countryside in Central Greece: Observations and Theories from the Boeotia Survey. In *Roman Landscapes: Archaeological Survey in the Mediterranean Region*, edited by G. Barker and J. Lloyd, pp. 122-132. Archaeological Monographs of the British School at Rome 2. British School at Rome, London.
   1992 The History of the Greek Countryside: As the Wave Breaks, Prospects for Future Research. Paper delivered to the conference "Rural Structures and Ancient Societies," held at the Ionian University, Corfu, Greece, 14-16 May 1992.

Bintliff, J., and A.M. Snodgrass
   1985 The Cambridge/Bradford Boeotian Expedition: The First Four Years. *Journal of Field Archaeology* 12:123-61.
   1988a The End of the Roman Countryside: A View from the East. In *First Millennium Papers: Western Europe in the First Millennium A.D.*, edited by R. Jones et al., pp. 175-217. BAR International Series 401. British Archaeological Reports, Oxford.
   1988b Mediterranean Survey and the City. *Antiquity* 62:57-71.
   1988c Off-Site Pottery Distributions: A Regional and Interregional Perspective. *Current Anthropology* 29:506-513.

Bommeljé, S., and P.K. Doorn (editors)

1987 *Aetolia and the Aetolians*. Studia Aetolica 1. Utrecht.

Braudel, F.
  1972 *The Mediterranean and the Mediterranean World in the Age of Philip II*. Collins, London.

Buck, C.E., W.G. Cavanagh, and C.D. Litton
  1988a The Spatial Analysis of Site Phosphate Data. In *Computer Applications in Archaeology*, edited by S. P. Q. Rahtz, pp. 151-160. BAR International Series 446(i). British Archaeological Reports, Oxford.
  1988b The Interpretation of Noisy Data from Archaeological Field Survey: Phosphate Analysis. *Environment, Geochemistry and Health* 10:92-95.
  1992 Tools for the Interpretation of Soil Phosphate Data from Archaeological Surveys. In *Geoprospection in the Archaeological Landscape*, edited by P. Spoery, pp. 75-87. Oxbow Monograph 18. Oxbow Books, Oxford.

Cavanagh, W.G., S. Hirst, and C.D. Litton
  1988 Soil Phosphate, Site Boundaries and Change Point Analysis. *Journal of Field Archaeology* 15:67-83.

Cavanagh, W.G., and C.B. Mee
  1993 Laconia: Rural Sites Project. *The British School at Athens, Annual Report of the Managing Committee for the Session 1992-1993*:30. British School at Athens, London.

Chang, C.
  1984 The Ethnoarchaeology of Herding Sites in Greece. *MASCA Journal* 3(2):44-48.
  1992 Archaeological Landscapes: The Ethnoarchaeology of Pastoral Landuse in the Grevena Region of Greece. In *Place, Time, and Archaeological Landscapes*, edited by J. Rossignol and L. A. Wandsnider, pp. 65-90. Plenum Press, New York.

Chang, C., and H. Koster
  1986 Beyond Bones: Toward an Archaeology of Pastoralism. In *Advances in Archaeological Method and Theory*, vol. 9, edited by M. B. Schiffer, pp. 97-148. Academic Press, New York.

Chang, C., and P.A. Tourtellotte
  1993 Ethnoarchaeological Survey of Pastoral Transhumance Sites in the Grevena Region, Greece. *Journal of Field Archaeology* 20:249-264.

Cherry, J.F.
  1982 Preliminary Definition of Site Distribution on Melos. In *An Island Polity: The Archaeology of Exploitation in Melos*, edited by

C. Renfrew and M. Wagstaff, pp. 10-23. Cambridge University Press, Cambridge.

1983   Frogs Round the Pond: Perspectives on Current Archaeological Survey Projects in the Mediterranean Region. In *Archaeological Survey in the Mediterranean Region*, edited by D. Keller and D. Rupp, pp. 375-415. BAR International Series 155. British Archaeological Reports, Oxford.

1986   The "New Wave" of Greek Surveys: Lessons and Future Directions. Paper presented to the British School at Athens Centennial Conference "Future Directions in Greek Archaeology", Cambridge, U.K., 28-30 August 1986.

1988   Pastoralism and the Role of Animals in the Pre- and Protohistoric Economies of the Aegean. In *Pastoral Economies in Classical Antiquity*, edited by C.R. Whittaker, pp. 6-34. Cambridge Philological Society Supplementary Volume 14. The Cambridge Philological Society, Cambridge.

Cherry, J.F., J.L. Davis, A. Demitrack, E. Mantzourani, T.F. Strasser, and L.E. Talalay

1988   Archaeological Survey in an Artefact-rich Landscape: A Middle Neolithic Example from Nemea, Greece. *American Journal of Archaeology* 92:159-76.

Cherry, J.F., J.L. Davis, and E. Mantzourani

1991   *Landscape Archaeology as Long-Term History: Northern Keos in the Cycladic Islands from Earliest Settlement to Modern Times.* Monumenta Archaeologica 16. Los Angeles, UCLA Institute of Archaeology, Los Angeles.

Constantine, D.

1984   *Early Greek Travellers and the Hellenic Ideal.* Cambridge University Press, Cambridge.

Davies, B.E., J.L. Bintliff, C.F. Gaffney, and A.T. Waters

1988   Trace Metal Residues in Soil as Markers of Ancient Site Occupance in Greece. In *Trace Substances in Environmental Health, XXII: A Symposium*, edited by D.D. Hemphill, pp. 391-98. University of Missouri, Columbia, MO.

Davis, J.L.

1991   Contributions to a Mediterranean Rural Archaeology: Historical Case Studies from the Ottoman Cyclades. *Journal of Mediterranean Archaeology* 4:131-216.

Davis, J.L., S.E. Alcock, J. Bennet, Y. Lolos, C.W. Shelmerdine, and E. Zangger

1993   The Pylos Regional Archaeology Project: Preliminary Report on the 1993 Season. Paper delivered to the 95th Annual Meeting of the Archaeological Institute of America, Washington D.C., 27-30 December 1993.

Darvill, T.
1986 *Upland Archaeology: What Future for the Past?* Council for British Archaeology, London.

Dyson, S.
1982 Archaeological Survey in the Mediterranean Basin: A Review of Recent Research. *American Antiquity* 47:87-98.

Elsner, J.
1994 From the Pyramids to Pausanias and Piglet: Monuments, Travel and Writing. In *Art and Text in Ancient Greek Culture*, edited by S. Goldhill and R. Osborne, pp. 224-254. Cambridge University Press, Cambridge.

Finley, M.I.
1985 *Ancient History: Evidence and Models.* Chatto and Windus, London.

Fish, S.K., and S.A. Kowalewski (editors)
1990 *The Archaeology of Regions: A Case for Full-Coverage Survey.* Smithsonian Institution Press, Washington, D.C. and London.

Foxhall, L.
1990 The Dependent Tenant: Land Leasing and Labour in Italy and Greece. *Journal of Roman Studies* 80:97-114.

French, E.B.
1990 Archaeology in Greece, 1989-90. *Archaeological Reports for 1989-1990* 36:3-82.
1993 Archaeology in Greece, 1992-93. *Archaeological Reports for 1992-1993* 39:3-81.

Gaffney, C.F., and V.L. Gaffney
1986 From Boeotia to Berkshire: An Integrated Approach to Geophysics and Rural Field Survey. *Prospezione Archeologiche* 10:65-71.

Jacobsen, T.W.
1984 Seasonal Pastoralism in the Neolithic of Southern Greece: A Consideration of the Ecology of Neolithic Urfirnis Pottery. In *Pots and Potters: Current Approaches in Ceramic Archaeology*, edited by P.M. Rice, pp. 27-43. U.C.L.A. Institute of Archaeology, Los Angeles.

Jameson, M. H.
1976 The Southern Argolid: The Setting for Historical and Cultural

Studies. In *Regional Variation in Modern Greece and Cyprus: Toward a Perspective on the Ethnography of Greece*, edited by M. Dimen and E. Friedl, pp. 74-91. The New York Academy of Sciences, New York.

Joyce, C.
1992 Archaeology Takes to the Skies. *New Scientist* (25 January 1992):42-46.

Koster, H.A., and J.B. Koster
1976 Competition or Symbiosis? Pastoral Adaptive Strategies in the Southern Argolid, Greece. In *Regional Variation in Modern Greece and Cyprus: Toward a Perspective on the Ethnography of Greece*, edited by M. Dimen and E. Friedl, pp. 275-285. The New York Academy of Sciences, New York.

Kvamme, K.L.
1989 Geographic Information Systems in Regional Research and Data Management. In *Archaeological Method and Theory*, vol. 1, edited by M.B. Schiffer, pp. 139-203. University of Arizona Press, Tucson.

Lock, G., and T. Harris
1992 Visualizing Spatial Data: The Importance of Geographic Information Systems. In *Archaeology and the Information Age: A Global Perspective*, edited by P. Reilly and S. Rahtz, pp. 81-96. Routledge, London.

Keller, D., and D. Rupp (editors)
1983 *Archaeological Survey in the Mediterranean Region*. BAR International Series 155. British Archaeological Reports, Oxford.

McDonald, W.A., and G.R. Rapp, Jr. (editors)
1972 *The Minnesota Messenia Expedition: Reconstructing a Bronze Age Regional Environment*. University of Minnesota Press, Minneapolis.

Mackenzie, D.
1897 Ancient Sites in Melos. *Annual of the British School at Athens* 3:71-88.

Mattingly, D.J.
1994 The Landscape of Imperialism. *Antiquity* 68:162-165.

Mee, C., D. Gill, H. Forbes, and L. Foxhall
1991 Rural Settlement Change in the Methana Peninsula, Greece. In *Roman Landscapes: Archaeological Survey in the Mediterranean Region*, edited by G. Barker and J. Lloyd, pp. 223-232. Archaeological Monographs of the British School at Rome 2. British School at Rome, London.

Mendoni, L., and P. Doukellis (editors)
   1994 Αγροτικές Δομές καί Αρχαίες Κοινωνίες.
   Proceedings of the conference "Rural Structures and Ancient
   Societies," held at the Ionian University, Corfu, 14-16 May 1992.
Morris, I. (editor)
   1994 *Classical Greece: Ancient Histories and Modern
   Archaeologies*. Cambridge University Press, Cambridge.
Murray, P., and C. Chang
   1981 An Ethnoarchaeological Study of a Contemporary Herders'
   Site. *Journal of Field Archaeology* 8:372-381.
Murray, P., and P.N. Kardulias
   1986 A Modern Site Survey in the Southern Argolid, Greece.
   Journal of Field Archaeology 13:21-41.
Nixon, L., J. Moody, S. Price, and O. Rackham
   1989 Archaeological Survey in Sphakia, Crete. *Echos du Monde
   Classique/Classical Views* 33(n.s.8):210-215.
Osborne, R.
   1985 Buildings and Residence on the Land in Classical and
   Hellenistic Greece: The Contribution of Epigraphy. *Annual of the
   British School at Athens* 80:119-28.
   1987 *Classical Landscape with Figures: The Ancient Greek City and
   its Countryside*. George Philip, London.
   1989 What Next? After the "New Wave" Has Broken. Paper
   presented to the meeting of the Greek Survey Group, University
   of Bradford, June 24, 1989.
Popham, M.
   1990 Reflections on An Archaeology of Greece: Surveys and
   Excavations. *Oxford Journal of Archaeology* 9(1):29-35.
Runnels, C.N., and T.H. van Andel
   1987 *Beyond the Acropolis: The Archaeology of the Greek
   Countryside*. Stanford University Press, Stanford.
Snodgrass, A.M.
   1982 La prospection archéologique en Grèce et dans le monde
   mediterranéen. *Annales: Economies, Sociétés, Civilisations*
   37(n.s.5-6):800-812.
   1987 *An Archaeology of Greece: The Present State and Future
   Scope of a Discipline*. University of California Press, Berkeley.
   1990 Survey Archaeology and the Rural Landscape of the Greek
   City. In *The Greek City from Homer to Alexander*, edited by O.
   Murray and S. Price, pp. 113-136. Clarendon Press, Oxford.
Snodgrass, A.M., and J.L. Bintliff

1991 Surveying Ancient Cities. *Scientific American* 264(3):88-93.
Snodgrass, A.M., and J.F. Cherry
   1988 On *Not* Digging Up the Past. *The Cambridge Review*
         109(no.2300):9-13.
Stein, C.A., and B.C. Cullen
   1994 Satellite Imagery and Archaeology: A Case Study from
         Nikopolis [Abstract]. *American Journal of Archaeology* 98:316.
Tsigakou, F.-M.
   1981 *The Rediscovery of Greece.* Thames and Hudson, London.
Watrous, L.V.
   1982 *Lasithi: A History of Settlement on a Highland Plain in Crete.*
         Hesperia Supplement 18. Princeton University Press, Princeton.
Wells, B. (editor)
   1993 *Agriculture in Classical Greece.* Paul Åströms Förlag,
         Stockholm.
Wells, B., C. Runnels, and E. Zangger
   1990 The Berbati-Limnes Archaeological Survey, The 1988 Season.
         Opuscula Atheniensia 18:207-38.
Wiseman, J., and A. Dousougli-Zachos
   1994 The Nikopolis Project 1991-1993: Overview of the
         Multidisciplinary Study of Southern Epirus [Abstract]. *American
         Journal of Archaeology* 98:315.
Wright, J. C., J.F. Cherry, J.L. Davis, E. Mantzourani, S.B. Sutton,
and R.F. Sutton
   1990 The Nemea Valley Archaeological Project: A Preliminary
         Report. *Hesperia* 59:579-659.
Zangger, E.
   1994 Landscape Changes around Tiryns during the Bronze Age.
         American Journal of Archaeology 98:189-212.

Chapter 6

Modeling Mortuary Behavior on a Regional Scale: A Case Study from Mainland Greece in the Early Bronze Age

Daniel J. Pullen

Introduction: Approaches to Social Organization Through Mortuary Behavior

The study of mortuary behavior has always been of central interest to archaeology, even in its early years under such pioneers as Schliemann whose excavations brought to light the royal Shaft Grave tombs of Mycenae in the 1870s. The study of mortuary behavior enjoyed a major role in the great changes through which archaeology went in the 1960s and 1970s (cf. Binford 1971; Brown 1971; Saxe 1970). In recent anthropology, too, there has been an importance placed upon mortuary behavior, as death is one of the few common human experiences (e.g., Bartel 1982; Bloch 1971).

Certainly in the archaeology of the Aegean area, both prehistoric and historic, tombs, burials, and cemeteries have long been of major interest. Indeed, some periods and cultures, such as the Sub-Mycenaean and Protogeometric periods in Athens or the third millennium B.C. cultures of the Cyclades, are known almost exclusively from their tombs. Despite this intense focus on burials, the study of mortuary behavior in Aegean archaeology remains relatively unsophisticated. While certain dimensions (dimensions in the sense of Goldstein 1981;

see below) of burials, such as tomb form and grave goods, are well studied, other dimensions, such as those dealing with the human remains and the spatial relationships among the human bodies, other tomb contents, and material outside the tombs proper, are often ignored, even in relatively recent excavations.

For the Early Bronze Age (EBA) of mainland Greece (known as the Early Helladic period or EH), roughly the third millennium B.C., the study of mortuary behavior is hampered by a number of problems, not the least of which is poor, incomplete, or summary publication of the data. At most any EH site, no more than a handful of graves are reported; rare are the sites such as Manika, Lithares, or Agios Kosmas with cemeteries. The study of mortuary behavior, more than most areas of archaeological interest, often focuses upon the individual, but the majority of EH tombs seem to have been used for serial or multiple burials which immediately raises methodological problems such as association of individual human remains with grave goods or other features of the tomb.

Regional analysis can play a role in the study of mortuary behavior, and, likewise, the study of mortuary behavior can help in the interpretation of data from a regional perspective. This interplay between the study of mortuary behavior and the study of archaeological data on a regional level has been especially helpful in understanding some of the dynamics of EH society.

My ultimate goal is to utilize pattern in mortuary behavior as one way of understanding the social organization of EH society as a whole. A regional approach, considering the EH social-cultural region as a single entity, will serve several purposes, not the least of which is to consider the full range of mortuary behavior in the society. This would include sites which are principally not "mortuary" in nature--here I consider the case of the intramural burial in a society which primarily uses the cemetery for placement of the dead. In addition, EH society was one where differentiation among sites in terms of size, location, and function became important and it is assumed the organization of society also became differentiated. The study of social organization of EH society as a whole would necessarily, then, encompass a region, not just a single site. A very practical consideration is that no single EH site has been fully excavated, and the consideration of more than one or two incompletely excavated sites will increase the data with which to work and lessen the chance of exceptional data skewing the picture. For the Aegean this is crucial as so many of our data on mortuary behavior are poor. With a judicious assessment, "old" data and incomplete data can be used in modelling mortuary behavior on a regional scale. Although social organization is often approached by studying differentiation of the individual, it should also include differentiation among groups of individuals (see below); by considering each tomb in EH Greece as a group of individuals, the regional approach to mortuary behavior also helps alleviate problems in interpretation of social status of individuals since burials in EH Greece are generally not individual but serial multiple in nature.

Ideally, a diachronic study of mortuary behavior in the Aegean EBA would be preferred. Much of the mortuary data cannot be precisely dated, however, and in any case the division of EH ceramics into stratigraphically based, and hence chronological, sequences has only just begun (cf. Wiencke 1989; Pullen 1988). Thus, I approach the problem from a chronologically static point of view, but the span of years (and possible changes through time) covered in the following discussion should be kept in mind. My focus is the EH II period, approximately 2700/2600 to 2300 B.C. in uncalibrated radiocarbon years. This cultural period, along with its contemporary cultures in the Cyclades, at Troy, and on Crete, is often regarded as a period of great changes in Aegean society. Many changes, of course, have their origins in the preceding Neolithic and EH I periods, but in the EH II period the results of these changes are more readily apparent in the archaeological record (cf. Renfrew 1972; Wiencke 1989).

Death and the disposal of the remains involve individuals; indeed the study of mortuary behavior over the last few decades has been seen as one of the primary ways in archaeology of getting at individuals and their position in the society. Nearly all the theoretical and methodological literature deals with discrete, individual acts of disposal of individuals which can be isolated archaeologically (e.g., Goldstein 1981). Such is generally not the case with the EBA Aegean, not only for the mainland EH culture, but also for the contemporary Early Cycladic and Early Minoan cultures where tombs are reused numerous times. As such, the individual burial usually cannot be the "unit" of analysis, unless it is part of an exception. Rather, the tomb or the site becomes the unit of analysis, and these units when compared to one another must take into consideration the region.

Social organization is concerned with differentiation among individuals or groups of individuals. Using Goodenough's (1965) model of the social persona composed of many different social identities, each identity coming into use in a different social situation, we can expand social organization to include not just "political" organization (that realm of activities related to the concept of "power"; cf. Haas 1982), but also ranking, economic, and indeed any relationship between two individuals or groups of individuals. Thus, emerging social complexity can be studied in many different realms or dimensions of human behavior, each with its own structure, whether hierarchical or not. This multidimensional approach avoids the single parameter "layer-cake" approach to social organization often taken by cultural evolutionists, systems theorists, Marxists, and other archaeologists (e.g., Johnson 1978; see McGuire [1983] for elucidation of the multidimensional approach, based ultimately upon Weber [1947]).

One such realm of behavior is mortuary activity. Within the study of mortuary behavior, the multidimensionality of differentiation observable in the archaeological record has long been recognized (e.g., Binford 1971). Goldstein's more systematic and practical set of dimensions of differentiation directly observable in the archaeological record are used here (1981:59):

(1) Treatment of the body itself
   a. degree of articulation of the skeleton
   b. disposition of the burial
   c. number of individuals per burial
   d. mutilations and anatomical modifications
(2) Preparation of the disposal facility
   a. form of the facility
   b. orientation of the facility and the body within the facility
   c. location of the facility in relation to the community
   d. location of the facility within the disposal area itself
   e. form of the disposal area
(3) Burial context within grave
   a. arrangement within grave of specific bones with relation to grave furniture and grave facility
   b. form of furniture
   c. quantity of goods (to which I would add *kinds* of goods, such as metals versus ceramics)
(4) Population profile and biological dimensions
   a. age
   b. sex
   c. disease status and/or circumstances of death
   d. nutritional evidence and environmental stress
   e. genetic relationships

Such criteria are fairly straightforward guidelines for observation of the archaeological record. The problem arises from the interpretation of these dimensions: how to transform the observed phenomena into meaningful statements reflecting the presence of social ranking and other organizing principles.

For the Aegean Bronze Age, grave associations are often the only information available apart from the form and location of the grave facility. Grave associations are only one dimension of the mortuary behavior system. Some have objected to using grave associations for determining status distinctions, claiming they are relatively unimportant (e.g., Tainter 1978:121, but citing for evidence his own unpublished paper). Renfrew (1972), however, has shown that there exists variation in the relative wealth of grave associations in the Aegean in the EBA and at other times. I argue that for the mortuary systems of the Aegean Bronze Age, the kinds and quantities of grave goods *do* reflect ranking; certainly the very existence of the Shaft Graves at Mycenae would preclude claims to the contrary.

I have found this method of approaching mortuary behavior on a regional scale relatively successful in that it has allowed me to construct a model of EH mortuary behavior which at least forms a basis upon which to compare other periods and regions of the Aegean. In this regional approach I consider all types of data, including "negative" data, of varying quality and reliability, from excavations, intensive surface surveys, and topographical reconnaissance surveys. Information from some 40 sites and findspots in central and southern Greece has been compiled in order to construct this model (Figure 6.1). Cemetery excavations are few; more common are isolated tombs at a site, sometimes intramural. Several sites known from surface survey are suggested to be mortuary sites based on their proximity to settlements and finds. Many sites were excavated prior to the 1970s, when the primary concern was the retrieval of grave goods, and the importance of other aspects of the burial was not generally recognized. Additionally several sites were "excavated" as part of salvage operations, sometimes after the destruction of the majority of the tomb and its contents.

A Regional Approach To Aegean Early Bronze Age Mortuary Behavior

This is not the place to review all the data (cf. Pullen 1985: Chapter 4), but a few examples will suffice to illustrate the variety of data avail-

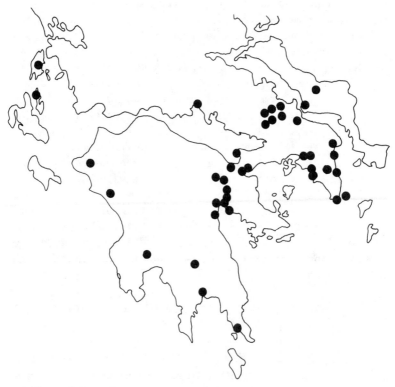

Figure 6.1. Sites in Central and Southern Greece with evidence for
Early Bronze Age burials.

able in the Aegean.

Manika, on the island of Euboea at the Strait of Chalchis, is probably the best known EH cemetery, with over 170 graves, some 50 excavated in 1904 (Papabasileios 1910) and the remainder since 1982 (Sampson 1985, 1988). As in most EH graves, there are multiple burials, and the poor preservation at this coastal site makes identification of skeletal material difficult, even for such a basic criterion as the number of skeletons in each grave. Preliminary analysis indicates that of the 111 recently excavated tombs, 17 (plus three uncertain) had one skeleton, seven had two skeletons, 34 had more than two skeletons (but usually mixed so exact number was uncertain), and 39 had "very little" bone (Sampson 1988:Table 7). These figures are slightly misleading, for five of the tombs with one or two skeletons also had bones pushed to the side, and other tombs have overlapping categories. Still, though, the primacy of multiple burials in one tomb is clear. An osteological analysis of the skeletal remains of 47 individuals from 22 graves excavated in 1982 (Fountoulakes 1985) revealed three infants, 11 children, five youths, and 26 adults; of the 31 adults and youths, 24 could be sexed as 13 female and 11 male. Even more interesting is the evidence for "operations" on the skeletons: 226 examples of cutmarks, holes, sections, and bone detachments were recorded (Fountoulakes 1985). These "operations" occur on all ages and sexes, in both "rich" and "poor" graves. Fountoulakes concludes that all the operations were performed post mortem on bones at points of insertion of muscles and tendons, usually in a bilaterally symmetrical pattern on the body. This suggests systematic dismemberment or disarticulation of the bodies. This evidence agrees in part with the suggestions of Mylonas for Agios Kosmas (see below).

The Manika tombs were usually rockcut chambers reached by a vertical to sloping shaft from the surface, sometimes with stairs; a stone slab often blocked a constricted doorway. The chambers averaged 2 m x 2 m in size, though there was a great range; likewise, there was a great variety in the shape of the chamber, from rounded to square to, perhaps more commonly, trapezoid. The tombs were often oriented on a north-south axis with the access shaft to the south, though again there is variety even within the same cluster (e.g., Sampson 1988:Figure 35); perhaps there is some chronological significance to the different orientations.

The quantity of grave goods was not great in the Manika tombs, but there is great variety, with many tombs containing no objects at all; there is also a great variety in quality and kind of object, e.g., pottery, metal, imported marble figurines and vessels (Sampson 1988:48-57, 59-62, Tables 12-14). Sampson grouped the graves into rich (more than 7 objects), mediocre, and poor (one or no object besides obsidian), and determined that some 60% of the tombs could be considered "poor."

Zygouries is more typical of the kind of data with which Aegean prehistorians have to work (Blegen 1928). Excavations in 1921-1922 revealed an extensive cemetery of EH II to Roman date located ca. 500 m west of the EH village, but only four tombs could be assigned to the EH II period on the basis of tomb type and contents. All four were irregular hollows in the soft bedrock, usually reached via a rather large shaft opening directly into the chamber. Skeletal fragments representing up to 15 adults were found in disarray in the chambers, with few grave goods interspersed. Tomb VII (Blegen 1928:43-47) was disturbed by a second, later grave built only 0.10-0.20 m above it, giving the impression of bones and objects arranged around the edges and leaving the center free. The oval chamber, 2.60 m north-south by 1.85 m east-west, at an average depth of 1.25 m below the surface, contained the remains of 12 and possibly 14 individuals (nos. 1, 3-6, 8-11, 13, 14, 16 on plan in Blegen 1928:Figure 38), probably all adults by the size of the bones (though no physical anthropologist examined the bones). Few grave goods were found.[1] Tomb XVI (Blegen 1928:47-48) was a small (1.33 m north-south by 1.05 m east-west) chamber, the floor of which, reached via a shaft, was 1.30 m below the surface. Blegen's notebook entries, however, seem to indicate the presence of a cist grave immediately to the north, which may have caused some disturbance of the tomb in question (Zygouries notebook CWB 1922 [on file in Korinth Museum], p.104, 112). To the north of the cist, a large part of an "EH vase" was uncovered, but no bones; therefore Blegen did not consider this spot a grave (Zygouries notebook CWB 1922, p.132). Only three skeletons (all adults?) were found, mostly in the western half (nos. 1-3 on plan, Blegen 1928:Figure 41), again in a disorderly state. A bronze pin (no. 4 on plan) and "three large potsherds" (nos. 5-7 on the sketch plan, perhaps sauceboats?) were the only other contents. Tomb XX (Blegen 1928:48-53) measured 1.96 m east-west by 1.78 m north-south; it was shallow, the floor varying in depth below surface from 0.70 to 1.00 m. Remains of at least 15 adults(?) were found mixed, mostly in the southern half (nos. 1-15 on plan, Blegen 1928:Figure 43), protected perhaps by the overhanging rock which formed part of the roof. The grave offerings are very similar to those of Tomb VII.[2] Tomb XXIII (Blegen 1928:53-54) was disturbed by a later Roman tile grave. The large chamber 2.50 m north-south by 2.40

m east-west, with a roof height of ca. 0.70 m, was empty except for one fragment of a human femur and a few sherds of EH type. On the basis of type and the presence of only EH sherds in the fill of the chamber, Blegen assigned this tomb to the EB period. Blegen prefers to call these tombs ossuaries (1928:54), but he does not imply that placement of the dead in these chambers was anything but primary. Their use must be for serial multiple burials to account for the extremely disordered nature of the skeletal remains. The absence of children (though they may have been unrecognized by the excavator or not preserved) implies a different place and/or method for their disposal. Blegen dismisses the possibility that the "numerous rectilinear shafts found everywhere about the hill" were originally EBA tombs, like Cycladic tombs or those at Korinth, which were later cleared out and reused by the Romans (1928:54). Sherd material from the fill of Graves VII, XVI, and XX was analyzed in 1981-82 by the present author (Pullen 1985:Table 4.1). As there is no EH settlement on the Ambelakia hill where the graves are located, it is reasonable to assume that the sherd material found in the fill of the graves is *in situ*, and perhaps represents the old offerings which were displaced when another body was interred. Those vessels mentioned above (given by Blegen as the contents) might then be assigned to the latest burial(s). Graves VII and XVI were disturbed by later graves, and thus the completeness of their contents (skeletal remains and grave goods) are suspect. It may be that Grave XX is the most representative, with an average of three vessels per skeleton. This average coincides with the mean number of vessels for the graves considered as a whole.

Isolated tombs, such as one at Kalamaki, have been discovered and salvaged. During construction of the National Road from Athens to Korinth to the west of Kalamaki, just east of the Isthmus of Korinth, one or more EBA tombs were destroyed (Broneer 1958:28). No settlement is known in the immediate vicinity. Twenty-one vessels were recovered, dating to EH II. Many of the vessels seem to have parallels from outside the Argolid and Korinthia (see Pullen 1985:154 note 13 for a summary of the vessels, their shapes, and their decoration). The numerous pedestalled bowls, the incurved flat rims, the micaceous fabric, and polished and burnished slips place this group of vessels outside the Korinthian EH II ceramic assemblage and more in line with Attic and Saronic Gulf assemblages.

Asine provides a good example of the value of "negative" data in understanding EH mortuary behavior (cf. Pullen 1990). Two (and a possible third) tombs dated to the EBA were found at Asine; both are children's graves on the "Pre-Mycenaean Terrace" (Frödin and Persson 1938:41-42, 338-340). The first grave was a square cavity in the rock, ca. 0.90 m square, 0.50 m deep, the northern edge of which was lined with stones. A "child's" skeleton consisting of skull, tibiae and femora was found, oriented east-west (Frödin and Persson 1938:338; on p.42, described with head to the northwest) and accompanied by three bowls[3] and four obsidian blades (Frödin and Persson 1938:Figure 230 no.5). The second grave was a "shallow concavity in the rock, about 0.90 m by 0.40 m" containing the "scanty remains of a child's skeleton" (Frödin and Persson 1938:339, but cf. contra, p. 42 "no skeletal remnants whatsoever could be identified") and three bowls[4]. The tombs are dated by Persson to his EH III which Caskey (1960) would rename EH II; they are undoubtedly quite late in EH II, probably equivalent to Lerna House of Tiles Phase (i.e., Lerna IIID), due to the shape and surface treatment of the shallow bowls (Wiencke 1989). They are probably contemporary with the Bothros from the same terrace. In Room II of House R on Terrace III, a cavity in the rock below the eastern wall was discovered, measuring 0.70 m by 0.30 m. If this was a tomb, it must have been destroyed when House R was built (see Pullen 1987 for discussion of problems in dating House R). All three tombs, then, are intramural. The lack of other burials, especially any adults, suggests the presence of a cemetery elsewhere at Asine.

Evidence from Isthmia suggests a burial, though no tomb was found: an eroded deposit excavated in the gully to the northwest of the Temple of Poseidon at the Isthmian Sanctuary included "two pieces of bone in extremely decayed condition" (Smith 1955). This, coupled with the presence of so many intact or complete vessels, may indicate a grave group (see Pullen 1985:156 note 16 for a summary of this pottery). Most of this group falls early in EH II, some into EH I; if this is a grave group, it is interesting to compare it with the very different assemblage from the nearby Kalamaki tomb. Part of the difference is, of course, chronological, with the Isthmia tomb being earlier, but the Isthmia assemblage falls fully within the Argolid-Korinthian tradition, unlike the Kalamaki group.

At Agios Kosmas in Attica (Mylonas 1959), on the coast immediately north of the narrow neck connecting the promontory on which the settlement is situated, 32 graves were excavated in what Mylonas called the North Cemetery; graves were also found (few of which were excavated) on the coast immediately to the south of the isthmus, forming the South Cemetery (Mylonas 1959:Chapter 3). Many more graves than were excavated were found in both cemeteries, but most had been subjected to erosion by the sea or to tomb robbers. Both cist and built tombs were found in the North Cemetery, with the cist graves *usually* located immediately along the shore and the built tombs slightly inland (plan, Mylonas 1959:Drawing 48), but Mylonas does not see any chronological or functional distinction in the placement of these two types. No overall orientation was observed in tomb or burial placement, though the entrances generally faced towards the settlement. The tombs varied in shape from quadrilateral tending towards trapezoidal to elliptical or semicircular, usually wider at one end (not consistently the door end). The walls, usually vertical or inclined, were topped by large capstones, counterbalanced on the exterior by short walls of stones (cf. Mylonas 1959:Drawings 18 and 19 for sections), though as evidenced by the numerous collapsed roofs the counterbalancing was insufficient to support the superstructure (cf. Mylonas 1959:Figure 75). One tomb (Grave 11) had a schist-paved floor; the others had floors of sand and/or pebbles. Small doorways (0.35 m to 0.68 m wide by 0.30 m to 0.46 m high) usually nearer the corners than the middle of a side, echoing contemporary house construction, were often preceded by a short "prothyron" or passage to the surface. That the tombs were often used for some time is evidenced by the reconstruction of several tombs to include a doorway, a feature perhaps not to be found in earlier phases of the tomb. The doorways, often with cut lintels and thresholds, were blocked by orthostates, and the prothyron filled with stones. Around many graves on the surface was an area marked off by lines of stones; it was in those areas that the majority of grave goods were found.

The skeletal material within the graves seemed to represent primary inhumation of up to 16 or more adults and children. In a few cases children were buried separately (Graves 9A, 11A, and 25). The older skeletons were pushed indiscriminately to the sides or arranged to create a level space when a new interment was to take place. No special care was taken for any part of the skeleton, not even the skull. Three instances of unusual treatment were discovered: outside Graves 3 and 14 were found the scattered remains of probably one individual each; the burial outside Grave 3 evidently had grave goods. To the north of Grave 30 is an area of scattered bones (Area A on Mylonas 1959:Drawing 49). To the west is an area (Area V) of 47 small vessels, all but two of which were one-handled cups (Mylonas' type C13; cf. Mylonas 1959:Figures 151-156) and two of which had remains of "red color" (cf. Mylonas 1959: Drawing 45 and Figure 110). South of Area V is an obsidian chipping floor (Area O) with cores and blades which were refitted to the cores (Mylonas 1959:Figure 167A for refitted cores). North of Area V were found eight very large vessels (Mylonas 1959:Figures 111-112): three bowls (Mylonas 1959:Figure 157), three large jars (Mylonas 1959:Figures 157-158), one large bowl (Mylonas 1959:Figure 158), and a tabbed bowl (Mylonas 1959:Figure 158). North of Area A was found an extended supine skeleton with some obsidian placed around the body. To the west of the body, Area B revealed much broken pottery, including many unusual types not found elsewhere on the site: a patterned ware sauceboat and pyxis (Mylonas 1959:Figure 160) and fragments of a red-slipped and incised jar (Mylonas 1959:Figure 161). Mylonas prefers to see the extended skeleton and surrounding area as evidence for a two-stage mortuary ritual, consisting of primary inhumation in an earth pit to allow partial decomposition, followed by secondary placement in the tombs (1959:118). Many of the skeletal fragments from the tombs are partially articulated, so that complete decomposition probably did not take place outside the tombs.

Due to the disturbed nature of much of this rather shallow site and because of the usual placement of grave goods outside the tomb (only seven had offerings inside the tomb), little can be said about individuals. Grave goods consisted primarily of pottery, usually the one-handled cup (shape C13, cf. Mylonas 1959:Drawing 57) but including most other Early Helladic/Early Cycladic shapes (cf. list, Mylonas 1959:68-71, Drawings 57-60); stone objects (bowls, figurines, palettes); obsidian; terracotta stands; sherds; shells; and only one piece of copper (tweezers, from Grave 3A). Several graves had few if any goods associated with them, although some, such as numbers 3, 7 and the Area of Extended Skeleton had over two dozen items. All the pottery and objects are contemporary with the settlement on the adjacent headland and date to the EH II period (Mylonas called the period EH III, but it should now be considered EH II in light of Caskey [1960]), though there is heavy Cycladic influence in the figurines and much of the pottery (frying pans, one-handled cups). A few vessel types do not occur in the settlement and some settlement vessel types do not occur in the cemetery (see list, Mylonas 1959:68-71). Based on the sequence of construction, the remodeling to include doorways, and the use of quern fragments in wall construction, Mylonas divides the graves into three chronological groups: Graves 1, 4, 7, 9, and 10 are placed as the oldest; Graves 3, 5, 6, 11, 16, and 21 as the middle group; and Graves 2, 8, 12, 13, 14, 15, 20, 22, 23, 24,

28, 31, 32, and Area of Extended Skeleton are the youngest. The actual burials probably continued to be placed in the oldest group after the youngest group of tombs had been built and put into use.

While we are not able to say anything about individual status as evidenced by the mortuary practices at Agios Kosmas, the presence of discretely bounded tombs used for multiple successive burial argues for family tombs. Whether the three anomalous burials discussed above represent stages in the mortuary ritual or differential treatment of individuals due to social differences is an open question. I prefer to see these anomalous burials as representing differential treatment, as there is little evidence from elsewhere (and the partially articulated skeletal material at Agios Kosmas would support this) to suggest more than one stage in the mortuary ritual.

In the plain of Marathon at the locality of Tsepi, an Early Bronze Age cemetery was discovered and partially excavated (Marinatos 1970a, 1970b, 1970c, 1970d, 1971, 1972). At least six parallel rows of cist tombs oriented northeast-southwest were found. Within each row tombs were separated from one another by rows of pebbles and a small passage. The cist tombs were small, usually less than 1 m in length, never more than 1 m deep, and built for the most part of upright slabs, only occasionally of fieldstone walls. On the southern side of each tomb was a small doorway, too small for actual use; the burial was effected by lowering the body into the grave from above when the roofing slabs had been removed. Above the area of the door at the surface was placed a pile of stones and one or two uprights as a grave marker, and the edge of the cist itself was marked by a low masonry wall. Up to 20 burials were placed in one tomb, in a strongly contracted position. Prior burials were pushed to the side, with some care usually taken in the replacement of the skull: e.g., Tomb 2, with at least 12 persons represented, had the skulls stacked along the side (Marinatos 1970c:Figure 3). Very few grave goods were found, and in all but one instance, within the tomb. No details of individual tomb contents have been published yet. Marinatos reports that in general when any grave goods were found they consisted of from one to three vases, all of Cycladic types (Pelos group, e.g., frying pan [Marinatos 1970c:Figure 4], incised shallow bowl [Marinatos 1970c:Figure 32]). Scraps of silver and copper are also mentioned as tomb contents. Again we see here discretely bounded tombs used for multiple successive burials, suggestive of family tombs. No settlement has been indicated nearby, but EBA habitation sites are known from the area.

A cemetery is surmised from surface finds of frying pans, Cycladic pottery and marble vessel fragments to the east of the headland where the fortified settlement of Asketario is located (Theochares 1955b:115). Two child burials came from the excavation of the settlement at Asketario: traces of a child's skeleton were found in a trial trench in the center of a mound; and by the west wall of Room 28 of House E (plan, Theochares 1955b:Figure 2), a child's skeleton was found on a paved floor, covered by a large fragment of a pithos, and unaccompanied by any other items.

At Chalandri, in the northeast suburbs of Athens, a shallow marble bowl was found, "typical of many Cycladic and E.H. graves" (Theochares 1955a:288). To the south of Chalandri, on the foothill of Hymettos called Tsakos, near Holargon, is an EBA settlement known from surface collections. The Chalandri find may indeed indicate a cemetery, placed at some distance from the settlement.

The evidence from these nine sites briefly summarized above illustrates the wide range in quality and completeness of mortuary data available from central and southern Greece. Only Manika and Agios Kosmas have data relating to all the dimensions outlined above. From other sites where excavations have yielded burials, data relating to the skeleton, even simple determinations of the minimum number of individuals in each tomb, are usually lacking. Some of the data are derived from surface explorations where the identification as "burial" or "cemetery" is sometimes questionable.

Despite these severe problems with the data, a systematic analysis of the archaeologically observable dimensions of mortuary behavior on the regional level does reveal a consistent pattern of mortuary practices in EBA Greece. The majority of the dead were buried in tombs located in cemeteries. Small infants, however, were sometimes buried intramurally, often in a vessel of some sort. Tomb types vary, but are generally of two types: earth or rock cut tombs entered by a passageway, or stone lined cists without an entrance. Examples in both categories can be quite regular in their form.

Cemeteries are discrete areas, separate from settlements. Cemetery and habitation areas may be contiguous, as at Manika, but usually a distance of several hundred meters separates the two areas, as at Zygouries or Agios Kosmas. A number of the sites included in this study apparently are cemetery sites without a known settlement in the immediate vicinity. This distance between settlement and cemetery may be part of the reason cemeteries are not well represented in the archaeological record of EBA Greece.

Cemeteries vary in the degree of formality of their layout. At Tsepi tombs are arranged in rows separated by "alleys." At Manika some clusters of tombs are formally laid out, others are relatively "random" in their placement with respect to one another. At Agios Kosmas the tombs are located with respect to the natural topography, and separated by lines of stones.

The dead are placed in a flexed position within the tomb chamber. Successive use of the same tomb for later burials is the norm. Previous burials were displaced to the sides, though sometimes reverence for the skulls is evident. At Manika shallow pits appear to have been used for the remains of earlier burials.

The desire for placement of the body in a flexed position was apparently strong, even when the tomb size would have allowed extended positions. Those skeletons for which details of articulation are available demonstrate flexed joints. The skeletal material from Manika shows signs of "operations," or severing of the ligaments and muscles so that the joints could be flexed. Mylonas suggested a two-stage burial ritual at Agios Kosmas on the basis of an extended adult skeleton in the cemetery. The first stage would be represented by the extended skeleton buried for purposes of partial desiccation, and the second stage by the flexed bodies within the tombs (Mylonas 1959:118). The Manika skeletons with cut marks would support Mylonas' theory. Many of the skeletal fragments from tombs are partially articulated, so that complete decomposition probably did not take place outside the tombs. The Agios Kosmas extended skeleton remains the only evidence for the two-stage interment.

The reuse of tombs for later burials presents a major obstacle to the study of individual burials and their relationships to grave goods. The broken nature of much ceramic material found in the tombs and the careless displacement of earlier burials and grave goods suggests that sanctions for removal of previous grave goods may not have been severe. It is likely that we do not have the total grave goods for each individual in a tomb.

There are disparities in the quantities of grave goods in tombs, especially when metal objects are counted separately. There are fewer metal objects than people buried in any one tomb, suggesting differences in both kinds and quantities of objects given to an individual. Renfrew (1972) demonstrated a similar phenomenon for Early Cycladic tombs. Ranking of individuals is suggested by this differential wealth of grave goods, although the multiple nature of the burials with disturbances of previous burials precludes quantification of this differential wealth.

Due to inadequate reporting, the demographics of the dead individuals are the least known dimensions. That only infants were buried intramurally indicates that a distinction was made on the basis of age. Children were buried with adults in the cemeteries at Agios Kosmas and Manika, but were not recognized at Zygouries, perhaps due to the poor preservation of bone. If there was indeed an age at which an individual was no longer buried intramurally but included in the cemetery with adults, that is a significant fact which suggests that age related distinctions had importance in EBA Greek society.

Exceptions to this model are few. One tomb at Lithares, in Boeotia, is reported to have held a cremation (Spyropoulos 1969). The tombs at Steno on Lefkas (Dörpfeld 1927) and at Ancient Elis (Koumouzelis 1980) also held cremations. Intramural adults have been found at Thebes (Touloupa 1964:192), Tiryns (Kilian 1983:318 and Figure 48), Strefi (Koumouzelis 1980:51), Pelikata (Heurtley 1934-5), Koufovouno (Rénard 1989:35-38) and Agios Stephanos (Taylour 1960, 1972) (Figure 6.2). Those at Tiryns and Thebes[5] are perhaps isolated instances, but the numerous Agios Stephanos burials cannot be so easily dismissed (see Forsén 1992:237-240 for a recent discussion of the problem of intramural versus extramural EH burials). The majority of the 24 burials from Agios Stephanos assigned to the EH II period are infants; only eight are adults. Of these eight, only one female is securely dated to EH II by the grave goods while the rest are apparently dated on stratigraphic grounds or the information given is contradictory. The preliminary report is not clear as to whether these burials are strictly contemporary with the buildings among which they were found, or if the burials represent a distinct phase in which this area of the site was used as a cemetery and not for habitation.

The major set of exceptions to the model are the burials in the northwest Peloponnesos and Ionian Islands. Adult pithos burials on Ithaka at Pelikata, on Lefkas at Steno, and at Strephi in Elis, and cremations at Steno and at Ancient Elis are not consistent with the mortuary practices of sites in the Argolid or Attica. Thus we have a regional difference, rather than a contradiction of the model for the other sites. It may be that Agios Stefanos and the unexcavated site of Pavlopetri in southern Lakonia (Harding et al. 1969), which may also have noninfant intramural burials, also form a regional group distinct from sites in the northeast Peloponnesos and east central Greece.

So far I have only described the mortuary practices of EBA Greece. As a conclusion I would like to suggest an interpretation of these mortuary practices in terms of what they can tell us about EBA social

Figure 6.2. Sites in Central and Southern Greece with evidence
for intramural burials. Solid circles indicate adults, hollow circles
indicate children.

organization. Individuals are buried in tombs which are maintained for some length of time. These tombs are probably to be thought of as the property of families or some other corporate group which continued in existence for more than one generation. The presence of both children and adults in the same tomb strongly supports the family nature of tombs. Goldstein (1981) has proposed a relationship between the presence of discrete cemetery areas and corporate groups based upon direct lineal descent. These corporate groups, much larger than a nuclear family in that they include several generations and branches ultimately related to a single ancestor, are a major means of organization in many societies. While Goldstein found that corporate groups which control crucial and restricted resources through lineal descent maintain discrete formal cemeteries, the converse, that cemeteries mean corporate groups that control crucial resources, is not necessarily true. The multiple use of tombs, however, strengthens the argument for the existence of corporate groups in EBA Greek society. Before a certain age individuals were not considered part of the community and were disposed of differently from their elders. This suggests that one's position in society changed with age, much as we have the concept of a certain age of majority. The differences in kinds and quantities of grave goods indicate ranking based upon wealth, but whether age and/or sex played a role in this form of ranking cannot be determined.

The regional approach to the study of mortuary behavior taken in this paper is an effective way of studying this realm of human behavior which is difficult to examine at individual EH sites. The construction of the model of EH mortuary behavior makes two major contributions to the study of EH society. The first is the identification of what appears to be a consistent pattern of mortuary behavior at numerous sites in east central and southern Greece, in contradistinction to separate regions of southern Peloponnesos and western Greece. This regional differentiation in mortuary behavior suggest we should look for regional differences in other realms of human behavior in the EBA. The pattern observed for east central and southern Greece can be explicated in terms of differentiation of individuals in EH society by the criteria of age and wealth and by the importance of identity with the family or corporate group after death. The second contribution is that of demonstrating the utility of using all kinds of data, on a regional level, especially data from earlier excavations and research which may not have been collected in a manner consistent with today's practice and standards. Viewing the mortuary data from a regional perspective is an important tool for trying to understand society and culture in Early Bronze Age Greece.

References Cited

Bartel, B.
  1982 A Historical Review of Ethnological and Archaeological
    Analyses of Mortuary Practice. *Journal of Anthropological
    Archaeology* 1:32-58.
Binford, L.R.
  1971 Mortuary Practices: Their Study and Their Potential. In
    Approaches to the Social Dimensions of Mortuary Practices, edited
    by James A. Brown, pp. 6-29. Society for American Archaeology
    Memoir 25. Society for American Archaeology, Washington, DC.
Blegen, C.W.
  1928 *Zygouries: A Prehistoric Settlement in the Valley of Cleonae.*
    Harvard University Press for the American School of Classical
    Studies at Athens, Cambridge, MA.
Bloch, M.
  1971 *Placing the Dead: Tombs, Ancestral Villages, and Kinship
    Organization in Madagascar.* Seminar Press, New York.
Broneer, O.
  1958 Excavations at Isthmia, Third Campaign, 1955-1956. *Hesperia*
    27:1-37.
Brown, J.A. (editor)
  1971 *Approaches to the Social Dimensions of Mortuary Practices.*
    Society for American Archaeology Memoirs 25. Society for
    American Archaeology, Washington, DC.
Caskey, J.L.
  1960 The Early Helladic Period in the Argolid. *Hesperia* 29:
    285-303.
Dörpfeld, W.
  1927 *Alt-Ithaka: ein Beitrag zur Homer-Frage.* Verlag Richarde
    Uhde, München.
Forsén, J.
  1992 *The Twilight of the Early Helladics: A Study of the
    Disturbances in East-Central and Southern Greece towards the
    End of the Early Bronze Age.* Studies in Mediterranean
    Archaeology and Literature Pocket-Book 116. Paul Åstroms
    Förlag, Jonsered, Sweden.
Fountoulakes, M.

1985 Τό Ανθρωπολογικό Υλικό τής Μάνικας Χαλκίδας. In
    Μάνικα:Μία Πρωτοελλαδική Πόλι στή Χαλκιδα, I, by
    Adamantios A. Sampson, pp. 393-458. Etaireia Euboïkon
    Spoudon, Athens.

Frödin, O., and A.W. Persson
    1938   *Asine:Results of the Swedish Excavations, 1922-1930.*
    Generalstabens litografiska anstalts forlag i distribution,
    Stockholm.

Goldstein, L.G.
    1981 One-Dimensional Archaeology and Multi-Dimensional People:
    Spatial Organisation and Mortuary Analysis. In *The Archaeology
    of Death*, edited by Robert Chapman, Ian Kinnes, and Klavs
    Randsborg, pp. 53-69. Cambridge University Press, Cambridge.

Goodenough, W. H.
    1965 Rethinking 'Status' and 'Role': Toward a General Model of
    the Cultural Organization of Social Relationships. In *The
    Relevance of Models for Social Anthropology*, edited by M.
    Blanton, pp. 1-24. ASA Monograph 1. Praeger, New York.

Haas, J.
    1982 *The Evolution of the Prehistoric State*. Columbia University
    Press, New York.

Harding, A., G. Cadogan, and R. Howell
    1969 Pavlopetri: An Underwater Bronze Age Town in Laconia.
    Annual of the British School at Athens 64:113-142.

Heurtley, W.A.
    1934-5 Excavations in Ithaca, II: The Early Helladic Settlement at
    Pelikata. *Annual of the British School at Athens* 35:1-44.

Johnson, G.A.
    1978 Information Sources and the Development of Decision-Making
    Organizations. In *Social Archeology: Beyond Subsistence and
    Dating*, edited by C.L. Redman, M.J. Berman, E.V. Curtin,
    W.T. Langhorne, N.M. Versaggi, and J.C. Wanser, pp. 87-112.
    Academic Press, New York.

Kilian, K.
    1983 Ausgrabungen in Tiryns, 1981: Bericht zu den Grabungen.
    Archäologischer Anzeiger 277-328.

Konsola, D.
    1981 Προμυκηναϊκή Θήβα: Χωροταξική καί Οικιστική Διάρθρωση.
    Unpublished dissertation, Department of Archaeology, University
    of Athens, Athens.
    1984 *Η Πρώϊμη Αστυκοποίηση στούς Πρωτοελλαδικούς Οικισμούς:*

Συστηματική Ανάλυση τών Χαρακτηριστικών τής. Athens.
Koumouzelis, M.
1980 *The Early and Middle Helladic Periods in Elis*. Unpublished Ph.D. dissertation, Brandeis University. University Microfilms (No. 80-24537), Ann Arbor.
Marinatos, S.
1970a From the Silent Earth. *Αρχαιολογικά Ανάλεκτα έξ Αθηνών* 3:61-68.
1970b Further News from Marathon. *Αρχαιολογικά Ανάλεκτα έξ Αθηνών* 3:153-166.
1970c Further Discoveries at Marathon. *Αρχαιολογικά Ανάλεκτα έξ Αθηνών* 3:349-366.
1970d Ανασκαφαί Μαρθώνος. *Πρακτικά τής έν Αθήναις Αρχαιολογικής Εταιρείας* 5-28.
1971 Ανασκαφαί Μαρθώνος. *Πρακτικά τής έν Αθήναις Αρχαιολογικής Εταιρείας* 5-6.
1972 Ανασκαφαί Μαρθώνος. *Πρακτικά τής έν Αθήναις Αρχαιολογικής Εταιρείας* 5-7.
McGuire, R.H.
1983 Breaking Down Cultural Complexity: Inequality and Heterogeneity. In *Advances in Archaeological Method and Theory* 6, edited by M. B. Schiffer, pp. 91-142. Academic Press, New York.
Mylonas, G.E.
1959 *Aghios Kosmas: an Early Bronze Age Settlement and Cemetery in Attica*. Princeton University Press, Princeton.
Papabasileios, G.
1910 Περί τών έν Εύβοια Αρχαίων Τάφων. Βιβλιοθήκη τής έν Αθήναις Αρχαιολογικής Εταιρείας 15. Archaiologike Etaireia, Athens.
Pullen, D.J.
1985 *Social Organization in Early Bronze Age Greece: A Multi-Dimensional Approach*. Ph.D. dissertation, Indiana University. University Microfilms (No. 85-16653), Ann Arbor.
1987 Asine, Berbati, and the Chronology of Early Bronze Age Greece. *American Journal of Archaeology* 91:533-544.
1988 The Early Phases of the Early Bronze Age at Tsoungiza Hill, Ancient Nemea. *American Journal of Archaeology* 92:252.
1990 Early Helladic Burials at Asine and Early Bronze Age Mortuary Practices. In *Celebrations of Death and Divinity in the Bronze Age Argolid, Proceedings of the 6th International*

Symposium at the Swedish Institute at Athens, 11-13 June, 1988, edited by R. Hägg and G. Nordquist, pp. 9-12. *Skrifter Utgivna av Svenska Institutet i Athen, 4°*, 40. Stockholm.

Rénard, J.
1989 *Le Site Néolithique et Helladique Ancien de Kouphovouno (Laconie): Fouilles de O.-W. von Vacano (1941)*. Aegaeum 4. Université de Liège, Liège.

Renfrew, C.A.
1972 *The Emergence of Civilisation: The Cyclades and the Aegean in the Third Millennium B.C.* Metheun, London.

Sampson, A.A.
1985 *Μάνικα:Μία Πρωτοελλαδική Πόλι στή Χαλκίδα*, I. Etaireia Euboïkon Spoudon, Athens.
1988 *Μάνικα:Ο Πρωτοελλαδικός Οικισμός καί τό Νεκροταφείο*, II. Ekdose Demou Halkideon, Athens.

Saxe, A.A.
1970 *Social Dimensions of Mortuary Practices*. Unpublished Ph.D. dissertation, University of Michigan. University Microfilms (No. 71-4720), Ann Arbor.

Smith, E.
1955 Prehistoric Pottery from the Isthmia. *Hesperia* 24:142-146.

Spyropoulos, T.G.
1969 *Ληθάρες Θηβών. Αρχαιολογικόν Δελτίον* 24 (A:Μελέται): 28-46.

Tainter, J.A.
1978 Mortuary Practices and the Study of Prehistoric and Social Systems. In *Advances in Archaeological Method and Theory*, vol. 1, edited by M.B. Schiffer, pp. 105-141. Academic Press, New York.

Taylour, Lord W.
1960 Laconia: Ayios Stephanos, 1960. *Αρχαιολογικόν Δελτίον* 16 (B:Χρονικά): 104-105.
1972 Excavations at Ayios Stephanos. *Annual of the British School at Athens* 67:205-270.

Theochares, D.R.
1955a Νέοι <Κυκλαδικοί> Τάφοι έν Αττική. *Νέον Αθηναίων* 1:283-292.
1955b Ανασκαφή έν Αραφένη. *Πρακτικά τής έν Αθήναις Αρχαιολογικής Εταιρείας* 109-117.

Touloupa, E.
1964 Αρχαιότητες καί Μνημεία Βοιωτίας, II: Ανασκαφικαί Ερευναι

εντός τής Πόλεως τών Θηβών, a. Καδμείον. Οικόπεδον Α. καί Σ. Τζορτζή (Πινδάρου καί Αντιγόνης). Αρχαιολογικόν Δελτίον 20 (Β:Χρονικά) 230-232.

Weber, M.
1947 *The Theory of Social and Economic Organization.* Translated and edited by Talcott Parsons. Free Press, Glencoe IL.

Wiencke, M.H.
1989 Change in Early Helladic II. *American Journal of Archaeology* 93:495-509.

Endnotes

1. Finds from Tomb VII: a gold ornament with a spiral of silver wire attached (Blegen 1928:Plate XX, no. 7; no. 1 on plan); two pieces of silver, one perhaps a diadem (Blegen 1928:Figure 176; nos. 7 and 21 on plan); a bronze pin (no. 21 on plan); two carnelian beads (identified as chalcedony, Blegen 1928:197; Plate XX, nos. 2 and 4; nos. 18 and 20 on plan); one cylindrical bead of soft green stone (Blegen 1928:Plate XX, no. 6); a stone amulet in the shape of a "foot" (Blegen 1928:Plate XX, no. 3; no. 17 on plan); one blade of obsidian (Blegen 1928:Plate XX, no. 5; no. 2 on plan); one "sea shell"; a sauceboat (no. Z-363, Blegen 1928:Figure 95; no. 15 on plan); a shallow bowl (no. Z-571, Blegen 1928:Figure 95; no. 12 on plan); an unpainted jar (no. Z-565, Blegen 1928:Figure 95); a small vessel shaped like the bowl of a pipe (Plate XX, no. 1; no. 1 on plan); and fragments of a small pyxis.

2. Finds from Tomb XX: one gold ornament (Blegen 1928:Plate XX, no. 11; no. 18 on plan); two fragments of silver, probably a diadem; one silver pin (Blegen 1928:Plate XX, no. 9; no. 19 on plan); one bronze pin (Blegen 1928:Plate XX, no. 8); one bronze "spatula" (Blegen 1928:Plate XX, no. 10; no. 20 on plan); one bead of carnelian (Blegen 1928:Plate XX, no. 12); one bead of steatite (Blegen 1928:Plate XX, no. 13); one whorl or button of bone (Blegen 1928:Figure 181, no. 3); a shallow bowl (no. Z-301, Blegen 1928:Figure 96); a patera or miniature bowl (no. Z-302, Blegen 1928:Figure 96; no. 21 on plan); and a few EH pot sherds.

3. Contents of grave on pre-Mycenaean Terrace: (1) shallow bowl, inturned rim, ring foot; red "paint" interior and exterior lip only (Frödin and Persson 1938:340 and Figure 230:1); (2) shallow bowl, incurved wall, ring foot smoothed onto body; slipped (Frödin and Persson 1938:340 and Figure 230:2-3); (3) shallow bowl, round base, plain rim; plain (Frödin and Persson 1938:340 and Figure 230:4).

4. Contents of second grave on pre-Mycenaean Terrace: (1) bowl with slightly incurving wall, "straight, sharply cut-off lip," ring foot; inside "thin, brownish varnish, the rim of the mouth [exterior?] with thick black varnish" (Frödin and Persson 1938:340 and Figure 231:left); (2) shallow

bowl, incurving wall, ring foot; interior thin glaze paint (Frödin and Persson 1938:340 and Figure 231:center); (3) shallow bowl, slightly flattened base, straight splayed sides, plain lip; inside thin glaze-paint (Frödin and Persson 1938:340 and Figure 231:right).

5. The designation of the Thebes adult burials reported by Touloupa (1964) as intramural is based on Konsola's delineation of the EH settlement of Thebes (1981, 1984); the paucity of graves from the numerous excavations in these limits established by Konsola which reached EH levels, though, would suggest the presence of an EH cemetery elsewhere.

Chapter 7

Archaeology and Theoretical Considerations on the Transition from Antiquity to the Middle Ages in the Aegean Area

Timothy E. Gregory

Introduction

In recent years archaeological research has come to play an increasingly important role in research strategies designed to increase our knowledge of Late Antiquity. This era was, of course, the period of the "decline and fall of the Roman Empire"--in the eastern Mediterranean, from the 3rd through the 8th century after Christ. The reason for this reliance on archaeology is, in part, the enormous increase in the amount of published archaeological material from Late Antiquity and the early (or proto-) Byzantine period, as more and more sites have been excavated and as excavators have become more conscious of their responsibility to record evidence from non-classical levels. In addition, the numerous regional archaeological surveys carried out in all areas of the Eastern Mediterranean have produced enormous quantities of material and identified a number of sites of all kinds that is truly amazing. To the surprise of classical archaeologists, many of these surveys have found that sites dating from Late Antiquity are among the most numerous of any of the periods represented. Thus, preliminary publication suggests that in Boeotia, Keos, and the Argolid the number of sites securely identified as Late Roman is second only to those of classical date, while on Melos the number of Late Roman sites is second to none. (For a summary, see the table in Alcock 1989a:106, 1989b:13; and van Andel and Runnels 1987:171, Figure 14; cf. Wright et al. 1990:617, Figure 11, where the "Byzantine" period has the largest number of components, followed by the classical and the Roman, which is apparently primarily late Roman in date). In the Late Antique Argolid "The economic improvement was slow at first...then peaked in the fifth and sixth centuries. A very large number of sites belong mainly to the later centuries of this period" (van Andel and Runnels 1987:115; cf. Cameron 1993:180, for the East).

By contrast, the material from the early Byzantine period (7th-8th centuries) is scant, and the number of sites falls from the heights of Late Antiquity to nearly zero: in the Argolid "our latest dated artifacts are coins belonging to the reign of Phokas ... after that nothing .... We have no evidence that from the middle of the seventh century on there were any settlements left in the area" (van Andel and Runnels 1987:121-122). This characterization of the archaeological evidence is, of course, directly in line with contemporary interpretation of the overall historical situation, at least among Byzantinists: prosperity in Late Antiquity followed by collapse in the late sixth century and a painfully slow recovery to a middle Byzantine zenith that was still at a level much lower than that of Late Antiquity. In fact, the archaeological evidence, when it first began to be used, from the 1950s onward, became a major underpinning of this now-dominant historical view (Foss 1975, 1977; Kazhdan 1954).

Contending Views on the Roman Decline

In the West the debate about the collapse of the Roman system is probably more advanced than it is in the East, and there, from the 1930s on, the Pirenne thesis has had an impact on scholarship, and "transformation" rather than "collapse" became an accepted way to describe the phenomenon. Nonetheless, until recently archaeological evidence even for the West played a relatively insignificant role, and the "fall" of the Roman Empire was still a valid paradigm for most scholars (see Bowersock 1988). Thus, the "fall" was central in the arguments of such great historians as Seeck (1901), Rostovtzeff (1926:476-477), Piganiol (1947), and A.H.M. Jones (1964:812 [cf. 1068 on the East], 1974:306). In recent years, some scholars have begun to make much greater use of archaeological data for an understanding of events in the West, and they have voiced serious misgivings about the traditional view: Whittaker (1976), for example, concerning the widespread belief that large amounts of land went out of production in Late Antiquity, and Dyson (1985) about the continuity in methods of agricultural exploitation. Nevertheless, most studies of the period continue to see "decline and fall" as the appropriate paradigm (for the extreme, see Ferrill 1986), including some analyses based primarily on archaeological sources (e.g., Hodges and Whitehouse 1983).

Many questions and problems, however, still remain, not least of which is the common ignorance of material evidence from the Byzantine Dark Ages, a factor which is likely to have influenced the identification of sites and activity from the period. As pottery, etc., from the Dark Ages becomes more generally known it should be possible to interpret the data from the period in a manner more independent of the literary texts, and the "darkness" may be dispelled a bit. One should note the new work being undertaken on Melos by G.A. Sanders, as yet unpublished, as well as important considerations on the economic, more particularly numismatic, evidence by Reece (1978, 1981), Hendy (1985:619-667), and Metcalf (1990).

Fully detailed knowledge of the Byzantine Dark Ages, however, will have to wait for further study and additional excavation. Perhaps more immediately to be considered is an analysis of the broader ramifications of the dramatic contrast between the huge amount of archaeological material from Late Antiquity and its near absence in the Byzantine Dark Ages. The easiest explanation is, of course, the current orthodoxy on historical development: "le grand brèche" in which a prosperous Late Antiquity--essentially continuous with the classical world--suddenly collapsed in the chaos of the late sixth and seventh centuries (in general, see Haldon 1985; Zakythinos 1966).

This reconstruction may well be correct, but there are several problems, not least of which is the explanation for the contrast: how are we to explain and characterize the collapse, especially given its apparent suddenness and the steepness of the decline? The question has rarely been answered and hardly even asked in precisely this form, despite its centrality in discussion of the "fall of the Roman Empire" and related issues (Bintliff and Snodgrass 1988; Fowden 1988; Wickham 1984). Perhaps closest in this respect is the important contribution of James Russell to the 1986 International Byzantine Congress in Washington (Russell 1986). Russell there argued that the decline of the city of Anemurion was not, in fact, sudden, but that it was preceded by a relatively long decline that lasted for up to a hundred years, throughout much of the sixth century. In Syria, likewise, current scholarly opinion now seems to hold that the collapse of the ancient synthesis was a slow phenomenon that began, perhaps, in the 550s, and that the Islamic conquest was merely one of many blows that put an end to the old way of life (Cameron 1993:177-182; Kennedy 1985a, 1985b). In the Balkans, however, the break is still generally seen as relatively sudden, and commonly connected directly with the barbarian, especially Slavic, invasions. Most modern accounts, however, seek to explain the collapse without consideration of the apparent prosperity that came immediately before--how can we explain the success of the invasions, given the archaeological evidence of the immediately preceding period? Sinclair Hood, writing in the volume on Byzantine Emporio (Ballance 1989:2) noted that "there are even hints of a marked increase of population in the region of the Emporio in the 6th century A.D .... and this suggest(s) the comparative prosperity of the area at the time." Hood, nevertheless, thinks that this apparent population increase and prosperity "could reflect the coming of refugees who had escaped from some part of the Balkan peninsula, ravaged by Goths and Huns at the end of the fourth and in the early fifth century, and from the time of Justinian (527-565) onwards subjected to massive raids by the Bulgars and later by the Avars and Slavs" (cf. Hood 1970).

Such an explanation for an individual site may, of course, be correct. On the other hand, the enormous quantity of archaeological data from Late Antiquity seems to be a generalized phenomenon, from urban to rural sites, from north to south in the Eastern Empire (at least until various parts were lost), and it is difficult to see all of these as refugee sites, absorbing population from everywhere else. In addition, although some sites of this period were remote and/or strongly fortified, many-- probably most--of the sites display no archaeological evidence that they were places of refuge; indeed, many were completely unfortified. One may therefore return to the more general question: how are we to explain the amount and diffusion of archaeological material from the fourth to the sixth century and its virtual disappearance in the later sixth and seventh centuries? The present paper will restrict itself almost entirely to the Aegean area, with a particular focus on the western shores of that sea, not because mainland Greece was any more important than other areas, but simply because a regional approach is likely to be the only one accurately to reflect actual conditions. In addition, Greece has largely been ignored in the broader studies of the transformation from antiquity to the Middle Ages, despite the long history of careful excavations that have been carried out there and the recent development of archaeological survey in Greece (Cherry, this volume).

Revised Models

Typically, the ubiquity of sites and physical material--especially coins and pottery--from Late Antiquity would be taken as an indication of prosperity and a flourishing economy and society. Snodgrass and Bintliff have no problem in accepting this conclusion: "From c. 300 A.D. onwards, and especially for the 5th-6th centuries A.D., there are plentiful signs throughout the East Mediterranean of a flourishing urban and rural life, even of expansion and/or recolonization of land and cultivation" (Bintliff and Snodgrass 1988:212). They point to a disappearance of the ancient pattern of settlement, based on the complementary town and farm, and its replacement by a "modern" settlement pattern, based on the nucleated village, and they connect this with the collapse of rural security and markets for non-subsistence products and services (cf. Halstead 1987). In the end they relate these events to the importance of the peasant landholder, on the model suggested by Ostrogorsky (1956, 1959), and to the "survival of the Greco-Roman way of life ... two centuries after its collapse in Italy" (Bintliff and Snodgrass 1988:216). This whole question, and the role of the peasant community, either derived from Late Antiquity or based on a supposed early Slavic institution, has been heatedly debated among Byzantinists (Gorecki 1986; Kazhdan 1960; Lipsic 1951). There is no full agreement on the issue, but the weight of scholarship today seems to emphasize the continuity of village life through the age of transition, although, of course, with some changes, and it downplays the importance of alleged Slavic institutions.

Alternatively, we may seek more complex explanations. One approach might be to take the model, based largely on data from regional surveys, recently proposed by Susan Alcock for the early Roman period in Greece and see how it fits, *mutatis mutandis*, for Late Antiquity. Thus, Alcock notes the scarcity of archaeological data for the Early Roman period--just the opposite of what we see for Late Antiquity (Alcock 1989a, 1989b; cf. Millar 1984)--and notes that if one were to rely on survey evidence alone the countryside would appear all but deserted during the 400 years between 200 B.C. and A.D. 200 (another period, one may note, in which ceramics are notoriously difficult to identify in a context of archaeological survey). The archaeological distributions, she argues, are best explained not by overall economic factors, but by broader Roman imperial social and political policy which favored the local aristocracies as the natural allies of Rome. This, in turn, led to an increase in the size of individual holdings (villas) and a concomitant nucleation of settlement. Land exploitation was concentrated in the best locations and the number of sites discovered in archaeological survey consequently declined to a remarkably low level.

By contrast, in Late Antiquity the central government took a complicated attitude toward the landed aristocracy. On the one hand, the economic policies of the state fell especially hard on the *curiales*, the local aristocracy who were made generally responsible for the fiscal needs of society as a whole (Petit 1955:284-294). On the other hand, at least after Diocletian, the emperors sought some accommodation with the upper levels of the aristocracy (the so-called senatorial aristocracy), since they provided much of the administrative talent necessary for the functioning of the state. In this regard, there was a clear differentiation between the eastern and the western parts of the empire, since in the latter the senatorial aristocracy was in large part identical with the old landowning aristocracy of the earlier empire, while in the East they were more commonly "new men," frequently Christians, who often fled to the Senate in Constantinople from their local curia (Arnheim 1972:4-6; Garnsey 1974; Jones 1940:192-209; Liebeschuetz 1972:174-192). These latter formed a "service elite" rather than a traditional hereditary aristocracy, although there were of course some old families still in power in the East (Haldon 1990:125-72). One should also remember that even members of the new aristocracy normally turned their position and success into landholding, and that, in the East as in the West, the church and the emperor were still the two largest individual landowners. Nevertheless, both the attitude of the state to the traditional aristocracy and the social makeup of the senatorial class varied widely between East and West and this had a profound effect on the history of the two halves of the empire (Arnheim 1972:169-171).

Throughout Late Antiquity the state thus maintained a crucial and, in some ways, contradictory attitude toward the large landowners. On the one hand, the state sought the support and the cooperation of the landowners since they were some of the most important officials of state and the representatives of traditional prestige culture (for an interesting analysis of the relationship between the aristocracy and the state see Brown 1992:3-70). On the other hand, the state commonly wished to control the landowning aristocracy, in their tendency to acquire ever larger landholdings, to turn the peasant proprietors into dependent *coloni*, and thus to deprive the state of important tax revenues. There certainly can be no doubt that in some provinces a significant nucleation of landholding in the form of *latifundia* occurred, with a concomitant decline in the number of peasant freeholders (Jones 1964:773-788), and the codes are clear in their concern about this phenomenon. The attitude of the state can be witnessed, in part, in the attempt to restrict the growth of patronage, a system in which peasant proprietors put their land and themselves under the protection and authority of a powerful person, usually a great landowner (Jones 1964:775-781). This broader development has often been seen in Marxist terms as part of the transformation of the antique economy based on slavery to the medieval economy based on feudalism, and modern forms of this argument have added considerable sophistication to the model (Haldon 1990:160-172; Siuziumov 1959; Wickham 1984).

Be this as it may, the variation in the success met by the state's effort to control the growth of *latifundia* may, in part, be explained by the distinction in the composition of the aristocracy in the two halves of the empire, mentioned above. Commonly, these efforts are thought to have been ineffectual, and presumably they were in the West, but in the East the situation was quite different, in large part because the state was stronger and because the senatorial aristocracy was much more completely dependent upon the will of the emperor. The archaeological evidence, at least from Greece and Syria, may be taken as support for such a reconstruction of the economic situation in which nucleated settlements were not the norm. Indeed, perhaps contrary to expectation, the examination of survey material reveals an agricultural economy based upon a widely dispersed settlement system, making use of marginal land that was exploited in hardly any other period, and engaged in specialized production of goods that seem destined for long--and short--distance markets.

The location and size of agricultural establishments in this period is particularly telling. They can be found not only in the better land along the coast, but also in nearly inaccessible locations, high on mountain slopes, and on waterless islands (van Andel and Runnels 1987:115-117). The imprecision of dating methods for survey material is an ever-present danger, but it seems clear that most of these remote settlements were occupied in periods of comparative peace. Greece, for example, experienced no serious invasion from the time of Alaric to the beginning of the Slavic incursions, i.e., from ca. 396 to 585, a period of nearly two hundred years--a factor which must certainly be borne in mind when considering the issues at hand--so we cannot explain remote settlements primarily as places of refuge, but as integral parts of the economic system (Gregory 1984a; Kardulias et al. 1994). Population may not have increased in this period, but it was clearly spread remarkably widely across the landscape.

Aside from the cities, most settlements were small and most were--as always--based primarily on agriculture. Yet, there is evidence that the agriculture of this period was not entirely subsistence, but based at least partially on exchange. Van Andel and Runnels (1987:116-117), speculating on the evidence from the Argolid, suggested that the fragmentation of the Roman Empire in the second and third centuries and afterward aided local and regional production and distribution, resulting in a boom in the economy of areas such as Greece which had earlier been overwhelmed by the mass-produced goods of great centers such as Italy, Gaul, and North Africa. It might be debated whether the market was ever free or whether the government played a leading role in the procurement and distribution of goods (Hopkins 1980, 1983)--but the effect would be the same in either case, and we see, in many parts of the Eastern Mediterranean, evidence of both specialization and trade. Thus, the work of Tchalenko (1953), beginning in the 1930s and now continued by excavation at selected sites, has shown that the northern Syrian plateau was a prosperous center for the production of oil for the cities of the coast (Kennedy 1985a, 1985b; Kennedy and Liebeschuetz 1988). Similar kinds of large-scale production facilities, with presses and large storage vats, have been noted throughout Greece, and the evidence of large-scale manufacture of transport amphoras in many areas along the Greek coast testifies to the mechanisms of trade on which the economy was apparently based (cf. van Andel and Runnels 1987:115-117). Likewise, there is plentiful direct evidence for trade, especially in the form of fine ceramics from Asia Minor and North Africa which turn up in all but the most impoverished sites, both inland and along the coast. I have elsewhere argued (1984a, 1986) that small Greek offshore islands were, at least in part, occupied to facilitate trade and transportation during this period.

The implications of this reconstruction are considerable. They suggest a degree of economic complexity that is not generally accepted for the period but that accords very well with the evidence. The magnitude of the many early Christian churches constructed in the fifth and sixth centuries, for example, cannot be explained simply as the result of the growth of the power of the church or the piety of the faithful. The basilica at Lechaion, the northern harbor of Korinth, was more than 200 m in length and decorated with rich marbles, many of them imported, and mosaics. In the same city and its suburbs there were at least six other churches of approximately the same date, many of them large and lavishly appointed (Pallas 1990:769-787). Certainly, there must have been some centralization of wealth in the hands of the Christian clergy, and the construction of churches may be seen as the corollary of the decline of construction in the secular civic centers and pagan sanctuaries. Furthermore, the emperor and the whole imperial apparatus may be seen as the source of funds for some of the construction. Nonetheless, the churches *were* built, frequently at considerable expense, and this could not have been done unless there was a relatively secure economic base. In most cases we cannot be certain who paid for these buildings, but the inscriptions attesting to private donations (often by the clergy) are many, and we cannot assume that the imperial government alone was responsible for the majority of church construction.

This model of expansion and economic complexity is both based on and in important ways at variance with the primitivist model of the ancient economy developed by Moses Finley (1973) and modified, among others, by Hopkins (1983), Hendy (1985:3-5), Garnsey and Saller (1987:43-63), and Gallant (1991). It is based on Finley in the sense that it avoids simple application of modern economic thought to an ancient setting and it accepts the proposition that cultural forces will affect economies in significant ways. Yet, it views the economy of the late Roman East as characterized by complexity, long-distance trade, and interdependence, perhaps on a scale not previously known in the ancient world.

Any discussion of the ancient economy necessarily raises the issue of the importance of trade. Generally, since Finley, the tendency has been to view the ancient economy as based almost entirely on subsistence agriculture, and there can be no doubt that the ancient economy was fundamentally different from any modern system (Hopkins 1983). Further, it is clear that traders, as independent operators and as a social class, were not a dominant factor in antiquity, and that this can be said for Late Antiquity as well as for earlier periods (Whittaker 1983). It is also clear that mechanisms other than trade were probably responsible for some, if not most, of the movement of goods in the period. Thus, the state certainly did intervene in the economy both to ensure the production and distribution of essential goods (especially foodstuffs for the cities and the army) and in its landowning policies and tax structure (Wickham 1984; 1988), and one should not view the economy as "free" in any modern sense (see Gallant 1991:8-10, 187-196). The tax structure of the state, however, may well have been a primary stimulus in the contemporary economy (Hopkins 1980) and its expenditure was certainly an important source of distribution, especially in the militarized areas of the empire. The growing wealth of the institutional church and its involvement in production and distribution, in part for charitable purposes, certainly resulted in the substantial exchange of goods over widely dispersed areas (Whittaker 1983:165-169). Finally, the well-attested phenomenon of aristocrats holding estates in various parts of the empire will also have added to this exchange and one should imagine that much of this exchange was conducted not through the mechanism of an open market, but by agents who were in the service of the landowners (Whittaker 1983:169-173).

Nonetheless, much of the discussion of ancient trade does seem based on an argument that no longer needs to be made: that the ancient economy was not based on a class system similar to that of early modern Europe. As Veyne has shown, the absence of an independent class of traders does not show that trade--or at least organized exchange--was unimportant in the ancient world (Veyne 1976:135; also see Pleket 1983:131-132). In fact, for the purposes of the analysis in this paper, it does not matter much whether the exchange of goods was carried out through a free market or through some tied economic medium. What the evidence shows is that there was a large volume of exchange in the Late Antique Eastern Mediterranean and that it was multi-directional, involving the transport of goods in various directions. It is also clear that the exchange is likely to have involved much more than large-scale gifts at the upper end of the social hierarchy. As we have seen, there seems to be evidence for the industrial-scale production of oil and transport amphoras; furthermore, the distribution of imported pottery throughout the landscape (where it has been revealed through systematic survey) is so broad that it would be hard to explain the phenomena as a result of exchange among wealthy landowners. There is, of course, some apparent correlation between the appearance of fine imported pottery (in Greece, especially African Red Slip and Phocaean Ware) and upper-level settlements, but these wares, as well as imported amphoras, turn up also in isolated farmsteads and broadly across the landscape (Jameson et al. 1994). These latter observations are still mostly impressions, and much more detailed quantitative work needs to be done with the survey material, but the broad outlines nevertheless seem clear.

This paper does not seek to address the means through which surpluses were extracted from the peasantry nor to engage in debate about the nature of the "political economy" of Late Antiquity (Gallant 1991:7-10). But the degree of such interchange and the conclusions that this requires about economic specialization and interdependence are impossible to ignore. One may compare the view of Greene (1986:170): "Quite simply, I believe that the level of economic activity revealed by archaeological research makes the 'minimalist' approach of historians such as Finley untenable" (cf. Whittaker 1983:178: "Plentiful evidence of the existence of trade and traders in the later Empire exists and does not in any sense support the hypothesis of a closed economy").

This analysis, further, contradicts the generally held assumption that there was a shortage of labor in Late Antiquity and that many fields were, in fact, deserted as a result of this (Boak 1955; Jones 1964:812, 1039, 1041). Our understanding of the question of these *agri deserti* is fundamental for any consideration of this period, since it involves the issue of the importance of the *latifundia* and the growth of a class of dependent *coloni*. Some scholars (Lewit 1991; Whittaker 1976), in fact, have begun to question this fundamental concept and it is clear that the archaeological evidence, from East and West alike, strongly contradicts the impression given by the literary sources of an abandoned and empty rural countryside (see the important new work of Kosso 1993, which I have not yet been able to consult systematically). This problem is almost certainly to be resolved by a consideration of the nature of the literary evidence, which is primarily legal or moralizing in nature. In the first instance, the state was naturally concerned to maximize its income, and given the nature of the Late Antique tax system, it was both necessary for the state to want to "tie" individual farmers to the land and for the farmers to seek to avoid such restraints: hence the focus of the codes on the flight of cultivators and empty fields. Secondly, Roman moralists of every age bemoaned the abandonment of the land and the disappearance of the noble peasantry from its traditional station. Such complaints must be put in the proper perspective and balanced by the archaeological evidence which shows intensive cultivation that was spread widely throughout the countryside.

Perhaps most importantly, the nature of the economic system proposed in this paper may help to explain the suddenness of the collapse when it came. Thus, if we view the Late Roman economy as a highly integrated system, based in part on specialized production and trade, it is easy to imagine the multiplied effect of small disturbances.

Earthquakes, disease, poor harvests, invasions, etc., that might in other periods have been easily overcome, would have disastrous repercussions and shake the entire system, leading to dramatically sudden collapse. A resort to subsistence agriculture would be possible, and the effect on traditional urban life would be catastrophic, since the cities naturally depended on the produce of the countryside for their food supply.

In addition, as we have seen, there is clear evidence for the use of marginal lands in Late Antiquity (Gregory 1984a; Bintliff and Snodgrass 1985:147-149; van Andel and Runnels 1987:113-117). This phenomenon would produce a short-term economic spurt, as large amounts of manpower were brought to bear on poor land, thus fostering an overall increase in production. Nonetheless, this effect would soon turn downward, in part because of the high cost of production and diminishing returns, but more significantly as a result of probable environmental damage. Thus, the opening of new land for grazing and cultivation would produce an immediate economic boom, especially if there was an available excess population to cut and burn trees and open the land to cultivation and/or grazing. But the utilization of these lands would require the continued investment of high levels of capital, especially to maintain such facilities as terrace walls and soil fertility. In a situation of economic opportunity these might not always be carefully maintained, since profits could be accrued quickly and easily. Over the long run, however, the fertility of the soil would be lost and terraces on high-altitude, steep land could suddenly shift, producing catastrophic results for both those living on them and those dwelling in the plains below. As is generally known, one school of geological historians sees the period of Late Antiquity as marked by serious environmental deterioration--large-scale erosion and the silting up of valleys and harbors (Vita-Finzi 1969)--and the model proposed here would fit well with such a scenario, although this would naturally not preclude environmental deterioration in other periods (see the discussion in van Andel et al. 1986; van Andel and Runnels 1987:143-144; cf. Kosso 1993).

Thus, in this view the invasions of the sixth and seventh centuries may have been a factor in the collapse of ancient civilization in the East, but as a catalyst rather than a cause. In fact, the cause of the difficulty was internal and, ironically, based on the very success of the economic system and imperial policy in regard to the large landowners. This is not to argue that the imperial authorities "should," or even could, have done something else: certainly the *dynatoi* were in a position where they represented a sustained threat to the imperial system, especially in certain parts of the empire. In Greece, perhaps, the nature of the landscape provided a certain natural brake on their power and it was significant that they were obviously the primary target of any barbarian raid that descended on the countryside. Powerful landowners in strongly fortified villas could possibly have provided a significant counter to the barbarian threat, but the pattern of events in the contemporaneous West does not hold out much hope along those lines (cf. Arnheim 1972:171).

Indeed, it is probably significant that the Byzantine revival, when it took place in the ninth century and later, was clearly based at least in part on the survival of the Greek-speaking communities that had maintained their existence from the period of Late Antiquity (Herrin 1973). Ironically, as a result of this situation, one of the difficulties of examining the archaeological evidence from the Byzantine Dark Ages is that so much of the ninth-century material looks very much like that of the late sixth century! These communities were in part located in places like Korinth and Athens that had probably preserved something of their urban character, but the survival of Greek place-names in remote locations shows that some of the marginal communities also survived (Koder and Hild 1976:105-106). Perhaps these were refugee settlements during the period of the invasions, but if so, the way had at least been paved by the establishment of settlements in these remote areas in the previous period of security and prosperity, thus providing an institutional infrastructure for the threads of continuity that stretched between antiquity and the Byzantine age.

In addition, the dispersed settlement system, to the extent that it survived the first onslaughts of invasion, probably served to help integrate the migrants into a new way of life and to pave the way for accommodation and acculturation. The course of that process is, naturally, most difficult to document since the sources--literary and archaeological--are so few and so difficult to interpret. Slowly, however, and with care, archaeologists are beginning to discern the dim outline of the process and, again, the primary focus of activity is not just the large city, but the outlying area. This is not the place to discuss the controversial question of the early Byzantine village communities (see Haldon 1990:132-141), but there can be little question that these were dynamic social and economic units that were based structurally on continuity with the period of Late Antiquity. As Haldon (1990:135) notes: "There is no reason to doubt either that such communities existed in an unbroken tradition throughout the seventh century" (cf.

Svoronos 1982; Kaplan 1985). In this regard witness the situation at Ancient Isthmia, where we are just now beginning to trace the shape of what appears to be a Dark-Age settlement on the ruins of the old Roman Bath. The remains were not carefully excavated in the 1970s and they were not recognized for what they were at the time, but we are now at work in an effort to reconstruct what must have been a significant point of contact between the new settlers and the older inhabitants, in a landscape that was apparently still populated as a result of conditions and policies of the preceding period (Gregory 1993).

Transformation as a General Model

One might reasonably conclude by asking how the model of transformation presented above accords with other theories of decline and fall. Obviously, it differs significantly from most of the "explanations" put forward by historians. Indeed, it seems more reasonable to compare it with broader models of collapse, such as that propounded recently by Joseph Tainter (1988). This latter theory starts from the principle that complex societies must make significant investments in order to increase or even maintain their complexity. At a certain point "investment in sociopolitical complexity as a problem-solving response often reaches a point of declining marginal returns," and collapse follows (1988:194). Tainter uses the (western) Roman empire as one of his primary examples to illustrate this phenomenon, but virtually any modern Roman historian would seriously question his use of evidence, interpretation of historical data, and unsophisticated reference to the complicated scholarship on the question. Thus, he sees the complexity and growth of Rome almost entirely in terms of territorial aggrandizement and he falls into the error of assuming that the territorial growth of the Roman empire was economically profitable and that "once the accumulated surpluses have been spent, a conqueror must thereafter incur costs to administer, garrison, and defend the province.... Costs rise and benefits decline" (Tainter 1988:128-52, at 149). He further concludes that the growth of the Roman administration was a response to the problems generated by the termination of the wars of conquest. When "complexity was no longer yielding benefits superior to disintegration," collapse was all but inevitable, and the collapse was, in fact, a positive development, since it "yielded at the same time both a reduction in the costs of complexity and an increase in the marginal return on its investment" (1988:151).

One may, in fact, question almost every aspect of Tainter's model, insofar as it applies to the Roman Empire, on historical grounds. Thus, no modern historian of Rome would maintain that Rome' territorial expansion was motivated by economic considerations, and most would argue that the military expansion never paid for itself, even at the time of the conquest itself, except that certain Roman generals enriched themselves at the expense of the conquered; the overall Roman economy certainly did not benefit directly. Furthermore, Tainter's view of the later Roman empire is at considerable variance with virtually all contemporary scholarship on the period. Thus, he observed that:

> The Empire that emerged under Diocletian and Constantine was administered by a government that was larger, more complex, more highly organized, and that commanded larger and more powerful military forces. It taxed its citizens more heavily, conscripted their labor, and regulated their lives and their occupations. It was a coercive, omnipresent, all-powerful organization that subdued individual interests and levied all resources toward one overarching goal: the survival of the State [Tainter 1988:141].

This view may be compared to a recent summary that reflects current historiography on the nature of this period (Cameron 1993:82, 83, 86):

> After all, if the structure of the state in the late fourth and fifth centuries was as top-heavy and as liable to collapse from its own internal contradictions as many scholars assert, why is it that the eastern empire seems to have gone from strength to strength? . . . . The older model depends on the view of a massive tightening up of government control and consequent increase of government expenditure, generally attributed to Diocletian. . . . The frequently repeated and often contradictory pronouncements of emperors do not signify authoritarian intrusions on the lives of individuals so much as vain attempts to regulate a situation which was in practice beyond their control. Once this is fully recognized it is easier to . . . discard the idea of Diocletian as the initiator of some kind of rigid and repressive regime.

Despite these serious errors in historical interpretation and an essentially flawed view of Late Antiquity, Tainter's broader idea of declining returns may yet be a useful theoretical framework in which to place events of this period. Thus, as we have seen, the growth of the economy, in the fourth and fifth centuries, led to expansion and the occupation of various environmental and, perhaps even economic, niches. This, almost certainly, provided increasing returns--but only to a point. The system was interdependent, and therefore fragile.

Continuing marginal investment in land and resources that were evermore poorer or more remote brought increasingly small returns. These might, for a time, still bring prosperity, but the least disturbance--natural or man-made--could bring the whole system down upon itself, quickly and catastrophically. Not, of course, that the entire system disappeared instantly or that the cultural consequences of this system disappeared as well--they certainly did not--but when the crises came the retraction was quick and the return to earlier modes of production was widespread.

References Cited

Adams, R. McC.
    1981 *Heartland of Cities*. University of Chicago Press, Chicago.
Alcock, S.E.
    1989a Archaeology and Imperialism: Roman Expansion and the Greek City. *Journal of Mediterranean Archaeology* 2:87-135.
    1989b Roman Imperialism in a Greek Landscape. *Journal of Roman Archaeology* 2:5-34.
    1991 Urban Survey and the Polis of Phlius. *Hesperia* 60:421-463.
    1993 *Graecia Capta. The Landscapes of Roman Greece*. Cambridge University Press, Cambridge.
Arnheim, M.T.W.
    1972 *The Senatorial Aristocracy in the Later Roman Empire*. Clarendon Press, Oxford.
Ballance, M., J. Boardman, S. Corbett, and S. Hood
    1989 *Excavations in Chios 1952-1955*. Byzantine Emporio. British School of Archaeology Supplementary Volume 20. London.
Bintliff, J.A., and A. Snodgrass
    1985 The Cambridge/Bradford Boeotian Expedition: The First Four Years. *Journal of Field Archaeology* 12:3-61.
    1988 The End of the Countryside: A View from the East. In *First Millenium Papers: Western Europe in the First Millenium A.D.*, edited by R.F. Jones, J.H.F. Bloemers, S.L. Dyson, and M. Biddle, pp. 175-217. BAR International Series 401. British Archaeological Reports, Oxford.
Boak, A.E.R.
    1955 *Manpower Shortage and the Fall of the Roman Empire in the West*. University of Michigan Press, Ann Arbor.
Bowersock, G.W.
    1988 The Dissolution of the Roman Empire. In *The Collapse of*

Ancient States and Civilizations, edited by N. Yoffee and G.L. Cowgill, pp. 165-175. University of Arizona Press, Tucson.

Brown, P.
1992 *Power and Persuasion in Late Antiquity. Towards a Christian Empire*. University of Wisconsin Press, Madison.

Carandini, A.
1983 Pottery and the African Economy. In *Trade in the Ancient Economy*, edited by P. Garnsey, K. Hopkins, and C.R. Whittaker, pp. 145-162. Chatto and Windus, London.

Callot, O.
1984 *Huileries antiques de Syrie du Nord*. Diffusion de Boccard, Paris.

Cameron, A.
1993 *The Mediterranean World in Late Antiquity A.D. 395-600*. Routledge, London.

Cherry, J.F., J.L. Davis, and E. Mantzourani (editors)
1991 *Landscape Archaeology as Long-Term History: Northern Keos in the Cycladic Islands*. UCLA Monumenta Archaeologica 16, UCLA Institute of Archaeology, Los Angeles.

Dyson, S.L.
1985 *The Creation of the Roman Frontier*. Princeton University Press, Princeton.

Ferrill, A.
1986 *The Fall of the Roman Empire. A Military Explanation*. Thames and Hudson, London.

Finley, M.I.
1973 *The Ancient Economy*. Hogarth Press, London.

Foss, C.
1975 The Persians in Asia Minor at the End of Antiquity. *English Historical Review* 90:721-743.
1977 Archaeology and the 'Twenty Cities' of Byzantine Asia. *American Journal of Archaeology* 81:469-486.

Fowden, G.
1988 City and Mountain in Late Roman Attica. *Journal of Hellenic Studies* 108:48-59.

Fulford, M.
1980 Carthage--Overseas Trade and Political Economy, AD 400-700. *Reading Medieval Studies* 6:68-70.

Gallant, T.W.
1991 *Risk and Survival in Ancient Greece. Reconstructing the Rural Domestic Economy*. Stanford University Press, Stanford.

Garnsey, P.
  1974 Aspects of the Decline of the Urban Aristocracy in the
     Empire. *Aufsteig und Neidergang der römischen Welt* ii, 1:229-
     252. Berlin and New York.
Garnsey, P., K. Hopkins, and C.R. Whittaker (editors)
  1983 *Trade in the Ancient Economy.* Chatto and Windus, London.
Garnsey, P., and R. Saller
  1987 *The Roman Empire. Economy, Society and Culture.*
     Duckworth, London.
Gorecki, D.
  1986 The Slavic Theory in Russian Pre-Revolutionary
     Historiography of the Byzantine Farmer Community. *Byzantion*
     56:77-107.
Greene, K.
  1986 *The Archaeology of the Roman Economy.* University of
     California Press, Berkeley.
Gregory, T.E.
  1984a Diporto: A Byzantine Maritime Settlement in the Gulf of
     Corinth. Δελτίον τῆς Χρηστιανικῆς Αρχαιολογικῆς Εταιρείας
     12:287-304.
  1984b Cities and Social Evolution in Roman and Byzantine South
     East Europe. In *European Social Evolution: Archaeological
     Perspectives*, edited by John Bintliff, pp. 267-276. University of
     Bradford Press, Bradford.
  1986 A Desert Island Survey in the Gulf of Corinth. *Archaeology*
     39(3):16-21.
  1993 An Early-Byzantine (Dark-Age) Settlement at Isthmia:
     Preliminary Report. In *The Corinthia in the Roman Period*, edited
     by T.E. Gregory, pp. 149-160. Journal of Roman Archaeology
     Supplementary Series No. 8, Ann Arbor.
Haldon, F.
  1985 Some Considerations on Byzantine Society and Economy in
     the Seventh Century. In *Perspectives in Byzantine History and
     Culture*, edited by J.F. Haldon, and J.T.A. Koumoulides, pp. 75-
     112. *Byzantinische Forschungen* 10. A.M. Hakkert, Amsterdam.
  1990 *Byzantium in the Seventh Century.* Cambridge University
     Press, Cambridge.
Halstead, P.
  1987 Traditional and Ancient Rural Economy in Mediterranean
     Europe: plus ça change. *Journal of Hellenic Studies* 107:77-87.
Hendy, M.

1985 *Studies in the Byzantine Monetary Economy.* Cambridge University Press, Cambridge.

Herrin, J.
1973 Aspects of the Process of Hellenization in the Early Middle Ages. *Annual of the British School at Athens* 68:113-126.

Hodges, R., and D. Whitehouse
1983 *Charlemagne, Mohammed and the Origins of Europe. Archaeology and the Pirenne Thesis.* Cornell University Press, Ithaca, New York.

Hopkins, K.
1980 Taxes and Trade in the Roman Empire. *Journal of Roman Studies* 70:101-125.

1983 Introduction. In *Trade in the Ancient Economy*, edited by P. Garnsey, K. Hopkins, and C.R. Whittaker, pp. ix-xxv. Chatto and Windus, London.

Hood, S.
1970 Isles of Refuge in the Early Byzantine Period. *Annual of the British School at Athens* 65:37-45.

Jameson, M., T.H. van Andel, and C.N. Runnels
1994 *A Greek Countryside: The Southern Argolid from Prehistory to the Present Day.* Stanford University Press, Stanford.

Jones, A.H.M.
1940 *The Greek City from Alexander to Justianian.* Clarendon Press, Oxford.

1964 *The Later Roman Empire. A Social, Economic and Administrative Survey.* Basil Blackwell, Oxford.

1974 *The Roman Economy. Studies in Ancient Economic and Administrative History.* Basil Blackwell, Oxford.

Kaplan, M.
1985 L'Exploitation paysanne byzantine entre l'antiquité et le moyen are (VIe-VIIIe siècles): affirmation d'une structure économique et sociale. In *From Late Antiquity to Early Byzantium*, edited by V. Vavrinek, pp. 101-105. Academia, Prague.

Kardulias, P.N., T.E. Gregory, and J. Sawmiller
1994 Bronze Age and Late Antique Exploitation of an Islet in the Saronic Gulf, Greece. *Journal of Field Archaeology*, in press.

Kazhdan, A.P.
1954 Vizantijskie goroda v VII-IX vv. *Sovietskaya Arkheologija* 21:164-188

1960 *Derevnja i Gorod v Vyzanyij, IX-X vv.* Izd-vo Akademii nauk SSSR, Moscow.

Kennedy, H.
  1985a The Last Century of Byzantine Syria: A Reinterpretation.
    In *Perspectives in Byzantine History and Culture,* edited by J.F.
    Haldon, and J.T.A. Koumoulides, pp. 141-183. *Byzantinische
    Forschungen* 10. A.M. Hakkert, Amsterdam.
  1985b From Polis to Madina: Urban Change in Late Antique and
    Early Islamic Syria. *Past and Present* 106:3-27.
Kennedy, H., and J.H.W.G. Liebeschuetz
  1988 Antioch and the Villages of Northern Syria in the 5th and 6th
    Centuries A.D. *Nottingham Medieval Studies* 32:65-90.
Koder, J., and F. Hild
  1976 *Hellas und Thessalia. Tabula Imperii Byzantini.* 1. Verlag der
    österreichische Akademie der Wissenschaft, Vienna.
Kosso, C.K.
  1993 *Public Policy and Agricultural Practice: An Archaeological
    and Literary Study of Late Roman Greece.* Unpublished Ph.D.
    Dissertation, Department of History, University of Illinois at
    Chicago.
Lewit, T.
  1991 *Agricultural Production in the Roman Economy A.D. 200
    -400.* BAR International Series 568. British Archaeological
    Reports, Oxford.
Liebeschuetz, J.H.W.G.
  1972 *Antioch. City and Imperial Administration in the Later Roman
    Empire.* Clarendon Press, Oxford.
Lipsic, E.E.
  1951 *Byzanz und die Slawen. Beiträge zur byzantinischen
    Geschichte des 6.-9. Jahrhunderts.* H. Bohlaus Nachfolger,
    Weimar.
Metcalf, D.M.
  1990 Avar and Slav Invasions into the Balkan Peninsula (c. 575
    -625): The Value of the Numismatic Evidence. *Journal of Roman
    Archaeology* 4:140-148.
Millar, F.
  1984 The Mediterranean and the Roman Revolution: Politics, War
    and the Economy. *Past and Present* 102:3-24.
Ostrogorsky, G.
  1956 *Quelques problèmes d'histoire de la paysannerie byzantine.*
    Editions de Byzantion, Brussels.
  1959 Byzantine Cities in the Early Middle Ages. *Dumbarton Oaks
    Papers* 13:45-66.

Pallas, D.
   1990   Corinth. *Reallexikon zur byzantinischen Kunst* 4:746-
   811. Berlin.
Parsons, J.R.
   1974   The Development of a Prehistoric Complex Society: A
   Regional Perspective from the Valley of Mexico. *Journal of Field
   Archaeology* 1:81-108.
Petit, P.
   1955   *Libanios et la vie municipale à Antioche au IVe siècle après
   J.-C.* P. Geuthner, Paris.
Piganiol, A.
   1947   *L'empire chrétien.* Presses universitaires de France, Paris.
Pletket, H.W.
   1983   Urban Elites and Business in the Greek Part of the Roman
   Empire. In *Trade in the Ancient Economy*, edited by P. Garnsey,
   K. Hopkins, and C.R. Whittaker, pp. 131-144. Chatto and
   Windus, London.
Randsborg, K.
   1991   *The First Millenium A.D. in Europe and the Mediterranean.
   An Archaeological Essay.* Cambridge University Press,
   Cambridge.
Reece, R.
   1978   Coins and Frontiers--or Supply and Demand. *Akten des XI
   internationalen Limeskongress*, pp. 643-646. Budapest.
   1981   Coinage and Currency in the Third Century. In *The Roman
   West in the Third Century*, edited by A. King and M. Henig, pp.
   79-78. BAR International Series 109. British Archaeological
   Reports, Oxford.
Renfrew, A.C., and J. Wagstaff (editors)
   1982   *An Island Polity.* University of Cambridge Press, Cambridge.
Rostovtzeff, M.
   1926   *The Social and Economic History of the Roman Empire.*
   Clarendon Press, Oxford.
Russell, J.
   1986   Transformations in Early Byzantine Urban Life: The
   Contribution and Limitations of Archaeological Evidence. *XVII
   International Byzantine Congress: Major Papers*, pp. 137-154. A.
   Caratzas, New Rochelle.
Seeck, O.
   1901   *Geschichte des Untergangs der antiken Welt.* Siemenroth and
   Troschel, Berlin.

Siuziumov, M.Y.
    1959 Nekotorye problemy istorii vizantii. *Voprosy istorii* 3:98-117.
Svoronos, N.
    1982 Notes sur l'origine et la date du Code Rural. *Travaux et
        Mémoires* 8:487-500.
Tainter, J.A.
    1988 *The Collapse of Complex Societies.* Cambridge University
        Press, Cambridge.
Tchalenko, G.
    1953 *Villages antiques de la Syrie du Nord.* P. Geuthner, Paris.
van Andel, T.H, and C. Runnels
    1987 *Beyond the Acropolis. A Rural Greek Past.* Stanford
        University Press, Stanford.
van Andel, T.H., C.N. Runnels, and K.O. Pope
    1986 Five Thousand Years of Land Use and Abuse in the Southern
        Argolid, Greece. *Hesperia* 55:103-128.
Veyne, P.
    1976 *Le Pain et le Cirque.* Penguin Press, London.
Vita-Finzi , C.
    1969 *The Mediterranean Valleys: Geological Change in Historical
        Time.* Cambridge University Press, Cambridge.
Weithmann, M.W.
    1978 *Die slavische Bevolkerung auf der griechischen Halbinsel. Ein
        Beitrag zu historischen Ethnographie Sudosteuropas.* R. Trofenik,
        Munich.
Whittaker, C.R.
    1976 Agri Deserti. In *Studies in Roman Property,* edited by M.I.
        Finley, pp. 137-165. Cambridge University Press, Cambridge.
    1983 Late Roman Trade and Traders. In *Trade in the Ancient
        Economy,* edited by P. Garnsey, K. Hopkins, and C.R. Whittaker,
        pp. 163-180. Chatto and Windus, London.
Wickham, C.
    1984 The Other Transition: From the Ancient World to Feudalism.
        Past and Present 103:3-36.
    1988 Marx, Sherlock Holmes and Late Roman Commerce. *Journal
        of Roman Studies* 78:183-193.
Wright, J.C., J. F. Cherry, J.L. Davis, E. Manzourani, S.B. Sutton,
and R.F. Sutton
    1990 The Nemea Valley Archaeological Project: A Preliminary
        Report. *Hesperia* 59:579-659.
Zakythinos, D.A.

1966 La grand brèche dans la tradition historique de l'hellénisme du septième au neuvième siècle. Χαριστήριον εἰς A.K. Ορλανδόν, pp. 300-327. Vivliotheke tes en Athenais Archaiologikes Etaireias No. 54, Athens.

Chapter 8

On Lithic Studies in Greece

Curtis N. Runnels

Introduction

Several chapters in this volume offer views of the ways that archaeology is breaking new ground in the collection of data useful for the construction of cultural histories of entire regions. The growing interest in regional studies and the field methods that make them possible is a significant departure from the traditional goal of studying individual archaeological sites. This advancing field is making important additions to the usual categories of data studied by archaeologists. The focus in such studies is upon complete regional settlement patterns, and the definition of archaeological sites has been expanded to incorporate not only larger settlements, but also the many sites that are not usually considered "settlements," for example individual farmsteads, shrines, animal folds, dumps, and many kinds of specialized activity areas. In a related move, regional surface investigations have been widened to include isolated features such as inscriptions, quarries, or wells, and also the most ephemeral traces of human activity often overlooked in the early days of topographic reconnaissance, particularly the low density scatters of artifacts that resulted from activities such as manuring agricultural fields or the dumping of refuse. Finally, regional surveys are having the effect of encouraging archaeologists to investigate the long term interaction of humans and the landscape, primarily, but not exclusively, through the study of soils and erosional deposits that were created, at least in part, by human agencies.

This expansion of the scope of regional studies may be compared with the application of scientific techniques of materials analysis in recent decades to the study of data retrieved by excavation. The inclusion of scientific analysis of materials into research designs requires a change in archaeological methods, for instance the introduction of sieving and flotation techniques, and also a change in the list of usual categories of artifacts and other materials that are recovered and studied by excavators. Today, in order to approach the ideal of investigating a site in the total systemic and depositional complexity that is made possible by the new scientific techniques, multidisciplinary archaeologists are adding the analyses of biological materials, studies of the sources of raw materials used on the site, analyses of anthropogenic sediments, and the taphonomy of site formation processes to the standard investigation of features and artifacts recovered in excavations.

The goal of the regional analyst is to reconstruct and to explain the record of the human past, but a change in the frame of reference from the single site to the much larger area that forms the context or setting for the site is necessary. The study of a typical regional framework, which may include an area of several hundred square kilometers, requires the reconstruction of the complicated history of human settlement and landscape over a period of many millennia. In turn, this cultural history is the result of the coevolution, in the technical sense used in biology and human ecology (e.g., Durham 1991), of a dynamic system. This system consists both of human settlements and the physical landscape, and it is the landscape which sets the stage, to a degree, for human activities by partly constraining the possibilities open to humans, and the landscape is in its turn transformed by the human settlements that are spread over it.

Regional Studies of Lithics

In an earlier paper (Runnels 1983) I attempted to make a case for studying lithic artifacts as part of regional studies programs of archaeological research, but that paper had little impact on the thinking of Mediterranean archaeologists, particularly those working in the recent historical periods. It is still rare for archaeologists to collect or analyze lithics discovered in field surveys with the same level of professional interest and enthusiasm that is shown for potsherds. Surely one reason for this attitude is the continuing scarcity of reference materials for use in the classroom and laboratory, but another reason, and here we must be brutally honest, is that many archaeologists who work in the Aegean think that stone artifacts are of little value for archaeological reconstruction or interpretation, particularly for historical periods when surviving architecture and well known types of decorated pottery bulk so large in the archaeological record. My purpose in this paper, therefore, is to counter such views, as far as can be done in this forum, and attempt again to persuade archaeologists working in all periods to collect and analyze lithic materials.

For the study of cultural history on a regional scale, lithic artifacts are an important part of the archaeological record because they are the most long-lived cultural materials that survive from antiquity. Lithics are sometimes the principal residues of human activity on many sites, and for some archaeological periods they are the only surviving evidence. This is particularly true for the prehistoric periods in Greece. An example is the Greek Palaeolithic. Evidence for early prehistoric inhabitation of Greece was established on a firm foundation only in the 1960s. The evidence for the Upper Palaeolithic and Mesolithic periods in the late Pleistocene and early Holocene are known primarily through excavations where the majority of recovered artifacts are stone tools. The Early Palaeolithic (before 40,000 B.P.), however, is known entirely from stone tools, the majority of which have been found on open-air sites in the Peloponnesos, Thessaly, and Epiros (see Runnels 1988 for a summary).

Lithics are important for more than indicating the presence or absence of a particular period. They can also be used to study cultural processes on a regional scale that are of general interest to archaeologists. One such process was the transition to the village farming economy that began in Greece in the seventh millennium B.C. For decades archaeologists have debated the question of whether agricultural origins in Greece were the result of experimentation by indigenous Mesolithic cultures, or the result of immigrants from Anatolia or the Near East who brought with them the fundamental economic elements of the agricultural way of life. New light has been thrown on this question by a recent technological evaluation of lithics from the Neolithic period that was used to identify different regional patterns of neolithization in Thessaly and the Peloponnesos. In an important and innovative paper, Perlès (1987) concentrated on the detailed study of the reduction techniques ("châines opératoires") that could be reconstructed from assemblages recovered from excavations of Early Neolithic sites in the Thessalian plain and from Franchthi Cave in the southern Argolid. Her analyses demonstrate that the Thessalian flintworkers used a sophisticated pressure technique to produce blades and that this method and the blades it produced owe nothing to the Mesolithic techniques that were present at sites such as Franchthi Cave and Sidari in Corfu. This finding is interpreted by Perlès to show that the blade technology of Thessaly was entirely a novel development, which supports the hypothesis that the earliest Thessalian agriculturalists were immigrants. As additional support for this thesis, Perlès shows that the contemporary Early Neolithic lithic assemblage from Franchthi Cave contains substantial technical elements that are derived from the earlier Mesolithic assemblage found at that site, which suggests that the earliest Neolithic community included flintknappers trained in the old traditions. Perlès uses this last discovery to support a hypothesis of two separate paths to the farming way of life, one based in the north on immigrant farmers, whatever their ultimate origin may turn out to be, and in the south a more complicated process that included the participation by, or acculturation of, indigenous people.

In a related technological study, Perlès (1990) uses lithics from a wide number of sites in northern and southern Greece to answer questions about the analysis of manufacturing techniques and raw material procurement practices in the Neolithic period. Her analyses show major differences in the acquisition and use of different raw materials for stone tools, particularly in obsidian, between the northern regions of Thessaly and Macedonia and the southern region consisting of Attika, the Peloponnesos, and the Cyclades. One of several interesting conclusions that result from this study is that specialists in stone tool production, in particular those who made fine blades with a pressure technique, were active primarily in the earlier phases of the Neolithic and largely disappear from the record in the later phases of the Neolithic. This conclusion has considerable significance for the study of craft specialization, regional interaction, trade, and economic development.

Classical archaeologists, however, have rarely used lithics in regional studies, despite the successes achieved by prehistorians. This is possibly because they are not aware that flaked stone tools and many older types of lithics continued to be made and used throughout the historical periods. If this is the case, it is unfortunate because lithics are an important part of the material culture of the historical periods in Greece and in all parts of the Old World. There are many types of historical lithics, but saddle querns and rotary querns are perhaps the most commonly occurring ones. Historical assemblages, however, include flaked stone tools of flint, chert, and obsidian that were used for gunflints, as parts of firemaking kits, as elements in threshing sledges, and for a variety of household tasks and ritual activities that range from circumcision to the gelding of animals (Rosen 1985; Runnels 1982; Torrence 1986, 1991).

One reason for the neglect of lithics by Classical archaeologists is perhaps the simple nature of many stone tools and their widespread temporal distribution. This limitation is often said to apply to the typical saddle querns found in large numbers on Mediterranean sites of virtually every period. Although it is true that saddle querns are not as sensitive chronological indicators as are styles of decorated pottery, it is incorrect to conclude, as did Childe (1956:73-74), that querns and handmills are useless for the construction of typological series or as type fossils because they persist for long periods of time without exhibiting marked technological or typological change. Recent research on saddle querns and rotary querns in Greece shows that querns and handmills undergo considerable change through time and are useful for typological and chronological studies. In a study of 300 querns excavated from stratified prehistoric and historic sites in Attika and the Argolid, for instance, I demonstrated that saddle querns, rotary querns, and other handmills could be classified on the basis of form, size, use, raw material, and method of manufacture, and that the different types of querns could be correlated with specific periods (Runnels 1981). Neolithic and Bronze Age saddle querns, for instance, could be readily identified, even when only small fragments were preserved. Saddle querns were produced in Classical Antiquity and in recent historical periods, but they are of different types than their prehistoric counterparts. In Greece, a major change in milling technology occurred in early Roman times when conclusive archaeological evidence shows that the use of rotary motion for turning millstones was introduced into the eastern Mediterranean from the West sometime in the second century B.C. During the course of the Roman period, rotary mills were modified in size, form, and raw materials, and different types of mills, from small rotary querns, large Pompeiian-type grain mills, and the mills used to crush olives, such as the *trapetum* or *mola olearia*, can be distinguished for every phase of the long Roman period (Moritz 1958; Runnels 1990). This study of querns and mills has been extended to surface sites found in regional surveys, and it has proved possible to recognize the different types of stone tools from very small fragments; these querns and mills not only supply useful chronological information about surface sites, but also can be used to infer something about the functions of the sites (Kardulias and Runnels 1994). Small rotary querns, for instance, may be found on any kind of site where food was prepared, but the large and expensive *trapeta* appear to belong only to later Roman villas that specialized in the production of olive oil.

Lithics cover the entire range of human history in the Mediterranean, and they constitute one of the few classes of artifacts which can be studied in every period of antiquity. As the few studies already cited can show, lithics have much to contribute to regional studies. There is one difficulty, however, that stands in the way of the use of lithics: *viz.*, the subject matter of "lithics" has never been adequately defined. For students who are unsure about the concept, the word "lithics" may conjure up an image of flint and obsidian chipped stone tools, but lithics must have a wider meaning referring to all stone artifacts, regardless of their forms, raw materials, or techniques of manufacture. Some archaeologists may also view lithics as a subject that begins and ends with flaked stone tools, and in an earlier paper I drew attention to a tendency to leave ground stone tools, cut and engraved stones, architectural elements, and many more categories of stone artifacts out of any definition of lithics (Runnels 1985). In my opinion, it is this narrowness of perspective which has been at the root of the neglect of lithics by regional archaeologists. A wider definition of lithics would allow archaeologists to expand their ability to reconstruct and explain the evidence for the human past. Such a definition would include stone artifacts that are not usually identified in excavations or published with other artifacts, and this would expand the number of materials useful for analysis. To cite examples of what can be gained by regarding lithics as more than chipped stone tools, we should include Pittinger's pioneering study of the surprising number and variety of rocks and minerals, such as alum, pumice, and sulphur, being extracted on an industrial scale from the island of Melos in the Roman period (Pittinger 1975), or Dworakowska's (1975) study of quarries for building stones in the Classical period. Although Pittinger's results were based chiefly on literary sources, and Dworakowska based her conclusions primarily on references to published quarries in the literature, these studies together demonstrate that the use of different rocks and lithic artifacts in ancient times was much greater than has been hitherto commonly accepted. It is also clear from these studies that in some periods prospecting, quarrying, and mining were undertaken on a large scale, and systematic efforts must be made to find the physical evidence for such activities in the archaeological record.

The limitations imposed by a narrow definition of the subject pale into insignificance, however, when we remember that analyses of lithic artifacts are often restricted to exercises in classification rather than to the broader study of the production, distribution, use, and discard of lithics. If the study of lithics was enlarged to include a variety of materials and processes usually treated as separate subjects, lithics could be used to expand existing approaches to include questions that go beyond the narrow ones of technological and economic activity to questions of a social or political nature. A good example that comes to mind of a study that has addressed technological and economic questions involving lithics is Torrence's analysis of the Melian obsidian quarries. In this pioneering study, Torrence studied the quarries in Melos that supplied sites throughout the Aegean during the Neolithic and Bronze Age with obsidian tools, chiefly in the form of fine pressure blades, in an attempt to determine whether the quarries had been controlled by specialist flintknappers as part of a developed commercial industry, or whether the quarries had been worked directly by consumers who came to the island in the course of other activities (Torrence 1986). Working entirely from literary and epigraphical evidence from a much later period, and on an entirely different problem, Wikander has demonstrated that there is evidence for the widespread use of watermills in the first two centuries of the Roman period. Previous studies contended that watermills became widespread only in the Late Roman period with the spread of Christianity and the decline of slavery (Wikander 1984), but Wikander's hypothesis has been confirmed by the discovery of early Roman watermills, mostly in the course of surface surveys (Wikander 1985). An interesting parallel study along entirely independent lines is represented by the identification of the sources for the raw materials for querns and mills in the Roman period by Thorpe and Williams-Thorpe. The chemical identification of the sources of Roman millstones in the Mediterranean has permitted them to reconstruct with a high degree of probability a complex and sometimes surprising picture of seaborne trade in the western Mediterranean, with the mills serving as ballast and cargo in empty grain ships returning to Africa from Italy (Williams-Thorpe 1988). This last study is especially important because the evidence is derived entirely from regional archaeological evidence, and this trade would be completely unknown if we were confined to the literary and epigraphical testimonia. The systematic study of the sources of stone for querns and mills has been widened to embrace the whole

Mediterranean from the Neolithic period to the end of Classical Antiquity (0. Williams-Thorpe, personal communication 1992), and the results of these studies will be of great importance.

What kinds of artifacts and materials should be included in an expanded definition of lithics? In Table 8.1, there are at least 13 different categories of archaeological lithics that are likely to be encountered in surveys and excavations. There are many interesting observations that could be made about these categories, but one striking feature is the widespread distribution of lithic categories in all time periods. To the best of my knowledge, the manufacture of ground stone cutting tools in the form of polished celts (unperforated axes and adzes) and shaft-hole axes, adzes, and battle axes, is the only category of lithics that belongs exclusively to one prehistoric period. The only artifacts that can be assigned exclusively to later historical periods are rotary querns and large rotary mills powered by animals, wind, or water. Apart from these two important exceptions, one category of stone tools or another may be said to occur in all, or at least the majority, of archaeological periods. To take one obvious example, flaked stone tools (the simple flakes produced by a single blow from a core) are found on the earliest Palaeolithic sites and in the modern threshing sledges and tinderboxes of traditional Greek life. In between these two chronological extremes, examples of utilitarian or decorative lithic artifacts stretch across the millennia, providing many potential data for all archaeologists.

Conclusions

The examples cited in passing above serve to indicate some of the ways that lithics may contribute significantly to the material record available for study on a regional scale. In closing, it is perhaps useful to speculate about some areas that have not yet been addressed systematically by lithic analysts, and to consider trends and future developments in the study of lithics.

The most useful connecting thread in lithic analyses is clearly the study of chronology. Stone artifacts appear to be indicators of chronology in the same way as are styles of decoration in pottery or changes in architectural orders. The durable nature of the raw materials along with the different forms of lithics make them easy to recognize

Table 8.1. Categories of Lithic Artifacts Found in the Mediterranean Area.

(1) Flaked tools of flint, obsidian, and other materials (includes cutting tools and a wide variety of other tools, e.g., tinderflints, threshing sledges, and gunflints).

(2) Axes, adzes, battle-axes, chisels, and other cutting tools shaped by pecking, grinding, polishing, and perforating hard rocks.

(3) Handstones used for abrading and percussion.

(4) Querns, which come in two major categories:
   a. saddle querns.
   b. rotary querns.

(5) Mills, which come in four major categories:
   a. large rotary grain mills.
   b. rotary millstones used in windmills and water-mills.
   c. large rotary mills for crushing olives.
   d. large rotary mills used for other industrial purposes, such as crushing salt.

(6) Mortars and Pestles.

(7) Pressing equipment for olives, grapes, and industrial materials.

(8) Vessels and palettes.

(9) Stones and minerals with magical, religious, and medicinal uses (e.g., quartz crystals, ochre, and alum).

(10) Cut stones or engraved stones used as parts of other artifacts or as sculptural or architectural elements (e.g., tesserae of mosaics, or loomweights).

(11) Architectural elements (cut stone, plaster, and cement).

(12) Ornamental stones (e.g., lapis lazuli, *lapis Lacedaemonius*, colored marble).

(13) Stones with other economic functions (e.g., molds for metallurgical use, fluxes, salt, and pigments).

and to date in the field. The wide distribution of querns, which are found in sites of all sizes and of all kinds, frequently occurring in dumps or built into later field walls or terraces, makes them especially valuable for Classical archaeologists.

In addition to their use for the dating of sites, lithics are useful indicators of the functions of sites or artifact scatters. One example will serve to illustrate the usefulness of even isolated lithic artifacts. In the course of the Berbati-Limnes regional survey in the Argolid carried out by members of the Swedish Institute, Neolithic stone tools, including ground stone celts, andesite saddle querns, and, most importantly, flint sickle elements, were discovered in tracts walked by survey teams on hillslopes and uplands in places where there is no longer any preserved soil. These artifacts were dated on typological grounds alone and are unassociated with any sites in the traditional sense, and in some cases they are not associated with any other cultural materials. These scattered finds provide valuable clues to the existence of prehistoric agricultural activities in areas that are unusable for agricultural production today, and these artifacts would not have been recovered in excavations or in the course of surveys that were directed chiefly towards the collection of datable potsherds (Wells et al. 1990:217-222).

The uses of lithics to which I have already drawn attention include the study of technological development and economic activities, including craft specialization, trade, and the many sides of production that can be reconstructed by finding the manufacturing sites of lithic artifacts and making detailed studies of the behavioral or structural features of production (chânes opératoires). There are many aspects of lithics, however, that have yet to attract serious study, but would provide evidence particularly beneficial for those engaged in regional studies. Among the topics awaiting future study I would include the processes by which stone tools become part of low density artifact scatters that are common in the Mediterranean landscape, and a related field of inquiry would be the ethnographic study of the general taphonomic processes by which lithics enter the archaeological record.

References Cited

Childe, V.G.
   1956 *Piecing Together The Past: The Interpretation of
      Archaeological Data.* Routledge and Kegan Paul, London.
Dworakowska, A.

1975 *Quarries in Ancient Greece.* Polish Academy of Sciences and the Institute of the History of Material Culture, Warsaw.

Durham, W.
1991 *Coevolution: Genes, Culture, and Human Diversity.* Stanford University Press, Stanford.

Kardulias, P.N., and C. Runnels
1994 The Lithic Artifacts. In *Artifact and Assemblage: The Finds from a Regional Survey of the Southern Argolid, Greece, Volume 1: The Prehistoric and Early Iron Age Pottery and the Lithic Artifacts,* edited by C. Runnels, D. Pullen, and S. Langdon. Stanford University Press, Stanford, in press.

Moritz, L.A.
1958 *Grain-Mills and Flour in Classical Antiquity.* Clarendon Press, Oxford.

Perlès, C.
1987 Les Industries du Néolithique 'Précéramique' de Grèce: Nouvelles Études, Nouvelles Interpretations. In *Archaeologia Interregionalis, Chipped Stone Industries of the Early Farming Cultures in Europe,* pp. 19-39. Warsaw University and Jagiellonian University, Cracow.

1990 L'Outillage de Pierre Taillée Néolithique en Grèce: Approvisionnement et Exploitation des Matières Premières. *Bulletin de Correspondence Hellénique* 114:1-42.

Pittinger, J.
1975 The Mineral Products of Melos in Antiquity and Their Identification. *Annual of the British School at Athens* 70:191-97.

Rosen, S.A.
1985 The Potentials of Lithic Analysis in the Historic Periods in Israel. *Mitekufat Haeven, Journal of the Israel Prehistoric Society* 18:37-43.

Runnels, C.
1981 *A Diachronic Study and Economic Analysis of Millstones from the Argolid, Greece.* Ph.D. dissertation, Indiana University. University Microfilms, Ann Arbor.

1982 Flaked-Stone Artifacts in Greece during the Historical Period. *Journal of Field Archaeology* 9:363-373.

1983 Lithic Artifacts from Surface Sites in the Mediterranean Area. In *Archaeological Survey in the Mediterranean Area,* edited by D.R. Keller and D.W. Rupp, pp. 143-48. BAR International Series 155. British Archaeological Reports, Oxford.

1985 Lithic Studies: Some Theoretical Considerations. *Lithic*

Technology 14:100-106.

1988 A Prehistoric Survey of Thessaly: New Light on the Greek Middle Palaeolithic. *Journal of Field Archaeology* 15:277-290.

1990 Rotary Querns in Greece. *Journal of Roman Archaeology* 3:147-154.

Torrence, R.

1986 *Production and Exchange of Stone Tools: Prehistoric Obsidian in the Aegean.* Cambridge University Press, Cambridge.

1991 The Chipped Stone. In *Landscape Archaeology as Long-Term History: Northern Keos in the Cycladic Islands from Earliest Settlement until Modern Times*, edited by J.F. Cherry, J.L. Davis, and E. Mantsourani, pp. 173-198. Institute of Archaeology, University of California, Los Angeles, Los Angeles.

Wells, B., C. Runnels, and E. Zangger

1990 The Berbati-Limnes Archaeological Survey. The 1988 Season. *Opuscula Atheniensia* 18:207-238.

Wikander, Ö.

1984 *Exploitation of Water-Power or Technological Stagnation? A Reappraisal of the Productive Forces in the Roman Empire.* Scripta Minora, Regiae Societatis Humaniorum Litterarum Lundensis, Studier utgivna av Kungl. Humanistiska Vetenskapssamfundet i Lund, 1983-84:3. CWK Gleerup, Lund.

1985 Archaeological Evidence for Early Water-Mills: an Interim Report. In *History of Technology*, edited by N. Smith, vol. 10, pp. 151-179. Mansell, London and New York.

Williams-Thorpe, 0.

1988 Provenancing and Archaeology of Roman Millstones from the Mediterranean Area. *Journal of Archaeological Science* 15:253-305.

IV.
SPECIALIZED STUDIES: FLORA, FAUNA, AND POPULATION STRUCTURE

Chapter 9

Palaeoethnobotany in Regional Perspective

Julie M. Hansen

Introduction

Palaeoethnobotanical studies use a variety of techniques to collect remains of plants from archaeological sites or from surrounding landscapes in order to address diverse questions about how people and plants interacted in the past. The remains involved in palaeoethnobotany include pollen, phytoliths, seeds, fruit, wood, plant impressions, and the chemical remains of plants. When brought together in a regional approach to understanding past human-plant interaction, these studies can provide valuable insight into, for example, the adaptation of people to changing environmental conditions, development and implementation of new subsistence practices, influxes of new peoples, or trade in exotic goods. In this chapter I will examine some of the important palaeoethnobotanical studies carried out in Greece that permit a discussion of the human-plant interrelationships through time in a regional perspective.

The Evidence by Period

Human presence in Greece is known from the Lower Palaeolithic (ca. 250,000 B.P.) onward. Although there are no botanical data from pollen studies or other sources for the earliest periods of occupation,

it is possible to discuss potential plant resources available from the
Middle Palaeolithic (125,000-30,000 B.P.). Sytze Bottema (1980; this
volume) has provided a detailed summary of the vegetation changes in
Greece from 15,000 B.P. to recent times based on nearly 30 pollen
cores from the mainland and Crete. It is against this backdrop that the
more site-specific palaeoethnobotanical studies of macroscopic plant
remains should be placed in order to understand the range of possible
options available and choices made by the inhabitants of Greece through
the prehistoric and early historic periods. The relationship between the
regional and site-specific studies, however, has rarely been explored to
its fullest extent. A brief overview of the types of palaeoethnobotanical
studies published to date will provide a basis for discussion of what
regional studies have been or could be done.

Pollen data are available from before 125,000 B.P. at the site of
Khimaditis IV (Bottema 1974). The lowest two zones, L and M,
indicate steppic vegetation at low elevations, with pine at higher
elevations. These zones are equated with the Riss Glacial period in
Europe and span some part of the late Lower Palaeolithic. In Greece,
this period is represented by finds in Epiros (Runnels and van Andel
1993a) and Thessaly (Runnels 1988; Runnels and van Andel 1993b).
I will discuss the potential botanical resources in this type of
environment below.

The Middle Palaeolithic (125,000-30,000 B.P.) is better represented
in Greece than the earlier period, although the earliest finds seem to
date to not more than 60,000 B.P., suggesting that there may be a
hiatus in occupation between the Lower and Middle Palaeolithic
(Runnels 1988). The palynological evidence available stretches back to
at least 125,000 B.P. at Khimaditis IV (Zone O) and perhaps to
sometime before 75,000 B.P. at Lake Ioannina I in Epiros (Zones N
and O; Bottema 1974) and Tenagi Philippon (Zone Q) in Macedonia
(Wijmstra 1969) . All of these areas were forested; Khimaditis with
deciduous oak, hornbeam, elm, and hazel at lower elevations and pine
and fir forest above; Ioannina with fir forest initially at 500 m and
above, changing to deciduous oak with hornbeam, ash, elm, and hazel;
and Tenagi Philippon with an oak forest changing gradually to more
open oak/pine woodland. Bottema (1974:91) relates these zones to the
Eem interglacial of Europe, a warm period with cool winters and
summers wetter than today. Among the resources available during this
period would have been the nuts of the oak and hazel, and the edible
sweet sap from the ash, in addition to a variety of herbaceous plants
including grasses and *Chenopodium*, at least at Khimaditis and

Ioannina. Unfortunately, there are as yet no secure archaeological data to indicate any occupation at these sites during this time.

At the time that Middle Palaeolithic hunter/gatherers were occupying various areas in Greece the palynological data indicate fluctuating periods of steppe, forest steppe, and forest. Pollen data from Tenagi Philippon, Ioannina, and Xinias in Thessaly (Bottema 1979) have spectra that cover the time period 60,000-30,000 B.P. In the area of Lake Ioannina, vegetation fluctuated between a steppe and steppe forest in the earlier stages of the period (closer to 75,000 B.P.), to forest by ca. 50,000 B.P. (Zone S). Within the basin Bottema suggests that open vegetation, including *Artemesia, Chenopodium,* and grasses, would have been found with scattered oaks and junipers forming a steppe forest. "At higher elevations, trees would have formed the closed deciduous forests" with oak, elm, lime, maple, and hazel (Bottema 1974:99).

During the initial Middle Palaeolithic occupation of Asprochaliko in Epiros the area would have been forested, at least around the Ioannina Basin at 470 m above sea level (masl), with fir dominant from elevations of 500 m and above. Below would have been more open vegetation down to the coast. The sea level at this time would have been about 35 or 40 m lower than today (Shackleton et al. 1984). The island of Corfu would have been attached to the mainland and the southern coast of Epiros would have been somewhat wider than today. It is probable that the Asprochaliko inhabitants would have been able to exploit not only some of the herbaceous species available in the steppe, but perhaps some arboreal resources in the form of acorns or hazel nuts in refugia along rivers and protected areas with greater moisture.

It is interesting that during this time of fluctuating vegetation, there should be greater evidence of human occupation. The less dense forests, areas of open herbaceous vegetation, and frequent ecotones between forest and steppe would have provided rich and varied plant and animal resources. Although none of the excavated sites that date to this period, such as Asprochaliko and Kokkinopilos in Epiros, have yielded any evidence of macroscopic plant remains, we can get an idea of the type of resources available to them from the pollen data at Ioannina. The steppe and steppe forest vegetation at low altitudes (0-500 masl) would have provided a variety of edible grasses, including various wild cereals, as well as legumes and *Chenopodium.* Along the rivers and lake edges, tubers of sedges or rushes might have been exploited (Hillman et al. 1989; Hillman 1989) while in protected refugia trees such as oak or hazel may have survived and provided protein and fats from their nuts.

The Upper Palaeolithic, 30,000-10,000 B.P., corresponds to the Pleniglacial and Late Glacial periods when vegetation in most of Greece was composed largely of steppe, with forest of pine, fir, or deciduous species only at high elevations or lowland refugia along rivers where moisture was sufficient (Bottema this volume). Recent palynological studies (Willis 1992a, 1992b, 1992c), although they extend back only to about 12,000 B.P., suggest that the rapid spread of forest at the end of the Pleistocene indicates that deciduous trees such as oak existed in the vicinity during the pleniglacial.

There are no palynological data available from the Peloponnesos that can be correlated with the Upper Palaeolithic occupation of Franchthi Cave. The macroscopic remains from the cave dating from before 25,000 to about 13,000 B.P. consist only of species of Boraginaceae which are steppic plants the seeds of which most likely blew into the cave or were deposited by animals, but can tell us nothing about plant exploitation by humans during this period (Hansen 1991). The remains of wood charcoal from these deposits consist almost entirely of juniper which may have been growing on the slopes of the Fourni valley or in protected areas. It is not until the Late Glacial period that carbonized plant remains begin to appear at Franchthi Cave. The earliest of these are dated to about 13,000 B.P. and consist of lentils, almonds and pistachios, suggesting that the climate had ameliorated to some extent with at least warmer temperatures and possibly moister conditions. Wild lentils typically grow on rocky or gravelly, shallow soils in open habitats so their presence at this period suggests that the area around Franchthi Cave still had a fairly open vegetation cover. The appearance of wild oats and barley by about 11,000 B.P. is a further indication that the vegetation of this area of the southern Argolid retained its open nature.

Steppe is composed predominantly of herbaceous vegetation, usually dominated by *Chenopodium* and *Artemesia* in the Pleistocene Eastern Mediterranean. While steppic vegetation may not appear to offer much in the way of botanical resources for human use, Hillman et al. (1989) have shown from their studies of the Mesolithic plant remains from Abu Hureyra in northern Syria, that there are often a wide variety of species that make up the steppe and many of these have edible, or otherwise useful, parts. In addition to *Chenopodium*, the leaves and seeds of which are edible, various grasses such as brome grass (*Bromus* sp.), ryegrass (*Lolium* sp.) and small seeded barely would have been available in the dry steppe. Along the rivers or lake edges tubers from sedges or rushes could have been gathered. The steppe also had species of Atriplex (e.g., *A. hortensis* = Mountain Spinach) that has edible seeds and leaves. *Artemesia* leaves can be used for a wide variety of medicinal purposes. The Gramineae species, noted on all of the Late Glacial diagrams, would have included many grasses with edible seeds. Cereal-type pollen is also identified and this could have included, for example, wild species of barley, rye, or oats that would have been edible. Several sites in Epiros dating to the Middle and Upper Palaeolithic have been excavated (Klithi, Asprochaliko, Kastritsa), although none of them has produced any macroscopic plant remains. We must not assume from this, however, that they would not have been exploiting some of the vegetational resources both for food and other uses during this time. In the steppe, the above-named species could have been collected, while in refugia in the higher altitudes species of hazel and oak would have supplied vegetable fats and protein to the diet. The kind of mosaic vegetation that the Mesolithic inhabitants of Abu Hureyra exploited may have been more similar to the environment around Ioannina during the Middle rather than the Upper Palaeolithic during the Pleniglacial, but some of the same species could have survived.

The Mesolithic period (10,000-8000 B.P.) corresponds to the early Postglacial which is represented in a number of pollen diagrams in Northern and Central Greece (Bottema this volume). Macroscopic remains for this period, like the Upper Palaeolithic, come only from the Southern Argolid site of Franchthi Cave, however, where there are no palynological data with which to correlate them. Throughout those areas where pollen data are available the climatic amelioration, warmer moister conditions in general, are characterized by expansion of predominantly oak forest. The type of forest, the time of its spread, and the density of forest differ from one area to another and were dependent on factors such as precipitation and temperature changes. In general, throughout Greece where the data are available the vegetational changes taking place between 13,000 and 10,000/9000 B.P. indicate an increase in available moisture, probably from an increase in precipitation, as well as an increase in temperature. We are still at a loss to connect much of these data to actual human habitation for most of Greece, however. No Mesolithic sites have been identified in Thessaly or Macedonia as yet, and those areas of southern Greece where Mesolithic sites have been identified have not provided any pollen data. Nor have most of the Mesolithic sites been excavated. The macroscopic plant remains from Franchthi Cave suggest that the Southern Argolid provided at least an open woodland vegetation by about 11,000 B.P. as indicated by the availability of pistachios, almonds, pears, and legumes such as lentils, while more open areas provided resources such as wild oats and barley.

For the Neolithic and Bronze Ages, several palynological studies can be more or less directly related to specific archaeological sites such as Giannitsa in Macedonia (Bottema 1974) near the Neolithic site of Nea Nikomedeia; Tenagi Philippon in the Plain of Drama, Macedonia (Greig and Turner 1974; Wijmstra 1969) that is relevant to the sites of Dikili Tash and Sitagroi; Kopaïs (Turner and Greig 1975) in Boeotia that covers the Bronze Age when sites such as Gla and Orchomenos flourished; Osmonaga Lagoon (Wright 1972) in Messenia near the Bronze Age palace of Pylos; and Kiladha Bay (Bottema 1990) that covers most of the Neolithic during which Franchthi Cave was occupied. The other cores that have been taken are not closely associated with any excavated sites, although many sites do exist in the region of the cores, especially those in Thessaly and Macedonia. Neolithic sites provide the opportunity to supplement the palynological data for regional vegetation with the macroscopic plant remains recovered from excavated contexts.

Figure 9.1 shows the number of sites per period from the Upper Palaeolithic through the Byzantine era that have yielded plant remains and Figure 9.2 shows the location of these sites in Greece. The data are drawn primarily from published site reports with palaeoethnobotanical studies, or from separate specialist reports, and do not include every mention of a chance seed found during excavations. The total number of sites represented here is 45. The Late Neolithic (16 sites) and the Late Bronze Age (16 sites) provide the bulk of data on macroscopic plant remains in Greece, while a number of periods are represented by only one or two sites with plant remains. The inconsistency in these data make it difficult to compare the palaeoethnobotany of one period with another. Some general conclusions can be drawn, however.

During the Neolithic the large number of villages in Thessaly would suggest a fairly large population of people with an agricultural subsistence base. Analysis of plant remains from several of these Neolithic sites confirms the presence of the Near Eastern assemblage of emmer and einkorn wheat, barley, lentils, peas, and vetch, along with sheep and goat from the earliest Neolithic occupation around 6500 B.C. The Neolithic assemblage of plant remains from Franchthi Cave is typical of those found throughout Greece for this period and provides

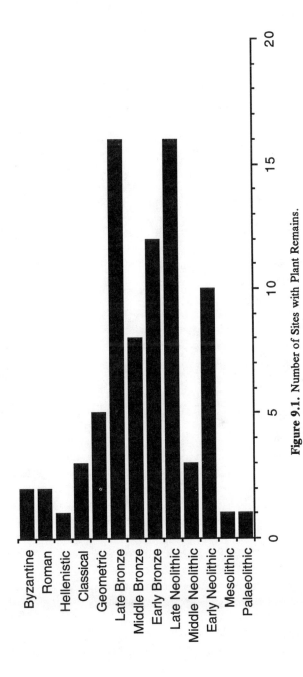

Figure 9.1. Number of Sites with Plant Remains.

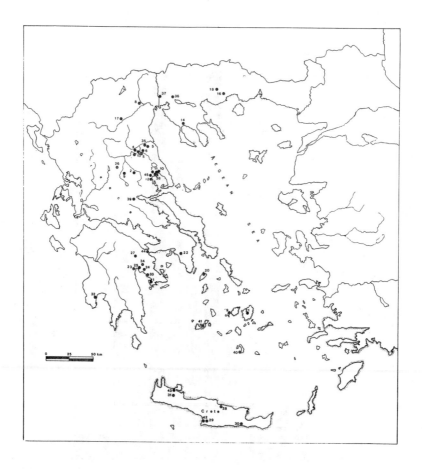

Figure 9.2. Aegean sites with plant remains.

Site #	Site Name	Periods Represented
1	Franchthi Cave	UP, M, EN, MN, LN, FN
2	Achillcion	EN
3	Argissa Magoula	AN/EN, EB, MB
4	Otzaki Magoula	EN, MN
5	Soufli Magoula	AN/EN
6	Gediki	AN/EN
7	Sesklo	AN.EN, MN, LN
8	Nea Nikomedeia	EN/MN
9	Prodromos	EN
10	Pefkakia	LN, EB, MB
11	Dimini	LN
12	Pyrassos	LN
13	Arapi Magoula	LN
14	Olynthus	LN
15	Rachmani	LN
16	Dikili Tash	LN
17	Servia	LN
18	Sitagroi	LN
19	Saliagos	LN, FN
20	Kephala	LN, FN
21	Naxos (Zas Cave)	LN, FN, EB
22	Athens (Agora)	LN, MB, LB, G, B
23	Lerna	LN, EB, MB, C
24	Synoro	EB
25	Tiryns	EB, LB, SM
26	Tsani	EB
27	Tsoungiza	EB, MB, LB
28	Knossos	EN, MB, LB
29	Phaistos	EB
30	Myrtos	EB
31	Debla	EB
32	Nichoria	MB, LB, PG, G, C, B
33	Iria	LB
34	Dendra	LB
35	Marmariani	LB
36	Assiros	MB, LB
37	Kastanas	EB, LB, G, A/C
38	Iolkos	LB, PG, G
39	Kalapodi	LB, G, R
40	Thera	LB
41	Melos	LB
42	Aghia Triadha	LB
43	Chania	LB
44	Isthmia	H
45	Demetrias	R

Abbreviations: UP = Upper Palaeolithic, M = Mesolihthic, AN = Aceramic Neolithic, EN = Early Neolithic, MN = Middle Neolithic, LN = Late Neolithic, FN = Final Neolithic, EB = Early Bronze (=Early Helladic, Early Cycladic, Early Minoan), MB = Middle Bronze (=Middle Helladic, Middle Cycladic, Middle Minoan), LB = Late Bronze (=Late Helladic, Late Cycladic, Late Minoan), SM = Sub-Mycenaean, PG = Proto-Geometric, G = Geometric, A = Archaic, C = Classical, H = Hellenistic, R = Roman, B = Byzantine

Key to Figure 9.2: Aegean sites with plant remains.

an opportunity to compare the Mesolithic hunter/gatherer plant exploitation pattern with that of early Neolithic farmers. One change that can be seen is the decrease in wild pistachio, almond, and pear in the Neolithic levels. This may be the consequence of taphonomic differences resulting from changes in how the cave was used between the two periods, but it is also possible that exploitation of wild plants in the Neolithic was less common. Wild plant species may have been reduced in number in the landscape through land clearance for fields, or simply ignored in favor of crop species.

In addition to Franchthi Cave, many Thessalian sites have yielded plant remains from the Neolithic period, to the extent that we may now begin to draw some general conclusions about the palaeoethnobotany of that region. The important sites of Sesklo, Pyrasos, Rachmani, Dimini, Achilleion, Soufli, and Ghediki are discussed by Jane Renfrew (1966) and several conclusions about the early appearance and development of agriculture in this part of Greece are proposed. One conclusion that she draws is that barley became a more important crop than wheat in the late Neolithic and Bronze Age. Unfortunately, the small amount of material she had to work with and the lack of contextual information to ascertain whether these remains were crops in their own right, part of a mixed cropping system, or weeds in the fields of other crops, makes it difficult to be certain of these conclusions. Recently, more material has been collected and published by Helmut Kroll (1979, 1981) for Sesklo, Dimini, and Argissa, as well as previously unreported sites such as Pefkakia, Otzaki, and Arapi. As a result, we now have a fairly good idea of the probable types of crops grown and some of the wild plants available from the Early Neolithic through the Late Neolithic in Thessaly. The new material recorded by Kroll (1981), however, was collected from scarps of previous excavations and may not be representative of the full range of plants exploited or available. In addition, no contextual information is available for these remains, so it is not possible to ascertain what they represent in terms of the agricultural system; nor is it possible to compare these remains with those from other sites because comparable contexts may not be represented. A storage context full of emmer wheat crops cannot be compared to a rubbish pit containing the cleanings from a crop.

If we examine the types of plants represented in each period, it is interesting to note that the number of legume species increases in the Late Neolithic. Whether this is an artifact of excavation, i.e., more sites with plant remains produce more legumes, or truly represents an increase in the types of plants utilized is unclear at this point. Nonetheless, the correlation of the appearance of certain toxic species such as fava beans (*Vicia faba*) and chickling vetch (*Lathyrus* spp.) with the apparent increase in evidence for cooking vessels (Vitelli 1993) is intriguing. This problem is discussed in detail elsewhere (Hansen 1994). It should be noted here, however, that it is just this type of problem that could be addressed with consistent, systematic collection of plant remains from every site that is excavated.

Among the other questions we would like to address for each site, as well as for a region, are the type of cropping system used, the length of fallow, if any, and the specific areas around the site or throughout the region that were planted. How much land clearance, for example, was done during the Neolithic and was this predominantly done early on as the area was being settled, or did it take place primarily in the Late Neolithic as population expanded and more agricultural land was required? Some help may come from pollen studies done in Thessaly, but these are not fine-tuned enough to answer such questions on a small scale and it is not always obvious from the pollen data whether the decrease in arboreal species is the result of land clearance, climatic fluctuation, or some other factor.

In most of the Greek pollen diagrams covering the Neolithic period it is not possible to associate directly vegetational changes with specific agricultural practices [Bottema 1982 (1985):282; Bottema and Woldring 1990]. Among the important cultural indicators are cereal types, including crop plants such as emmer wheat or barley, but these could also represent wild cereals such as wild barley, goat grass (*Triticum aegilopoides*) or wild rye (*Secale montanum*), all of which are present in the Late Pleistocene as well. Another critical type is plantain (*Plantago lanceolata* type). In northern Greek diagrams such as those from Edessa, Khimaditis I and III, and Giannitsa this type begins to show up around 8000 B.P. and may be correlated with the spread of agriculture into Thessaly at this time. In the south, however, the data are inconclusive because plantain occurs in the Pleistocene levels of the diagrams as part of the natural vegetation. Other species, such as asphodel, may be indicators of naturally open vegetation or the result of overgrazing [Bottema 1982 (1985):282]. Many of the other species that are potential indicators of human activity do not occur in significant quantity to allow any definite conclusions to be drawn. Thus, Bottema [1982 (1985):284] concludes that it is not possible to trace the beginning of farming in Greece through palynological data.

The macroscopic plant remains from a site can help answer these questions, provided the remains are systematically collected from securely identified contexts, and that similar contexts are compared through time to allow a discussion of probable changes in plant use, areas exploited, etc. For example, Glynis Jones (1981, 1987; Jones et al. 1986) has begun the analysis of the massive quantity of plant remains from the Late Bronze Age component at Assiros in Macedonia. Because of the careful method of excavation and systematic recovery of the carbonized remains from several rooms in a structure she was able to conclude that these were the remains of at least seven stored crops (*Triticum monococcum, T. dicoccum, T. spelta, T. aestivum/durum, Hordeum vulgare, Panicum miliaceum, Vicia ervilia*) in various stages of processing. The einkorn, millet and bitter vetch were shown to have been stored separately and were, therefore, most likely grown as separate crops. Among the other plants, bread/macaroni wheat and barley were probably crops in their own right, while the consistent appearance of emmer wheat with spelt wheat suggests that they were grown together. The distribution of crops within the rooms, certain species in one room with other species in the other rooms, as well as the estimated capacity lead to the conclusion that these facilities were communal storage rather than the storerooms of a single household. This conclusion leads to the consideration of the relationship of Assiros to the surrounding region. To what extent were the crops in these storerooms redistributed only within the village of Assiros, and to what extent did they travel beyond the site? Were all of the identified crops grown by the people living at Assiros, or do they represent produce paid into the central store from the region?

By examining the weed assemblage associated with the crops, Jones (1992) was able to suggest that garden cultivation rather than field cultivation was more common at this site. The range of crops grown, each with different edaphic requirements, and different sowing and harvesting times, suggests that the inhabitants of Assiros were ensuring some return even in bad years, and spreading the work load over much of the year (Halstead 1989). Perhaps such an intensive garden system was sufficient to produce the surplus necessary to allow, or perhaps require, communal storage for the village. Further analysis will undoubtedly provide answers to many other questions about the nature of the agricultural system at this important site.

The question of the origins of olive and grape cultivation in Greece has been addressed elsewhere (Runnels and Hansen 1986; Hansen 1988) and will be briefly summarized here. The macroscopic plant remains and pollen data from Greece do not yet provide positive evidence for the large scale exploitation or cultivation of olives prior to the Late Bronze Age. The primary problem in understanding the development (or introduction) of domesticated olives and olive cultivation is the fact that it is not possible to distinguish on morphological grounds between a wild and a domesticated olive. Wild olives, however, grow fairly sparsely in the landscape and it would be more difficult to collect massive quantities of them than it would be if they were cultivated in groves. Therefore, a case for cultivation of olives can best be made on the basis of the presence of either massive quantities of plant remains, or substantial processing implements and features, such as presses and storage facilities. These types of evidence, together with written texts and pollen data, most strongly point to a Late Bronze Age development of olive cultivation.

Olive oil, from both wild and domesticated trees, is mentioned in the Linear B texts (see Melena 1983 for an overview of these data) but the information is insufficient to establish a per capita consumption rate. Historical texts verify the importance of the olive and the export of olive oil (Boardman 1976), and it is assumed that olives and olive oil played an important role in the diet by this time. Aschenbrenner (1972:59) noted that the per capita consumption of olive oil in the village of Karpafora, Messenia in 1969 was between 35 and 125 kg. Once olives were made palatable by pickling and could be pressed efficiently to make oil it is probable that these resources were utilized on a daily basis by the people of Greece. Evidence available so far suggests that the latter did not happen until the Late Bronze Age; while the former may have occurred earlier, no evidence is forthcoming.

Grapes, on the other hand, may have been cultivated by the Middle Bronze Age, at least in Macedonia. The primary evidence for grape cultivation has usually been the morphological changes in size and shape of the seed, but studies have shown (Hopf 1964; Kroll 1983) that there is a significant overlap in the dimensions of wild and domesticated grape seeds and little clear demarcation in the sizes within large populations of archaeological specimens. Nonetheless, the quantity of remains found in Middle Bronze Age levels at sites such as Lerna, outside the current geographical distribution of the wild grape, may suggest some form of manipulation at that time. The best evidence for domesticated grapes, based on quantity of remains as well as size changes, comes from Late Bronze Age Kastanas (Kroll 1983), which lies within the range of the natural distribution of wild grapes. Grapes probably played a relatively insignificant role in the diet until wine was initially produced. When this may have taken place is as yet unknown, but it certainly happened by the Late Bronze Age.

The role that grapes and olives, or any other plant for which we have archaeological evidence, played in the diet of ancient peoples of Greece is impossible to determine with any certainty using botanical remains alone. Ubiquity, the appearance of the species throughout a site in relatively high quantities and throughout deposits in many sites of a region, would indicate that the plant in question played a significant role in the culture concerned. The presence of associated artifacts such as (in the case of olives or grapes) presses, storage vessels, and the residues from those vessels, would also provide more certain evidence of the importance of these plants. Ethnographic evidence and historical texts can also provide some information but should be used with caution since there is no reason to assume that prehistoric peoples utilized the plants in the same ways as historic or present populations.

Conclusion

As already noted, with appropriate botanical data it is possible to identify the type of agricultural system on a given site. This can be translated to similar sites within the same geographic and ecological area and thus a picture of the regional agricultural system, including seasonal calendars, fallowing systems, and irrigation practices can be provided. This broader perspective can then begin to provide answers to regional questions, such as the nature of the subsistence system within a specific period or diachronically. Because of the diversity of regional environments in Greece it is to be expected that subsistence systems would differ to some extent. Macedonia, for example, could not rely on olive oil production and export, while the Cyclades could not have produced sufficient wheat to export. Trade relations among the different regions of mainland Greece, the Cyclades, and Crete must have, to some extent, depended on the control of certain agricultural products such as oil, wine, and wheat. These commodities would have played an important role in the overall economic systems that included, at least since the Bronze Age, trade in ceramics, textiles, and metals. The rise and fall of these economic systems would surely have been tied to some extent to the uncertainties of agricultural production on a regional scale; the demise of civilizations such the Mycenaean may have been linked, in part, to poor production in some areas.

Neither the palynological data nor the macroscopic remains alone can give us the range of information that we require in order to address these and other questions posed in this paper, but a combination of these two lines of inquiry can bring us closer to an answer. A great deal more data are needed, however, to be able to address many of the questions about prehistoric society that we wish to ask. It is imperative that *all* projects at all sites adopt a regular, systematic approach to plant collection from the very start of excavation. It is only in conjunction with comparable bodies of data in the form of macroscopic remains that we can begin to put together accurate, local, site-by-site pictures, which, in turn, can be combined with palynological data to provide a regional perspective on the interrelationship between people and plants in Greece.

References Cited

Aschenbrenner, S.
  1972 A Contemporary Community. In *The Minnesota Messenia Expedition: Reconstructing a Bronze Age Regional Environment*, edited by W.A. McDonald and G.R. Rapp, Jr., pp. 47-63. University of Minnesota Press, Minneapolis.
Boardman, J.
  1976 The Olive in the Mediterranean: Its Culture and Use. *Philosophical Transactions of the Royal Society, London* 275:187-196.
Bottema, S.
  1974 *Late Quaternary Vegetation History of Northwestern Greece.* Ph.D. dissertation, University of Groningen, Groningen.
  1979 Pollen Analytical Investigations in Thessaly (Greece). *Palaeohistoria* 21:19-40.
  1980 Palynological Investigations on Crete. *Review of Palaeobotany and Palynology* 31:193-217.
  1982 (1985) Palynological Investigations in Greece with Special Reference to Pollen as an Indicator of Human Activity. *Palaeohistoria* 24:257-289.
  1990 Holocene Environment of the Southern Argolid: A Pollen Core from Kiladha Bay. In *Franchthi Paralia: The Sediments, Stratigraphy, and Offshore Investigations*, edited by T.J. Wilkinson and S.T. Duhon, pp. 117-138. Excavations at Franchthi Cave, Greece, Fascicle 6. Indiana University Press, Bloomington.
Bottema, S., and H. Woldring
  1990 Anthropogenic Indicators in the Pollen Record of the Eastern Mediterranean. In *Man's Role in the Shaping of the Eastern Mediterranean Landscape*, edited by S. Bottema, G.

Entjes-Nieborg and W. van Zeist, pp. 231-264. Balkema, Rotterdam.

Greig, J., and J. Turner
1974 Some Pollen Diagrams from Greece and their Archaeological Significance. *Journal of Archaeological Science* 1:177-194.

Halstead, P.
1989 The Economy Has a Normal Surplus: Economic Stability and Social Change among Early Farming Communities of Thessaly, Greece. In *Bad Year Economics*, edited by P. Halstead and J. O'Shea, pp. 68-80. Cambridge University Press, Cambridge.

Hansen, J.M.
1988 Agriculture in the Prehistoric Aegean: Data versus Speculation. *American Journal of Archaeology* 92:39-92.
1991 *The Palaeoethnobotany of Franchthi Cave.* Excavations at Franchthi Cave, Greece, Fascicle 7. Indiana University Press, Bloomington.
1994 Palaeoethnobotany and Palaeodiet in the Aegean Region. In *Aspects of Palaeodiet in the Aegean*, edited by S. Vaughan and W. Coulson. Weiner Laboratory Monographs in Archaeometry, vol. 1. Oxbow, forthcoming.

Hillman, G.C.
1989 Late Palaeolithic Plant Foods from Wadi Kubbaniya in Upper Egypt: Dietary Diversity, Infant Weaning, and Seasonality in a Riverine Environment. In *Foraging and Farming: The Evolution of Plant Exploitation*, edited by D.R. Harris and G.C. Hillman, pp. 207-239. Unwin and Hyman, London.

Hillman, G.C., S.M. Colledge, and D.R. Harris
1989 Plant-Food Economy During the Epipalaeolithic Period at Tell Abu Hureyra, Syria: Dietary Diversity, Seasonality, and Modes of Exploitation. In *Foraging and Farming: The Evolution of Plant Exploitation*, edited by D.R. Harris and G.C. Hillman, pp. 240-268. Unwin and Hyman, London.

Hopf, M.
1964 Nutzpflanzen vom Lernäischen Golf. *Jahrbuch des Romisch-Germanischen Zentralmuseums* 11:1-19.

Jones, G.
1981 Crop Processing at Assiros Toumba--A Taphonomic Study. *Zeitschrift für Archäologie* 15:105-111.
1987 A Statistical Approach to the Archaeological Identification of Crop Processing. *Journal of Archaeological Science* 14:311-323.
1992 Weed Phytosociology and Crop Husbandry: Identifying a

Contrast between Ancient and Modern Practice. *Review of Palaeobotany and Palynology* 73:133-143.
Jones, G., K. Wardle, P. Halstead, and D. Wardle
1986 Crop Storage at Assiros. *Scientific American* 254:3:96-103.
Kroll, H.
1979 Kulturpflanzen aus Dimini. In *Festschrift Maria Hopf*, edited by U. Körber-Grohne, pp. 173-189. Rheinland-Verlag GMBH, Köln.
1981 Thessalische Kulturpflanzen. *Zeitschrift für Archäologie* 15:97-103.
1983 *Kastanas: Ausgrabungen in einem Siedlungshügel der Bronze-und eisenzeit Makedoniens 1975-1979: Die Pflanzenfunde.* Prähistorische Archäologie in Südosteuropa Band 2, Vorlag Volker Spiess, Berlin.
Melena, J.
1983 Olive Oil and Other Sorts of Oil in the Mycenaean Tablets. *Minos* 18:89-123.
Renfrew, J.M.
1966 A Report on Recent Finds of Carbonized Cereal Grains and Seeds from Prehistoric Thessaly. Θεσσαλικά 5:21-36.
Runnels, C.N.
1988 A Prehistoric Survey of Thessaly: New Light on the Greek Middle Paleolithic. *Journal of Field Archaeology* 15:277-290.
Runnels, C. N., and J. M. Hansen
1986 The Olive in the Prehistoric Aegean: The Evidence for Domestication in the Early Bronze Age. *Oxford Journal of Archaeology* 5:299-307.
Runnels, C.N., and T.H. van Andel
1993a A Handaxe from Kokkinopilos, Epirus, and Its Implications for the Paleolithic of Greece. *Journal of Field Archaeology* 20:191-203.
1993b The Lower and Middle Paleolithic of Thessaly, Greece. *Journal of Field Archaeology* 20:299-317.
Shackleton, J.C., T.H. van Andel, and C.N. Runnels
1984 Coastal Paleogeography of the Central and Western Mediterranean during the Last 125,000 Years and Its Archaeological Implications. *Journal of Field Archaeology* 11:307-314.
Turner, J., and J. Grieg
1975 Some Holocene Pollen Diagrams from Greece. *Review of Palaeobotany and Palynology* 20:171-204.

Vitelli, K.D.
  1993 *Franchthi Neolithic Pottery: Volume 1. Classification and Ceramic Phases 1 and 2.* Excavations at Franchthi Cave, Greece, Fascicle 8. Indiana University Press, Bloomington.
Wijmstra, T.A.
  1969 Palynology of the First 30 m of a 100 m Deep Section in Philippi, Northern Greece. *Acta Botanica Neerlandica* 18:511-527.
Willis, K.J.
  1992a The late Quaternary Vegetational History of Northwest Greece. I. Lake Gramousti. *New Phytologist* 121:101-117.
  1992b The Late Quaternary Vegetational History of Northwest Greece. II. Rezina marsh. *New Phytologist* 121:119-138.
  1992c The late Quaternary Vegetational History of Northwest Greece. III. A Comparative Study of Two Contrasting Sites. *New Phytologist* 121:139-155.
Wright, H.E., Jr.
  1972 Vegetation History. In *The Minnesota Messenia Expedition: Reconstructing a Bronze Age Regional Environment*, edited by W.A. McDonald and G.R. Rapp, Jr., pp. 188-199. University of Minnesota Press, Minneapolis.

Chapter 10

Recent Work in Greek Zooarchaeology

David S. Reese

Introduction

In 1985 Sebastian Payne published his "Zooarchaeology in Greece: A Reader's Guide," providing a major service to those interested in Greek zooarchaeology. It has recently been translated into Japanese (Uzawa et al. 1993). His paper included a bibliography of animal bone reports published through 1983; it did not include references on invertebrate remains.

Here I update Payne's bibliography, listing several bone reports not recorded by him, papers published after 1983, articles dealing with invertebrates, and reports on relevant textual and iconographic evidence. The present paper should be used in conjunction with Payne's article; I do not duplicate his bibliographic references unless the article is specifically referred to here.

The first bone studies performed by zoologists in the Aegean were done for H. Schliemann on his material from Troy (Schliemann 1880:114-116, 317-323, 431-32). The first such study actually published by a zoologist was on about 50 bones from the 1901 excavation in the Late Minoan III and Early Iron Age Dictaean cave on Crete excavated by D.H. Hogarth and studied by W. Boyd-Dawkins (1902). The record of zoological study is then rather spotty until the mid-1950s when the late J. Boessneck began his work on the fauna from Neolithic sites in Thessaly.

Most of the published research (i.e., more than one published paper as of the time of writing [March 1994]). on animal bones from Greek sites has been done by the British (Bedwin, Coy, Gamble, Halstead, Jarman, Jones, Payne), the Germans (Becker, Boessneck, von den Driesch, Nobis), and the Americans (Klippel, Reese, Schwartz, Snyder). Several other individuals have also made significant contributions: Bökönyi (Hungarian), Gejvall (Swedish), Jullien (French), and Trantalidou (Greek). Other individuals have specialized in certain animal types or products--birds (Mourer-Chauviré), fish (Rose), and ivory (Krzyszkowska). For shells, most of the work has been by Chevallier, Karali-Yannacopoulou, Reese, N.J. Shackleton and J.C. Shackleton, and Tsuneki. Supporting work comes from textual research (Godart, Jameson, Killen, Palaima, Raulwing, van Straten, Young) and artifact studies (Cline, Gill, Guest-Papamanoli, Karali-Yannacopoulou, Porter, Vanschoonwinkel).

Most faunal analyses have been performed on Neolithic and Bronze Age remains, particularly Neolithic Thessaly and the Bronze Age in the Argolid and on Crete. Here I shall focus on the fauna from Iron Age and later sites in Greece (and Aegean Turkey).

For many years faunal remains were not actively collected from historic Greek sites, so the record is quite poor. Where they have been collected, the samples differ as to size because of the number of years of excavation, the number of years of study of the fauna (some reports are only on part of the sample excavated), and because of the recovery methods used (hand-collection, dry-sieving, water-sieving, flotation).

Faunal remains have not generally been collected on surface surveys as it is usually impossible to determine accurately the date of the bone or shells. There are a few cases where concentrations of crushed *Murex trunculus* shells have been found on the surface, and are considered to be good evidence for shell purple-dye production at the site as some time in the past (Reese 1987d, ms.e).

Table 10.1 is a listing of the post-Bronze Age sites known to me which have fauna published or under study. It is arranged geographically and then alphabetically by site. For completeness, it also includes sites with similarly dated fauna (ca. 1000 B.C. to ca. A.D. 1300) from the Aegean coast of Turkey. Many of the Greek sites were excavated to uncover their pre-Iron Age components, with the later material being of much less interest (i.e., Lerna, Midea, Tiryns, Asine, Agios Stephanos, Chania, Pseira).

Looking at Table 10.1 it is clear that very few geographic regions have more than one to three faunal samples studied. This makes any attempt at regional interpretations very difficult. Some of the faunal collections were excavated so long ago or are so small as to be unreliable as to the true picture of faunal exploitation at that site (Thorikos, Lerna, Tiryns, Asine, Phocis-Doris sites, Chania, Dictaean cave, Karphi, Knossos [Glaukos shrine], Delos, Lindos).

There are more sites with studied fauna in the Argolid and on Crete; but most of these are from scrappy post-Bronze Age occupation on top of the major Mycenaean or Minoan sites.

A large number of these post-Bronze Age collections come from religious (sanctuary/temple) sites rather than residential or industrial sites: Athens, Korinth (possibly), Akrokorinth, Isthmia, Halieis, Thebes, Kalapodi, Corycien cave, Dictaean cave, Dreros, Kato Syme, Knossos, Kommos, Pseira [a monastery], Delos, Zagora, Koukounaries, Heraion, Mytilene (includes two Demeter altars), Ephesus, and Miletus. As these various sites are dedicated to at least seven different deities and are of various dates, they might be expected to produce very different faunal remains. However, some generalizations can be made.

A few of these sites have good evidence for burnt sacrifice, producing substantial quantities of burnt bones (Athens, Isthmia, Kommos, Mytilene, Miletus). These are generally the hind-quarters of ovicaprids or cattle, or very young complete pigs. Some of the sites have significant numbers of astragali (knuckle-bones), often modified and probably used in divination (Athens, Akrokorinth, Halieis, Thebes, Corycien cave, Kommos). Some have produced exotic fauna, like ostrich eggshells or imported shells or bones (Korinth, Isthmia, Halieis, Kalapodi, Kommos, Heraion, Ephesus [Reese 1984d, 1985b, 1985d]). Several of these sites have large concentrations of ovicaprid (mainly goat) horncores (Halieis, Dreros, Kato Syme, Delos, Ephesus).

Several of these faunal collections are from cemetery sites (Lefkandi, Vroulia, Theologos, Halikarnassos [unique burial sacrifice]). Some Hellenistic and/or Roman sites, have major quantities of bone-working debris (Korinth, Knossos, Pergamon).

It is clear that many more post-Bronze Age faunal samples need to be collected, analyzed, and published before we will be in a position to answer more than very basic site-specific questions.

Table 10.1. Post-Bronze Age Greek (and Aegean Turkish) Sites with Analyzed Faunal Remains. Counts Given Are for Post-Bronze Age Sample only.

Greek Mainland

Attica

Athens, altar of Aphrodite Ourania in the Agora (c500-400 B.C; c3300 burnt bones; Foster 1984; Jameson 1988; Reese 1989a)

Thorikos (5th-4th c. B.C.; c100 bones; Gautier 1967)

Korinthia

Korinth (2nd c. A.D.; 4500 bones and 50 shells; Reese 1987a; Rielly 1987 [bird]; Rose 1987 [fish]; Williams 1979:117-118 [fish])

Akrokorinth, Sanctuary of Demeter and Kore (7th c. B.C. to 4th c. A.D.; c1600 bones, c450 shells; Reese ms.a, ms.b)

Isthmia (6th c. B.C. to Roman; Gebhard and Hemans 1992:15, 17-18, 42, 46, 57, 63-65, 66-68, 70, 71-73, 74-75, 76; Reese 1989a:69, 1993 [4th-3rd c. B.C. well-fill; c200 remains])

Argolid

Lerna* (Geometric to Roman; Gejvall 1969)

Midea* (Roman and Byzantine; Gejvall 1983 [c500 bones, c30 shells]; Waldén 1983 [shells]; personal analysis)

Tiryns* (5th c. B.C.; 55 bones; von den Driesch and Boessneck 1990:89)

Prophitis Elias, Tiryns* (Archaic; 75 bones and 7 shells; von den Driesch and Boessneck 1990:153)

Asine* (Moberg 1992 [c100 Geometric to Roman bones from the 1926 season]; Reese 1982c [c20 shells])

Halieis, Sanctuary of Apollo (8th c. B.C. to Roman; c1300 fragments; c800 shells; personal analysis; Jameson 1988)

Halieis, Acropolis (8th-4th c. B.C.; c850 fragments; personal analysis)

Euboea

Lefkandi tombs* [shell only] (Jones 1980; Reese 1992d:123, 125, 126 and personal analysis)

Boeotia

Kástron Khóstia (7th c. B.C. to 4th c. A.D.; personal analysis)

Thebes, Kabeirion sanctuary (Classical to Roman; c5000 identified bones; Boessneck 1973; Jameson 1988)

Phocis/Doris

Kalapodi, Sanctuary of Artemis and Apollo* (Proto-Geometric to Byzantine, c1300 identified bones and c125 shells; Stanzel 1991)

Corycien cave (22,800 astragali, 430 shells; Amandry 1984; Poplin 1984a, 1984b)

Phocis-Doris sites: Lilaia [mixed Geometric Classical, Hellenistic], Panaghia [mixed Classical, Hellenistic, Roman, Byzantine], Kouvela [Hellenistic], Keramidario and Khani Zaghana (Hellenistic, Roman], Agios Dimitrios [Roman], Palaiochorio [Byzantine] (personal analysis)

Macedonia

Assiros Toumba* (Early Iron Age; Halstead and Jones 1980, 1994b)

Kastanas* (Early and Middle Iron Age; Becker 1986)

Porto Lagos [shell only] (Byzantine; Karali-Yannacopoulou 1981a, 1982, 1989a [22,400 shells])

Lakonia

Agios Stephanos* (Frankish [ca. 1250-1320 A.D.]; c2000 bones and c2000 shells; Mourer-Chauviré 1994; Reese 1994f; Rose 1994b)

Messenia

Nichoria* (Early Iron Age and Byzantine; Sloan and Duncan 1978 [c1000 identified bones; Mancz 1989]; Reese 1992a [c12 shells])

Epiros

Kassope (4th-1st c. B.C.; c36,000 bones and c9500 shells; Friedl 1984; Boessneck 1986)

Greek Islands

Crete

Chania* (Persson 1993, ms.; Reese in 1994h [shell], personal analysis)

Chersonisos [shell only] (Roman; Boekschoten 1962)

Dictaean cave* (c50 bones of the LM III and Geometric; Boyd-Dawkins 1902)

Dreros, Temple of Apollo (Deonna 1940; Marinatos 1936)

Gortyn (Hellenistic and Byzantine; c950 bones and c50 shells; Wilkins 1994)

Karphi (Early Iron Age; Students of the BSA 1937-38:70, 76, 78, 80-83, 85, 92-93, 95-97, 104, 107, 133-34)

Kato Syme* (Lembessi and Reese 1990 [shells]; Nobis 1988a [169 identified bones from all periods]; personal analysis)

Kavousi, Kastro* (mainly Late Geometric; c2800+ identified bones; Klippel and Snyder 1991; personal analysis [shells])

Knossos, Unexplored Mansion* (mainly Roman; Bedwin 1992 [c6500 bones]; Reese 1992c [34 shells]; Sackett 1992)

Knossos, Shrine of Glaukos (Iron Age to Roman; c140 bones identified; Jones 1978)

Knossos, Sanctuary of Demeter* (8th c. B.C. to 2nd c. A.D.; c600 bones; Hägg 1994; Jameson 1988; Jarman 1973; personal analysis;)

Kommos, sanctuary complex* (ca. 1000 B.C. to Roman; c25,000 bones and 93,400 shells; Jameson 1988:92; Payne 1994; Reese 1984e, 1989a:68-70, 1994b-e; Reumer and Payne 1986)

Mochlos* (personal analysis)

Pseira* (6th-11h c. A.D. monastery; c1100 bones, c1600 shells; personal analysis)

Other Islands

Delos (Deonna 1940)

Zagora on Andros (Geometric; Cambitoglou 1981:81-82, 99)

Koukounaries on Paros* (personal analysis)

Heraion on Samos (7th c. B.C.; c17,500 bones, 20+ shells; Boessneck and von den Driesch 1981, 1983a, 1988)

Mytilene (Reese 1989a:68-69; bone analysis by D. Ruscillo)

Vroulia tombs on Rhodes (Kinch 1914:160-61)

Lindos on Rhodes (Archaic; Blinkenberg 1931:183-84)

Theologos cemeteries on Thassos (c100 bones; Halstead and Jones 1992; Karali-Yannacopoulou 1992b)

Kastri on Thassos* (Halstead and Jones 1994a)

Mikaleph (Palaeopolis) on Corfu (c500 remains, Cordy ms.a, b)

Aegean Turkey

Didyma (Hellenistic to Medieval; c6800 bones and c850 shells; von den Driesch and Boessneck 1982; Boessneck and von den Driesch 1983b; Boessneck and Schaeffer 1986)

Ephesus, Artemision (7th-4th c. B.C.; c3400 bones and c60 shells; Wolff 1976; Jameson 1988; Hägg 1994)

Halikarnassos, maussolleion (350-400 B.C.; Aaris-Sorensen 1981;

Højlund 1981, 1983)

Miletus - Kalabak Tepe (7th-5th c. B.C.; c3800 bones and c4200 shells; Peters 1994; Peters and von den Driesch 1994)

Miletus - Zeytin Tepe, an Aphrodite sanctuary (7th-5th c. B.C.; c6000 bones and c325 shells; Peters 1994; Peters and von den Driesch 1994)

Pergamon (Hellenistic and Roman; von den Driesch and Boessneck 1982 [c700 worked bones]; Boessneck and von den Driesch 1985 [fauna from various cisterns of Hellenistic to 12th-15th c. A.D. date], 1994)

Troy* (Schliemann 1880; Gejvall 1938, 1939; Uerpmann et al. 1992 [Hellenistic-Roman, c1100 identified bones])

* site also has Late Bronze Age material

198   *Beyond the Site: Regional Studies in the Aegean*

References

Aaris-Sorensen, K.
> 1981 A Zoological Analysis of the Osteological Material from the Sacrificial Layer at the Maussolleion at Halikarnassos. *The Maussolleion at Halikarnassos* I, pp. 91-110. Jutland Archaeological Society Publications 15:1. Nordisk Forlag, Copenhagen.

Aloupi, E., Y. Maniatis, T. Paradellis, and L. Karali-Yannacopoulou
> 1990 Analysis of a Purple Material Found at Akrotiri. In *Thera and the Aegean* World III(1), edited by D.A. Hardy et al., pp. 488-490. Thera Foundation, London.

Amandry, P.
> 1984 Os et Coquilles. Chaptre IX in *L'Antre Corycien* II, pp. 347-380. BCH Supplemental Volume IX. École française d' Athènes, Paris.

Åström, P., and D.S. Reese
> 1990 Triton Shells in East Mediterranean Cults. *Journal of Prehistoric Religion* III-IV: 5-14.

Becker, C.
> 1986 *Kastanas, Ausgrabungen in einem Siedlungshügel der Bronze und Eisenzeit Makedoniens 1975-1979. Die Tierknochenfunde.* Prähistorische Archäologie in Südosteuropa 5. Wissenschaftsverlag Volker Spiess, Berlin.
> 1991 Die Tierknochenfunde von der Platia Magoula Zarkou--neue Untersuchungen zu Haustierhaltung, Jagd und Rohstoffverwendung im neolithisch-bronzezeitlichen Thessalien. *Praehistorische Zeitschrift* 66(1):14-78.

Bedwin, O.
> 1984 The Animal Bones. Appendix 2 in *The Minoan Unexplored Mansion at Knossos*, by M.R. Popham, et al., pp. 307-308. BSA Supplemental Volume 17. Thames and Hudson, London.
> 1992 The Animal Bones. Appendix 1 in *Knossos, From Greek City to Roman Colony. Excavations at the Unexplored Mansion* II(2), by L.H. Sackett, pp. 491-492. BSA Supplemental Volume 21. Thames and Hudson, London.

Blinkenberg, C.
> 1931 *Lindos, Fouilles de l'acropole, 1902-1904* I *Les petits objets*. Walter de Gruyter, Berlin.

Bloedow, E.
> 1987 Mycenaean Fishing in Troubled Waters. *Classical Views*

31:179-185.
Boekschoten, G.J.
  1962 Note on Roman Purple Winning at Chersonisos, Crete.
       Basteria 26(3-4):59-60.
Boessneck, J.
  1973 *Die Tierknochenfunde aus dem Kabirenheiligtum bei
       Theben (Böotien)*. Institut für Palaeoanatomie,
       Domestikationsforschung und Geschichte der Tiermedizin der
       Universität München, München.
  1986 Zooarchäologische Ergebnisse an den Tierknochen- und
       Molluskenfunden. In *Haus und Stadt im Klassischen Griechenland*,
       edited by W. Hoepfner and E.-L. Schwandner, pp. 136-140.
       Deutscher Kunstverlag, München.
Boessneck, J., and A. von den Driesch
  1981 Reste exotischer Tiere aus dem Heraion auf Samos.
       *Mitteilungen des Deutschen Archäologischen Instituts, Athenische
       Abteilung* 96:245-248.
  1983a Weitere Reste exotischer Tiere aus dem Heraion auf
       Samos. *Mitteilungen des Deutschen Archäologischen Instituts,
       Athenische Abteilung* 98:21-24.
  1983b Tierknochenfunde aus Didyma. *Archäologischer Anzeiger*:
       611-651.
  1984 Die Zoologische Dokumentation der Reste von vier Pferden
       und einem Hund aus einem Mykenischen Schachtgrab in Kokla bei
       Argos (Peloponnes). *Spixiana* 7:327-333.
  1985 *Knochenbfunde aus Zisternen in Pergamon*. Institut für
       Palaeoanatomie, Domestikationsforschung und Geschichte der
       Tiermedizin der Universität München, München.
  1988 *Knochenbfall von Opfermahlen und Weihgabenaus Heraion von
       Samos* (7. Jh. v. Chr.). Institut für Palaeoanatomie,
       Domestikationsforschung und Geschichte der Tiermedizin der
       Universität München, München.
Boessneck, J., and J. Schäffer
  1986 Tierknochenfunde aus Didyma II. *Archäologischer
       Anzeiger*:251-301.
Boessneck, J., and R. Thessing
  1994 Die Tierknochenfunde aus drei griechischen Häusern
       der klassischen Zeit, in press.
Bökönyi, S.
  1986 Faunal Remains. In *Excavations at Sitagroi, A Prehistoric
       Village in Northeast Greece* I, edited by C. Renfrew, M.

Gimbutas, and E. Elster, pp. 63-132. Monumenta Archaeologica 13. Institute of Archaeology, Los Angeles.

1989 Animal Remains. In *Achilleion, A Neolithic Settlement in Thessaly, Greece, 6400-5600 B.C.*, edited by M. Gimbutas, S. Winn, and D. Shimabuku, pp. 315-332. Monumenta Archaeologica 14. Institute of Archaeology, Los Angeles.

Bown, W.
1990 Old Bones Reveal Legendary Minotaur Was All Bull. *New Scientist* 128(1747):21.

Boyd-Dawkins, W.
1902 Remains of Animals Found in the Dictaean Cave in 1901. *Man* 114:162-165.

Broodbank, C., and T.F. Strasser
1991 Migrant Farmers and the Neolithic Colonization of Crete. *Antiquity* 65:233-245.

Buchholz, H.-G., G. Jöhrens, and I. Maull
1973 *Jagd und Fischfang* (Archaeologia Homerica II:J). Vandenhoeck and Ruprecht, Göttingen.

Cambitoglou, A.
1981 *Guide to the Finds from the Excavations of the Geometric Town of Zagora.* Archaeological Museum of Andros, Athens.

Cherry, J.
1988 Pastoralism and the Role of Animals in the Pre- and Protohistoric Economies of the Aegean. In *Pastoral Economies in Classical Antiquity*, edited by C.R. Whittaker, pp. 6-34. Cambridge Philological Society, Supplemental Volume 14, Cambridge.

Chevallier, H.
1973 (Rapport sur les travaux de l'École française en 1970). Grotte de Kitsos (Laurion), IV: Mollusques. *Bulletin de Correspondence Hellenique* 97:443-459.

1975 Coquilles Marines. Chapter IX in *Études Crétoises* XX *Fouilles exécutées à Mallia, sondages au Sud-Ouest du palais (1968)*, edited by H. Chevallier, pp. 157-159. P. Geuthner, Paris.

1981 Les Mollusques de gisement Préhistoriques de Kitsos (Attique). In *La grotte Préhistorique de Kitsos (Attique)* II, edited by N. Lambert, pp. 611-632. École française d'Athènes, Paris.

Chevallier, H., G. Richard, P. Salvat, and B. Salvat
1971 (Rapport sur les Travaux de l'École française en 1970). Grotte de Kitsos (Laurion), Vc: Mollusques. *Bulletin de Correspondence Hellenique* 95:732-735.

Cline, E.H.
1991 Monkey Business in the Bronze Age Aegean: The Amenhotep II Faience Figurines at Mycenae and Tiryns. *The Annual of the British School at Athens* 86:29-42.

Coote, H.C.
1869 The Scallop Shell, Considered as a Symbol of Initiation into the Eleusinian Mysteries. *Archaeologia* 42:322-326.

Cordy, J.-M.
ms.a. Recherches archéozoologiques dans la Palaeopolis de Corfou.
ms.b. Archéozoologie du site de Mikaleph (Corfou).

Darcque, P.
1983 Les Coquillages en pierre en tierre cuite et en faïence dans le Monde Égéen. Appendix in C. Baurain and P. Darcque, Un Triton en pierre à Malia. *Bulletin de Correspondence Hellenique* 107:59-73.
1986 Un Triton en Pierre Trouvé à Malia. *Archeologia* 211:32-38.

Day, L.P.
1984 Dog Burials in the Greek World. *American Journal of Archaeology* 88:21-32.

Deith, M.R.
1988a A Molluscan Perspective on the Role of Foraging in Neolithic Farming Economies. In *The Archaeology of Prehistoric Coastlines*, edited by G. Bailey and J. Parkington, pp. 116-124. Cambridge University Press, Cambridge.
1988b The Contribution to Site Interpretation: Approaches to Shell Material from Franchthi Cave. In *Conceptual Issues in Environmental Archaeology*, edited by J.L. Bintliff, D.A. Davidson, and E.G. Grant, pp. 49-58. University of Edinburgh Press, Edinburgh.

Deith, M.R., and N.J. Shackleton
1988 Oxygen Isotope Analyses of Marine Molluscs from Franchthi Cave. In *Marine Molluscan Remains from Franchthi Cave*, by J.C. Shackleton. Excavations at Franchthi Cave, Greece, Fascicle 4, pp. 133-187. Indiana University Press, Bloomington.

Deonna, W.
1940 Les Cornes Gauches des Autels de Dréros et de Délos. *Revue des Études Anciennes* 42:111-126.

Detournay, B.
1980 Éléments de Parure et de Decoration. In *Études Crétoises* XXVI *Fouilles exécutées à Mallia. Le Quartier Mu 2*, by B.

Detournay, J.-C. Poursat, and F. Vandenabeele, pp. 133-146.
P. Geuthner, Paris.

von den Driesch, A.
  1987 Haus- und Jagdtiere im vorgeschichtlichen Thessalien.
  Praestorische Zeitschrift 62:1-21.

von den Driesch, A., and J. Boessneck
  1982 Tierknochenbfall aus einer spätrömischen Werkstatt in
  Pergamon. *Archäologischer Anzeiger* 20: 563-574.
  1983 Schneckengehäuse und Muschelschalen aus Didyma.
  Archäologischer Anzeiger 21: 653-672.
  1990 Die Tierreste von der Mykenischen burg Tiryns bei
  Nauplion/Peloponnes. In *Sonderdruck aus Tiryns Forschungen und
  Bericht* XI, edited by K. Kilian, pp. 87-164. Verlag Philipp von
  Zabern, Mainz am Rhein.
  1994 Tierreste aus einem Kultsaal in Pergamon, in press.

Evely, D.
  1984 The Other Finds of Stone, Clay, Ivory, Faience, Lead etc.
  Section 8 in *The Minoan Unexplored Mansion at Knossos*, by
  M.R. Popham, et al., pp. 223-259, 288-300. BSA Supplemental
  Volume 17. Thames and Hudson, London.

Friedl, H.
  1984 *Tierknochenfunde aus Kassope/Griechenland (4.-1. Jh. v.
  Chr.).* Unpublished Ph.D. thesis, Universität München, München.

Foster, G.V.
  1984 The Bones from the Altar West of the Painted Stoa.
  Hesperia 53:73-82.

Gamble, C.
  1982a Animal Husbandry, Population and Urbanization. In *An
  Island Polity: The Archaeology of Exploitation in Melos*, edited by
  C. Renfrew and J.M. Wagstaff, pp. 161-171. Cambridge
  University Press, Cambridge.
  1982b Leadership and 'Surplus' Production. In *Ranking, Resource
  and Exchange*, edited by C. Renfrew and S. Shennan, pp. 100-
  105. Cambridge University Press, Cambridge.
  1985 Formation Processes and the Animal Bones from the
  Sanctuary at Phylakopi. In *The Archaeology of Cult, The
  Sanctuary at Phylakopi*, edited by C. Renfrew, pp. 479-483. BSA
  Supplemental Volume 18. Thames and Hudson, London.

Garnsey, P., and I. Morris
  1989 Risk and *Polis*: The Evolution of Institutionalised Responses
  to Food Supply Problems in the Ancient Greek State. In *Bad Year*

Economics: Cultural responses to Risk and Uncertainty, edited by
P. Halstead and J. O'Shea, pp. 98-105. Cambridge University
Press, Cambridge.

Gautier, A.
1967 Analyse des Restes Osseux de l'Insula 3. In Thorikos 1965,
Préliminaire sur la Troisième Campagne des Fouilles, pp. 72-73.
Comité des Fouilles Belges en Grece, Bruxelles.

Gebhard, E.R., and F.P. Hemans
1992 University of Chicago Excavations at Isthmia, 1989:I.
Hesperia 61:1-77.

Gejvall, N.-G.
1938 The Fauna of the Different Settlements of Troy. Bulletin
de la Société Royale des Lettres de Lund 1937-1938 II:51-57.
1939 The Fauna of the Successive Settlements of Troy. Bulletin
de la Société Royale des Lettres de Lund 1938-1939 I:1-7.
1969 Lerna, A Preclassical Site in the Argolid. I. The Fauna.
American School of Classical Studies, Princeton.
1983 Animal Bones from the Acropolis. Appendix VII in The
Cuirass Tomb and other Finds at Dendra 2 by P. Åström, pp. 51-
54. SIMA IV. Paul Åströms Förlag, Göteborg.

Gill, M.
1985 Some Observations on Representations of Marine Animals in
Minoan Art, and Their Identification. In L'Iconographie
Minoenne, edited by P. Darcque and J.C. Poursat, pp. 63-81.
BCH Supplemental Volume XI. École française d'Athènes, Paris.

Godart, L.
1971 Valeur des Idéogrammes OVIS^m, OVIS^f, CAP^m, CAP^f,
SUS^m, SUS^f, BOS^m et Bos^f dans les tablettes de Cnossos et de
Pylos. Κρητηκά Χρονικά 23:89.

Grieg, J.R.A., and P. Warren
1974 Early Bronze Age Agriculture in Western Crete. Antiquity
48:130-132.

Guest-Papamanoli, A.
1983 Pêche et pêcheurs minoens: proposition pour une
recherche. In Minoan Society (Proceedings of the Cambridge
Colloquium, 1981), edited by O. Krzyszkowska and L. Nixon, pp.
101-111. Bristol Classical Press, Bristol (Reprinted 1990).
1985 Une pêche au guet: le Taliani, origines et distribution
géographique. In L'Exploitation de la Mer (VIèmes Recontres
Internationales d'Archéologie et d'Histoire, Antibes, Octobre
1984), pp. 185-203. Recontres Internationales d'Archéologie et

d'Histoire, Antibes, Juan-les-Pins.

1986 Archéologie, ethnographie ou ethnoarchéologie des
ressources marines des sites côtièrs. In *L'Exploitation de la Mer*
(VIèmes Recontres Internationales d'Archéologie et d'Histoire,
Antibes, Octobre 1985), pp. 281-303. Recontres Internationales
d'Archéologie et d'Histoire, Antibes, Juan-les-Pins.

Hägg, R.

1994 Cult Practice and Archaeology: Some Examples from
Early Greece. In *Actes du IX' Congrès de la Fédération
Internationale des Associatione d'Études Classiques, Pisa, 24-30
VIII 1989*, pp. 81-97. Studi Italiana di Filologia Classica, in press.

Halstead, P.

1984 *Strategies for Survival: An Ecological Approach to Social
and Economic Change in Early Farming Communities of Thessaly,
N. Greece.* Unpublished Ph.D. thesis, Department of
Archaeology, University of Cambridge.

1987 Man and Other Animals in Later Greek Prehistory.
Annual of the British School at Athens 82:71-83.

1989 The Economy Has a Normal Surplus: Economic Stability and
Social Change among Early Farming Communities of Thessaly,
Greece. In *Bad Year Economics: Cultural Responses to Risk and
Uncertainty*, edited by P. Halstead and J. O'Shea, pp. 68-80.
Cambridge University Press, Cambridge.

1992a Dimini and the 'DMP': Faunal Remains and Animal
Exploitation in Late Neolithic Thessaly. *Annual of the British
School at Athens* 87:29-59.

1992b From Reciprocity to Redistribution: Modelling the Exchange
of Livestock in Neolithic Greece. In *Animals and their Products
in Trade and Exchange (Anthropozoologica 16)*, edited by A.
Grant, pp. 19-30.

1992c Agriculture in the Bronze Age Aegean: Towards a Model
of Palatial Economy. In *Agriculture in Ancient Greece*, edited by
B. Wells, pp. 105-117. Skrifter utgivna av Svenska Institutet i
Athen, 4°, XLII, Stockholm.

1992d Banking on Livestock: Indirect Storage in Greek Agriculture.
Bulletin on Sumerian Agriculture 7:63-75.

1993 *Spondylus* Shell Ornaments from Late Neolithic Dimini,
Greece: Specialized Manufacture or Unequal Accumulation.
Antiquity 67:603-609.

1994 Lost Sheep? On the Linear B Evidence for Breeding Flocks at
Mycenaean Knossos and Pylos. *Minos* 25-26, in press.

Halstead, P., and G. Jones
    1980 Bio-Archaeological Remains from Assiros Toumba. Appendix.
        In Excavations at Assiros, 1975-9, by K.A. Wardle. *Annual of the
        British School at Athens.* 75:265-267.
    1987 Bioarchaeological Remains from Kalythies Cave, Rhodes.
        Appendix I in *Η Νεολιθική Περίοδος στά Δωδεκάνησα*, edited by
        A. Sampson, pp. 135-152. Ministry of Culture, Publications of the
        Archaiologikon Deltion 15, Athens.
    1992 Animal Bones and Burial Customs in Early Iron Age Thasos:
        the Faunal Remains from the Cemeteries of Kastri Settlement. In
        Πρωτοϊστορική Θάσος, edited by H. Koukouli-Hrysanthaki, pp.
        753-755. Ministry of Culture, Athens.
    1994a The Fauna and Economy of Late Neolithic-Early Iron Age
        Kastri, Thasos. In preparation.
    1994b Faunal remains and animal exploitation at Assiros Toumba.
        In preparation.
Halstead, P., and J. O'Shea
    1982 A Friend in Need is a Friend Indeed: Social Storage and the
        Origins of Social Ranking. In *Ranking, Resource and Exchange,*
        edited by C. Renfrew and S. Shennan, pp. 92-99. Cambridge
        University Press, Cambridge.
Hayward, L.G.
    1990 The Origin of the Raw Elephant Ivory Used in Greece and
        the Aegean during the Late Bronze Age. *Antiquity* 64:103-109.
Højlund, F.
    1981 The Deposit of Sacrificed Animals at the Entrance to the
        Tomb Chamber. In *The Maussolleion at Halikarnassos* I, pp. 23-
        89. Jutland Archaeological Society Publications 15:1. Nordisk
        Forlag, Copenhagen.
    1983 The Maussolleion Sacrifice. *American Journal of Archaeology*
        87:145-152.
Jameson, M.H.
    1988 Sacrifice and Animal Husbandry in Classical Greece. In
        Pastoral Economies in Classical Antiquity, edited by C. R.
        Whittaker, pp. 87-119. Cambridge Philological Society,
        Supplementary Volume 14, Cambridge.
Jarman, M.R.
    1973 Preliminary Report on the Animal Bones.In *Knossos, The
        Sanctuary of Demeter* by J.N. Coldstream, pp. 177-179. BSA
        Supplemental Volume 8. Thames and Hudson, London.
    1974 Human Influences in the Development of the Cretan Fauna.

Unpublished manuscript.

Jones, G.

1978 Appendix: Bone Report. In KRS 1976: Excavations at a Shrine of Glaukos, Knossos by P.J. Callaghan. *Annual of the British School at Athens* 73:29-30.

1980 Shells. In *Lefkandi I The Iron Age*, edited by M.R. Popham, L.H. Sackett, and P.G. Themelis, pp. 229-230. BSA Supplemental Volume 11. Thames and Hudson, London.

Jullien, R.

1974 L'industrie de l'os chez les Minoens de Malia (1800 BC) Crête. In *L'Industrie de l'Os de Préhistoire*, p. 105. Universite de Provence.

1975 Faune. Chapter VIII in *Études Crétoises XX Fouilles exécutées à Mallia, sondages au Sud-Ouest du palais (1968)*, pp. 155-156, edited by H. Chevallier. P. Geuthner, Paris.

Kadletz, W.

1976 *Animal Sacrifice in Greek and Roman Religion*. Unpublished Ph.D. dissertation, University of Washington, Seattle.

Karali-Yannacopoulou, L.

1979 *L'Utilisation des Mollusques dans la Protohistoire de l'Egée*. Unpublished thèse de 3e cycle, Universite de Paris.

1981a The Malacological Material of Porto Lagos. In *Fondation Européenne de la Science, Activité byzantine, Rapport de Missions, 1981*, edited by C. Bakirtzis, pp. 8-9.

1981b Μαλακολογικό Υλικό. Appendix III in Ανασκαφή σέ Οικισμό τής Εποχής Χαλκού (Πρώιμης) στήν Πεντάπολη τού Νομού Σερρών, by D. Grammenos. *Αρχαιολογική Εφημερίς*:115-118.

1982 The Malacological Material of Porto Lagos. In *Fondation Européenne de la Science, Activité byzantine, Rapport de Missions, 1982*, edited by C. Bakirtzis, pp. 71-74.

1985 La Représentation des Mollusques sur les Sceaux Minoens. In *L'Iconographie Minoenne*, edited by P. Darcque and J.C. Poursat. BCH Supplemental Volume XI. École française d'Athènes, Paris.

1986 Η Αρχαιολογία καί ή Μελέτη τών Θαλασσινών Οστρέων. *Αρχαιολογία* 19:57-59.

1988 Le Rôle des Mollusques a l'ère Préhistorique dans l'île de Thassos. In *Actes de Symposium International Thracia Pontica* IV (6-12 October 1988), pp. 309-320. Sozopol.

1989a Les Mollusques de Porto-Lagos. *Zeitschrift für Byzantinische Forschungen* 14:247-256.

1989b Purple, a Valuable Dye in Antiquity. Πρακτικά τής
      Ανθρωπολογικής Εταιρίας:92-96.
1990a Sea Shells, Land Snails and other Marine Remains from
      Akrotiri. In *Thera and the Aegean* III(2), edited by D.A. Hardy,
      et al., pp. 410-415. Thera Foundation, London.
1990b Σημασία καί Χρήσεις τών Θαλασσινών Οστρέων στό
      Προϊστορικό Αιγαίο. Πρακτικά Τριήμερου Αιγαίου: 21-23
      Δεκεμβρίου 1989. Ανάτυπον έκ τού ΛΒ' Τομού (1990) τού
      Περιοδικού Παρνασσός, pp. 123-128. Athens.
1991a Parure en Coquillage du Site de Dimitra en Macédoine
      Protohistorique. In *Thalassa, L'Egee Prehistorique et la Mer*
      (*Aegaeum* 7), edited by R. Laffineur and L. Basch, pp. 315-322.
      Université de Liège, Liège.
1991b Ανάκγη καί Σημασία τής Μαλακολογικής Ερευνας τών
      Αρχαίων Οικισμών τής Αιτωλοακαρνανίας. Πρακτικά, 228-232.
1992a Βραχιόλια από Σπόνδυλο. Ανθρωπολογικά Ανάλεκτα (2nd
      Anthropological Congress in Athens, December 1987) 50(2):57-
      61.
1992b Μελέτη τού Μαλακολογικού Υλικού από τά Νεκροταφεία
      Καστρί καί Λάρνακι. Appendix III in Πρωτοϊστορική Θάσος: Τά
      Νεκροταφεία τού Οικισμού Καστρί, by H. Koukouli-Hrisanthaki,
      pp. 756-759. Ministry of Culture, Publications of the
      Archaiologikon Deltion 45, Athens.
1992c Τό Μαλακολογικό Υλικό. In *Ακρωτήρι Θήρας*, by L. Karaly-
      Giannakopoulou, pp. 163-170. Archaiologike Etaireia, Athens.
1992d Sources of Ivory in the Aegean Bronze Age: An
      Environmental Approach. In *Ivory in Greece and the Eastern
      Mediterranean from the Bronze Age to the Hellenistic Period*,
      edited by J. Lesley Fitton, pp. 57-60. British Museum Occasional
      Paper 85. British Museum, London.
1993a Τό Μαλακολογικό Υλικό από τήν Καλογεροβρύση. In
      Kaloyerovrisi, A Bronze Age Settlement at Phylla, Euboea, by A.
      Sampson, pp. 169-173. Eleftheroudakis, Athens.
1993b Θαλάσσια Οστρεα καί Χερσαία Μαλάκια από τό Σπήλαιο
      Σκοτεινή. In *Skoteini, Tharrounia: The Cave, the Settlement and
      the Cemetery*, by A. Sampson, pp. 370-377. Eleftheroudakis,
      Athens.
Keller, C.
1909 Die ausgestorbene Fauna von Kreta und ihre Beziehungen
      zu Minotaurus-Sage. *Vierteljahresschrift der naturforschenden
      Wissenschaft in Zürich, Jahrgaug* 54(1-2):424-435.

1911 Studien über die Haustiere der Mittelmeer-Inseln. *Neue Denskahriften der schweizerischen Gesellschaft* 44.

Kinch, K.F.
   1914 *Fouilles de Vroulia (Rhodes)*. Greg Reimer Libraire Éditeur et Imprimeur, Berlin.

Klippel, W.E., and L.M. Snyder
   1991 Dark Age Fauna from Kavousi, Crete. The Vertebrates from the 1987 and 1988 excavations. *Hesperia* 60:179-186.

Kosmetatou, E.
   1994 Horse Sacrifice in Greece and Cyprus. *Journal of Prehistoric Religion* 7, in press.

Kotjabopoulou, E., and K. Trantalidou
   1993 Faunal Analysis of the Skoteini Cave. In *Skoteini, Tharrounia; the Cave, the Settlement and the Cemetery*, by A. Sampson, pp. 392-434. Eleftheroudakis, Athens.

Krzyszkowska, O.H.
   1981 *The Bone and Ivory industries of the Aegean Bronze Age: A Technological Study*. Unpublished Ph.D. dissertation, University of Bristol, Bristol.
   1983 Wealth and Prosperity in Pre-Palatial Crete, the Case of Ivory. In *Minoan Society (Proceedings of the Cambridge Colloquium 1981)*, edited by O. Krzyszkowska and L. Nixon, pp. 163-170. Bristol Classical Press, Bristol (reprinted 1990).
   1984 Ivory from Hippopotamus Tusk in the Aegean Bronze Age. *Antiquity* 58:123-125.
   1988 Ivory in the Aegean Bronze Age: Elephant Tusk or Hippopotamus Ivory? *Annual of the British School at Athens* 83:209-234.
   1989 Early Cretan Seals. New Evidence for the Use of Bone, Ivory and Boar's Tusk. *Corpus der Minoischen und Mykenischen Siegel 3 Fragen und Probleme der bronzezeitlichen ägaischen Glyptik*, edited by W. Müller, pp. 111-126. Mann, Berlin.
   1990 *Ivory and Related Materials. An Illustrated Guide*. BICS Supplement 59. Classical Handbook 3. Institute of Classical Studies, London.
   1992 Aegean Ivory Carving: Towards an Evaluation of LBA Workshop Material. In *Ivory in Greece and the Eastern Mediterranean from the Bronze Age to the Hellenistic Period*, edited by J. Lesley Fitton, ed. British Museum Occasional Paper 85. British Museum, London.
   1994 Ivories from Tiryns. In *Sonderdruck aus Tiryns Forschungen*

und Bericht XIII, edited by K. Kilian. Verlag Philipp von Zabern, Mainz am Rhein, in press.

Lamberton, R.D., and S.I. Rotroff
1985 *Birds of the Athenian Agora*. Picture Book No. 22. American School of Classical Studies at Athens, Princeton.

Larje, R.
1987 Animal Bones. In *Paradeisos, A Late Neolithic Settlement in Aegean Thrace*, edited by P. Hellström, pp. 89-118. Memoir 7. Medelhavsmuseet, Stockholm.

Lax, E.M., and T.F. Strasser
1992 Early Holocene Extinctions on Crete: The Search for the Cause. *Journal of Mediterranean Archaeology* 5:205-228.

Lembessi, A., and D.S. Reese
1990 Recent and Fossil Shells from the Sanctuary of Hermes and Aphrodite, Syme Viannou, Crete. *Αρχαιολογική Εφημερίς 1986*: 183-188.

Lepiksaar, J.
1975 Fischreste aus der Magula Pevkakia. In *Tierknochenfunde aus der Magula Pevkakia in Thessalien*, by B. Jordan, pp. 181-188. Unpublished Ph.D. dissertation, Universität München, München.

Loulloupis, M.C.
1979 The Position of the Bull in the Prehistoric Religions of Crete and Cyprus. *Acts of the International Archaeological Symposium "The Relations Between Cyprus and Crete, ca. 2000-500 B.C.,"* pp. 215-222. Department of Antiquities, Nikosia.

Mancz, E.A.
1989 *An Examination of Changing Patterns of Animal Husbandry of the Late Bronze and Dark Ages of Nichoria in the Southwestern Peloponnese*. Ph.D. dissertation, University of Minnesota, Minneapolis. University Microfilms (No. 89-18286), Ann Arbor.

Marinatos, S.
1936 Le Temple Géométrique de Dréros. *Bulletin de Correspondence Hellenique* 60:214-285.

Michaelides, D., and D.S. Reese
1994 *Pinctada* Shells from the Mediterranean Basin and Near East, in preparation.

Moberg, K.
1992 The Animal Bones. Appendix in Excavations in the Levandis Sector at Asine, 1989 by R. Hägg and G.C. Nordquist. *Opuscula Atheniensia* 19:5, 66-68.

Moody, J.A.
  1987 *The Environmental and Cultural Prehistory of the Khania
       Region of West Crete: Neolithic through Late Minoan III.*
       Unpublished Ph.D. thesis, University of Minnesota, Minneapolis.
Mourer-Chauviré, M.
  1994 The Bird Remains from Agios Stephanos. In *Agios
       Stephanos, Results of Excavations in Laconia, 1973-77*, edited by
       W. Taylour and R. Janko. BSA Supplemental Volume. Thames
       and Hudson, London, in press.
Nobis, G.
  1988a Die Haus-und Wildtiere aus dem Berheiligtum Kato
       Syme/SO-Kreta - Grabungen 1972 bis 1984 -. *Tier und Museum*
       1(2):42-47.
  1988b Archäozoologische Untersuchungen in Griechenland. *Tier
       und Museum* 1(2):49-50.
  1989 Tierreste aus Knossos auf Kreta. *Archäologische
       Informationen* 12(2):216-223.
  1990 Der 'Minotaurus' von Knossos auf Kreta - im Lichte
       moderner archäozoologischer Forschung. *Tier und Museum*
       2(1):15-19.
  1991 Das Gastmahl des Nestor, Herrscher über Pylos - Mythos
       und Wahrheit über mykenische Tafelfreuden-. *Tier und Museum*
       2(3):67-77.
  1992 Forschungsstelle für klassische Archäozoologie in
       Griechenland. *Tier und Museum* 3(2):62-70.
  1993 Archäozoologische Untersuchungen von Tierresten aus dem
       "Palast des Nestor" bei Pylos in Messenien, SW-Peloponnes. *ZfA
       Z. Archäol* 27:151-173.
Palaima, T.G.
  1989 Perspectives on the Pylos Oxen Tablets: Textual (and
       Archaeological) Evidence for the Use and Management of Oxen
       in Late Bronze Age Messenia (and Crete). In *Studia Mycenaea
       (1988)*, edited by T.G. Palaima, C.W. Shelmerdine, and P.H.
       Ilievski, pp. 85-124. Ziva Antika Monographies 7, Skopje.
  1991 Maritime Matters in the Linear B Tablets. In *Thalassa,
       L'Egee Prehistorique et la Mer (Aegaeum 7)*, edited by R.
       Laffineur and L. Basch, pp. 273-310. Université de Liège, Liège.
  1992 The Knossos Oxen Dossier: The Use of Oxen in Mycenaean
       Crete. Part I: General Background and Scribe 107. In *Mykenaïka*,
       edited by J.-P. Olivier, pp. 463-474. BCH Supplemental Volume
       XXV. École française d'Athènes, Paris.

Payne, S.
1985 Zoo-Archaeology in Greece: A Reader's Guide. In
*Contributions to Aegean Archaeology: Studies in Honor of William
A. McDonald*, edited by N.C. Wilkie and W.D.E. Coulson, pp.
211-244. Kendall/Hunt, Dubuque.
1990 Appendix: Field report on the Dendra horses. In E.
Protonotariou-Deilaki, The Tumuli of Mycenae and Dendra. In
Celebrations of Death and Divinity in the Bronze Age Argolid,
edited by R. Hägg and G.C. Nordquist, pp. 103-106. Skrifter
utgivna av Svenska Institutet i Athen, 4°, XL, Stockholm.
1994 The Small Mammals. Appendix 5.1 in *Kommos* I(1) *The
Kommos Region and Houses of the Minoan Town*, edited by J.W.
Shaw and M. Shaw. Princeton University Press, Princeton, in
press.
Pelon, O.
1966 Maison d'Hagia Varvara et Architecture Domestique a
Mallia. *Bulletin de Correspondence Hellenique* 90:552-585.
Pendlebury, H.W., J.D.S. Pendlebury, and M.B. Money-Coutts
1935-36 Excavations in the Plain of Lasithi. I. The Cave of
Trapeza. *Annual of the British School at Athens* 36:5-131.
1937-38 Excavations in the Plain of Lasithi. II. *Annual of
the British School at Athens* 38:1-56.
Persson, P.O.
1993 Ure in Chania auf Kreta. *Tier und Museum* 3(3):121-123.
ms. Preliminär Rapport om Undersökning av Skelettmaterial från
Chania.
Peters, J.
1994 Archaic Milet: Daily Life and Religious Customs from
an Archaeozoological Perspective, in press.
Peters, J., and A. von den Driesch
1994 Siedlungsabfall *versus* Opferreste, Eßgewohnheiten in
archaischen Milet. In G. Von Graeve et al. *Istanbuler
Mitteilungen*, in press.
Pollard, J.
1977 *Birds in Greek Life and Myth*. Thames and Hudson,
Plymouth.
Poplin, F.
1984a Contribution Ostéo-Archéologique à la Connaissance des
Astragales de l'Antre Corycien. In Os et Coquilles. *L'Antre
Corycien* II, edited by P. Amandry, pp. 381-393. BCH
Supplemental Volume 9. École française d'Athènes, Paris.

1984b Astragales des Delphes et Relations Quantitatives des
Ossements Droits et Gauches Trouvés en Fouille. *Revue
f'Archeometrie.*

Porter, R.
1988 The Living Subjects of Minoan Marine Style Art.
American Journal of Archaeology 92:251-252 (abstract).

Poursat, J.-C.
1984 Poissons minoens Mallia. In *Aux origines de l'Hellenisme,
La Crete et la Grèce. Homage a Henri van Effenterre presenté par
le Centre G. Glotz,* pp. 25-28. Publications de la Sorbonne, Paris.

Powell, J.
1992a Archaeological and Pictorial Evidence for Fishing in the
Bronze Age: Isssues of Identification and Interpretation. In *IKON,
Aegean Bronze Age Iconography (Aegaeum 8),* edited by R.
Laffineur and J. Crowley, pp. 307-316. Université de Liège,
Liège.
1992b Fishing in the Prehistoric Aegean. *Ancient History: Resources
for Teachers* 22:5-24.

Protonotariou-Deilaki, E.
1990 The Tumuli of Mycenae and Dendra. In *Celebrations of
Death and Divinity in the Bronze Age Argolid,* edited by R. Hägg
and G.C. Nordquist, pp. 85-102. Skrifter utgivna av Svenska
Institutet i Athen, 4°, XL, Stockholm.
1994 *The Horse in Prehistoric Greece.* Athens, in press.

Pullen, D.J.
1992 Ox and Plow in the Early Bronze Age Aegean. *American
Journal of Archaeology* 96:45-54.

Raulwing, P.
1992 Die Haustierhaltung in Pylos/Messenien am Ende des
2.Jahrtausends v.Chr. nach den Aussagen der frühgriechischen
Linear B-Tafeln. *Tier und Museum* 3(2):48-61.

Reese, D.S.
1982a Recent and Fossil Shells from Tomb XVIII, Gypsades
Cemetery, Knossos, Crete. *Annual of the British School at Athens*
77:249-250.
1982b The Use of Cone Shells in Neolithic and Bronze Age
Greece. *Athens Annals of Archaeology* 15(l):l25-129.
1982c The Molluscs from Bronze Age to Post-Geometric Asine
in the Argolid, Greece. Appendix 2 in *Asine II. Results of the
Excavations East of the Acropolis 1970-74* l by S. Sietz, pp. 139-
142. Skrifter utgivna av Svenska Institutet i Athen, 4°, XXIV:1,

Stockholm.

1983a The Use of Cone Shells in Neolithic and Bronze Age Greece. *Annual of the British School at Athens* 78:353-357.

1983b Bibliography on Shells from Archaeological Sites in Greece. *The Conchologists' Newsletter* 87:126-128.

1984a Shark and Ray Remains in Aegean and Cypriote Archaeology. *Opuscula Atheniensia* 15:188-192.

1984b Topshell Rings in the Aegean Bronze Age. *Annual of the British School at Athens* 79:237-238.

1984c Molluscs from Early Bronze Age Lithares. Appendix 4 in *Lithares* by H. Tzavella-Evjen, pp. 197-201 (Greek), 219-220 (English summary). Deltion Supplement 32. Athens.

1984d Strange and Wonderful: Exotic Fauna from Sanctuary Sites. *Newsletter of the American School of Classical Studies at Athens*. Fall, 13.

1984e Faunal Remains from the Kommos Temples, Crete. *American Journal of Archaeology* 88:257 (abstract).

1985a The Late Bronze Age to Geometric Shells from Kition. Appendix VIII(A) in *Excavations at Kition* V(II), by V. Karageorghis, pp. 340-371. Department of Antiquities, Nicosia.

1985b The Kition Ostrich Eggshells. Appendix VIII(B) in *Excavations at Kition* V(II) by V. Karageorghis, pp. 371-382. Department of Antiquities, Nicosia.

1985c The Kition Astragali. Appendix VIII(C) in *Excavations at Kition* V(II) by V. Karageorghis, pp. 382-391. Department of Antiquities, Nicosia.

1985d Hippopotamus and Elephant Teeth from Kition. Appendix VIII(D) in *Excavations at Kition* V(II) by V. Karageorghis, pp. 391-408. Department of Antiquities, Nicosia.

1985e The Kition Tortoise Carapace. Appendix VIII(E) in *Excavations at Kition* V(II) by V. Karageorghis, pp. 409-415. Department of Antiquities, Nicosia.

1985f Molluscs from Early Bronze Age Lithares. Appendix I in *Lithares: An Early Bronze Age Settlement in Boeotia*, by H. Tzavella-Evjen, pp. 50-53. Occasional Paper 15. Institute of Archaeology, Los Angeles.

1987a A Bone Assemblage at Corinth of the Second Century after Christ. *Hesperia* 56:255-274.

1987b Marine and Fresh-water Molluscs. In *Paradeisos, A Late Neolithic Settlement in Aegean Thrace*, edited by P. Hellström, pp. 119-134. Memoir 7. Medelhavsmuseet, Stockholm.

1987c The EM IIA Shells from Knossos, with Comments on Neolithic to EM III Shell Utilization. *Annual of the British School at Athens* 82:207-211.

1987d Palaikastro Shells and Bronze Age Purple-dye Production in the Mediterranean Basin. *Annual of the British School at Athens* 82:201-206.

1988 *Marine Invertebrates and Mediterranean Archaeology.* Unpublished Ph.D. dissertation, Department of Archaeology, University of Cambridge, Cambridge.

1989a Faunal Remains from the Altar of Aphrodite Ourania, Athens. *Hesperia* 58:63-70.

1989b On Cassid Lips and Helmet Shells. *Bulletin of the American Schools of Oriental Research* 275:33-39.

1990a Analysis of Shell Material. In J.A. Gifford, Analysis of Submarine Sediments off Paralia, Chapter 7 in *Franchthi Paralia: The Sediments, Stratigraphy, and Offshore Investigations* by T.J. Wilkinson and S.T. Duhon, pp. 103-106. Excavations at Franchthi Cave, Greece, Fascicle 6. Indiana University Press, Bloomington.

1990b Triton Shells from East Mediterranean Sanctuaries and Graves. In P. Åström and D.S. Reese, Triton Shells in East Mediterranean Cults. *Journal of Prehistoric Religion* III-IV:7-14.

1990c Paleocryptozoology and Archaeology: A Sivathere no Longer. *Cryptozoology* 9:100-107.

1990d Review of *Marine Molluscan Remains from Franchthi Cave, with a Report on the Oxygen Isotope Analysis of Marine Molluscs from Franchthi Cave* by J.C. Shackleton, M.R. Deith and N.J. Shackleton. *American Journal of Archaeology* 94:682-683.

1991 The Trade of Indo-Pacific Shells into the Mediterranean Basin and Europe. *Oxford Journal of Archaeology* 10:159-196.

1992a Recent and Fossil Invertebrates (with a Note on the Nature of the MH I fauna). Appendix I in *Excavations at Nichoria in Southwest Greece* II *The Bronze Age Occupation*, edited by W.A. McDonald and N.C. Wilkie, pp. 770-778. University of Minnesota Press, Minneapolis.

1992b Fauna from the Poros Tomb. Appendix G in Μινωικός Λαξευτός Τάφος στόν Πόρο Ηρακλείου (Ανασκαφής 1967), by P. Muhly, pp. 180-181. Bibliotheke tis en Athenais Archaiologikes Etaireias 129, Athens.

1992c Recent and Fossil Marine Invertebrates. Appendix 2 in *Knossos, From Greek City to Roman Colony. Excavations at the Unexplored Mansion* II.2, by L.H. Sackett, pp. 493-496. BSA

Supplemental Volume 21. Thames and Hudson, London.

1992d Shells and Animal Bones. In *La Nécropole d'Amathonte Tombes 113-367* VI (Études Chypriotes XIV), edited by V. Karageorghis, O. Picard, and C. Tytgat, pp. 123-144. A.G. Leventis Foundation, Nicosia.

1993 Faunal Remains from the Well. Appendix in V.R. Anderson-Stojanović, A Well in the Rachi Settlement at Isthmia. *Hesperia* 62:301-302.

1994a The Fauna. In *Pseira* I *The Minoan Buildings on the West Side of Area A*, edited by P.P. Betancourt and C. Davaris. The University Museum, Philadelphia, in press.

1994b The Larger Mammals. Chapter 5.2 in *Kommos* I.1 *The Kommos Region and Houses of the Minoan Town*, edited by J.W. Shaw and M. Shaw. Princeton University Press, Princeton, in press.

1994c The Bird Remains. Chapter 5.3 in *Kommos* I.1 *The Kommos Region and Houses of the Minoan Town*, edited by J.W. Shaw and M. Shaw. Princeton University Press, Princeton, in press.

1994d The Marine Invertebrates. Chapter 5.5 in *Kommos* I.1 *The Kommos Region and Houses of the Minoan Town*, edited by J.W. Shaw and M. Shaw. Princeton University Press, Princeton, in press.

1994e Land Snails and Insects. Chapter 5.6 in *Kommos* I.1 *The Kommos Region and Houses of the Minoan Town*, edited by J.W. Shaw and M. Shaw. Princeton University Press, Princeton, in press.

1994f The Mammal Bones and Invertebrates from Agios Stephanos in *Agios Stephanos, Results of Excavations in Laconia, 1973-77*, edited by W. Taylour and R. Janko. BSA Supplemental Volume. Thames and Hudson, London, in press.

1994g Shells. Fascicle 33 in *Well Built Mycenae: The Helleno-British Excavations within the Citadel at Mycenae, 1959-1969*, edited by W.D. Taylour, E.B. French, and K.A. Wardle. Oxbow Books, Oxford, in press.

1994h The Shells. In *The Greek-Swedish Excavations at the Agia Aikaterini Square, Kastelli, Khania, 1970-1987* I *Geometric to the Greek Period*, edited by E. Hallager, Y. Tzedakis, and C.G. Styrenius, in press.

ms.a The Astragali from the Sanctuary of Demeter and Kore, Acrocorinth.

ms.b Marine Shells from the Sanctuary of Demeter and Kore,

Acrocorinth.
ms.c The LH III Shells from Lerna in the Greek Argolid.
ms.d Land Snails from Neolithic and Bronze Age Lerna, Greece.
ms.e Iron Age Purple-dye Production in Greece.
ms.f Molluscs from Tomb VII at the Ailias Cemetery, Knossos, Crete.

Reese, D.S., and O.H. Krzyszkowska
1996 Elephant Ivory at Minoan Kommos. In *Kommos* I(2) *The Kommos Region and Houses of the Minoan Town*, edited by J.W. Shaw and M. Shaw. Princeton University Press, Princeton, in press.

Reisch, L.
1976 Beobachtungen an Vogelknochen aus dem Spätpleistozän der Höhle von Kephalari (Argolis, Griechenland). *Archäologisches Korrespondenzblaatt* 6:261.

Reumer, J.W.F., and S. Payne
1986 Notes on the Soricidae (Insectivora, Mammalia) from Crete. II. The Shrew Remains from Minoan and Classical Kommos. *Bonner zoologische Beiträge* 37(3):173-182.

Rielly, K.
1987 The Bird Bones. Appendix A in D.S. Reese, A Bone Assemblage at Corinth of the Second Century after Christ. *Hesperia* 56:265-266, 272-273.

Rizza, G.
1979 Tombes de Chevaux. In *Acts of the International Archaeological Symposium "The Relations Between Cyprus and Crete, ca. 2000-500 B.C."*, pp. 294-297. Department of Antiquities, Nikosia.

Rose, M.J.
1986 Prehistoric Fishing in the Aegean. New Evidence from Franchthi Cave. *American Journal of Archaeology* 90:177 (abstract).
1987 The Fish Bones. Appendix B in D.S. Reese, A Bone Assemblage at Corinth of the Second Century after Christ. *Hesperia* 56:266-267, 273-274.
1994a The Fish Remains. Chapter 5.4 in J.W. Shaw and M. Shaw, eds., *Kommos* I.1 *The Kommos Region and Houses of the Minoan Town*. Princeton University Press, Princeton, in press.
1994b Fish Remains from Agios Stephanos. In *Agios Stephanos, Results of Excavations in Laconia, 1973-77*, edited by W. Taylour and R. Janko. BSA Supplemental Volume. Thames and Hudson,

London, in press.

1994c Fish Remains, Buildings AC and AD. In *Pseira I The Minoan Buildings on the West Side of Area A*, edited by P.P. Betancourt and C. Davaris. The University Museum, Philadelphia, in press.

1994d Early Fishing in the Aegean. In *Fish and Archaeology*, edited by A. Jones and R. Nicholson. BAR International Series. British Archeological Reprints, Oxford, in press.

Ruche, C., and P. Halstead

1987 The Animal Bones from Ayios Dimitrios. In *Ayios Dimitrios, a Prehistoric Settlement in the Southwestern Peloponnesos: The Neolithic and Early Helladic Periods* by C.L. Zachos. Unpublished Ph.D. dissertation, Department of Archaeology, Boston University.

Sackett, L.H.

1992 Objects in Bone and Bone Working. Section 12 in *Knossos, From Greek City to Roman Colony. Excavations at the Unexplored Mansion II.2*, by L.H. Sackett, pp. 379-389. BSA Supplemental Volume 21. Thames and Hudson, London.

Sakellarakis, J.

1971 Das Kuppelgrab A von Archanes und das Kretisch-mycenische Tieropferritual. *Praestorische Zeitschrift* 45:135-219.

1974 Le thème du Pecheur dans l'Art Prehistorique de l' Égée. *Athens Annals of Archaeology* VII:370-390.

1979 *Τό Ἐλεφαντόδοντο καί ἡ Κατεργασία τοῦ στά Μυκηναϊκά Χρόνια*. Athens.

Schliemann, H.

1880 *Ilios, The City and Country of the Trojans*. John Murray, London.

Schwartz, C.A.

1985 Agios Petras, The Vertebrate and Molluscan Fauna. Final Report. Appendix II in *Agios Petras, A Neolithic Site in the Northern Sporades*, by N. Efstratiou, pp. 151-163. BAR International Series 241. British Archaeological Reports, Oxford.

Shackleton, J.C.

1983 An Approach to Determining Prehistoric Shellfish Collecting Patterns. In *Animals and Archaeology 2 Shell Middens, Fish and Birds*, edited by C. Grigson and J. Clutton-Brock, pp. 77-85. BAR International Series 183. British Archaeological Reports, Oxford.

1985 Macro- and Micro-level Approaches to the Reconstruction of

Palaeoshorelines. In *Palaeoenvironmental Investigations: Research Design, Methods and Data Analysis*, edited by N.R.J. Fieller, D.D. Gilbertson, and N.G.A. Ralph, pp. 221-228. BAR International Series 258. British Archaeological Reports, Oxford.

1986 Prehistoric Shore Environments, Shellfish Availability, and Shellfish Gathering at Franchthi, Greece. *Geoarchaeology* 1:127-143.

1988a *Marine Molluscan Remains from Franchthi Cave*. Excavations at Franchthi Cave, Greece, Fascicle 4. Indiana University Press, Bloomington.

1988b Reconstructing Past Shorelines as an Approach to Determining Factors Affecting Shellfish Collecting in the Prehistoric Past. In *The Archaeology of Prehistoric Coastlines*, edited by G. Bailey and J. Parkington, pp. 11-21. Cambridge University Press, Cambridge.

Shackleton, J., S. Hood, and J. Musgrave

1987 The Ashmolean Shell Plaque (AM 1938.537). *Annual of the British School at Athens* 82:284-295.

Shackleton, J.C., and T.H. van Andel

1980 Prehistoric Shell Assemblages from Franchthi Cave and Evolution of the Adjacent Coastal Zone. *Nature* 288(5788):357-359.

Shackleton, N.J.

1968a Knossos Marine Molluscs (Neolithic). In Knossos Neolithic Part II by J.D. Evans. *Annual of the British School at Athens* 63:264-266.

1968b The Molluscs, the Crustacea, the Echinodermata. Appendix IX in *Excavations at Saliagos near Antiparos*, by J.D. Evans and A.C. Renfrew, pp. 122-138. BSA Supplemental Volume 5. Thames and Hudson, London.

1969 Preliminary Observations on the Marine Shells. Appendix I in T.W. Jacobsen, Excavations at Porto Cheli and Vicinity, Preliminary Report II: The Franchthi Cave, 1967-68. *Hesperia* 38:379-380.

1972a The Shells. Appendix VII in *Myrtos, An Early Bronze Age Settlement in Crete*, edited by P. Warren, pp. 321-325. BSA Supplemental Volume 7. Thames and Hudson, London.

1972b Stable Isotope Study of the Paleoenvironment of the Neolithic Site of Nea Nikomedeia, Greece. *Nature* 227(5261):943-944.

ms.a Shells from the Neolithic site of Nea Nikomedeia.

ms.b Sitagroi: Mollusca.

Sloan, R.E., and M.A. Duncan
1978 Zooarchaeology of Nichoria. Chapter 6 in *Excavations at Nichoria in Southwest Greece* I *Site, Environs and Techniques*, edited by G. Rapp, Jr. and S. E. Aschenbrenner, pp. 60-77. University of Minnesota Press, Minneapolis.

Snyder, L.M., and W.E. Klippel
1991 Dark Age Subsistence in East Crete: The Fauna from Vronda and Kastro. *American Journal of Archaeology* 95:292-293 (abstract).

Stanzel, M.
1991 *Die Tierreste aus dem Artemis-/Apollon-Heiligtum bei Kalapodi in Böotien/Griechenland.* Unpublished Ph.D. dissertation, Ludwig-Maximilians-Universität, München.

van Straten, F.
1988 The God's Portion in Greek Sacrificial Representations: Is the Tail Doing Nicely? In *Early Greek Cult Practice*, edited by R. Hägg, N. Marinatos, and G.C. Nordguist, pp. 51-68. Skrifter utgivna av Svenska Institutet i Athen, 4°, XXXVIII, Stockholm.

Students of the British School of Archaeology at Athens
1937-38 Excavations in the Plain of Lasithi. III. Karphi, A City of Refuge of the Early Iron Age in Crete. *Annual of the British School at Athens* 38:57-145.

Taramelli, A.
1897 The Prehistoric Grotto at Miamu. *American Journal of Archaeology* 1:287-312.

Thomas, K.D.
1987 Prehistoric Coastal Ecologies: A View from Outside Franchthi Cave, Greece. *Geoarchaeology* 2:231-240.

Thessing, R.
1977 *Die Großenentwicklung des Haushuhns in vorund Frühgeschichtlicher Zeit.* Unpublished Ph.D. dissertation, Universität München.

Tranier, M.
1973 Antre Corycien; Note sur la Fauna des Vertébrés Associiée au Gisement Préhistorique. *Bulletin de Correspondence Hellenique* 97:528-535.

Trantalidou, C.
1990 Animals and Human Diet in the Prehistoric Aegean. In *Thera and the Aegean World* III.2, edited by D.A. Hardy, et al., pp. 392-405. Thera Foundation, London.

220   *Beyond the Site: Regional Studies in the Aegean*

1992 Τό Οστεολογικό Υλικό. In Μία Νέα Προϊστορική Θέση στή Μύκονο: Ο Τύμβος τής Φτελιάς, Τάφος τού Αίαντος. Αρχαιογνωσία 5:133-134.

1993 Παρατηρήσεις σέ Μικρά Ανασκαφικά Σύνολα:Τό Οστεολογικό Υλικό τής Καλογεροβρύσης. In *Kaloyerovrisi, A Bronze Age settlement at Phylla*, Euboea by A. Sampson, pp. 163-169. Eleftheroudakis, Athens.

1994 Ελληνιστική Ταφή Ζώου. In Ελληνικά Κέας, edited by L. Mendoni, in press.

Tsuneki, A.

1987 A Reconsideration of *Spondylus* Shell Rings from Agia Sofia Magoula, Greece. *Bulletin of the Ancient Orient Museum* 9:1-15.

1989 The Manufacture of *Spondylus* Shell Objects at Neolithic Dimini, Greece. *Orient* 25:1-21.

1994 Shells and Shell Objects from Neolithic Dimini. *Ανθρωπολογικά*, in press.

Uerpmann, H.-P., K. Köhler, and E. Stephen

1992 Tierreste aus den Neuen Grabungen in Troia. *Studia Troica* 2, pp. 105-121. Verlag Philipp von Zabern, Mainz am Rhein.

Uzawa, K., Y. Nishiaki, A. Matsutani, A. Nobayashi, M. Yoneda, K. Yoshida, and T. Akazawa

1993 Translation: Zoo-Archaeology in Greece: A Reader's Guide. (In Japanese). *Al-Rafidan* 14:275-302.

Vanschoonwinkel, J.

1990 Animal Representations in Theran and Other Aegean Arts. In *Thera and the Aegean* III.2, edited by D.A. Hardy, et al., pp. 327-347. Thera Foundation, London.

Vialou, D.

1981 La Parure. In *La Grotte Prehistorique de Kitsos (Attique)* I, edited by N. Lambert, pp. 391-419. École française d'Athènes, Paris.

Vickery, K.P.

1936 *Food in Early Greece*. Illinois Studies in Social Studies XX(3). University of Illinois Press, Urbana.

Waldén, H.W.

1983 Mollusca. Appendix III in *The Cuirass Tomb and other Finds at Dendra* 2 by P. Åström, p. 46. SIMA IV. Paul Åströms Förlag, Göteborg.

Wilkins, B.

1994 I Resti Faunistici di Gortina (scavi dal 1978 al 1980), in press.

Williams, C.K., II.

1979 Corinth 1978. Forum Southwest. *Hesperia* 48:105-144.
Winder, N. P.
1986 *Faunal Analysis: Studies in the Analysis and Interpretation of Animal Bones from Large, Multi-Phase Archaeological Excavations*. Unpublished Ph.D. dissertation, University of Southampton, Southampton.
1991 Interpreting a Site: The Case for a Reassessment of the Knossos Neolithic. *Archaeological Review from Cambridge* 10:37-52.
Wolff, P.
1976 Die Tierreste. In Das Tieropfer am Artemisaltar von Ephesos by A. Bammer, F. Brein, and P. Wolff in *Studien zur Religion und Kultur Kleinasiens*, edited by S. Şahin, E. Schwertheim, and J. Wagner, pp. 107-115. E.J. Brill, Leiden.
Yannouli, E.
1994 Dhimitra, a Neolithic and Late Bronze Age Village in Northern Greece: The Faunal Remains. In Νεολιθική Μακεδονία by D.B. Grammenos. T.A.Π.A, Athens, in press.
Young, D.
1965 Some Puzzles about Minoan Woolgathering. *Kadmos* 4:111-122.

Chapter 11

Regional Population Diversity and the Archaic to Early Byzantine Cranial Remains from Isthmia, Greece

Joseph L. Rife and Myra J. Giesen

Introduction

Any study which merges physical anthropology with classical archaeology crosses into a virtual *terra incognita* in the scholarship. Although archaeologists of other periods and areas have routinely addressed the osteology and taphonomy of human burials, archaeologists of ancient Greece and Rome have by and large remained moored to the literary, architectural, and art historical aspects of burials, grave goods, and mortuary practice. The fate of bones at classical sites is often one of desultory excavation and deplorable storage conditions. Despite the breadth and depth of recent publications on the cultural dimensions of the ancient world, the attention given the biocultural dimensions such as demography, nutrition, pathology and biodistance has been limited. While significant research has been conducted on these topics in the past two decades, further investigations in this fertile region could shed new light on the biological context of classical culture. The present study integrates the approaches of the classical archaeologist and the physical anthropologist in addressing regional population diversity over time in terms of the cranial morphology of burials from Isthmia, Greece.

The few studies which have applied osteological methodologies to problems in classical archaeology and ancient history fall into two categories in the broader discipline of physical anthropology. Buikstra et al. (1990) recently discussed the frequency of these two general types. The first type is perhaps best represented by the work of the late J. Lawrence Angel, who for nearly half a century catalogued osteometric data from various classical sites. Angel's prolific research initiated a serviceable data base for skeletal morphology in the Aegean from Neolithic to Medieval times, but with a particular focus on the earlier periods (1939, 1941, 1942, 1943, 1944, 1945, 1946a, 1946b, 1951, 1955, 1959, 1966, 1968, 1970, 1971, 1973a, 1973b, 1975, 1976, 1977, 1986). Not unlike most research during the formative stages of the discipline of physical anthropology, Angel's surveys of ancient Greek osteology as well as the surveys of his predecessors and contemporaries concerning, for instance, prehistoric and dynastic Nubian and Egyptian populations (e.g., Batrawi 1945, 1946; Collett 1933; Crichton 1966; Dudley Buxton 1921; Morant 1925) described ranges of variation among specific "racial" types. The notion of races adopted by Angel and others of his generation is no longer considered valid because it presumed a direct correlation between ethnicity and morphology and underestimated the elasticity of physical variation in human populations. Nonetheless, the work of Angel and his successors is useful in approximating the biodistance, or the degree of phenotypic separation of polygenic traits (such as cranial shape), between distinct sample groups. Some studies in the wake of Angel's pioneering research have established a foundation for future biodistance analyses by presenting osteometric assessments of burials from pre-classical and classical sites in Italy (Becker 1985, 1987, 1992; Bisel 1987; Fornaciari and Mallegni 1986; Manzi and Sperduti 1988), in Gaul (Buchet 1978; Pilet 1980), in Hungary (Éry 1981), in England (Warwick 1968), in North Africa (Berry et al. 1967; Berry and Berry 1973; Carlson 1976; Osbourne 1992; Van Gerven 1982; Van Gerven et al. 1976), and in Greece and Asia Minor (Bisel 1992, 1983; Casey and Downey 1969:190-193; Musgrave and Evans 1980; Panagiaris 1992; Prag 1989, 1990; Prag et al. 1984; Wall et al. 1986).

Studies of the second type have largely addressed questions of paleopathology, paleonutrition, and the various nonmetric features of human remains. Some salient examples are the recent investigations of behaviorally-induced auditory exostoses in ancient Rome and its environs (Manzi et al. 1991); of hyperparathyroidism and other disorders in Ptolemaic and Roman burials from Dakleh oasis, Egypt

(Cook et al. 1988; Dzierzykray-Rogalski 1980); of the skeletal biology of burials from Carthage (Brisko and Dozier 1986; Fornaciari et al. 1983; Kilgore and Jurmain 1988; Schwartz and Dirkmaat 1984; Walth and Miller 1993); of the dental pathology of Roman populations (Smith and Tau 1978; Whittaker and Stack 1984; Whittaker et al. 1987); of health and mortality in Egypt and Nubia (Armelagos et al. 1981; Bassett et al. 1980; Carlson et al. 1974; Harris and Ponitz 1980; Hummert 1983; Kilgore 1984; Morse et al. 1964; Sandford et al. 1983; Sandison 1980; Van Gerven et al. 1981); of porotic hyperostosis (Angel 1978; Fornaciari and Mallegni 1980); of kinship (Bondioli et al. 1986; Salamon and Legyel 1980); of nutrition in early Greece and Roman Italy (Bisel 1980, 1983, 1988, 1992; Bisel and Angel 1985); and of disease in general (Grmek 1989; Jackson 1988; Manchester 1984).[1]

These two categories reflect a trend in physical anthropology toward intrasite versus intersite studies and toward trait evaluation versus biodistance analysis. Moreover, the development of these two categories of research has been attended by a steady increase in the implementation of quantitative strategies primarily in the form of computer and statistical applications, an increase which has been widely recognized and discussed (e.g., Renfrew 1983; Ruggles and Rahtz 1988; Walsh and Patton 1985). As is also the case for the broader discipline of physical anthropology, quantitative studies which address the health of Greek and Roman populations have outnumbered those which address the morphological variability of those populations. There is a persistent need for more investigation in both directions at classical sites. Reconsideration of the osteometric data base on the local as well as on the regional levels would allow for a clearer understanding of the distribution of morphological traits and how such a distribution relates to other local or regional patterns of variation, both biological and cultural.

This study, affiliated most closely with the former of these two categories, is a morphometric comparison of adult crania from Isthmia. Located on the Isthmus of Korinth in the northeastern Peloponnesos, Isthmia was at a crossroads between southern Greece and mainland Europe, between the Orient and the Roman West (Figure 11.1). As a Panhellenic sanctuary under the sponsorship of nearby Korinth featuring the Temple of Poseidon, athletic facilities, and a theater, it was a significant site from Archaic times on both the regional and the international levels. Korinth was colonized by Julius Caesar in 44 B.C. and soon became both a thriving commercial emporium and the chief polity of Roman Achaea. This regional prosperity was reflected at Isthmia by

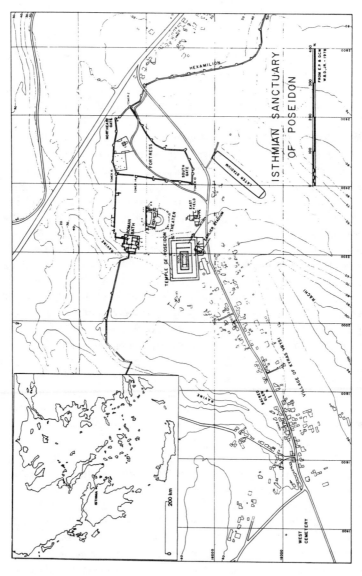

Figure 11.1. Plan of Isthmia. Inset shows location of Isthmia in Greece.

a bath complex of the middle second century A.D. which boasted lavish interior decor and a magnificent monochrome mosaic. Because of its strategic location between the Saronic and Korinthian Gulfs on the peninsular threshold, Isthmia was the site of a fortification program undertaken by the emperor Theodosius II ca. 410-420 and renovated a century later by the emperor Justinian. The fortifications entailed an impressive rampart spanning 6,000 *passus* from shore to shore, the so-called "Hexamilion," and a fortress with a garrison of up to 2,000 troops to patrol and defend the region (Gregory 1993; Kardulias 1992).

The University of California at Los Angeles (UCLA) Excavations under the direction of Paul A. Clement recovered over 200 individual burials between 1967 and 1976 from various sectors of the site. The burials were in storage at the Archaeological Museum and the excavation house in Kyras Vrysi since the time of exhumation. Myra J. Giesen, with the assistance of Mary Beth Parisi and Joseph L. Rife, conducted the first detailed examination of the material during the 1989, 1990, and 1991 field seasons of the Ohio State University Excavations at Isthmia under the direction of Timothy E. Gregory. Their procedure for each burial included reconstructing fragmentary bones, recording measurements and pathologies, resorting the material in a more organized and readily accessible fashion, and creating a computerized data base. A crucial first step was to modify the UCLA numbering scheme which only designated the interment units, or the graves, in sequence of excavation, and not the individuals interred in those units, or the burials (see Table 11.1 for a concordance of old grave numbers with new burial numbers). Some subsequent conservation and examination was carried out during the 1992 and 1993 seasons. A complete catalogue of the material is now being prepared. Of all human remains, only 43 adult crania were sufficiently preserved to qualify for the morphometric comparison presented here. These crania comprise two sample groups which represent two periods in the site's history: 13 date to the sixth to early fifth centuries B.C., or the Archaic to Classical era, and 30 date to the late fourth to sixth centuries A.D., or the Late Roman/Early Byzantine era.

The morphometric comparison will examine diachronic trends in the population diversity of the region through an analysis of the biodistance between the two sample groups in terms of cranial morphology. Despite the shortcomings due to the small sample size, the results of this preliminary analysis suggest that biological stability in one segment of the population accompanied the various changes which characterized the Korinthia from the Archaic to the Early Byzantine periods. This con-

Table 11.1. Index of Old Grave Numbers and New Burial Numbers. M=Males, F=Females.

Area	Old Grave Number	New Burial Number	M	F
W Cemetery	I-36	68-136A	0	1
W Cemetery	I-42	68-142A	1	0
W Cemetery	II-42	68-242A	1	0
W Cemetery	II-48	68-248A	1	0
W Cemetery	II-50	68-250A	1	0
W Cemetery	II-61	68-261A	1	0
W Cemetery	II-72	68-272A	1	0
W Cemetery	II-77	68-277B	0	1
W Cemetery	?	68-991A	1	0
W Cemetery	1	70-001A	0	1
W Cemetery	3	70-003A	1	0
W Cemetery	7	70-007A,B	2	0
NE Gate	1	67-001B,C,D	1	2
NE Gate	2	67-003B	1	0
NE Gate	3	69-103A,B	2	0
NE Gate	4	69-004B,C,D,E	1	3
NE Gate	5	69-005B,C	1	1
NE Gate	6	69-001A,C,D	1	2
NE Gate	7	69-007A	1	0
Tower 14	1	67-002A	1	0
Tower 14	2	69-002A	0	1
Tower 14	3	69-003A	1	0
Tower 14	?	69-701A	1	0
Tower 2	1	68-006A	1	0
Tower 2	2	68-002A	1	0
Tower 2	3	68-003A	1	0
Loukos Field	1	69-801A	1	0
Roman Bath	1	76-002B	0	1
Roman Bath	2	76-002A	0	1
Roman Bath	3	76-002C	0	1
Gully Bastion	2	70-901A,B,C	1	2

clusion differs from the conclusion reached by Angel (1941)concerning some human remains from the site of Korinth. The apparent discrepancy between the material from Korinth and the material from Isthmia suggests divergent patterns of morphological variance within the region. These results are significant in that they imply not only the existence of some biological continuity, but also of some culturally-defined selective factors at work within subgroups of the regional population.

By initiating a data base of Isthmian cranial morphology and by outlining one basic procedure for confronting the osteological record at the classical site, this study aims to stimulate further consideration of both the skeletal morphology of the ancient Korinthians on a regional scale and its relationship with their history and behavior. As Buikstra (1977:67) has stated, "In a regional context, the investigation of the human biological system is critical to the investigation and development of local histories and the derivation of deductively testable models of human behavior." Future studies along these lines may well be on the horizon. Burns (1982:19) reports that the 300 Roman and Byzantine graves discovered by the American School of Classical Studies Excavations at Korinth over the past several decades have yielded 1,485 burials, few of which have received systematic osteological analysis. More recent explorations at Korinth have uncovered additional material (Williams and Zervos 1990:38-40, 1991:135-137, 161-162, 169-171). A full examination of this material and a comparison with the Late Roman/Early Byzantine material from Isthmia would allow for a more comprehensive analysis of regional population diversity. The present study initiates this process by presenting the information from one site, to which it is hoped that others will soon add their information in order to create a regional osteological profile.

The Context and Chronology of the Burials

Before comparing the two populations it is first necessary to establish the chronology of the burials through a brief examination of the associated artifacts and architectural features. Since the two sample groups are temporally isolated, we can suppose that any significant differences or similarities evident in the morphometric analysis reflect a pattern of biological stasis or change in the cranial morphology of the burial community over time. Although pottery was plentiful in the earlier burials from the West Cemetery, few graves contained well-preserved skeletal material. The graves with crania can be dated by the ceramic evidence to the sixth to early fifth centuries B.C. The later burials from the Fortress gates and towers, from the Roman Bath, and from the Hexamilion outworks contained fewer artifacts but substantial cranial remains. Nonetheless, they can be dated by the associated artifacts and features to the late fourth to sixth centuries A.D.

The West Cemetery is located at the western edge of the village of Kyras Vrysi on either side of the road that leads to the village of Hexamilia; the ancient road from Korinth to Isthmia probably followed the same route. Beginning in 1967, UCLA recovered 131 graves north of the road, of which only eight contained adult cranial remains complete enough for analysis (Clement 1968:142-143, 1969:119). Explorations south of the road in 1970 uncovered seven additional graves (Clement 1971:102-105). Although the artifacts from these burial areas await full publication, Dickey (1992) has provided some dates for the graves with preserved cranial remains. Based primarily on the ceramic evidence, he dated Grave I-36 (containing 68-136A), Grave II-42 (containing 68-242A), and Grave II-48 (containing 68-248A), to the Archaic period (1992:A-112, 117-118); Grave II-77 (containing 68-277B) to the Middle Korinthian period (1992:A-122); and Grave II-61 (containing 68-261A) to the Late Korinthian I period (1992:A-120). Although there are no diagnostic artifacts to indicate the dates of interment for Grave I-42 (containing 68-142A), Grave II-50 (containing 68-250A), and Grave II-72 (containing 68-272A), the group of vessels from an adjacent grave without human remains suggests a similar date for these burials. The vessels, deposited as funerary offerings outside the sarcophagus wall of Grave I-37, compare closely with many from the North Cemetery at Korinth which date from the middle to late sixth century B.C. (Clement 1969:119; Clement and Thorne 1974; Dickey 1992:A-113). Dickey suggested similar dates for the four burials with substantial cranial remains from the area of the West Cemetery south of the road. Because of the design and thickness of the sarcophagi, he suggested a date of no later than the middle sixth century for the interment of Grave 1 (containing 70-001A) and Grave 3 (containing 70-003A; 1992:A-122-123). From diagnostic pottery he dated Grave 7 (containing 70-007A and 70-007B) to the Late Korinthian I period (1992:A-124). A temporal bone from the West Cemetery not associated with other cranial remains, 68-991A, was discovered in storage and is presumably contemporary with the burials already described. These cranial remains from 13 individuals recovered from 11 graves in the West Cemetery thus date to the Archaic to Classical period, or the sixth to early fifth centuries B.C.

The burials from various locales around the fortifications and adjoining structures which are situated along the east-west axis of the ravine and the Hexamilion rampart date from a later phase in the history of the site. In 1967 and 1969 UCLA excavated eight graves in the vicinity of the Northeast Gate of the Fortress (Clement 1968:139-143, 1970:164-167). The Northeast Gate, which was constructed on the site of a monumental Early Roman tripylon during the second decade of the fifth century A.D., was flanked by two rounded towers and commanded both the Hexamilion and the chief entrance into the Fortress (Gregory 1993:52-56). Grave 1 (containing 67-001B, 67-001C, and 67-001D) was located just south of the inner staircase and the lower platform of Tower 19. Grave 2 (containing 67-003B) displaced the bottom step of the inner staircase near Tower 19. Grave 3 (containing 69-103A and 69-103B) was located west of Tower 1. Grave 4 (containing 69-004B, 69-004C, 69-004D, and 69-004E) was located along the interior face of the Hexamilion near Tower 1 and adjacent to Grave 3. Grave 5 (containing 69-005B and 69-005C) was located near Tower 19 and just west of Grave 2; its cover slabs rested snugly on a groove cut into the interior face of the Hexamilion. Grave 6 (containing 69-001A, 69-001C, and 69-001D) was located near Tower 19 and just west of Grave 5. Grave 7 (containing 69-007A) was located ca. 15 m. north of Tower 19 along the escarpment of the ravine. Grave 8 was located near Tower 1 and just northwest of Grave 3, but contained no burial.

Associated artifacts and features indicate that the Northeast Gate burials date to the late fourth to late fifth centuries A.D. (Gregory 1993:77-79). Since the lowest courses of the inner face of the Hexamilion near Tower 1 overran Graves 3, 4, and 8, the burials predate the Theodosian construction of the Northeast Gate, a date supported by their design and the diagnostic artifacts. The other burials inside the curtain wall, however, incorporate both the Hexamilion and the North Wall and therefore postdate the construction of the Hexamilion rampart around the gateway. It is clear from their corresponding stratigraphy that the burials in Graves 1, 2, 5, and 6 were interred at the same time, probably in the middle to late fifth century (Clement 1970:163-164). The displacement of the lower staircase by Grave 2 suggests that during this period the Northeast Gate complex was either abandoned as a military installation or had fallen into some state of disrepair during a period of relaxed defensive employment (Gregory 1993:79; Gregory and Kardulias 1990:505-506; Kardulias 1992:284). The chronological relationship between Grave 7 and the other Northeast Gate graves is not easily defined because Grave 7 is outside the gateway and some distance from the other burials. The level and character of the interment would suggest that it postdates Graves 1, 2, 5, and 6 and may belong to the late decades of the fifth century (cf. Gregory 1993:78). A reasonable deduction is that all human remains from the Northeast Gate area date to between A.D. 375 and sometime after 457, a *terminus post quem* provided by a coin of the emperor Marcian (A.D. 450-457) from Grave 1.

Explorations in 1967 and 1969 around Tower 14 and the West Gate revealed an intricate pattern of settlement which lasted from Roman Imperial times well into the Byzantine and Frankish periods (Clement 1968:142, 1970:163-164). Grave 1 (containing 67-002A), Grave 2 (containing 69-002A), and Grave 3 (containing 69-003A) all postdate a wall which runs roughly northwest-southeast just west of the Fortress wall and parallel to the so-called Long Wall. Diagnostic pottery and coins indicate that the Long Wall, which may represent some large athletic structure, and the northwest-southeast wall, which begins right where the Long Wall breaks off, date respectively to the late first and the late third to early fourth centuries A.D. (Clement 1968:142; Gregory 1993:107-108; Peppers 1969:211-212). Because it was situated in the robbed-out footing trench of a rubble wall which overran the wall parallel to the Long Wall, Grave 2 must postdate the early fourth century. If the three burials are in fact contemporary, as their uniform level suggests, they are datable by a coin depicting the emperor Theodosius I, Valentinian II, or Arcadius (A.D. 383-392) which was found in the grave enclosure near the right scapula and cervical vertebrae of 69-002A (cf. Gregory 1993:109). Another burial from Tower 14, 69-701A, was discovered in storage and is presumably contemporary with the burials already described. These burials, and those from Graves 1, 2, 5, and 6 at the Northeast Gate, which date to the late fourth to late fifth centuries, may share the same phase in the occupation of the Fortress.

In 1968 UCLA excavated three graves near Tower 2 in the northeast corner of the Fortress (Clement 1969:116-118). Grave 1 (containing 68-006A) and Grave 2 (containing 68-002A) were located in the corner where the Hexamilion and the east wall of the Fortress meet. These two graves cut through a level of debris which may represent the occupation of the Fortress during the sixth century. Without a better understanding of their context, it is difficult to provide a more precise date for the burials than Byzantine, or the sixth century at the earliest (cf. Clement 1969:118; Gregory 1993:115-116). The foundations of the

Hexamilion adjacent to Tower 2 overran another grave, Grave 3 (containing 68-003A). Late Roman pottery and a coin of the House of Valentinian (A.D. 364-379) from the construction fill on the bedrock suggest that Grave 3 predates Graves 1 and 2 to the late fourth to early fifth centuries A.D., roughly contemporary with or preceding Graves 3, 4, and 8 at the Northeast Gate (Gregory 1993:114).

While exploring the Loukos Field outside the South Gate, the main entrance into the Fortress opposite the Northeast Gate, in 1969, UCLA discovered Grave 1 (containing 69-801A) ca. 24 m. southwest of the gateway (Clement 1970:163). Although Grave 1 abutted a cement pavement, without associated artifacts and a reliable stratigraphic profile it is difficult to assign a date to either the floor surface or the burial. Grave 1 may represent a period of habitation during the sixth century and well after the construction of the Fortress, but there is no clear chronological marker.

During explorations in 1976 of the Roman Bath, which is located west of the Fortress along the rampart of the Hexamilion, UCLA discovered Grave 1 (containing 76-002A, 76-002B, and 76-002C; Clement 1976:67). The three individuals were deposited one after another in a narrow, subterranean channel .68 m east from a vertical drainage shaft in the southwest corner of Room II. Since there were no artifacts associated with the grave, a precise date of interment for the burials is unclear. The drainage shaft, however, cuts through a thin layer over the mosaic floor which represents a period of disuse early in the fifth century before the construction of the Hexamilion piers along the north wall of the Bath (Wohl 1981:112-140). Sixth century pottery from the strata above that level and below the Bath collapse suggests that this area of the dilapidated structure was occupied at that time by those who utilized the drainage shaft (Gregory 1993:41; Wohl 1981:116). Grave 1 may date to this period, roughly contemporary with Graves 1 and 2 from Tower 2 and Grave 1 from the Loukos Field.

In 1970 UCLA explored the Hexamilion outworks near the Roman Bath and uncovered Grave 2 ca. 25.5 m. north of Room I (containing 70-901A, 70-901B, and 70-901C; Clement 1971:109-110). These burial numbers are based on an inferential pairing of cranial and vertebral members: because of their mixing during excavation and storage, it was difficult to identify which vertebral columns and which skulls belonged together. The rubble walls which here adjoin the Hexamilion along the edge of the ravine seem to have functioned as defensive outworks, or a "gully bastion" (Gregory 1993:44). Grave 2 was divided into two compartments, the northern containing two burials and the southern containing eight. The artifacts associated with the burials date to the late fourth or the early fifth centuries A.D., the same period as Graves 3, 4, and 8 at the Northeast Gate (Clement 1971:110; Gregory 1993:43-44; Peppers 1979: 296-298).

The 28 burials associated with the fortifications thus date to the late fourth to late fifth centuries, or A.D. 375-475, with some from the sixth century. Without clearer indications of the dates of interment for nine burials from Tower 14 (67-002A, 69-003A, 69-701A), Tower 2 (68-006A, 68-002A), the Loukos Field (69-801A), and the Roman Bath (76-002A, 76-002B, 76-002C), it is difficult to assess the chronological relationship between these individuals and those from the Northeast Gate and the Hexamilion outworks. Nevertheless, some associated artifacts and features, as well as the analogous nature of their inhumation, suggest that all burials from the Isthmian fortifications date to within ten generations of one another, primarily during the active construction phases of the Northeast Gate and the fortifications near the Roman Bath.

The Morphometric Comparison

A comparison of the two sample groups will elucidate general trends in the morphology of the population which utilized the site during two distinct phases separated by over 825 years. This comparison will test for significant differences between the group means for each variable used. If no statistically significant difference appears, the groups may well be drawn from the same population. This is the null hypothesis. A significant difference in variable means would indicate either that the sample groups are derived from separate populations, and thus the null hypothesis would not be supported, or that the sample groups represent a single population which has undergone widespread, or macroevolutionary, changes. This study attempts to follow Corrucini's prescriptions for practical morphometric analysis (1978:136), namely, that such a study should define and standardize comparative criteria, provide an objective comparison, and synthesize, or recognize patterns. Under these guidelines, the basic procedure was to record the cranial measurements, to compute descriptive statistics, and to employ Student's t-test using the Statistical Package for the Social Sciences Revision 4 (SPSS[4]).

The 21 cranial measurements which were commonest in the data set, including all mandibular and mastoideal measurements, were used as variables for this analysis (Figure 11.2; Tables 11.2 and 11.3). The initial assessment of the cranial measurements included 44 measurements which osteologists typically use to define the morphology of the vault, the basicranium, the face, and the mandible (Howells 1973:165-190; Hrdlička 1939:119-148; Martin and Saller 1957:362-384). But using measurements which are in most cases unreliable due to the poor state of the bone would further increase the uncertainty of the analysis. It was often impossible to record measurements because of the fragmentary state of the remains. While some individuals were intact at the time of exhumation, seasonal extremes of wetness and dryness as well as constant abrasion by coarse-grained sediments had often pulverized the cancellous tissue and delicate surfaces at epiphyses and articulations. Wesolowsky (1973:342, 350-351) noted the similarly poor state of preservation of the Late Roman/Early Byzantine material from Lerna Hollow at Korinth and attributed it to hydrological shifts. The best preserved skeletal elements at Isthmia were mandibles and mastoid processes of the temporal, as is often the case at archaeological sites. The resilience of the mandible and the mastoid when subjected to post-depositional disturbance results from the structural durability of the bone fabric at these locations (Binford and Bertram 1977:109; Brain 1976:109; Maltby 1982:81). Although the mastoid process is used to measure cranial shape less often than other elements, there have been significant studies which include or discuss mastoideal measurements as variables in comparative analysis (e.g., Giles and Eliot 1963:56-59; Howells 1973:176-177; Panagiaris 1992; Turner 1986:274). Moreover, although a greater susceptibility to morphological differentiation over time for mandibular shape as opposed to facial shape has been noted (Droessler 1981:149; Friedlaender 1975:117; Howells 1969:453), some influential biodistance studies have included mandibular measurements as variables (e.g., Angel 1971:96; Chung et al. 1986:466; Droessler 1981:86-87; Kennedy et al. 1984:110; Sanghvi 1953:353; Spielman et al. 1972:395). While the mandible is technically not part of the cranium, osteologists typically group mandibular measurements with measurements of the cranium proper (e.g., Steele and Bramblett 1988:65-69). Howells (1973:6-7, 1989:3) would have included mandibular measurements in his global surveys of cranial variation, but in most of the museum and university collections which he used as sample groups individual mandibles and crania had not been paired.

The archaeological record often furnishes a less than ideal skeletal sample for comparative study, and Isthmia is no exception. It is impos-

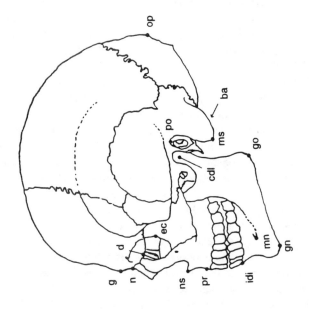

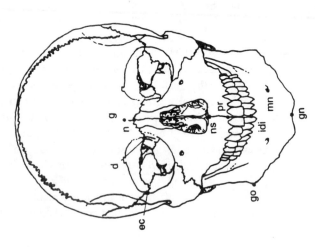

Figure 11.2. Diagram of the human skull showing points of measurement (see Table 11.2).

Table 11.2. The Measurements (with Abbreviations) Used in the Morphometric Comparison.

Glabello-Occipital Length (GOL)	Glabella (g) to Opisthocranion (op)
Maximum Cranial Breadth (XCB)	Maximum distance between parietals perpendicular to sagittal plane
Nasion-Prosthion Height (NPH)	Nasion (n) to Prosthion (pr)
Bizygomatic Breadth (ZYB)	Maximum distance between zygomatic arches perpendicular to median plane
Nasal Breadth (NLB)	Maximum distance across nasal aperture perpendicular to sagittal plane
Nasal Height (NLH)	Nasiospinale (ns) to Nasion (n)
Minimum Frontal Breadth (WFB)	Minimum distance between temporal crests of frontal
Orbital Height (ORH)	Maximum height between upper and lower orbital margins perpendicular to axis
Orbital Breadth (ORB)	Ectoconchion (ec) to Dacryon (d)
Basion-Nasion Length (BNL)	Basion (ba) to Nasion (n)
Mastoid Height (MDH)	Porion (po) to Mastoidale (ms)
Mastoid Breadth (MDB)	Maximum distance from digastric groove to base of mastoid process of temporal
Maximum Mandibular Length (XML)	Gnathion (gn) to Gonion (go)
Bicondyloid Breadth (BCB)	Condylion Laterale (cdl) to Condylion Laterale (cdl)
Minimum Ramus Breadth (WRB)	Minimum distance between anterior and posterior ascending ramus
Ascending Ramus Height (RMH)	Gonion (go) to Condylion Laterale (cdl)
Bigonial Breadth (BGB)	Gonion (go) to Gonion (go)
Coronoid Height (CRH)	Maximum height from base of coronoid process of ascending ramus
Symphysial Height (SYH)	Gnathion (gn) to Infradentale (idi)
Bimental Breadth (BMB)	Mentale (mn) to Mentale (mn)
Mandibular Body Height (MBH)	Maximum height from mandibular margin to buccal surface between 2nd and 3rd molars

Table 11.3. The Morphometric Data for the Isthmia Crania.

Location	68-136A	68-142A	68-242A	68-248A	68-250A	68-261A	68-272A	68-277A	68-991A	70-001A	70-003A
	W Cem	W Cem	W Cem	W Cem	W Cem	W Cem	W Cem	W Cem	W Cem	W Cem	W Cem
Old number	I-36	I-42	II-42	II-48	II-50	II-61	II-72	II-77	?	1	3
Sex & Age	F ± 37	M? ± 42	M ± 37	M 40-44	M + 20	M + 20	M? + 20	F? + 20	M? + 20	F? + 20	M ± 35
GOL [1]	-	-	193.0	188.0	-	-	-	-	-	-	-
XCB	-	-	142.0	126.0	-	-	-	-	-	-	-
NPH	61.0	-	-	-	-	-	-	-	-	-	-
ZYB	133.0	-	-	-	-	-	-	-	-	-	-
NLB	-	-	-	-	-	-	-	-	-	-	-
NLH	-	-	-	-	-	-	-	-	-	-	-
WFB	92.0	-	-	95.0	-	-	-	90.0	-	-	-
OBH	37.0	-	-	-	-	-	-	-	-	-	-
OBB	36.0	-	-	-	-	-	-	-	-	-	-
BNL	-	-	-	102.0	-	-	-	-	-	-	-
MDH	-	-	38.0	-	-	-	-	-	33.0	-	33.0
MDB	-	-	24.0	-	-	-	-	-	16.0	-	19.0
XML	-	-	-	-	-	-	-	-	-	-	-
BCB	-	-	-	-	-	-	60.0	-	-	-	-
WRB	26.5*	28.0	37.0	-	-	36.0	28.0	26.0	-	31.0	27.5
RMH	-	-	69.0	-	-	-	-	61.0	-	51.5*	55.0
BGB	-	-	-	-	-	-	-	-	-	-	-
CRH	55.0	64.5	68.0	-	59.0	-	-	58.0	-	-	-
SYH	25.0	27.0	-	31.0	-	36.0	29.0	-	-	-	-
BMB	40.0	37.0	-	32.0	45.0	-	38.5	-	-	-	-
MBH	24.0	20.0	-	26.0	21.0	31.0	26.0	27.0	-	-	-

[1] See Table 11.2 for abbreviations of measurements; all measurements are in millimeters; asterisks (*) indicate approximations.

Table 11.3. Continued.

Location Old number Sex & Age	70-007A W Cem 7 M ± 37	70-007B W Cem 7 M? + 20	67-001B NE Gate 1 F 35-37	67-001C NE Gate 1 M 24-29	67-001D NE Gate 1 F 22-23	67-003B NE Gate 2 M ± 35	69-001A NE Gate 6 F ± 47	69-001C NE Gate 6 F ± 23	69-001D NE Gate 6 M + 20?	69-103A NE Gate 3 M 30-35	69-103B NE Gate 3 M ± 40
GOL	-	-	-	-	-	-	172.5	175.0	173.0	-	-
XCB	-	-	-	-	-	-	141.0	-	-	-	-
NPH	-	-	68.0	65.0*	67.0	-	-	-	-	-	67.0
ZYB	-	-	120.0*	125.0*	119.0*	-	-	-	-	-	-
NLB	-	-	22.5	24.5	23.0	-	-	-	-	-	24.0
NLH	-	-	50.0	54.0	51.0	-	-	-	-	-	52.0
WFB	-	-	-	105.0*	93.5*	-	101.0	-	-	-	-
OBH	-	-	36.0	32.0	34.0	32.0	-	-	-	-	-
OBB	-	-	39.0	42.5	36.5	38.5	-	-	-	-	39.0
BNL	-	-	-	105.0	-	-	-	-	-	-	-
MDH	27.0*	-	39.0	35.0	40.0	32.5*	29.0	34.5	36.0	-	-
MDB	17.5	-	36.0	23.0	26.0	29.0	21.0	27.0	19.0	-	-
XML	-	-	-	106.0	-	-	-	-	-	-	-
BCB	-	-	-	119.5	-	-	-	-	-	-	-
WRB	-	-	30.5	35.0	32.5	-	-	27.0	34.0	30.5	31.0
RMH	-	-	59.0	63.0	57.0	-	-	60.0	-	58.0	59.0
BGB	-	-	-	105.0	-	-	-	-	-	-	-
CRH	-	-	61.0	65.0	60.0	-	-	57.5	-	-	56.0
SYH	-	-	28.5	-	-	-	-	-	-	-	-
BMB	-	47.0*	46.0	45.0*	-	-	44.0	39.0	45.0	-	-
MBH	-	-	27.5	28.5	25.0	-	25.0	27.0	27.5	-	-

Table 11.3. Continued.

	69-004B	69-004C	69-004D	69-004E	69-005B	69-005C	69-007A	67-002A	69-002A	69-003A	69-701A
Location	NE Gate	NE Gate	NE Gate	NE Gate	NE Gate	NE Gate	NE Gate	Tower 14	Tower 14	Tower 14	Tower 14
Old number	4	4	4	4	5	5	7	1	2	3	?
Sex & Age	F 35-40	M 30-35	F 25-30	F 30-35	F 17-23	M 25-29	M 45-50	M + 40	F 30-34	M 20-25	M ± 23
GOL	183.0*	-	-	-			172.0	196.0	187.0	-	174.5
XCB	-	-	-	-			119.0	-	143.0	147.0	148.0
NPH	121.0	73.0	60.0	-		57.0	64.0	71.0	67.0	68.0*	60.0
ZYB	-	136.0	-	-			105.0	-	121.0*	128.0	130.0
NLB	-	27.0	23.5	-		26.0	23.0	24.5	26.0	28.0	21.0
NLH	-	55.0	47.0	-		36.5	46.0	41.0	48.0	48.0*	49.0
WFB	98.0	103.0	91.0	-		96.0	86.0	-	101.0	98.0	94.0
OBH	-	34.0	33.0	-			36.0	31.0	31.0	-	35.0
OBB	-	43.0	38.0	-			37.5	40.0	36.0	-	39.0
BNL	-	101.0	95.0	-			93.0	109.0	96.0	-	101.0
MDH	32.5	35.5	33.5	-			24.0	27.0	36.0	43.0	39.0
MDB	21.0	18.0	21.0	-			16.0	27.0	22.0	22.0	37.0
XML	98.0	-	-	-			95.0	-	-	-	101.0
BCB	123.0	-	-	-			119.0*	-	-	-	119.0
WRB	30.0	-	-	33.0	-	30.5	30.0	31.0	34.5	34.0	29.0
RMH	53.0	-	-	60.0	-	61.0	47.0	67.0	53.0	69.0	60.0
BGB	85.0	-	-	-	-	-	90.0	102.0	91.0*	111.0	105.0
CRH	56.0	-	-	64.0	52.0	60.0	46.0	66.0	56.0	69.5	66.5
SYH	-	-	-	-	-	-	27.0	30.0	32.0	-	27.5
BMB	48.0	-	-	-	42.0	-	42.5	42.0	43.0	46.0	46.5
MBH	23.0	-	-	-	21.0	-	-	31.0	25.0	30.5	25.0

Table 11.3. Continued.

	68-002A	68-003A	68-006A	69-801A	76-002A	76-002B	76-002C	70-901A	70-901B	70-901C
Location	Tower 2	Tower 2	Tower 2	Loukos	Bath	Bath	Bath	G Bast	G Bast	G Bast
Old number	2	3	1	1	2	1	3	2	2	2
Sex & Age	M ± 35	M + 20?	M ± 37	M 25-30	F 35-39	F? + 20	F 20-25?	F ± 40	F 30-35	M 45-55
GOL	-	187.0	-	181.5	-	-	-	-	177.0	-
XCB	138.5	-	-	-	-	-	-	-	130.0	-
NPH	-	-	-	-	-	-	-	-	-	64.0*
ZYB	126.0*	-	-	-	-	-	-	-	65.0	114.0
NLB	24.0	-	-	-	-	-	-	-	-	22.5
NLH	-	-	-	-	-	-	-	-	51.0	46.0
WFB	-	100.0	-	-	-	-	-	97.0	94.5	82.0
OBH	-	-	-	-	-	-	-	-	31.0	31.5
OBB	-	-	-	-	-	-	-	-	37.0	37.0
BNL	-	-	-	-	-	-	-	-	-	-
MDH	32.0	39.0	30.0	41.0	32.0	28.5	23.0*	31.0	36.0	34.0
MDB	23.0	27.0	23.0	23.0	18.0	20.5	13.0	20.0	19.0	21.0
XML	-	-	106.0	106.0	-	90.0*	-	99.0	-	103.0
BCB	-	-	129.0	116.0	-	125.0*	-	102.0	-	-
WRB	29.0	32.0	34.0	38.0	-	33.0	32.0	32.0	-	-
RMH	58.5	59.5	57.0	66.0	-	59.0*	50.0*	43.0	-	-
BGB	110.0	106.0*	98.0	108.5	-	112.0	-	90.0	-	-
CRH	64.0	-	58.5	71.0	-	-	-	58.0	-	-
SYH	30.0	-	34.5*	-	-	-	34.0*	-	-	-
BMB	45.5	-	45.0	43.0	-	25.0	-	44.0	-	-
MBH	27.5	26.0	30.0	30.0	-	43.0	-	25.0	-	-

sible to determine whether the two sample groups are representative of their respective populations or whether those populations were uniformly distributed, although these are assumptions of the t-test. Angel was confronted with a similar problem in his analysis of the sparse material from Lerna (1971:39-41, 66-86). He acknowledged the deficit for certain periods and proceeded with reconstructing the biological profile of the population from the Neolithic to the Roman period even though it was based on a "laughably small" sample size (1971:69). Similarly, as long as the inadequacies of the data set are observed, the Isthmia crania can provide a reasonable sample on which to base a morphometric comparison and some preliminary conclusions concerning biodistance. A cautious approach, tempered with the understanding that future additions to the sample groups may prove or disprove earlier hypotheses, would seem a better alternative than either setting aside or excluding wholesale evaluations of human remains from classical sites.

The mean, standard deviation, and mean standard error were calculated and applied to the t-test to determine the statistical significance of discrepancies between the means for each variable from the two sample groups by sex. The t-value for each cranial measurement for the two sample groups was then calculated based on pooled variance estimates. This was a two-tailed test, meaning that computations included deviation in the direction of both extremes from the means. Of the 21 measurements used as variables, no variable had more than ten cases in the Archaic to Classical sample group and only seven variables occurred with a high enough frequency to qualify for the t-test. For males these were mastoid height, mastoid breadth, minimum ramus breadth, coronoid height, symphysial height, bimental breadth, and mandibular body height, and for females minimum ramus breadth. Finally, the t-value for each variable at the given degrees of freedom was translated into a universal p-value which was then compared to the standard significance level of .05.[2] For all eight variables, except male bimental breadth and female minimum ramus breadth, the p-value was greater than .05. Therefore, the null hypothesis could not be rejected for all variables.[3] Notwithstanding the deficiencies of the data set, the results of this analysis tentatively indicate the likelihood of biological similarity between the two sample groups for this site. There is, thus, some evidence for continuity between the two historic populations at the site. In addition, the information from the morphometric analysis provides an important comparative database which future research can use as an initial starting point (Tables 11.4 and 11.5).

Discussion

This morphometric comparison suggests that there was no significant difference between the Archaic to Classical and the Late Roman/Early Byzantine burials, at least in terms of mandibular and mastoideal morphology. It is important to note that significant differences in one, a few, or even several of the morphological traits do not necessarily imply that the two populations are biologically distinct. Such a distinction is only demonstrable when a constellation of traits shows significant variation. Minor variations in cranial shape throughout such a small sample group and over such an extensive interval of time are to be expected, as in the case of male bimental breadth and female minimum ramus breadth. Discrepancies can arise from the preferential selection of mates or other factors such as disease and differential fertility, demographic shifts, microevolution, or sampling error. If the West Cemetery or Fortress burials are atypical of their respective periods, the degree of biodistance indicated by such an analysis would not adequately represent the distribution of morphological traits in the original populations. Particularly in the case of the West Cemetery sample, the crania could be either hyperrobust or uncommonly gracile. Any conclusions based on the morphometric data thus depend on the distribution of the measurements in the actual range of variability. If the mandibular and mastoideal measurements are at all indicative of the constellation of measurements which comprise the cranial morphology of the two sample groups, one can posit a biological continuity between the Archaic to Classical and the Late Roman/Early Byzantine populations represented at Isthmia.

The results of this morphometric comparison differ from the conclusions of the only other comprehensive analysis of cranial remains from the Korinthia, Angel's examination of 74 skeletons recovered by the American School of Classical Studies over the first 40 years of excavation at Korinth (1941; cf. Burns 1982; Davidson 1937:230; Gejvall and Henschen 1968; Wesolowsky 1973; Wiseman 1969:86). From his published abstract it is clear that his examination tested for cranial traits which were diagnostic of certain "racial" types. He envisioned the Roman to Byzantine era as a period of transformation during which an influx of Dinaric and Eastern Alpine morphological characteristics was evident, as opposed to the Ancestral Nordic element which predominated in Classical times. In sum, Angel argued that the

Table 11.4. The Descriptive Statistics, t-values, and p-values for the Adult Male Crania.

Measurement	n[1]	X	sd	se	df	t	p
Glabello-occipital length AC[2]	2	190.50	3.54	2.50	6	-	-
Glabello-occipital length RB	6	180.67	9.46	3.86			
Maximum cranial breadth AC	2	134.00	11.31	8.00	4	-	-
Maximum cranial breadth RB	4	138.13	13.44	6.72			
Nasion-prosthion height AC	0	-	-	-	9	-	-
Nasion-prosthion height RB	9	65.44	5.03	1.68			
Bizygomatic breadth AC	0	-	-	-	7	-	-
Bizygomatic breadth RB	7	123.43	10.49	3.96			
Nasal breadth AC	0	-	-	-	10	-	-
Nasal breadth RB	10	24.45	2.10	0.66			
Nasal height AC	0	-	-	-	9	-	-
Nasal height RB	9	47.50	6.01	2.00			
Minimum frontal breadth AC	1	95.00	-	-	7	-	-
Minimum frontal breadth RB	8	95.50	8.00	2.83			
Orbital height AC	0	-	-	-	7	-	-
Orbital height RB	7	33.07	1.92	0.73			
Orbital breadth AC	0	-	-	-	8	-	-
Orbital breadth RB	8	39.56	2.18	0.77			
Basion-nasion length AC	1	102.00	-	-	4	-	-
Basion-nasion length RB	5	102.60	6.07	2.71			

	n	X	sd	se	df	t	p
Mastoid height AC	4	32.75	4.50	2.25	15	0.57	0.578
Mastoid height RB	13	34.46	5.45	1.51			
Mastoid breadth AC	4	19.12	3.47	1.74	15	1.57	0.138
Mastoid breadth RB	13	23.69	5.42	1.50			
Maximum mandibular length AC	0	-	-	-	6	-	-
Maximum mandibular length RB	6	102.83	4.36	1.78			
Bicondyloid breadth AC	1	60.00	-	-	6	-	-
Bicondyloid breadth RB	5	120.50	4.95	2.21			
Minimum ramus breadth AC	5	31.30	4.76	2.13	16	0.48	0.631
Minimum ramus breadth RB	13	32.15	2.66	0.74			
Ascending ramus height AC	2	62.25	9.55	6.75	12	-	-
Ascending ramus height RB	12	60.42	5.72	1.65			
Bigonial breadth AC	0	-	-	-	9	-	-
Bigonial breadth RB	9	103.94	6.59	2.20			
Coronoid height AC	3	63.83	4.54	2.62	11	0.13	0.898
Coronoid height RB	10	63.25	7.14	2.26			
Symphysial height AC	4	30.75	3.86	1.93	7	0.42	0.688
Symphysial height RB	5	29.80	2.97	1.33			
Bimental breadth AC	5	39.90	6.11	2.73	12	2.19	0.049
Bimental breadth RB	9	44.50	1.60	0.53			
Mandibular body height AC	5	24.80	4.44	1.98	12	2.12	0.056
Mandibular body height RB	9	28.44	2.10	0.70			

[1] n = number of crania; X = mean; sd = standard deviation; se = standard error; df = degrees of freedom; t = t-value; p = p-value.

[2] AC = Archaic to Classical burials; RB = Late Roman/Early Byzantine burials.

Table 11.5. The descriptive statistics, t-values, and p-values for the adult female crania.

Measurement	n	X	sd	se	df	t	p
Glabello-occipital length AC	0	-	-	-			
Glabello-occipital length RB	5	166.90	28.51	12.75	5	-	-
Maximum cranial breadth AC	0	-	-	-			
Maximum cranial breadth RB	3	138.00	7.00	4.04	3	-	-
Nasion-prosthion height AC	1	61.00	-	-			
Nasion-prosthion height RB	5	65.40	3.21	1.44	4	-	-
Bizygomatic breadth AC	1	133.00	-	-			
Bizygomatic breadth RB	4	120.25	0.96	0.48	3	-	-
Nasal breadth AC	0	-	-	-			
Nasal breadth RB	4	23.75	1.56	0.78	4	-	-
Nasal height AC	0	-	-	-			
Nasal height RB	5	49.40	1.82	0.81	5	-	-
Minimum frontal breadth AC	2	91.00	1.41	1.00	7	-	-
Minimum frontal breadth RB	7	96.57	3.79	1.43			
Orbital height AC	1	37.00	-	-			
Orbital height RB	5	33.00	2.12	0.95	4	-	-
Orbital breadth AC	1	36.00	-	-			
Orbital breadth RB	5	37.30	1.20	0.54	4	-	-
Basion-nasion length AC	0	-	-	-			
Basion-nasion length RB	2	95.50	0.71	0.50	2	-	-

Mastoid height AC	0	-	-	-	12	-	-
Mastoid height RB	12	32.92	4.74	1.37			
Mastoid breadth AC	0	-	-	-	12	-	-
Mastoid breadth RB	12	22.04	5.66	1.63			
Maximum mandibular length AC	0	-	-	-	3	-	-
Maximum mandibular length RB	3	95.67	4.93	2.85			
Bicondyloid breadth AC	0	-	-	-	3	-	-
Bicondyloid breadth RB	3	116.67	12.74	7.36			
Minimum ramus breadth AC	3	27.83	2.75	1.59	10	2.45	0.034
Minimum ramus breadth RB	9	31.61	2.19	0.73			
Ascending ramus height AC	2	56.25	6.72	4.75	9	-	-
Ascending ramus height RB	9	54.89	5.73	1.91			
Bigonial breadth AC	0	-	-	-	4	-	-
Bigonial breadth RB	4	94.50	11.96	5.98			
Coronoid height AC	2	56.50	2.12	1.50	8	-	-
Coronoid height RB	8	58.06	3.65	1.29			
Symphysial height AC	1	25.00	-	-	3	-	-
Symphysial height RB	4	29.88	3.97	1.98			
Bimental breadth AC	1	40.00	-	-	7	-	-
Bimental breadth RB	8	43.63	2.67	0.94			
Mandibular body height AC	2	25.50	2.12	1.50	8	-	-
Mandibular body height RB	8	24.81	2.07	0.73			

Korinth material reflected "a cyclic correlation of racial and cultural change" in which "genetic homogeneity in phases of mature culture follows (and precedes) inbreeding and great genetic variability during periods of confusion and racial invasion" (1941:88). This conforms with a model of racial transitions in the classical world which he proposed elsewhere (1944:329-368, 1946b:505-514). While his correlation of cranial types with "racial" types was typical of the scholarship at that time, it is no longer considered a viable association because ethnicity is a cultural and cranial morphology a biological construct. Furthermore, his model of "periods of confusion and racial invasion," a commonplace for past historians of Late Antique and Early Medieval Korinth (e.g., Finley 1932; Davidson 1937), would now require drastic revision. Despite these theoretical misinterpretations, Angel's conclusions were based on a well-constructed scientific analysis of cranial morphology. He was able to identify shifting proportions of "races" among the earlier and later burials from Korinth because there existed statistically significant morphological differences between the sample groups. Unfortunately, his abstract does not provide the actual measurements; the only measurement he mentions is skull circumference, a variable not used in this morphometric comparison.

Given the numerous pressures for biological change generated by populational changes in the region from Archaic to Byzantine times, it is remarkable that mandibular and mastoideal morphology varied only slightly in the sample groups from Isthmia, and in this way demonstrated a pattern unlike that observed by Angel. During the Archaic to Classical era, Isthmia was a religious hub under the patronage of Korinth which flourished on account of the Panhellenic festival. The establishment of a Macedonian garrison ἐν Κορίνθῳ καθάπερ πύλαις τὴν Πελοπόννησον ἀποκλείουσαν ("at Korinth as though closing the gates to the Peloponnesos," Appian, *Macedonica* fr. 8), a garrison which was instrumental in the struggle with the Achaean League from the late fourth century until the Roman victory at Cynoscephalae in 197 B.C., introduced peoples native to the northern Balkan peninsula. The destruction of Korinth at the hands of Lucius Mummius in 146 B.C. ushered in a century of little or no growth when Sikyon assumed the administrative responsibilities of the territory as well as the Games. Korinth was, as Cicero observed (*Tusculanae Disputationes* 3.53), all but deserted and in ruins. According to Appian's later account (*Punica* 136), Julius Caesar in his last days ordered the centuriation of a fresh settlement on the site, *Colonia Laus Julia Corinthiensis*. Thereafter, a few thousand urban plebs, mostly freedmen, in addition to a possible cadre of Roman retirees and their families, imported into the regional population a novel range of physical attributes. This enfranchisement of the Korinthia led to an incursion of foreign administrators, military personnel, and merchants (Williams 1993:31-33). As a great crossroads between the Orient and Rome, settlers brought to Korinth not only new artistic tastes, as embodied in the Pergamene baroque figural pillars of captives or client princes which once adorned the façade west of the Propylaea (Vermeule 1986), but also exotic morphological traits from across the Mediterranean. By the second half of the second century, when the bathing facility at Isthmia was in full operation, Korinth had secured a position of supremacy among the Roman cities of Greece. As Apuleius attests, *Corinthus est totius Achaeae provinciae caput* ("Korinth is the capital of the whole province of Achaea," *Metamorphoses* 10.18). It was commonly thought at this time that the destruction and rebirth of Korinth as *ager publicus* had caused the complete replacement of aborigines by foreigners. Pausanias displayed this notion when he wrote, Κόρινθον δέ οἰκοῦσι Κορινθίων μὲν οὐδεὶς ἔτι τῶν ἀρχαίων, ἔποικοι δὲ ἀποσταλέντες ὑπὸ Ῥωμαίων ("No one of the ancient Korinthians still inhabits Korinth but rather colonists sent out by the Romans," *Periegeta* 2.1.2). The gradual reorientation of the infrastructure of the Roman world with the rise of Constantinople created new trade networks, especially with the East. A steady inflow of outsiders from throughout the incipient Byzantine state helped to maintain Korinth as the largest city in the Peloponnesos. St. John Chrysostom (*In Epistulam I ad Corinthios* 1-2) attests that Korinth was a commercial and intellectual center as the see of the metropolitan bishop by A.D. 396, when Alaric and the Visigoths invaded. Both the prosperity and size of the regional population encouraged the development of new defensive strategies for the Greek peninsula during the fifth and sixth centuries which centered around the Hexamilion and the Fortress at Isthmia (Gregory 1993). From these oscillations in settlement and use across the region, it is clear that the history of the Korinthia was one of dynamic change and not stasis in the constituency of the regional population.

However, despite the deficiencies of this analysis, the morphological uniformity of the Isthmia mandibles and mastoid processes indicates some degree of biological continuity in the face of momentous regional changes, particularly during the Roman period. The morphological uniformity further suggests that the two sample groups may represent the same subgroup of the indigenous population. It seems safe to assume that since the funerary offerings associated with the West Cemetery burials are of local manufacture, the Archaic to Classical group lived at least in and around Korinth, if not out as far as Isthmia itself. While the identification of the West Cemetery burials as Korinthian presents little difficulty, Binford (1971) and O'Shea (1984), among others, have discussed the problems involved with interpreting ethnicity from mortuary practice. The numerous Korinthians buried in the West Cemetery over a long period may have selected that locale out of religious as well as social interest, both because of its proximity to the Temple of Poseidon and because of the international exposure afforded by the ceremonies every two years. While none of the sister sanctuaries at Olympia, Delphi, and Nemea had a *nekropolis* closely bordering on the area of the main attractions, none seems to have drawn as many spectators, vendors, priests, and pilgrims as Isthmia due to its location. In any event, with the exception of the Hellenistic settlement on the Rachi, it is doubtful that the site sustained a resident population for any great length of time before the construction of the Fortress. With the first substantial fortifications on the Isthmus came the need for forces not only to defend but also to maintain a sizable installation. This analysis suggests that it was not a standing army from overseas but rather the Late Roman/Early Byzantine group of these same native Korinthians who provided the manpower to fulfill both functions.

The difference between the results of this morphometric comparison and the results of Angel's study suggests that there existed at least two distinct routes for population diversity over time in the Korinthia, one represented by the two sample groups from Isthmia and one represented by the material from Korinth examined by Angel. In other words, certain segments of the indigenous population remained morphologically homogeneous and others became morphologically heterogeneous. While the burials from Korinth represent the actual urban population, there is no clear indication of whether the individuals interred at the West Cemetery and the fortifications lived in Korinth or in the hinterland. In either case, the Isthmia burials reflect one diachronic pattern of cranial morphology within the regional population which was preserved throughout Classical Antiquity by some significant barriers to interbreeding. The mechanisms of these assortative agents, or "barriers," is unclear, but they need not have been limited to geographic factors alone. It is certainly possible that they may have been defined by socioeconomic status as well as regional settlement. It would not be surprising to discover that they were influenced by a complex network of sociocultural factors.

That there were two courses of biological variation over time in the Korinthia does not mean that the two groups were ethnically isolated. The patent uniformity in the manufacture of material goods and architectural styles at both the urban nucleus and its satellite suggests a uniform ethnicity. The cranial remains from Isthmia therefore do not reflect "a cyclic correlation of racial and cultural change." Moreover, the inference of Pausanias, a shrewd observer with no recourse to the osteological record, could not have applied to all Korinthians. Although among a certain subgroup of the population the morphological elements of the Archaic to Classical period persisted into the Late Roman/Early Byzantine period, these Greeks had identified themselves as οἱ 'Ρωμαῖοι ("Romans") from the days of the Empire to the age of Byzantium.

Acknowledgements. An earlier version of this paper was presented at the 57th Annual Meeting of the Society for American Archaeology. The field research for this paper was conducted under the auspices of the American School of Classical Studies at Athens and the supervision of the Fourth Eforeia of Prehistoric and Classical Antiquities at Nauplion. We were supported at various stages by a Kenyon College Summer Science Scholar Grant and a discretionary grant from the Rackham Graduate School of the University of Michigan, for which we express our gratitude. The authors wish to thank foremost P. Nick Kardulias and Timothy E. Gregory for their encouragement and criticism. We also thank Susan Kirkpatrick Smith, Marshall J. Becker, Richard Yerkes, Paul W. Sciulli, J. Kenneth Smail, George S. Hammond, and S. Rex Stem as well as the anonymous reader for the Press for their suggestions in particular concerning the statistical analysis and skeletal morphology and in general concerning logic and style. As significant as their contributions have been, any errors are the fault of the authors alone.

References Cited

Angel, J.L.

1939 Geometric Athenians. In *Late Geometric Graves and a Seventh Century Well in the Agora*, edited by R.S. Young, pp. 236-246. *Hesperia* supplement 2. American School for Classical Studies at Athens, Princeton.

1941 Physical Types of Ancient Corinth. *American Journal of Archaeology* 45:88.

1942 Classical Olynthians. In *Excavations at Olynthus XI. Necrolynthia: A Study in Greek Burial Customs and Anthropology*, edited by D.M. Robinson, pp. 211-240. Johns Hopkins University Press, Baltimore.

1943 Ancient Cephallenians: The Population of a Mediterranean Island. *American Journal of Physical Anthropology* 1:229-60.

1944 A Racial Analysis of the Ancient Greeks: An Essay on the Use of Morphological Types. *American Journal of Physical Anthropology* 2:329-76.

1945 Skeletal Material from Attica. *Hesperia* 14:279-363.

1946a Skeletal Change in Ancient Greece. *American Journal of Physical Anthropology* 4:69-97.

1946b Social Biology of Greek Culture Growth. *American Anthropologist* 48:493-533.

1951 Troy: the Human Remains. In *Troy Excavations 1932-1938*, edited by C.W. Blegen. Supplementary monograph 1. Princeton University Press, Princeton.

1955 Roman Tombs at Vasa: The Skulls. In *Report of the Department of Antiquities, Cyprus 1945-1948*, edited by J.DuP. Taylor, pp. 68-76. The Department of Antiquities, Nicosia.

1959 Early Helladic Skulls from Aghios Kosmas. In *Aghios Kosmas: an Early Bronze Age Settlement and Cemetery in Attica*, edited by G.E. Mylonas, pp. 167-179. Princeton University Press, Princeton.

1966 Appendix: Human Skeletal Remains at Karataş. *American Journal of Archaeology* 70:255-257.

1968 Appendix: Human Skeletal Remains at Karataş. *American Journal of Archaeology* 72:260-263.

1970 Appendix: Human Skeletal Remains at Karataş. *American Journal of Archaeology* 74:253-259.

1971 *The People of Lerna: Analysis of a Prehistoric Aegean Population*. American School of Classical Studies at Athens, Princeton.

1973a Human Skeletons from Grave Circles at Mycenae. In *The Grave Circle B at Mycenae*, edited by G.E. Mylonas, pp. 379-397. Library of the Archaeological Society of Athens 73. The Archaeological Society of Athens, Athens.

1973b Skeletal Fragments of Classical Lycians. *American Journal of Archaeology* 77:303-307.

1975 Human Skeletons from Eleusis. In *The South Cemetery of Eleusis*, edited by G.E. Mylonas, pp. 301-312. Library of the Archaeological Society of Athens 81. The Archaeological Society of Athens, Athens.

1976 Early Bronze Age Karataş Peoples and Their Cemeteries. *American Journal of Archaeology* 80:385-391.

1977 Human Skeletons. In *Kephala: A Late Neolithic Settlement and Cemetery*, edited by J.E. Coleman, pp. 133-156. American School of Classical Studies at Athens, Princeton.

1978 Porotic Hyperostosis in the Eastern Mediterranean. *Medical College of Virginia Quarterly* 15:10-16.

1986 The Physical Identity of the Trojans. In *Troy and the Trojan War*, edited by M.J. Mellink, pp. 63-76. Bryn Mawr College Press, Bryn Mawr.

Armelagos, G.J., K.H. Jacobs, and D.L. Martin

1981 Death and Demography in Prehistoric Sudanese Nubia. In *Mortality and Immortality: The Anthropology and Archaeology of Death*, edited by S.C. Humphreys and H. King, pp. 33-58. Academic Press, New York.

Bassett, E.J., M.S. Keith, G.J. Armelagos, D.L. Martin, and A.R. Villanueva

1980 Tetracycline-labeled Human Bone from Ancient Sudanese Nubia (A.D. 350). *Science* 209:1532-1534.

Batrawi, A.M.

1945 The Racial History of Egypt and Nubia Part 1. *Journal of the Royal Anthropological Institute* 75:81-101.

1946 The Racial History of Egypt and Nubia Part 2. *Journal of the Royal Anthropological Institute* 75:81-101.

Becker, M.J.

1985 Metric and Non-Metric Data from a Series of Skulls from Mozia, Sicily and a Related Site. *Antropologia contemporanea* 8:211-228.

1987 Analisi antropologiche e paleontologiche: Soprintendenza di Roma. In *Le urne a capanne rinvenute in Italia*, edited by G. Batoloni, F. Buranelli, V. D'Atri, and A. De Santis, pp. 235-246. Giorgio Bretschneider, Rome.

1992 The Human Remains. In *Excavations at Otranto I. The Excavations*, edited by D. Michaelides and D. Wilkinson, pp. 153-165. The British School at Rome, Congedo Editore, Lecce.

Berry, A.C., and R.J. Berry

1973 Origins and the Relations of the Ancient Egyptians. In *Population Biology of the Ancient Egyptians*, edited by D.R. Brothwell and B.A. Chiarelli, pp. 200-208. Academic Press, New York.

Berry, A.C., R.J. Berry, and P.J. Ucko

1967 Genetical Change in Ancient Egypt. *Man* n.s. 2:551-568.
Binford, L.R.
   1971 Mortuary Practices: Their Study and Their Potential. In
   Approaches to the Social Dimensions of Mortuary Practices, edited
   by J.A. Brown, pp. 6-29. Memoirs of the Society for American
   Archaeology 25. Society for American Archaeology, New York.
Binford, L.R., and J.B. Bertram
   1977 Bone Frequencies and Attritional Processes. In *For Theory
   Building in Archaeology: Essays on Faunal Remains, Aquatic
   Resources, Spatial Analysis, and Systemic Modeling*, edited by
   L.R. Binford, pp. 77-153. Academic Press, New York.
Bisel, S.C.
   1980 *A Pilot Study in Aspects of Human Nutrition in the Ancient
   Eastern Mediterranean with Special Attention to Trace Elements
   in Several Populations from Different Time Periods*. Unpublished
   Ph.D. dissertation, Department of Anthropology, University of
   Minnesota, Minneapolis.
   1983 The Dark Age Burials: Analysis of Skeletal Material. In
   *Excavations at Nichoria in Southwest Greece III. The Dark Age
   and Byzantine Occupation*, edited by W.A. McDonald, W.D.E.
   Coulson, and J. Rosser, pp. 263-265. University of Minnesota
   Press, Minneapolis.
   1987 Human Bones at Herculaneum. *Rivista di studi pompeiani*
   1:123-129.
   1988 Nutrition in First-Century Herculaneum. *Anthropologie* 26:61-
   66.
   1992 The Human Skeletal Remains. In *Excavations at Nichoria in
   Southwest Greece II. The Bronze Age Occupation*, edited by W.A.
   McDonald and N.C. Wilkie, pp. 345-358. University of
   Minnesota Press, Minneapolis.
Bisel, S.C., and J.L. Angel
   1985 Health and Nutrition in Mycenaean Greece: A Study in Human
   Skeletal Remains. In *Contributions to Aegean Archaeology*, edited
   by N.C. Wilkie and W.D.E. Coulson, pp. 197-209. University of
   Minnesota Press, Minneapolis.
Bondioli, L., R.S. Corrucini, and R. Macchiarelli
   1986 Familial Segregation in the Iron Age Community of Alfdena,
   Abruzzo, Italy, Based on Osteodental Trait Analysis. *American
   Journal of Physical Anthropology* 71:393-400.
Brain, C.K.
   1976 Some Principles in the Interpretation of Bone Accumulations

Associated with Man. In *Human Origins: Louis Leakey and the East African Evidence*, edited by G.L. Isaac and E.R. McCown, pp. 97-116. W.A. Benjamin, Menlo Park, California.

Brisko, J.A., and K. Dozier
1986 Evidence of the Surgical Skills of Roman Physicians from Sixth Century A.D. Carthage. *American Journal of Physical Anthropology* 69:131-138.

Buchet, L.
1978 La nécropole gallo-romaine et mérovingienne de Frénonville (Calvados). Étude anthropologique. *Archéologie médiévale* 8:5-53.

Buikstra, J.E.
1977 Biocultural Dimensions of Archaeological Study: A Regional Perspective. In *Biocultural Adaptation in Prehistoric America*, edited by R.L. Blakely, pp. 67-84. Southern Anthropological Society Proceedings 11. University of Georgia Press, Athens.

Buikstra, J.E., S.R. Frankenburg, and L.W. Konigsberg
1990 Skeletal Biological Distance Studies in American Physical Anthropology: Recent Trends. *American Journal of Physical Anthropology* 82:1-7.

Burns, P.E.
1982 *A Study of Sexual Dimorphism in the Dental Pathology of Ancient Peoples*. Unpublished Ph.D. dissertation, Department of Anthropology, Arizona State University, Tempe.

Carlson, D.S.
1976 Temporal Variation in Prehistoric Nubian Crania. *American Journal of Physical Anthropology* 45:467-484.

Carlson, F., G.J. Armelagos, and D.P. Van Gerven
1974 Factors Influencing the Etiology of *Cribra Orbitalia* in Prehistoric Nubia. *Journal of Human Evolution* 3:405-410.

Casey, A.E., and E.L. Downey
1969 *Compilation of Common Physical Measurements on Adult Males of Various Races*. Amite and Knocknagree Historical Fund, Birmingham.

Chung, E.S., D.W. Rumck, S.E. Bilben, and M.C.W. Kau
1986 Effects of Interracial Crosses on Cephalometric Measurements. *American Journal of Physical Anthropology* 69:465-472.

Clement, P.A.
1968 Isthmia Excavations. Ἀρχαιολογικόν Δελτίον Χρονικά 23 Β'1 [1968]:137-143.
1969 Isthmia. Ἀρχαιολογικόν Δελτίον Χρονικά 24 Β'1 [1969]:116-119.

1970 Isthmia Excavations. 'Αρχαιολογικόν Δελτίον Χρονικά 25 Β'1 [1970]:161-167.

1971 Isthmia Excavations. 'Αρχαιολογικόν Δελτίον Χρονικά 26 Β'1 [1971]:100-111.

1976 Isthmia. 'Αρχαιολογικόν Δελτίον Χρονικά 31 Β'1 [1976]:65-70.

Clement, P.A., and M.MacV. Thorne
1974 From the West Cemetery at Isthmia. *Hesperia* 43:401-411.

Collett, M.A.
1933 A Study of 12th and 13th Dynasty Skulls from Kerma (Nubia). *Biometrika* 25:254-285.

Cook, M., E. Molto, and C. Anderson
1988 Possible Case of Hyperparathyroidism in a Roman Period Skeleton from the Dakleh Oasis, Egypt, Diagnosed Using Bone Histomorphometry. *American Journal of Physical Anthropology* 75:23-30.

Corruccini, R.S.
1978 Morphometric Analysis: Uses and Abuses. *Yearbook of Physical Anthropology 1977* 21:134-150.

Crichton, J.M.
1966 A Multiple Discriminant Analysis of Egyptian and African Negro Crania. In *Craniometry and Multivariate Analysis*, pp. 45-67. Papers of the Peabody Museum of Archaeology and Ethnology 57. Harvard University Press, Cambridge.

Davidson, G.R.
1937 The Avar Invasion of Corinth. *Hesperia* 6:227-239.

Dickey, K.
1992 *Corinthian Burial Customs, ca. 110-550 B.C.* Unpublished Ph.D. dissertation, Department of Near Eastern and Classical Archaeology, Bryn Mawr College, Bryn Mawr.

Droessler, J.
1981 *Craniometry and Biological Distance: Biocultural Continuity and Change in the Late Woodland-Mississippian Interface.* Center for American Archaeology at Northwestern University, Evanston.

Dudley Buxton, L.H.
1921 The Inhabitants of the Eastern Mediterranean. *Biometrika* 13:92-112.

Dzierzykray-Rogalski, T.
1980 Paleopathology of the Ptolemaic Inhabitants of Dakleh Oasis (Egypt). *Journal of Human Evolution* 9:71-74.

Éry, K.

1981 Anthropologische Analyse der Population von Tokod aus dem
5. Jahrhundert. In *Die spätrömische Festung und das Gräberfeld
von Tokod*, edited by A. Mócsy, pp. 223-263. Akadémiai Kiadó,
Budapest.

Finley, J.H.
1932 Corinth in the Middle Ages. *Speculum* 7:477-499.

Fornaciari, G., and F. Mallegni
1980 Iperostosi porotica verosimilmente talassemica in due scheletri
rinvenuti in un gruppo di tombe del III secolo a.C. di San
Giovenale (Viterbo). *Quaderni scienza antropologica* 4:21-50.
1986 Si un gruppo di inumati della necropoli di Cornus. In
*L'archeologia romana e altomedievale nell'Oristanese: Atti del
convegno di Cuglieri*, pp. 213-229. Scorpione, Taranto.

Fornaciari, G., F. Mallegni, D. Bertini, and V. Nuti
1983 *Cribra Orbitalia* and Elemental Bone Iron in the Punics of
Carthage. *Ossa* 8:63-77.

Friedlaender, J.S.
1975 *Patterns of Human Variation. The Demography, Genetics, and
Phenetics of Bougainville Islanders*. Harvard University Press,
Cambridge.

Gejvall, N.-G., and F. Henschen
1968 Two Late Roman Skeletons with Malformation and Close
Family Relationship from Ancient Corinth. *Opuscula Atheniensia*
8:179-193.

Giles, E., and O. Eliot
1985 Sex Determination by Discriminant Function Analysis of
Crania. *American Journal of Physical Anthropology* 21:53-68.

Gregory, T.E.
1993 *Isthmia V. The Hexamilion and the Fortress*. American School
of Classical Studies at Athens, Princeton.

Gregory, T.E., and P.N. Kardulias
1990 Geophysical and Surface Surveys in the Byzantine Fortress at
Isthmia, 1985-1986. *Hesperia* 59:467-511.

Grmek, M.D.
1989 *Diseases in the Ancient Greek World*. Johns Hopkins
University Press, Baltimore.

Harris, J.E., and P.V. Ponitz
1980 Dental Health in Ancient Egypt. In *Mummies, Diesease, and
Ancient Cultures*, edited by A. and E. Cockburn, pp. 45-51.
Cambridge University Press, Cambridge.

Howells, W.W.

1969 Criteria for Selection of Osteometric Measurements. *American Journal of Physical Anthropology* 30:451-458.

1973 *Cranial Variation in Man: A Study by Multivariate Analysis of Patterns of Difference Among Recent Human Populations.* Papers of the Peabody Museum of Archaeology and Ethnology 67. Harvard University Press, Cambridge.

1989 *Skull Shapes and the Map: Craniometric Analyses in the Dispersion of Modern Homo.* Papers of the Peabody Museum of Archaeology and Ethnology 79. Harvard University Press, Cambridge.

Hrdlička, A.

1939 *Practical Anthropometry.* The Wistar Institute of Anatomy and Biology, Philadelphia. Reprinted by AMS Press, New York.

Jackson, R.

1988 *Doctors and Diseases in the Roman Empire.* British Museum, London.

Kardulias, P.N.

1992 Estimating Population at Ancient Military Sites: The Use of Historical and Contemporary Analogy. *American Antiquity* 57:276-287.

Kennedy, K.A.R., J. Chiment, T. Disotell, and D. Meyers

1984 Principal-Component Analysis of Prehistoric South Asian Crania. *American Journal of Physical Anthropology* 64:105-118.

Kilgore, L.

1984 *Degenerative Joint Diseases in a Medieval Nubian Population.* Unpublished Ph.D. dissertation, Department of Anthropology, University of Colorado, Boulder.

Kilgore, L., and R. Jurmain

1988 Analysis of the Human Skeletal Remains. In *The Circus and a Byzantine Cemetery at Carthage* I, edited by J.H. Humphrey, pp. 257-283. University of Michigan Press, Ann Arbor.

Maltby, J.M.

1982 The Variability of Faunal Samples and Their Effects upon Ageing Data. In *Ageing and Sexing Animal Bones from Archaeological Sites,* edited by B. Wilson, C. Grigson, and S. Payne, pp. 81-90. BAR British Series 109. British Archaeological Reports, Oxford.

Manchester, K.

1984 Tuberculosis and Leprosy in Antiquity: An Interpretation. *Medical History* 28:162-173.

Manzi, G., and A. Sperduti

1988 Variabilità morfologica nei campioni cranici di Isola Sacra e Lucus Feroniae (Roma, I-III secolo d. C.). *Rivista antropologica* 66:201-206.

Manzi, G., A. Sperduti, and P. Passarello
1991 Behavior Induced Auditory Exostoses in Imperial Roman Society: Evidence from Coeval Urban and Rural Communities near Rome. *American Journal of Physical Anthropology* 85:253-260.

Martin, R., and K. Saller
1957 *Lehrbuch der Anthropologie in systematischer Darstellung mit besonderer Berücksichtigung der anthropologischen Methoden* I. 4th ed. Gustav Fischer, Stuttgart.

Morant, G.M.
1925 A Study of Egyptian Craniology from Prehistoric to Roman Times. *Biometrika* 17:1-52.

Morris, I.
1992 *Death-Ritual and Social Structure in Classical Antiquity.* Cambridge University Press, Cambridge.

Morse, D., D.R. Brothwell, and P.J. Ucko
1964 Tuberculosis in Ancient Egypt. *American Review of Respiratory Diseases* 90:524-541.

Musgrave, J.H., and S.P. Evans
1980 By Strangers Honor'd: A Statistical Study of Ancient Crania from Crete, Mainland Greece, Cyprus, Israel and Egypt. *Journal of Mediterranean Anthropology and Archaeology* 1:22-40.

Osbourne, C.
1992 The Human Skeletal Remains from Site 10 (1990). In *Leptiminus (Lamta): A Roman Port City in Tunisia*, edited by N. Ben Lazreg and D.J. Mattingly, pp. 269-270. *Journal of Roman Archaeology* supplement 4. University of Michigan Press, Ann Arbor.

O'Shea, J.M.
1984 *Mortuary Variability: An Archaeological Investigation.* Academic Press, Orlando.

Panagiaris, G.
1992 Φυσιοανθρωπολογική Μελέτη Σκελετικού Υλικού Νεολιθικής μέχρι Ελληνιστικής Εποχής τῆς Κεντρικῆς Ἑλλάδας καί τῆς Εὐρύτερης Περιοχῆς Αὐτῆς. Unpublished Ph.D. dissertation, Department of Biology, University of Athens, Athens.

Peppers, J.M.
1979 *Selected Roman Pottery, Isthmia Excavations 1967-1972.*

Unpublished Ph.D. dissertation, Department of Classical Archaeology, University of Pennsylvania, Philadelphia.

Pilet, C. (editor)
1980 La nécropole de Frénouville: Étude d'un population de la fin du IIIe a la fin du VIIe siècle I. BAR International Series 83. British Archaeological Reports, Oxford.

Prag, A.J.N.W.
1989 Reconstructing King Midas: A First Report. *Anatolian Studies* 39:159-166.
1990 Reconstructing King Philip II: The "Nice" Version. *American Journal of Archaeology* 94:237-247.

Prag, A.J.N.W., J.H. Musgrave, and R.A.H. Neave
1984 The Skull from Tomb II at Vergina: King Philip II of Macedon. *Journal of Hellenic Studies* 104:60-78.

Renfrew, C.
1983 Divided We Stand: Aspects of Archaeology and Information. *American Antiquity* 48:3-16.

Ruggles, C.L.N., and S.P.Q. Rahtz (editors)
1988 *Computer and Quantitative Technology in Archaeology 1987.* BAR International Series 393. British Archaeological Reports, Oxford.

Salamon, Á., and I. Lengyel
1980 Kinship Interrelations in a Fifth-Century "Pannonian" Cemetery: an Archaeological and Palaeobiological Sketch of the Population Fragment Buried in the Mösz Cemetery, Hungary. *World Archaeology* 12:93-104.

Sandford, M.K., D.P. Van Gerven, and R.R. Meglen
1983 Elemental Hair Analysis: New Evidence on the Etiology of *Cribra Orbitalia* in Sudanese Nubia. *Human Biology* 55:831-844.

Sandison, A.T.
1980 Diseases in Ancient Egypt. In *Mummies, Disease, and Ancient Cultures*, edited by A. Cockburn and E. Cockburn, pp. 29-44. Cambridge University Press, Cambridge.

Sanghvi, L.D.
1953 Comparison of Genetical and Morphological Methods for a Study of Biological Differences. *American Journal of Physical Anthropology* 11:385-404.

Schwartz, D.C., and D.C. Dirkmaat
1984 Human Remains. In *Excavations at Carthage. The British Mission* I, i: *The Avenue du President Habib Bourguiba, Salammbo. The Site and Finds Other than Pottery*, edited by H.R.

Hurst and S.P. Roskams, pp. 222-228. The University of Sheffield Department of Prehistory and Archaeology, Sheffield.

Smith, P., and S. Tau
1978 Dental Pathology in the Period of the Roman Empire: A Comparison of Two Populations. *Ossa* 5:35-41.

Spielman, R.S., F.J. de Rocha, L.R. Weitkamp, R.H. Ward, J.V. Neel, and N.A. Chagnon
1972 The Genetic Structure of a Tribal Population, the Yąnomamö Indians VII: Anthropometric Differences among the Yąnomamö Villages. *American Journal of Physical Anthropology* 37:345-356.

Steele, D.G., and C.A. Bramblett
1988 *The Anatomy and Biology of the Human Skeleton.* Texas A&M University Press, College Station.

Turner, K.R.
1986 Morphological Variants of the Temporal Bone and Biological Distance. *American Journal of Physical Anthropology* 69:274.

Van Gerven, D.P.
1982 Contribution of Time and Local Geography to Craniofacial Variation in Nubia's Batn el Hajar. *American Journal of Physical Anthropology* 59:307-316.

Van Gerven, D.P., G.J. Armelagos, and A. Rohr
1976 Continuity and Change in Cranial Morphology of Three Nubian Archaeological Populations. *Man* n.s. 12:270-277.

Van Gerven, D.P., M.K. Sandford, and J.R. Hummert
1981 Mortality and Culture Change in Nubia's Batn el Hajar. *Journal of Human Evolution* 10:395-408.

Vermeule, C. C.
1986 Figural Pillars: From Asia Minor to Rome to Corinth. In *Corinthiaca: Studies in Honor of Darrell A. Amyx*, edited by M.A. Del Chiaro, pp. 71-80. University of Missouri Press, Columbia.

Wall, S.M., J.H. Musgrave, and P.M. Warren
1986 Human Bones from a Late Minoan 1b House at Knossos. *Annual of the British School at Athens* 81:333-388.

Walsh, V.A., and P.C. Patton
1985 Future developments in Computer-Aided Aegean Archaeology. In *Contributions to Aegean Archaeology*, edited by N.C. Wilkie and W.D.E. Coulson, pp. 245-258. University of Minnesota Press, Minneapolis.

Walth, C.K., and L. Miller
1993 Burials and Disarticulated Human Bone (1990). In *Bir El Knissia at Carthage: A Rediscovered Cemetery Church Report no.*

1, edited by S.T. Stevens, pp. 191-200. *Journal of Roman Archaeology* supplement 7. University of Michigan Press, Ann Arbor.

Warwick, R.
    1968 The Skeletal Remains. In *The Romano-British Cemetery at Trentholm Drive, York,* edited by L.P. Wenham, pp. 113-176. Longman, London.

Wesolowsky, A.B.
    1973 The Skeletons of Lerna Hollow. *Hesperia* 42:340-351.

Whittaker, D.K., and M.V. Stack
    1984 The Lead, Cadmium and Zinc Content of Some Romano-British Teeth. *Archaeometry* 26:37-42.

Whittaker, D.K., S. Ryan, K. Weeks, and W.M. Murphy
    1987 Patterns of Approximal Wear in Cheek Teeth of a Romano-British Population. *American Journal of Physical Anthropology* 73:389-396.

Williams, C. K.
    1993 Roman Corinth as a Commercial Center. In *The Corinthia in the Roman Period,* edited by T.E. Gregory, pp. 31-46. *Journal of Roman Archaeology* supplement 8. University of Michigan Press, Ann Arbor.

Williams, C.K., and O.H. Zervos
    1990 Corinth, 1990: Southeast Corner of Temenos E. *Hesperia* 60:1-58.
    1991 Frankish Corinth: 1991. *Hesperia* 61:133-191.

Wiseman, J.R.
    1969 Excavations at Corinth, The Gymnasium Area, 1967-1968. *Hesperia* 38:64-106.

Wohl, B.L.
    1981 A Deposit of Lamps from the Roman Bath at Isthmia. *Hesperia* 50:112-140.

Endnotes

1. This is only a summary of the scholarship. For another recent discussion and a more complete bibliography including the important publications on mortuary practice and the social dimensions of death in ancient Greece and Rome, see the excellent study by Ian Morris (1992:70-102, 205-257).

2. The standard significance level of .05 means that, in 5% of the cases tested, discrepancies between variable means can be attributed to random factors or sampling error. Values greater than .05 therefore indicate that

discrepancies are insignificant, and values less than .05 indicate that discrepancies are significant. So, if the p-value is greater than .05, there is no significant difference between the two populations in terms of a morphological characteristic. If the p-value is less than .05, there is a significant difference between the variable means in the sample groups and the null hypothesis is not supported.

3.   A nonparametric, or distribution-free, statistical test does not assume that the data follow a uniform distribution. The Mann-Whitney U test, a nonparametric equivalent of the t-test, was later applied to the morphometric data to check the results of this analysis. The p-values from the U test for seven variables, including male bimental breadth, were greater than the .05 significance level; the p-value from the U test for female minimum ramus breadth was only slightly greater than 0.5.

V.
COMPUTER MODELLING

Chapter 12

The Site within the Region: Architectural Reconstruction Using Computer Technology

Michael G. Stys

Introduction

Over the past 30 years various researchers have conducted studies in different areas of Greece. These studies examine the interaction between humans and the environment through time by means of the choices humans had to make in response to their environment. These studies basically fall into two categories. The first category is that of regional analysis, which examines a broad geographical expanse that has boundaries defined by major sites. Regional studies routinely take into account environmental variables such as topography, weather, soil conditions, elevation, and any resource upon which humans were dependent. The second category is that of site-specific analysis, which involves a detailed study of the places humans occupied, and examines structures, monuments, temples, and gathering areas. Regions, however, are made up of sites, so the latter is the indispensable building block for any regional study.

A definition of region is in order. Of considerable concern for archaeologists over the years has been the problem of how to delineate the spatial elements they study. In one of the first and most influential systematic discussions of this issue, Willey and Phillips devised a hierarchy of size. Their system recognized as the smallest unit the site, defined as a fairly continuous distribution of the remains of a former "single unit of settlement" (Willey and Phillips 1958:18). Next in extent is the locality, "a geographical space small enough to permit the working assumption of complete cultural homogeneity at any given time" (Willey and Phillips 1958:18). A region encompasses a space that could be settled by a "social unit larger than the community" (Willey and Phillips 1958:19). A region also constitutes a particular physiographic unit. The largest unit, the area, is a major physiographic zone (e.g., the Great Basin, the Levant, or the Aegean Basin). The present study focuses on a single site as a means of demonstrating how a more refined understanding of the specific features (in this case, a complex building) informs our reconstruction of the various levels embedded in a settlement hierarchy.

Computer graphics technology facilitates the interpretation of specific sites and this paper describes a process that is applied to the Roman Bath at Isthmia, Greece (see Figure 11.1). The technology that was implemented at Isthmia allowed us to envision better what buildings looked like, and how they fit into the surrounding environment. From such analysis one can more clearly discuss social function.

The case study for examination is the Roman Bath at Isthmia, Greece. The Bath is almost completely excavated, yet many important problems concerning its construction and form remain. Roman bathing establishments possessed vast and complicated structural, hydraulic, and thermal components (Yegül 1993). In complicated buildings such as these, the ruins can be interpreted in a wide variety of ways. Computer Aided Design/Drafting (CADD or CAD) and sophisticated technical survey technology were used to record extant architectural features and to examine, analyze, and interpret the Bath's remains. In addition, the flexibility that this computer technology offers allows for the hypothetical reconstruction of the Bath, which will lead to a better interpretation of how the structure was utilized.

Site Background

Isthmia is located on the Isthmus of Korinth, a narrow land-bridge (about six miles wide) that connects Central Greece with the Peloponnesos. To the east is the Saronic Gulf which provides a link to Asia Minor, Cyprus, Syria, the Phoenician mercantile states, and Egypt. To the west is the Korinthian Gulf allowing contact with Italy, North Africa, Spain, and France. All land transportation between central Greece and the Peloponnesos had to pass through the Isthmus, and the two harbors, Lechaion (on the Korinthian Gulf) and Kenchreai (on the Saronic Gulf) were filled with ships from throughout the Mediterranean world. Isthmia was, thus, located at an important crossroad. Travellers, merchants, prophets, soldiers, thieves, pilgrims, and others passed through the site, making it an ideal center for communication, trade, worship, and religious practice.

In antiquity, Isthmia was a religious sanctuary (dedicated to Poseidon, the god of the sea and earthquakes). According to the second century A.D. traveller Pausanias (1964), Poseidon won control of the Isthmus in a contest with the sun-god Helios. It was one of the four Panhellenic sanctuaries of Greece along with Olympia, Delphi, and Nemea.

Athletic contests were an important part of Greek religion, and in the spring of every second year people from all of Greece gathered to celebrate the Isthmian games. The games included running, wrestling, boxing, and throwing events. These games also featured music and theatrical performances. Pine wreaths were the prizes for victory at the Isthmus (Broneer 1973:4).

The Roman Bath is located on the north end of the site, at the edge of a ravine, where cool breezes from the north would have provided relief in the middle of a Greek summer day. Just to the west of the Bath was a small stream that ran north from the area of the Temple and debouched into the ravine. This stream may have provided some of the water for the users of the Bath.

Earlier Greek Bath

The Bath was apparently constructed in the latter years of the first century after Christ (Gregory 1994; Gregory and Kardulias 1989). It underwent several renovations and redecorations, the most important of which was in the early second century. A series of impressive mosaic floors were laid at this time. The Bath continued to function until the end of the fourth century, but it was seriously damaged at that time, and by the late third century it was no longer being used for its original purpose (Gregory 1989, 1990).

The Bath was constructed in typical Roman manner with walls made either of brick or of small stones laid in courses; the surfaces were covered with decorative material, either plaster or marble revetment. The floors of the rooms were paved with mosaics, including the great monochrome mosaic in Room VI (Packard 1980). Details such as these need to be recorded as they provide clues to the use of the site.

Examination of the Bath at Isthmia reveals much about the routine that was followed in the Roman practice of bathing. This practice was not simply a means to get clean; it was much more a social exercise, an opportunity for individuals to meet with friends, to discuss business, politics, or other issues of the day. The function of the individual rooms is as interesting as the entire structure (Yegül 1993).

The bathers would presumably have entered the Bath from the north, going through Room XII into the long corridor of Room VII (Figure 12.1). From there one would have proceeded into Room VI, the great vaulted hall. On either end of the room were pedestals supporting sculpture that were over-life-size, while on the floor was the monochrome mosaic depicting various forms of sea life. From Room VI the bather would go to Room VIII, which was the apodyterium, or "changing room", and from there to Room IX, the tepidarium, or "warm room". The floors of Rooms IX, X, and XII were supported by hypocausts, which allowed the hot air from the furnaces at the south end of the building to circulate under the floor and through the walls, making the rooms much like a modern sauna. The bather would cleanse himself (or would have recourse to a slave), using a basin of hot water. From the tepidarium the bather would continue on to the caldarium, or "hot room" (Room XI), also heated by a hypocaust system. This process would be leisurely and a bather would probably wander among the rooms during the process. From the caldarium, he would pass into the laconicum (Room X) or "steam room" and finally go on to Room III, which was the frigidarium, or "cold room". The latter included plunge baths (Rooms IV and V), which were the only places where the bather could actually be immersed in water. After this, an individual might go on to one of the subsidiary rooms (Rooms I and II), to relax further and converse. These rooms, and others in the complex, might have also been used for exercise and as "lecture halls" where local or itinerant teachers could present their ideas to an interested public.

Methodology

Generating accurate and realistic architectural reconstructions requires an efficient production method. The illustration and reconstruction of archaeological features will be broken down into three phases: (1) demonstrate how state-of-the-art technology can aid field techniques for gathering data; (2) demonstrate how CAD is used to construct extant features of the Bath; and (3) demonstrate how CAD is used to produce hypothetical reconstructions of the Bath.

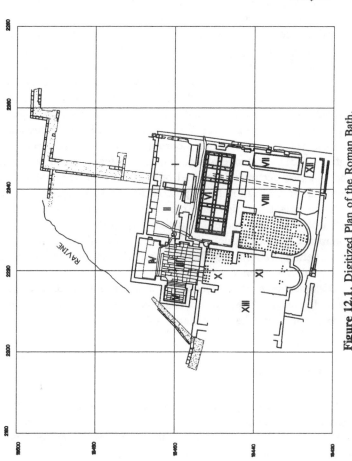

Figure 12.1. Digitized Plan of the Roman Bath.

The use of CAD to illustrate and create hypothetical reconstructions of the Bath begins with data that were collected during the 1990 field season. The author conducted a technical survey.[1]

Over 1500 point coordinates, describing strategically identified positions among the features of the Bath, were recorded during a 5-week field season. These point coordinates were chosen to illustrate best the "character" of the fragments. In other words, the principle used to select points was to survey any point that characterized a significant change in direction or elevation. This process requires a critical judgement by the operator to select the best points so that the subsequent drawings do not generalize or smooth the actual surfaces. The combination of the points will then represent the features that give an object its texture, form, and size. These data were then entered into AutoCAD as three-dimensional (3D) points. This requires insertion of a drawing entity (point) into the AutoCAD file by using the surveyed coordinates as the insertion coordinate. Then by connecting these entities, a 3D wireframe model of extant features can be generated. In short, a very accurate 3D model of existing conditions was created to serve as the foundation for hypothetical reconstructions.

After extant remains are recorded, they are evaluated by the archaeologist for accuracy, and then hypothetical reconstruction can commence. Reconstruction involves extending walls upward, constructing various roofing scenarios, and recreating probable structural components.

Documentation of the techniques and conventions used to produce these hypothetical reconstructions can include drawings, sequential slides, and computer generated animations of the reconstruction scenarios.

Field Techniques

Typical archaeological surveying techniques include manual methods that have been commonplace for many years. CAD was used in this case study to create a 3D data base that represents the present condition of the site as reflected in the 1990 field survey (Stys 1991).

The technical survey of the Bath included two principal tasks. First, the survey recorded excavation data (i.e., trench corners, artifact and feature locations, and stratigraphic levels). Second, the survey recorded the coordinate points that represent the extant remains of the Bath structure. This was done by surveying remaining walls, floors, corners, blocks, stones, and drains. All coordinate points were on the same x,y,z grid and so provided a three-dimensional description of extant conditions for the entire project area. Use of CAD, specifically AutoCAD, greatly enhanced both of these tasks.

Equipment used in the field included a Topcon laser theodolite, a reflecting prism, a prism rod, a tripod, and a laptop computer. Software packages included the GTS-Topo survey program and AutoCAD R.10. The survey computer program, running on the laptop computer linked by cable to the theodolite, uses the information provided by the theodolite to calculate coordinates of surveyed points.[2]

At this point, the data were simply points with 3D coordinates; they did not illustrate anything. This is when the AutoCAD software was utilized. The surveyed points should be manually entered into a drawing at their proper coordinates (with attributes--verbal information--attached to each graphic entity in the drawing). These attribute descriptions correspond to the descriptions used in the field survey. Consequently, it becomes simpler to "connect the dots" and create a wire-frame model of the surveyed area.

AutoCAD permits the creation of an unlimited number of layers (a "sheet" in a drawing file to which entities are attached). Layering was imperative to the management of the large amount of data in the drawing. For example, after the points were connected there was no need for the points to be displayed. Therefore, the points and the wire-frame model parts were placed on different layers, and the layer that contained just the entered points was "frozen" (turned off and ignored by AutoCAD until "thawed").

Digital data gathered in the field and entered into AutoCAD, plus photographs and field notes, were then used to recreate each room of the Bath individually. Separating the Bath model into individual room models made the actual data manipulation simpler. Managing smaller sized drawings (byte size) and perceiving the rooms individually ultimately increases computing speed and drawing simplicity. The individual files have been merged into a single AutoCAD drawing to form a composite model of the Bath. Photographs become an important visual aid in understanding how the points relate to each other.

In conclusion, the above mentioned technologies have been available for some time, but archaeologists have made little use of them until recently. The use of a state-of-the-art theodolite accompanied with a computer-based survey program (e.g., GTS-Topo) serves as a very fast and accurate data collection tool. A 3D visual database can be developed from collected data using AutoCAD. These techniques will provide more accurate data collection, which results in more precise illustrations and reconstructions than previously possible. The following section will illustrate, in more detail, how the data were converted into an AutoCAD database representing extant features of the Roman Bath.

Construction of Extant Features

Electronic drawing files can be created from the data collected via survey of the existing site conditions and visible ruins. The previous section discussed in detail how the data were collected and converted to a CAD format. This phase of the case study demonstrates how these data are manipulated using CAD to construct and illustrate the extant features of the Bath and surrounding topography.

Usually, it is desirable to collect other data for conversion in a CAD format (e.g., topography), in addition to data collected via field survey. Before the collected survey data of the Bath were manipulated in AutoCAD, the site's topography was converted to a CAD format.

CAD Topographic Plans

The following will explain the process of digitizing an existing topographic map into AutoCAD to create a two dimensional plan. Then the process of converting this CAD drawing into a three dimensional topo model will be addressed.

These maps have typically been manually drafted, which limits them in terms of changing scales or editing. With the advent of CAD not only can these plans be created at a convenient size in their computer format and plotted at any scale desired, but they can also be converted into a 3D representation of site conditions. In other words, the CAD topo model becomes another visualization tool to help understand the site's surroundings.

The initial step involved digitizing the existing site map (Figure 12.2). AutoCAD drawings of the topography and site provide a computer drawing file that facilitates data editing and permits flexible plotting of different sectors at various scales. In addition, the 3D model created from the drawing file serves as a visual tool to aid in the presentation of the site. Most importantly, one can insert features and artifact location directly into the site plan.

Figure 12.2. CAD drawing digitized from the existing site plan.

CAD Drawing of Extant Features of the Roman Bath

Archaeological features are typically fragmentary and incomplete. Consequently, illustrating them becomes a tedious chore. The survey technique described above (Field Techniques) was used to record the extant architectural features of the Bath. This technique greatly improved the efficiency of archaeological data recording and illustration when compared to traditional methods of survey and drafting.

Drawings of excavation trenches are very important, as these record the locations of features and artifacts prior to removal. Consequently, the accuracy and speed of drawing are crucial factors. Currently the archaeologist must measure and draw the features as they are excavated. This has proven to be effective, but slows excavation significantly. In addition to the artifact and trench data, the architectural features, specifically walls, floors, door openings, and ornamentation, need to be recorded. Shortcomings of this method are the inability to edit drawings without manual drafting and the inability to view the features from multiple perspectives.

When the points, strategically selected to best capture the character of the feature, were surveyed and successfully stored in the computer, the reconstruction of these features using AutoCAD commenced. Surveyed data for each room and feature are stored in individual files to simplify the input into AutoCAD. The principle used to select points was to survey any point that characterized a change in direction or elevation. This process requires a critical judgement by the operator to select the best points so that the subsequent drawings do not generalize or smooth the actual surfaces. The combination of the points thus represent the features that give an object its texture, form, and size.[3]

Using the above techniques for each room and feature created a series of computer drawing files that can be merged together to form a composite AutoCAD drawing. This drawing is a 3D database that can be rotated, viewed from any conceivable angle, and edited. It also serves as an illustrative database which has information such as bearing, length, etc., attached to each entity (line). This information can be recalled or "listed" for further analysis. Figure 12.3 illustrates the composite AutoCAD database of the extant Bath features. The survey data needed to construct this model took approximately 120 hours to gather in the field (Stys 1991).

The technology described above also served other purposes for the illustration of architectural features at Isthmia. During the 1990 excavation season, a third corner of a Greek Pool, located under the

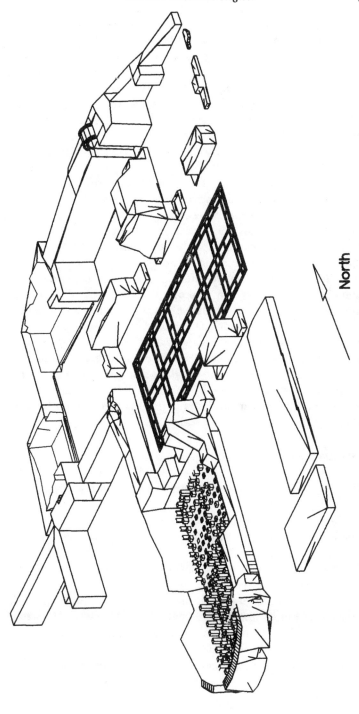

North

Figure 12.3. CAD drawing of extant features of Roman Bath.

Roman Bath, was revealed. Two other corners had been discovered in previous excavations. After surveying the wall that continued from this corner and inserting the data into AutoCAD it became apparent where the fourth corner was located. AutoCAD aided the reconstruction through its ability to quickly illustrate the bearing of that wall in relation to other walls already known. Consequently, the architect was able to determine the probable function of the newly excavated features. In other words, the constructed lines in AutoCAD could be "listed", making information such as bearing and length readily apparent. This not only facilitated the analysis of the feature but also provided a convincing illustration. Figure 12.4 illustrates the Greek Pool under the Roman Bath as uncovered during the 1990 field season.

The use of state-of-the-art survey equipment for data collection and AutoCAD for illustrating these data is a welcome addition to the excavation process because of its ease of use and accuracy. The combination of methods can aid in recording important excavation data, such as trench and artifact location, and stratigraphic contexts. In addition, this technology can improve the collection of data about architectural features, both in relation to other features and the site as a whole. The use of an AutoCAD database serves as a recording tool as well as an illustrative drawing. This drawing can be viewed in 3D from any angle to aid in the understanding of the architectural remains.

Figure 12.1 shows a plan of the Bath that was digitized from an existing plan drafted in 1978 by the late William Dinsmoor. The significance of this drawing is that it is flexible in that it can be edited quickly or plotted at any desired scale.

Illustrative Reconstructions

Archaeological illustrative reconstructions aid in visualizing a site and thereby provide an understanding of the ancient architectural forms. The AutoCAD database of extant features at Isthmia became the foundation for the reconstruction of the Bath as it may have appeared in the first century A.D.

The AutoCAD drawing of the extant features will serve as the base for a hypothetical reconstruction of the Bath in its complete form (Figure 12.5). From Figure 12.5, the major walls, foundations, apse, and doorways can be traced onto a new AutoCAD layer. The tracing assumes the walls are orthogonal or straight. This new plan provides the base for the hypothetical reconstruction.

Information on wall heights, arch distances, door heights, room con-

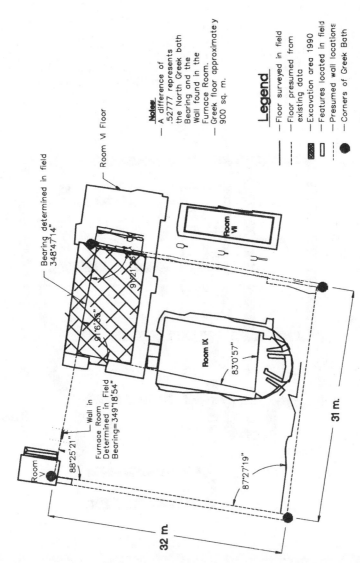

Figure 12.4. CAD drawing depicting Greek period architectural features under the Roman Bath.

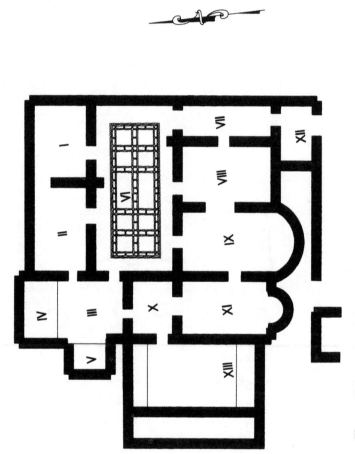

Figure 12.5. Plan of Bath traced from CAD drawing of extant features of the Bath.

nections, etc. was derived from a literature review, and interviews with the site director and several architects.

The first step in reconstructing the Bath was to create a drawing of the structure in three dimensions (Figure 12.6). Lines that represent the walls were extended upward, and arches, which represent the skeleton of the roof, were inserted to produce a wireframe model of the Bath. AutoCAD "surfaces" were then placed on this wireframe drawing to illustrate better the Bath architecturally (Figure 12.7).

Two roofing scenarios were created to explore the hypothetical differences among the possible reconstructions. Figure 12.7 illustrates the reconstructed structure with a wireframe of roofing scenario #1. (Note the arches that will later be shown as barrel vaults and cross vaults).

Making the roofs look as realistic as possible is accomplished by placing surfaces on the wireframe model. A drawback of using AutoCAD for drawing the roofs is that the surfaces that are placed on the wireframe appear as a series of rectangles placed around selected edges (i.e., arches, walls). For schematic illustrative purposes this appears adequate. However, it will be difficult to add details that better represent a Roman Bath roof in AutoCAD. Adding these details, such as sculpture, roof tiles, etc. can be accomplished manually after the drawing is plotted. Figure 12.8 presents a final hypothetical illustration of the Roman Bath with an initial roofing scenario.

Consultation with the site director (Gregory, personal communication 1991) indicated a need to change the roof structure to fit architectural conventions and comparanda. This is when the real power of AutoCAD is evident. By using the previous drawing a new roofing scenario can be created as an AutoCAD "layer."

AutoCAD layering can be thought of as electronic sheets of clear acetate laid one over the other. When working in two dimensions, one can look down through the sheets. The drawing represents all of the entities built from the superimposed sheets. The user can pull a single sheet to examine. In 3D, these electronic layers become more of an organizational tool. The layers can contain any group of objects. These layers can be superimposed in space to coexist with other groups. Electronic layering was essential when reconstructing the Roman Bath.

For the Bath drawing, names were given to a layer that would be indicative of the objects that would be placed on that layer. The first series of layers contained the wireframe objects that make up the specific rooms of the Bath. For example, layer "rm12" would contain the objects that represented room XII of the Bath; layer "rm12s" was

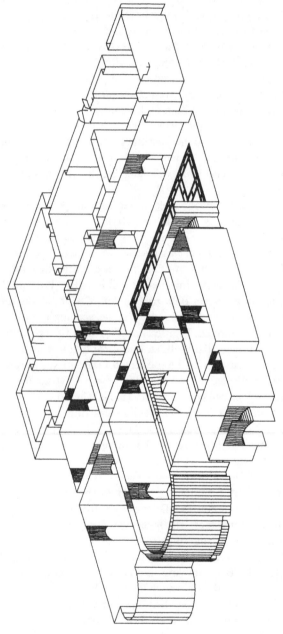

Figure 12.6. CAD drawing showing hypothetical wall and door construction.

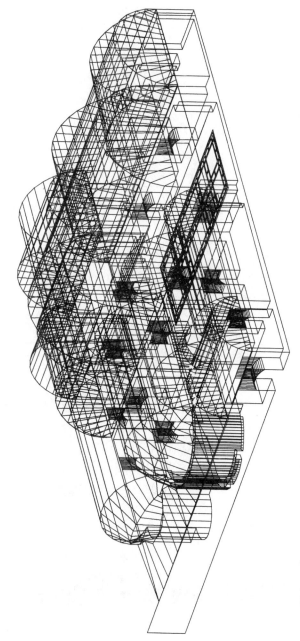

Figure 12.7. CAD wireframe drawing showing initial roofing model. Arches represent the vaulting schematically.

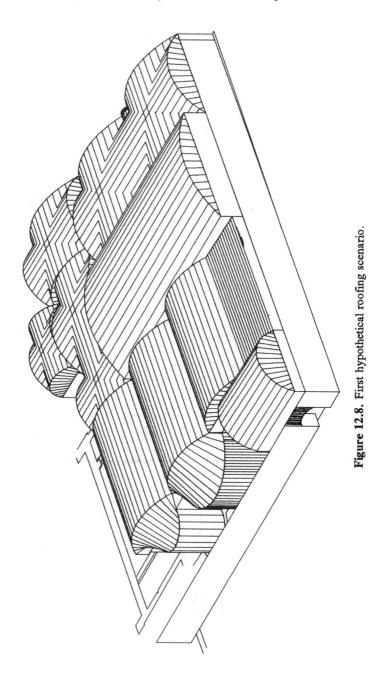

Figure 12.8. First hypothetical roofing scenario.

added to place the "surfaces" or "faces" of room XII ("surfaces" or "faces" are the AutoCAD entities that enhance 3D modelling). This process permits one to illustrate any combination of Bath features. The next set of layers are for the wireframe of the roofing scenario. Finally, a layer for the roofing "surfaces" is needed. These simple layering conventions proved to be effective in separating the drawing into its constituent parts. Because of this "layering" ability a second roofing scenario can be added easily to the existing database. "Freezing" the layers that have the first roofing scenario clears them from the screen, but not from the database.

At this point, a second roofing scenario was created on the existing 3D Bath drawing. New layers were created to place these objects. Figure 12.9 illustrates a second hypothetical roofing scenario. This second roof compensated for probable oversights in the first roofing scenario.

In summary, the hypothetical reconstructions shown above are preliminary drawings that illustrate how the Roman Bath at Isthmia, Greece may have appeared in the first century A.D.

Conclusion

This study attempted to provide a more intensive analysis of site specific conditions. Technology, such as a laser theodolite (surveying) and CAD (illustration), provides a flexible tool to interpret better the human-site relationship. The major benefits include expedited survey, efficient and accurate recording of data, and enhanced graphical display.

The rapidity with which readings can be taken allowed us to record elevations, distances, features, etc., very quickly and thoroughly. This ability allowed the excavation to proceed rapidly with few major interruptions. In addition, the ability to see drawings, contours, etc., shortly after the survey allowed us to assess the validity of contemplated steps in the excavation. They also provided working plans which facilitated the process of interpretation in the field. In the future, such aids will assist in making decisions concerning where to invest valuable excavation time. This provides a flow to the excavation, as well as improved accuracy in the readings.

The process of converting site specific survey data to a CAD database requires some special skill, but this can be learned quite easily. The advantage of the CAD system for graphical display is that it provides much greater flexibility than traditional drawing. Each tra-

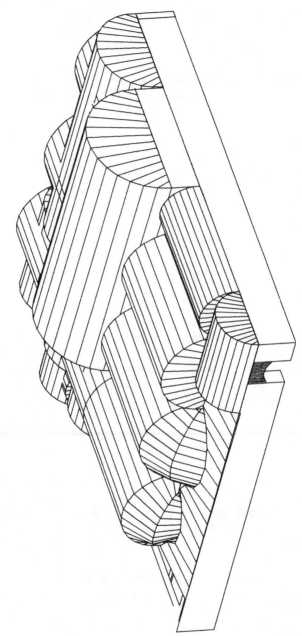

Figure 12.9. Second hypothetical roofing scenario.

ditional drawing is a single inflexible piece of information. Each view requires great investment in time to create. With CAD we can visualize the site, and individual features within it, very quickly in a variety of ways. In addition, preparation of publication quality plans is enhanced.

Even more important than the immediate benefits created using this technology, are the long-term prospects. The metrical nature of the CAD database makes it an invaluable repository of archaeological data. For example, now that the Bath is on CAD, we can much more easily compare it in a precise and quantifiable fashion to other baths. There is the potential, for example, for split screen comparisons that allow one to align and realign buildings for direct comparison. Questions that one may ask and be able to get answers to very quickly include: how do the various rooms compare? are plunge baths the same as in other buildings? how do the orientations compare? etc. In addition, gathering data from other sites will add to the database. Then, for example, the architectural elements can be categorized in terms of their overall dimensions. Because of the metrical nature of the CAD system one can query the computer to find all rooms of specific dimensions and then compare them on screen.

This project is the first step in a long term investigation in which we can, in a more sophisticated manner than before, examine the factors that influence the location of settlements. With CAD and Geographic Information Systems (GIS) we can model the settlement regime at different points in time to see what factors may have been key determinants of site location in different periods. We can also look inside sites to determine the particular elements that influenced the layout of settlements, the positioning of residences, etc. Also, we can begin to reconstruct formation processes (natural and cultural) to predict where there may be sites that have been buried by various natural events. With this ability we can begin to merge the site specific analysis with an understanding of the regional settings.

Using these various techniques allows us to look at specific sites (and entire regions) in a much more precise manner. This ability will be critical for understanding site use and abandonment. Thus, by examining specific sites within regions, we can begin to predict, for example, movement from site to site by season for specific resource exploitation.

In conclusion, improved survey techniques, graphical illustration, and data storage provide a better means to analyze site specific human conditions. The flexibility of the system permits inclusion of new data derived from excavation and survey. In the future this system can grow with other methods of regional analysis (GIS; see Dann and Yerkes, this volume) and provide a unified system of recording archaeological data.

References Cited

Broneer, O.
   1973 *Isthmia*. II. *Topography and Architecture*. American School of Classical Studies at Athens, Princeton.
Gregory, T.E.
   1993 In *The Corinthia in the Roman Period*, edited by T.E. Gregory, pp. 149-160. Journal of Roman Archaeology Supplementary Series No. 8, Ann Arbor.
   1994 The Roman Bath at Isthmia, 1972-1992: A Preliminary Report. *Hesperia*, in press.
Gregory, T.E., and P.N. Kardulias
   1989 The 1989 Season at Isthmia. *Old World Archaeology Newsletter* 13(3):14-17.
Packard, P.
   1980 A Monochrome Mosaic at Isthmia. *Hesperia* 49:326-346.
Pausanias
   1964 *Description of Greece*. Translated by W. H. S. Jones. 4 vols. Harvard University Press, Cambridge.
Stys, M.G.
   1991 *The Illustration and Proposed Reconstruction of the Roman Bath at Isthmia, Greece Using Computer Technology*. Unpublished Master's thesis, Department of Landscape Architecture, Ohio State University, Columbus.
Willey, G.R., and P. Phillips
   1958 *Method and Theory in American Archaeology*. University of Chicago Press, Chicago.
Yegül, F.
   1993 The Roman Baths at Isthmia in their Mediterranean Context. In *The Corinthia in the Roman Period*, edited by T.E. Gregory, pp. 95-112. Journal of Roman Archaeology Supplementary Series No. 8, Ann Arbor.

Endnotes

1. Phase 1 examines the use of a technology that has been available for some time. This traditional technology (survey) coincides well with the use of AutoCAD in drawing archaeological features. Data collection in the Bath involved the use of a laser theodolite (Topcon GS-4 Total Station) and a lap-top computer (Zenith Supersport 286) to provide the most efficient means of surveying the structure in three dimensions. The laser theodolite operates by sending out a laser beam which bounces off a prism. (The prism's location represents the precise location whose coordinates must be determined.) The lap-top computer accompanied by the GTS-Topo surveying program, performs all survey calculations and recording in the field. The program has the capability of "communicating" with the theodolite via a RS-232 cable. The GTS-Topo program was written by Warren B. Watts & Perpetual Motion Software with minor editing by the author in response to the requirements of this project. As a result, the surveying program controlled the theodolite and calculated and recorded the UTM (Universal Transverse Mercator) coordinates and elevations immediately as they were shot. These point coordinate data were in a format that can be input easily to AutoCAD (a leading computer aided design/drafting software package), and thus, provide 3D data ready for enhancement.

2. All trigonometric functions typical of survey mathematics are a part of the program, and no calculations are required in the field. In addition, the computer program allows the user to identify each coordinate point with a description. This capability is convenient; it means that efficient note taking in the field is available. Additionally, this capability reduces error due to distractions from heat and wind, common to the Mediterranean climate.

3. A problem occurred during this process of constructing a wireframe drawing of the Bath's features. An AutoCAD file soon becomes confusing when these points are entered as 3D data. At times they appear on top of each other if the view point of the drawing is in 2-D plan when they may actually be 1-2 m apart vertically. A way to alleviate this problem is to enter the data in manageable increments and then connect the points before continuing. Also, by editing the drawing at an oblique angle view, point positions on the screen become more obvious because changes in elevation are then evident. The accuracy of the AutoCAD drawing is limited by how many survey points are taken for that feature. Experience from the 1990 field season demonstrated no mechanical constraints in collecting any number of points, but one must consider the human factors of boredom, concentration level, and the availability of assistants.

Chapter 13

Use of Geographic Information Systems for the Spatial Analysis of Frankish Settlements in the Korinthia, Greece

Mark A. Dann and Richard W. Yerkes

Introduction

The archaeological record has three dimensions: space, time and form (Spaulding 1960), but archaeologists have had difficulty dealing with all three dimensions simultaneously (Green 1990). Studies of past human behavior require the investigation of the temporal and spatial distributions of artifacts, features, and sites in the landscape. To accomplish this, we must overlay, compare, and correlate multidimensional maps of the cultural and natural variables that define the landscape contexts of ancient settlement systems (Butzer 1982). Recently, a number of archaeologists have recognized that Geographic Information Systems (GIS) can be used to analyze archaeological data without compromising their three-dimensional qualities (Green 1990). GIS are software systems specially designed to handle data with spatial or mappable attributes, and facilitate problem solving through the description and interpretation of spatial relationships (Clarke 1986; Kvamme 1989). GIS-based regional studies can improve the way site catchments are investigated and facilitate the statistical analysis of site location tendencies (Allen et al. 1990; Brandt et al. 1992; Gaffney and Stancic 1991; Hunt 1992; Kvamme 1989).

In this study, a GIS was developed and used to identify the landscape contexts of thirteenth century Frankish settlements in the Korinthia, Greece (Dann 1992). By manipulating the GIS database, Frankish land use patterns were reconstructed, and a predictive model for Frankish settlement locations in the Korinthia was developed. Most archaeological models have noted the correlations between natural landscape features and site locations, suggesting that ancient people selected specific types of terrain, soils, and elevations for their settlements and activity areas (Brandt et al. 1992; Jochim 1976; Kvamme 1985; Parker 1985). Our study places equal emphasis on the cultural landscape (Johnson 1977; Romano and Schoenbrun 1993), and weighs the importance of defense, agricultural production, and proximity to transportation corridors on decisions about site locations (cf. Bon 1969; Gregory 1994a). The use of the GIS made it possible to combine multiple sets of spatial data and analyze their relationships. Data from geological, topographic, and historic maps were used to classify the soils around the known Frankish settlements, to determine the slope and aspect of these sites, and their proximity to sources of fresh water, ancient roadways, and other settlements. The geographical attributes that were shared by the known sites were identified, and the GIS was employed to identify similar geographic settings in the Korinthia where other Frankish settlements may be discovered (Proposals have been submitted requesting funds that will allow us to examine the areas of the Korinthia where these probable Frankish sites may be located).

Regional Studies in Southern Greece and the Potential for GIS

The pioneering work of the University of Minnesota Messenia Expedition (UMME) demonstrated how historic records and geographic information can be combined with archaeological and geomorphological investigations to reconstruct past environments and examine how the settlement patterns of a region in southern Greece changed through time (McDonald and Rapp 1972). Other multidisciplinary studies of ancient settlement systems have been conducted in the Argolid (Jameson et al. 1994; van Andel and Runnels 1987; Wells et al. 1990, 1993; Zangger 1992a, 1992b), Boeotia (Bintliff and Snodgrass 1985; Gregory 1992), and the Nemea Valley (Wright et al. 1990). However, these important studies did not have the benefit of a GIS analysis of the spatial (and statistical) relationships between landscape features, land use patterns, and settlement locations in antiquity.

The use of a GIS is not a substitute for systematic archaeological survey in a region, but can save much time and money in the planning of a survey and the analysis of the spatial data collected in the field. For example, in their regional analysis of ancient settlement systems on the island of Hvar in Dalmatia, Gaffney and Stancic (1991) used a GIS to analyze the published environmental data and the cultural information that had been gathered through decades of archaeological survey and excavation. The workers on the Hvar Project were compiling a register (or inventory) of the prehistoric and historic sites and monuments on the island, and they realized that a GIS is an ideal tool for managing the copious amounts of data that they were accumulating. The Hvar Project employed a GIS system that was developed by the Arkansas Archaeological Survey for research and data management. From Arkansas to Yugoslavia, a GIS has been applied to archaeological data sets that were compiled through regional surveys (Allen et al. 1990; Brandt et al. 1993; Kvamme 1989; Wansleeben 1988). These survey/data management applications have been successful, but would a GIS-assisted study be fruitful in a region where systematic archaeological survey has not yet been conducted? In regions like the Korinthia the recorded sites may not be a representative sample of the sites that comprised ancient settlement systems. The inventory of known sites may be biased toward larger, more obvious sites, and certain types of sites may be underrepresented or overlooked. We wanted to learn if a GIS could be developed to help us formulate a predictive model of site location even if our sample of known sites is limited and potentially biased.

We chose the Frankish period (thirteenth century) for our test case, since this brief episode in the long archaeological record of the Korinthia has been neglected. This part of the Peloponnesos (or Morea) witnessed a significant Medieval occupation (Kordosis 1981) and there are numerous historical documents (for certain phases), but relatively little analytical work has been conducted on this important "transitional period" from classical antiquity to the modern era. We have a historical outline of events in the Morea during the Frankish period, but our knowledge of the Frankish settlement system is incomplete. Topping (1972) noted that in Messenia, forty Medieval villages that were mentioned in the historic literature cannot be relocated, and it is likely that there are similar numbers of settlements in the Korinthia that are unaccounted for. We believe that the best way to relocate these "missing" sites and to create a more representative model of the Frankish settlement system is through the development of a predictive model that can guide our search. The development and application of a GIS would be the most economical means to accomplish that goal.

The Study Area

The Korinthia is the land around the ancient city of Korinth in the northeastern section of the Peloponnesos (an area of 30 x 46 km, or approximately 1,380 km²). It is a rich and strategic place, with a long history of human occupation. Ancient Korinthians controlled the Isthmus of Korinth (the major land route connecting central and southern Greece), exploited the resources of the Gulf of Korinth and the Saronic Gulf, and established trade relations with commercial centers in the eastern and western Mediterranean. Cultural exchange between the Aegean, Asia Minor, and the Adriatic and central Mediterranean often passed through a Korinthian filter.

The area is subject to earthquakes, and its soils are fragile and prone to erosion, but it contains one of the most fertile alluvial plains in southern Greece (Gregory 1994a; Rothaus 1994; Sakellariou and Faraklas 1971). However, rainfall records show that it is one of the driest places in Greece with a mean annual precipitation of only 38 - 44 cm. Much of the rain falls in heavy showers during the winter, so it rarely penetrates the soil, but rapidly flows to the sea. In spite of the limited rainfall, the area is "well-watered" by the abundant springs that bring water north to the plateaus and plains. However, the water must be collected in cisterns or diverted through channels from the springs for farming. Cultivation of the relic red soils and recent gray-brown soils of southern Greece can lead to a decline in fertility and severe erosion on steep hill slopes (van Andel and Runnels 1987). However, the rich soils of the Korinthian lowlands are enriched by the alluvium brought down by the larger streams that flow toward the Gulf from the southern mountains.

Frankish Occupation in the Peloponnesos

Between the eleventh and twelfth centuries, several crusades were organized to free the Holy Land (Jerusalem) from the control of the Turks. However, the crusaders were often able to acquire lands in the Middle East for their personal use and benefit. The most extreme example of this land acquisition was the Fourth Crusade (1202-1204), which never reached the Holy Land, but did result in the occupation of

Greece by the Franks (a generic term for westerners, but in the case of the Korinthia it refers specifically to French knights). The Franks could not pay for the Venetian ships that they had hired to take them to the Holy Land, so they were taken to Constantinople instead, where they sacked the Byzantine capital and established a Frankish state (Cheetham 1981). These land-hungry nobles partitioned their new Latin empire into the feudal kingdom of Thessaloniki and great fiefs such as the Duchy of Athens. With the fall of Korinth (the Byzantine capital of the Morea) and the conquest of the Greek strongholds of Akrokorinth, Argos, and Nauplia, the Frankish knight Villehardouin became Prince of Achaea. The Franks were never really accepted by the Greek population in the Korinthia (or the rest of the Morea), but the Principality of Achaea became the most brilliant and viable of the Latin states in the east (until the Byzantine reconquest at the end of the thirteenth century; cf. Bon 1969). Four of the Frankish settlements in the Korinthia have been identified: Akrokorinth, Agios Vasilios, Agionori, and Sophiko (Figure 13.1).

Akrokorinth

The fortified settlement of Akrokorinth is located atop a mountain southwest of the Isthmus of Korinth in the northern portion of the study area. Akrokorinth overlooks both the Korinthian Gulf and Saronic Gulf, as well as the fertile coastal plain. The military importance of the heights of Akrokorinth have been recognized since the sixth century B.C., and its fortifications were described as one of the shackles of Greece, the goal of every invader who wished to conquer the Peloponnesos (Carpenter and Bon 1936; Gregory 1994a; Papahatzis 1977; Salmon 1984; Tozer 1882; Wiseman 1978).

Agios Vasilios

The settlement at Agios Vasilios sits on a small mountain in the southern Korinthia. This mountain is faced with steep cliffs on the west and north. A larger mountain is located several hundred meters to the south. Agios Vasilios overlooks the main roads from Korinth to the Argolid and the southern Peloponnesos (through the Dervenaki pass). The fertile plain of Kleonai spreads north of the settlement. Coins and ceramics recovered during recent investigations at the site indicate that the fortified settlement was established in the thirteenth century (Gregory 1994a; Kardulias and Shutes 1992).

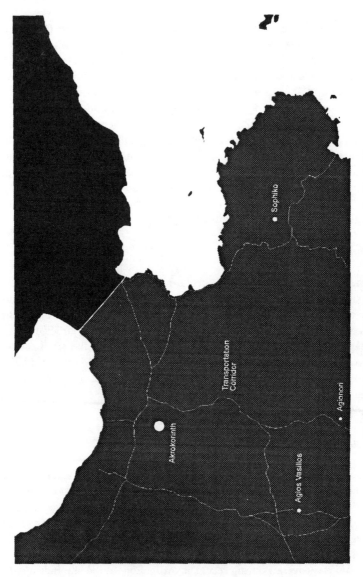

Figure 13.1. Known Frankish Settlements in the Korinthia.

Agionori

The Frankish site at Agionori is located southeast of Agios Vasilios and just east of the largest mountain in the Korinthia (Bon 1969:478-484). The Agionori pass lies just north of the site. The main road going south from Korinth to the plain of Argos winds through this pass. Fertile plains are found southwest of the settlement.

Sophiko

The rugged mountains along the Saronic Gulf in the eastern Korinthia contain the Frankish settlement at Sophiko. The site overlooks the road from Korinth (via Loutra Elenis) that runs to Korelias (on the southern shore of a small peninsula in the Saronic Gulf). A small fertile plain lies just below the site (Gregory 1994b).

Methodology

The study began with (1) a review of cultural data and natural landscape characteristics of the Frankish communities, followed by (2) the design and development of the GIS, (3) the utilization of the GIS in a spatial analysis of the Frankish settlements, and (4) the development of a predictive model of Frankish site locations (Dann 1992). In phase 1, cultural data were obtained from Medieval tax documents (Topping 1977), descriptions of Frankish settlements in the Morea (Bon 1969; Cheetham 1981), and from visits to Frankish sites in the Korinthia and Mystra (near Sparta). We tried to identify the amount of agricultural land that was taxed in the Morea, learn what crops were being grown on the hillsides and on the plains, what lands were set aside for grazing, etc., and how much land was needed to support the settlements. We also tried to isolate the criteria that were used to choose the locations of the Frankish sites (e.g., defensive considerations, access to roads, locations with a reliable source of water, etc.).

The natural characteristics of the Frankish settlements were tabulated from data taken from 1:50,000 scale maps produced by the Greek Institute of Geology and Mineral Exploration (Athens). These maps provided information on general topography, geology, mineralogy, and surface hydrology (as well as modern road and village locations). Detailed maps of the soils, subsurface hydrology, and topography of the study area were not available. The soils were classified, following

U.S.D.A. standard classifications, based on climate, slope, geology, and topography. Landsat images of the study area were also examined to determine if the known Frankish settlements had a common spectral signature (cf. Allen et al. 1990; Gaffney and Stancic 1991). All of these data had to be digitized (except for Landsat data) and incorporated into the GIS (Figures 13.2 and 13.3).

During the second phase of the study, Mark Dann determined that the design of the GIS would require both a vector- and a raster-based module. Raster-based GIS store spatial data as an array of grid cells (or pixels), while vector systems store data as points, lines and polygons (Burrough 1986; Gaffney and Stancic 1991). The vector system was required to manage the large digitized files, and to develop nonexistent topographic related data sets (e.g., digital elevation model, slope, directional orientation, etc.). The raster system was used due to its ability to easily incorporate Landsat data into the GIS data base, and its cartographic modeling capabilities. It was determined that the ARC/INFO software, a vector-based system, and the ERDAS software, a raster-based system, would be used for the required modules in the GIS. However, with the availability of GRID, a raster software module, in the ARC/INFO system, the Korinthian data base is now being converted to ARC/INFO. The GRID software will allow us to increase the processing speed for future modeling while at the same time allowing us to take advantage of many preprogrammed cartographic modeling algorithms. Other advantages of the system include the ability to develop a graphical user interface (GUI) that will make it easier for individuals that are not expert in GIS techniques to utilize the system and its data.

Common Spatial Features of the Frankish Sites

In the third phase of the study, the cultural data were examined using the GIS, and similar features of the four Frankish sites were listed. Table 13.1 is an example of a statistical report generated from the GIS database. It was found that the Frankish lords were concerned with defending their settlements from attacks by the Greeks (and other Franks), with creating a network of castles in the Morea that could be linked by the main roads (transportation corridors), and with locating sites near prime agricultural lands (Bon 1969; Cheetham 1981; Lurier 1964; Miller 1908; Topping 1977). During our visits to the sites, we noticed that four of the five settlements had been built in areas where they could be easily defended. Akrokorinth, Agios Vasilios, Agionori,

Legend

■ Tm-S.K	■ Q.el		
■ SH1	■ Q.Sc1		
■ H.SI	■ SH2		
■ H.CD	■ Js.K		
■ SC	■ al		
■ Pt.Sq	■ Pl.m,l,c		
■ Pl-Pt.m	■ oO		
■ Q.Cn1	■ Q.cn		
■ Q.t	■ Pt.St,c		
■ SC.CS	■ Pt.Cs		
■ Pl.M	■ Q.dl2		
■ Rl-M.K	■ Rm-j.K		
■ Q.Sc	▒ c		
■ Jm.K	▒ FT		
■ Q.dl	▒ El-M.K		
■ Q.al	▒ KS.K		
■ Q.al1	▒ M.t		
■ Pz.K	▒ S		
■ Pl.C1	░ Q.al2		
■ Ts-Jm.K	░ Q.dl2		
	░ Qdl3		

Figure 13.2. Geology map layer.

Figure 13.3. Digital elevation map layer with Landsat image overlaid. View facing southwest.

Table 13.1. Aspect Data for the Korinthia Generated by the GIS.

Category	Aspect	Points	Hectares	% of Area
Study Area	north	146062.	9128.875	14.18%
	northeast	169869.	10616.812	16.49%
	east	231920.	14495.000	22.51%
	southeast	77069.	4816.812	7.48%
	south	37349.	2334.312	3.63%
	southwest	53836.	3364.750	5.23%
	west	181108.	11319.250	17.58%
	northwest	132907.	8306.687	12.90%
	TOTALS:	1030120.	64382.500	
Akrokorinth	north	26.	1.625	5.90%
	northeast	13.	0.812	2.95%
	east	36.	2.250	8.16%
	southeast	63.	3.937	14.29%
	south	50.	3.125	11.34%
	southwest	52.	3.250	11.79%
	west	157.	9.812	35.60%
	northwest	44.	2.750	9.98%
	TOTALS:	441.00	27.562	
Agios Vasilios	north	0.	0.000	0.00%
	northeast	5.	0.312	16.13%
	east	8.	0.500	25.81%
	southeast	2.	0.125	6.45%
	south	0.	0.000	0.00%
	southwest	0.	0.000	0.00%
	west	11.	0.687	35.48%
	northwest	5.	0.312	16.13%
	TOTALS:	31.	1.937	
Agionori	north	4.	0.250	16.67%
	northeast	4.	0.250	16.67%
	east	6.	0.375	25.00%
	southeast	1.	0.062	4.17%
	south	0.	0.000	0.00%
	southwest	3.	0.187	12.50%
	west	5.	0.312	20.83%
	northwest	1.	0.062	4.17%
	TOTALS:	24.	1.500	
Sophiko	north	2.	0.125	4.08%
	northeast	13.	0.812	26.53%
	east	8.	0.500	16.33%
	southeast	0.	0.000	0.00%
	south	2.	0.125	4.08%
	southwest	4.	0.250	8.16%
	west	12.	0.750	24.49%
	northwest	8.	0.500	16.33%
	TOTALS:	49.	3.062	

and Mystra were all located on mountain summits, in rugged terrain with difficult access for attackers. Only Sophiko was not located in what was obviously a naturally defensive location. All five sites were located where they could view the fertile plains and transportation corridors below the settlements.

The Medieval sources describe the Morea as rich and profitable, where vines, olives, wheat, and flax were grown on the plains, and mulberry trees were cultivated for the silk industry. The extensive forests were full of game, and oak groves supplied acorns for vast herds of pigs. Large herds of sheep and goats grazed in the mountain pastures, while horses and cattle were raised on a more modest scale (Cheetham 1981). Topping (1977:544-549) discussed a tax record from Kephalonia (west of the Morea), where in 1267, a settlement of 25 families was required to pay tax on six vineyards with an area of 13.5 *modii*, arable fields covering 56.5 *modii*, two other fields (2 *modii*), fields and trees covering 9 *modii*, and two gardens (size not specified).

Land in Greece has been measured in *modii* since the Frankish period, and one *modius* can represent between 800 and 1,200 square meters (depending on the source). For this study, one *modius* equals 1,000 square meters. Topping's study of the tax record from Kephalonia suggests that 25 families required at least 81 *modii*, or an average of 3.24 *modii* per family. If we round this up to 4 *modii* per family (or 4,000 square meters), we can estimate the agricultural lands that were needed by the inhabitants of the Frankish sites in the Korinthia. The First Register for the Korinthia lists the population of three of the four Frankish settlements: Korinth had 330 families, and would require 1.32 square km of agricultural land, Agios Vasilios had 85 families that would require 0.34 square km of arable land, and Agionori had 52 families requiring 0.21 square km of farm land (Kordosis 1981). Sophiko was not mentioned in the First Register, but Gregory (1994b) recorded 200 structures at the site. A population of 200 families at Sophiko would need 0.8 square km of agricultural land.

Hypothesis Testing

In the third phase of the study, Dann began processing the landscape data sets in the GIS to test our hypothesis that the Frankish sites shared common spatial characteristics related to (1) defense, (2) proximity to transportation corridors, and (3) proximity to adequate amounts of fertile agricultural land. The spatial characteristics that relate to defense include slope, geology, soils, and topographic setting. The history of the Morea reveals a state of nearly constant warfare during the Frankish period (Cheetham 1981; Lurier 1964; Miller 1908). The Franks had to be concerned about defending the land that they won by arms and campaigning. It was our hypothesis that the Frankish settlements would be located in areas with moderate slopes that would provide a "natural" defense. Severe slopes would be difficult to build on, and would render difficult access to the sites. Gentle slopes would make the sites difficult to defend.

The geology of the Korinthia may also have influenced the choice of locations for Frankish sites. Areas with rock types that can be used for building materials (e.g., limestone, dolomite) may be favored. In addition, certain bedrock classes may be associated with ridge or mountain top areas that would provide natural defenses. Specific classes of thin and rocky soils may also be associated with these areas. Thin soils would also expose rock that can be used for building material. The topographic setting of the sites relates to their elevation, but locations on ridge tops and mountain summits can also be identified from map contours. We believed that the Franks would build their settlements on ridge and mountain tops, but that they would select locations that are high enough to be easily defended, but low enough to provide access to roads, crossroads, and agricultural lands on the plains.

Maps of the major Medieval transportation routes and crossroads in the Korinthia were made by consulting historical sources (Salmon 1984; Wiseman 1978). The site's proximity to transportation corridors and crossroads could be measured with reference to this map-layer. We believed that the sites would be located within a short walking distance from the roadways and crossroads since the Franks wished to keep in close communication with other sites, and create a network of settlements. Dann used a travel-time figure of 5 km per hour to convert distance to time in the calculations. Proximity to other Frankish sites was also considered in this aspect of the analysis. We predicted that there would be a regular spacing of the sites if a network of settlements were created.

In order to determine if the Frankish sites were located in close proximity to adequate amounts of fertile agricultural land, Dann created map-layers that reflected the proximity to surface water (stream drainage systems), prime agricultural land, and prime range land. The land classification was created by combining slope, aspect, and soil data. Fifteen categories were defined, with category (or class) XV representing lands with soils, slopes, and aspect (e.g., south-facing) that are best suited for growing grain (prime agricultural land). Class I is the inverse of class XV, and was classified as prime range land (since it was not suitable for cultivation, it was assumed that the land would be used for grazing). Classes II-VI were classified as good range land, and classes X-XIV would be considered good agricultural lands. Classes VII-IX would be neither prime agricultural nor prime range lands. The classification was subjective, but it was based on field observations of modern land use in the Korinthia (Kardulias and Shutes 1992) and U.S.D.A. standard classifications (Dann 1992).

The proximity studies also considered the quantity of agricultural land with a six km catchment area around each Frankish site (a 5-6 km radius defines the standard catchment area for agricultural societies, cf. Gaffney and Stancic 1991). As noted earlier, it was determined that 4,000 square meters of agricultural land were need to sustain one family. In the GIS database, this would equal about six pixels on the map of the study area. If we factor in the populations of the Frankish settlements, Akrokorinth would require 1980 pixels of prime agricultural land within its six km catchment. Agios Vasilios would need 510 pixels, Agionori 312 pixels, and Sophiko would require 900 pixels.

The amount of prime range land needed by each family was not recorded in the tax records. Dann used the amount of prime range land located within a 2 km radius of sites to determine if the sites were found near lands suitable for grazing.

The aspect data (Table 13.1) reveals how the site was oriented with relation to features of interest, such as agricultural lands and transportation corridors. Aspects were classified as eight compass directions: north, north-east, east, south-east, south, south-west, west, and north-west.

Landsat Data

Data obtained from Landsat images were analyzed to determine if the Frankish site locations have any common spectral reflectance (Dann 1992). If there was a common spectral reflectance, or signature, among the settlements and this signature was unique from other features in the image, it would enable us to identify other "missing" settlements in the image. The Landsat images provided views of the topography and vegetation cover in the study area, but their was no signature in these data that could be associated with Frankish sites. The lack of a unique signature could be the result of the resolution of the Landsat image compared to the average size of a settlement (the settlements were too small to be picked up by the Landsat sensors).

Results of the Spatial Analysis

The search for commonalties between the spatial characteristics of the Frankish sites in the Korinthia revealed that there were no correlations between the Landsat images, geology, elevation, aspect, and type of land (range land-agricultural land) found at the four sites. This means that there was no unique type of bedrock or type of land associated with the Frankish sites, and that they were located at different elevations. The data on aspect reveals that the orientation of the site towards features of interest was site specific but each site had a commanding view of the plains and transportation corridor below, and this should be taken as a common characteristic.

There are some additional data sets that reveal no correlation, but some commonalty. For example, all of the sites are located within 675 m of the nearest sources of water, but since drainage channels are evenly distributed throughout the study area, there are many other locations in the Korinthia that are just as close to water. All of the Frankish sites were located in close proximity to prime range land, but this type of land is very common in the hills and mountains of the Korinthia, and we do not think that it was an important factor when site locations were selected.

The following characteristics were found to be minimally correlated with Frankish site locations: slope, soil, and proximity to transportation corridors. The sites were usually located on areas with thin soils, with slopes between 12% and 26% (Sophiko was located in an area with gentler slopes) and within 1.5 km of a major roadway. The sites were all located within two km of a crossroad (this was listed as an average correlation). It was also found that each site was located between 9 and 13 km from its nearest neighbor. These proximity data suggest that a network of Frankish settlements was established in the Korinthia to facilitate communication between the sites.

The maximum correlations between landscape attributes and Frankish site locations involved the choice of mountain or ridge tops (for defense) and the proximity to prime agricultural lands. The result of the spatial analysis indicate that the Frankish sites did share common spatial characteristics related to (1) defense, (2) proximity to transportation corridors, and (3) proximity to adequate amounts of fertile agricultural land.

The Predictive Model

The spatial analysis provided us with some insights into how the Frankish sites were distributed in the Korinthia and which cultural and natural factors were given the most consideration during the process of selecting a location for a settlement. The results of the analysis were used to develop a predictive model of where Frankish sites are likely to be found. This involved the use of a modified weighted map-layer approach (Burrough 1986; Brandt et al 1992) in the analysis of the cultural and natural data. In a "typical" map-layer approach, a series of map-layers of the study area are generated, and within a map-layer, each pixel or grid location is assigned a value that indicates if it is favorable or unfavorable for the location of a site. Then the map-layer is assigned a weighted value that indicates the importance that the landscape feature has for site location, compared to other map-layers. The process is repeated for each of the map-layers, and for the final result, a sum is computed for all of the maps at the same grid location. A map that combines all categories and shows the sum would indicate which parts of the study area would be "archaeologically sensitive" and most favorable for site locations (Brandt et al. 1992; Kvamme 1985).

The problem with the weighted map-layer approach is the subjective nature of the process of assigning weights to the categories within each map-layer. For this reason, Dann (1992) decided to modify the approach. Our goal was to try to discover the common landscape features of the known Frankish sites. To accomplish this, the exploratory spatial analysis was conducted. We wanted to learn if the sites were located in similar settings and what the common values of these spatial attributes were. After this exploratory analysis was completed, and common features of the sites were identified, Dann (1992) employed the weighted map-layer approach selectively to create a predictive model.

Dann developed a routine to assign weights to the classes in the following landscape categories: slope, soil, defensive locations, and proximity to agricultural lands, transportation corridors, crossroads, and other settlements. These weights were based on the presence or absence of landscape characteristics at each settlement location. The categories were weighted, with defensive locations, proximity to agricultural lands, and proximity to other settlements, each receiving a weight of three; while proximity to crossroads was given a weight of two, and the other categories (slope and soil) were give a weight of one. This means that proximity to agricultural land is considered three times as important as soil in the sum of the weighted values (Figure 13.4).

This modified weighted map-layer analysis produced a map of probable Frankish site locations in the Korinthia, which can be combined with the map of known Frankish sites to reconstruct the settlement system that may have existed in the thirteenth century (Figure 13.5). These locations need to be field checked to determine if all of these locations were actually occupied.

Conclusion

The GIS proved to be an efficient tool for the documentation and analysis of Frankish site locations in the Korinthia. In utilizing the GIS it was possible to quickly create secondary landscape data layers from the original source layers (e.g., digital elevation model, slope and aspect created from digitized topography layer). Although the system is undergoing further refinement, the case study demonstrated the value of incorporating cultural and natural data in the study of complex settlement systems. The quantification and analysis of the spatial data provided new insights into how the Frankish sites relate to their environment. The GIS was also used to develop the predictive model that can guide future field studies and may result in the identification of previously unrecorded sites.

Figure 13.4. Map layer showing results of predictive analysis.

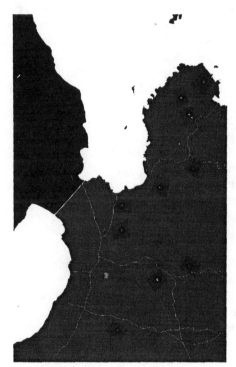

Figure 13.5. Hypothetical reconstruction of the Frankish settlement pattern, ca. A.D. 1220. Circles indicate predicted site locations.

References Cited

Allen, K.M.S., S.W. Green, and E.B.W. Zubrow (editors).
  1990 *Interpreting Space: GIS and Archaeology.* Taylor and
  Francis, London.
Bintliff, J.L., and A.M. Snodgrass
  1985 The Cambridge/Bradford Boeotian Expedition. The First Four
  Years. *Journal of Field Archaeology 12:125-161.*
Bon, A.
  1969 *La Moree Franque: Recherches Historiques, Topographiques
  et Archeologiques sur la Principaute d'Achaie (1205-1430).* E. de
  Boccard, Paris.
Brandt, R., B.J. Groenewoudt, and K.L. Kvamme
  1992 An Experiment in Archaeological Site Location: Modeling in
  the Netherlands Using GIS Techniques. *World Archaeology*
  24(2):268-282.
Burrough, P.A.
  1986 *Principles of Geographic Information Systems for Land
  Resource Assessment.* Clarendon Press, Oxford.
Butzer, K.W.
  1982 *Archaeology as Human Ecology.* Cambridge University Press,
  Cambridge.
Carpenter, R., and A. Bon
  1936 The Defenses of Acrocorinth and the Lower Town. *Corinth
  III, Part II,* American School of Classical Studies at Athens,
  Harvard University Press, Cambridge.
Cheetham, N.
  1981 *Mediaeval Greece.* Yale University Press, New Haven.
Clarke, K.C.
  1986 Advances in Geographic Information Systems. *Computers,
  Environment, and Urban Systems* 10:175-184.
Dann, M.A.
  1992 *The Use of a Geographic Information System to Study the
  Thirteenth Century Frankish Settlement Pattern in the Korinthia,
  Greece.* Unpublished Master's thesis, Department of Landscape
  Architecture, The Ohio State University, Columbus.
Gaffney, V., and Z. Stancic.
  1991 *GIS Approaches to Regional Analysis: A Case Study of the
  Island of Hvar.* Znanstveni institut Filozofske Fakultete, Ljubljana.
Green, S.W.
  1990 Sorting Out Settlement in Southeastern Ireland: Landscape

Archaeology and Geographic Information Systems. In *Interpreting Space: GIS and Archaeology*, edited by K.M.S. Allen, S.W. Green and E.B.W. Zubrow, pp. 356-363. Taylor and Francis, London.

Gregory, T.E.

1992 Archaeological Explorations in the Thisbe Basin. In *Boeotia Antiqua II*, edited by J.M. Fossey, pp. 17-34. J.C. Gieben, Amsterdam.

1994a From Kleonai to Agios Vasilios: Journey through an Ancient Landscape. In *International Scientific Colloquium on Rural Structures and Ancient Societies*. Ionian University, in press.

1994b The Medieval Settlement on Mt. Tsalika near Sophiko. In *Studies in Medieval and Post-Medieval Greece*, edited by G.D.R. Sanders and P. Lock, in press.

Hunt, E.D.

1992 Upgrading Site-Catchment Analysis with the Use of GIS: Investigating the Settlement Pattern of Horticulturalists. *World Archaeology* 24(2):283-309.

Jameson, M., T.H. van Andel, and C.N. Runnels

1994 *A Greek Countryside*. Stanford University Press, Stanford, in press.

Jochim, M.A.

1976 *Hunter-Gather Subsistence and Settlement: A Predictive Model*. Academic Press, New York.

Johnson, G.A.

1977 Aspects of Regional Analysis in Archaeology. *Annual Review of Anthropology* 6:479-508.

Kardulias, P.N., and M.T. Shutes

1992 Regional Study in the Korinthia--the Korinthia Exploration Project 1991. *Old World Archaeology Newsletter* 15(2):20-26.

Kordosis, M.

1981 Συμβολή στήν Ιστορία καί Τοπογραφία τής Περιοχής Κορίνθου στούς Μέσους Χρόνους. Viivliothiki Istorikon Meleton No. 159, Dionisiou Noti Karavia, Athinai.

Kvamme, K.L.

1985 Determining Empirical Relationships between the Natural and Environment and Prehistoric Site Locations: A Hunter-Gatherer Example. In *For Theory Building in Archaeological Analysis*, edited by C. Carr, pp. 208-238, Westport, Kansas City, KS.

1989 Geographic Information Systems in Regional Archaeological Research and Data Management. In *Archaeological Method and*

Theory, vol. 1, edited by M.B. Schiffer, pp. 139-203, University of Arizona Press, Tucson.

Lurier, H.E.
    1964 *Crusaders as Conquerors--The Chronicle of Morea*. Columbia University Press, New York.

McDonald, W.A., and G.R. Rapp Jr. (editors)
    1972 *The Minnesota Messenia Expedition*. University of Minnesota Press, Minneapolis.

Miller, W.
    1908 *The Latins in the Levant--A History of Frankish Greece (1204-1566)*. London.

Papahatzis, N.
    1977 *Ancient Korinth*. Ekdotike Athenon S.A., Athens.

Parker, S.C.
    1985 Predictive Modeling of Site Settlement Systems Using Multivariate Logistics. In *For Theory Building in Archaeological Analysis*, edited by C. Carr, pp. 173-207. Westport, Kansas City, KS.

Romano, D.G., and B.C. Schoenbrun
    1993 A Computerized Architectural and Topographic Survey of Ancient Corinth. *Journal of Field Archaeology* 20:177-190.

Rothaus, R.M.
    1994 Urban Space, Agricultural Space and Villas in Late Roman Corinth. In *International Scientific Colloquium on Rural Structures and Ancient Societies*. Ionian University Press, in press.

Sakellariou, M., and N. Faraklas
    1971 *Korinthia-Kleonaea*. Athens Technological Organization, Athens.

Salmon, J.B.
    1984 *Wealthy Corinth*. Clarendon Press, Oxford.

Spaulding, A.C.
    1960 The Dimensions of Archaeology. In *Essays in the Science of Culture in Honor of Leslie C. White*, edited by G.E. Dole and R.L. Carneiro, pp. 437-456, Thomas Y. Crowell, New York.

Topping, P.
    1972 The Post-Classical Documents. In *The Minnesota Messenia Expedition*, edited by W.A. McDonald and G.R. Rapp, Jr., pp. 64-80. University of Minnesota Press, Minneapolis.
    1977 *Studies on Latin Greece, A.D. 1205-1715*. Variorum Reprints, London.

Tozer, H.F.

1882 *Lectures on the Geography of Greece.* London (reprints 1974 by Ares Pubs., Chicago)
van Andel, T.H., and C.N. Runnels
1987 *Beyond the Acropolis: A Rural Greek Past.* Stanford University Press, Stanford.
Wansleeben, M.
1988 Geographic Information Systems in Archaeological Research. In *Computer and Quantitative Methods in Archaeology*, edited by S.P.Q. Rahtz, pp. 435-451. BAR International Series 446(2). British Archaeological Reports, Oxford.
Wells, B., C. Runnels, and E. Zangger
1990 The Berbati-Limnes Archaeological Survey. The 1988 Season. *Opuscula Atheniensia* 18(15):207-237.
1993 In the shadow of Mycenae. *Archaeology* 46(1):54-63.
Wiseman, J.
1978 *The Land of the Ancient Corinthians.* Studies in Mediterranean Archaeology 50, Paul Åströms Forlag, Göteborg, Sweden.
Wright, J.C., J.F. Cherry, J.L. Davis, E. Mantzourani, S.B. Sutton, and R.F. Sutton
1990 The Nemea Valley Archaeological Project: A Preliminary Report. *Hesperia* 59:579-659.
Zangger, E.
1992a Prehistoric and Historic Soils in Greece: Assessing the Natural Resources for Agriculture. In *Agriculture in Ancient Greece,* edited by B. Wells, pp. 13-19. Paul Åströms Forlag, Göteborg, Sweden.
1992b Neolithic to Present Soil Erosion in Greece. In *Past and Present Soil Erosion,* edited by M. Bell and J. Boardman, pp. 133-147. Oxbow Monographs 22, Oxford.

VI.
THE MODERN SETTING: ETHNOGRAPHIC AND ETHNOARCHAEOLOGICAL STUDIES

Chapter 14

Settlement Patterns, Settlement Perceptions: Rethinking the Greek Village

Susan Buck Sutton

Introduction

Just as archaeologists may have overused single site studies in organizing their understandings of ancient Greece (Cherry et al. 1991; van Andel and Runnels 1987), cultural anthropologists may have overemphasized the village community in taking their measure of modern Greek life. Working in collaboration with archaeological surveys of three Greek regions has transformed my thinking on the nature of villages in specific and the broader Greek social landscape in general. Invited to study recent settlement shifts in these three areas, I was forced to confront the mutability of villages both as settlements and social formations, and to place them within a broader spectrum of settlement options for Greek peasants. A more historicized, more problematized approach to the place of villages in Greek social relations emerged from this process.

Several aspects of survey research encouraged this rethinking. Shifting the gaze from a single settlement to an entire region, recognizing the different sites historically succeeding each other in an area, and exploring forces of settlement formation and dissolution all required a different approach than had been standard in village ethnography. Long-standing assumptions of stability, longevity, and essential uniformity among Greek villages gave way in the face of such investigations. The more fluid view of village life that has resulted has meaning for both ethnographic understandings and ethnoarchaeological comparisons. At the same time it throws into relief the ways in which academic, nationalistic, and local perceptions of villages have played off each other.

Anthropological Understandings of the Greek Village

Founded on the pioneering work of Friedl (1962) and Campbell (1964), the anthropology of modern Greece has developed into a rich discourse on a variety of issues pursued from both interpretive and materialist perspectives. Even a cursory examination of this research, however, reveals a strong bias for village studies. The need to broaden the discussion to the urban and national spheres with more work such as that by Hirschon (1989), Kenna (1983), and Herzfeld (1991) is obvious to all who work in Greece. The parallel but less obvious issue considered here, however, is the extent to which the dominance of village-based studies has skewed even our understanding of rural life.

In most ethnographies, the village has been a background constant rather than an object of investigation. As Lawrence and Low (1990) might say, Greek village research has consisted of studies in places, but not of the places themselves. Most ethnographers have used the village largely to bound and define the group to be examined. Even investigations of peasants leaving the countryside have generally posited a previously fixed village base from which this migration only recently began. Other settlement forms and allegiances, and the plasticity of villages themselves have almost never been at issue. The topic has been so foreclosed that few, if any, ethnographies have even bothered to define what was meant by the term village (χωριό, *horio*). Equally telling, a close reading of 25 well-known ethnographic studies reveals that over half focused on villages either founded or experiencing significant inward migration in the last 100 years, yet neither fact was generally taken as significant in understanding these settlements (Sutton 1988).

DuBoulay's (1974) classic study of a Pelion village thus both mentioned the foundation of this village in the early nineteenth century, and characterized it as isolated, untouched, and traditional until quite recently. Herzfeld's (1985) outstanding analysis of the poetics of manhood in a Cretan village observed in a footnote that this village more than tripled its size in the last 75 years, but did not pursue the impact of this growth on social relations. My own work on migrants from the island of Amorgos now living in Athens similarly held the village base from which they had moved as largely fixed and stable until quite recently (Sutton 1978, 1983).

While anthropological writings have thus revealed much about village social life and current trends of cityward migration, they have been relatively mute on the processes that form, shape and reshape villages over time, as well as the varying allegiances which their inhabitants hold toward them. When are villages important in people's lives and when are they not? Whose interests are served in promoting the stability of a particular village? How stable has the population of villages been over time? Why do villages sometimes form and why do other settlement types sometimes appear? Indeed, what other settlements are there in the Greek countryside? Such questions have not only gone unanswered in the anthropology of Greece, they have gone largely unasked.

This situation has certainly arisen from concern for other issues rather than deliberate oversight. The result, however, has been a misleading assumption of long-term village stability. Such an assumption has encouraged those seeking ethnoarchaeological analogies for Greek antiquity to focus on villages of great longevity, even though, as is discussed later, more fleeting settlements may actually have been more typical in Greek rural life, both past and present.

Anthropological inattention to Greek village history has also allowed sentimental, ideological, and political claims of an idealized village past to go uncontested. The authentication of the timeless peasant village has been an important theme in Greek nationalism since the mid-nineteenth century (Herzfeld 1982; Vryonis 1978). Establishing an unbroken continuity between modern Greek peasants and the glories of ancient Greece was critical to legitimation of the new Greek state. Nineteenth century Greece depended upon the support of European nations which idealized the ancient Greek past, but were also susceptible to Fallmerayer's theories (1965) that the contemporary population was no longer truly Greek. Even though population changes and cultural continuity are not logically exclusive, most nationalistic theories took the course of asserting a fixed village base of eternal Greek peasants to make their claims.

Even when divorced from the desire to articulate with antiquity, this postulation of the primordial folk village has carried forward to the present in support of various efforts to identify "the essential Greece" in the midst of the dislocations of rapid urbanization and commercialization. In this regard, the image of the timeless village has been harnessed with the dichotomies and distortions of the modernization paradigm (e.g., McNall 1974), which even if discredited in anthropology is still alive in the ways many urban Greeks view their rural past, planners conceive rural development policies, and preservationists attempt to stabilize the dynamic architectural traditions of rural Greece (Herzfeld 1991; Moore 1992).

The possibility that the inhabitants of the Greek countryside have actively participated in international economic systems for centuries (Evangelinides 1979; Hadjimichalis 1987; Kremmydas 1972; Mouzelis 1978) is precluded by such thinking. To those laboring under theories of modernization, Greek rural life has been a traditional, isolated and very localized system, routinely reproducing itself generation after generation until very recently. As one scholar working within this paradigm phrased it, rural Greek culture is "traditional, slow-changing, provincial and fatalistic" (Baxevanis 1972:62). While few anthropologists support such arguments, their assumptions of an unchanging village base have lent inadvertent support to them.

MacFarlane (1977) and Lowenthal (1985:122-123) have each demonstrated that such a belief in tightly-knit and semi-isolated communities of the past is a powerful myth of contemporary industrial society in general. It is a fiction, furthermore, which masks the considerable geographical mobility of many of the historical peasantries of Europe (see also Standing 1984:13). Anthropologists are in a position to confront the assumptions behind such myths and also to expand their own understandings by combining their detailed investigations of local social relations with both regional and historical perspectives. In this light, attention could profitably be directed toward the kind of social formations villages have been at various points in Greek history, how they have fit within a range of rural settlement types, why they form and dissolve, and how their inhabitants have legitimated and explained village existence; in short, issues well-suited for investigation by regional surveys.

Regional Surveys and Conceptual Reformulations

Indeed, the ethnographic work done in conjunction with several archaeological surveys has already yielded considerable insight into extra-village land use, regional relationships, and settlement change in rural Greece. The precise ecological studies of Clark (1976), Forbes (1976), Gavrielides (1976), and Koster and Koster (1976), for example, have revealed the importance of economic activities beyond the village proper. Chang's (1981) work on the geographical distribution of sheepfolds served further notice that significant construction sometimes occurs outside a settlement. Aschenbrenner's documentation (1986) of a Messenian village re-establishing itself along a new road, well below the original settlement, made it impossible any longer to think of villages as fixed in space. Done on a regional basis, although not part of a regional survey, Bialor's study (1976) of the gradual downward movement of population along the slopes of the northwestern Peloponnesos also supported this idea, as did Currier's (1976) examination of the movement of the Ios population back and forth between their main villages and seasonal hamlets.

The archaeological components of regional surveys have, of course, given a broader context and meaning to these ethnographic findings of rural settlement fluidity, for they have established a record of small settlements coming and going over the Greek landscape for millennia (e.g., Cherry et al. 1991; McDonald and Rapp 1972; Renfrew and Wagstaff 1982; van Andel and Runnels 1987; Watrous 1982). The work of several geographers and demographic historians similarly confirms that this has been as true for the last four centuries as it was for the ancient past. The rural Greek population has been in motion for some time (Kayser 1963; McNeill 1978). Panayiotopoulos (1985:43), Antondiadi-Bibicou(1965:376), and Laiou-Thomadakis(1977:223-266), for example, have discussed the repeated migrations that swept the Greek countryside during the Byzantine and Ottoman periods. Several other scholars, including Burgel (1965:11), Kolodny (1974), McGrew (1985), Sivignon (1981), Spirinodakis (1977:122-137), and Zakynthos (1976:88-91) have detailed how the lowland population increased as the Turks gradually fell from power and the modern Greek state became established.[1]

Also encouraging a reconceptualization of the Greek village is the evidence of both recent geographers and nineteenth-century travelers that settlements other than villages have shared the rural landscape. A careful reading of this literature uncovers at least two settlements smaller than villages. The first is a καλύβι (*kalivi*), or seasonal habitation, such as those used by shepherds. Καλύβια sometimes became more permanent residences as groups moved their base from one region to another, something noted by such geographers as Beuermann (1954), Sivignon (1981), and Handmann (1981), and also by such early nineteenth century travellers as Gell (1810:xiii).

A second sub-village type, noted only by a few, has generally been called by foreign observers a hamlet, a vague term seeming to indicate a very small, but year-round settlement lacking some of the amenities of a village (e.g., Philippson 1892; Pouqueville 1826). In this sense, the term seems applicable to what Rangavis, in his encyclopedic discussion of the modern Greek state (1853), called "places of few inhabitants", and Miliarakis (1886) referred to as κομίδια (*komidia*, little settlements). Along these lines, Panayiotopoulos reports that Venetian records for the Peloponnesos in 1700 showed 47 settlements with only one to two families living in them (1985:156).[2]

While many of these insights into rural settlement were just surfacing when I began working with regional surveys, my own thinking quickly moved into convergence with them. My work on the Argolid Exploration Project in 1982-83 disabused me of the assumption that all rural Greek regions had recently experienced population declines due to migration toward Athens.[3] Indeed, the southern Argolid actually experienced as much inward population movement during the last few centuries as it lost to other regions (van Andel and Sutton 1987). By the mid-1980s, there were at least 10 new villages in the region which had not existed two hundred years earlier. Despite the off-hand comments of my Athenian friends that this was a very backward region, I found considerable economic and demographic energy. Somewhat different, but still significant, patterns of rural-to-rural migration emerged from my subsequent study of modern land use for the Keos Archaeological Survey,[4] a project for which Whitelaw's detailed examination (1991) of isolated farmsteads greatly extended our understanding of the range of rural settlements.

By the time I joined the Nemea Valley Archaeological Project in 1985, my thinking on rural settlement patterns had thus changed significantly.[5] My goal was to develop some understanding of settlement strategies and perceptions among the many people passing through the valley during modern times; that is, the period from the Greek Revolution of the 1820s to the present. The results, after five seasons of field research, have provided some insight into the social relations behind the processes of village formation and abandonment that have increasingly become established as a repetitive theme in the rural Greek past.

Modern Settlement in the Nemea Valley

The Nemea Valley Archaeological Project involved both excavation and surface survey, with input from specialists in geomorphology, anthropology, paleobotany, history, and osteology (see Wright et al. 1990). My work on modern settlement and land use was greatly assisted by the archaeological field walkers who painstakingly recorded contemporary land use and collected modern materials while searching for signs of ancient activity. Such efforts yielded a field by field description of recent and contemporary land use for the entire area that far exceeded what could otherwise have been known. Indeed several sites abandoned only within the last two centuries were first identified by the field walkers, and then further investigated through interviews, local records, national and provincial listings, Venetian archives, historical travelers' accounts, nineteenth century newspaper files, the records of past excavations, and aerial photographs.

The Nemea Valley and its surrounding hillsides, an area roughly 10 km^2 in extent, is located midway between Korinth and Argos and slightly to the west of the National Road. It is one of several upland basins, each surrounded by mountains, moving progressively westward and upward from the National Road to the Lake Stymphalia region. As of the 1991 census, it contained two villages, Iraklio with a population of 487, and Koutsoumadi with a population of 135. Smaller, outlying settlements contained 82 people. Both villages and most of the valley fall within the present-day κοινότης (*koinotis*) of Archaia Nemea.

The regional and historical perspective adopted in this project has yielded a broader understanding of settlement in the Nemea region than would have appeared by focusing on just one, or even both, of its contemporary villages. Indeed its various transformations can only be understood by placing them in the context of wider systems of both settlement and political economy and the shifts which have occurred in these. The work done thus far has revealed the following series of developments in the valley.

In the early nineteenth century just prior to the Greek Revolution, the valley's population looked largely westward, over the ridge of Profitis Ilias to the market town of Agios Georgios (today known also as Nea Nemea) and its nearby monastery of the Koimiseos Theotokou Vrachou. The valley's inhabitants obtained supplies and sold produce in the town, and the monastery owned some land in the valley. At this time, the Nemea region was, in some respects, a buffer between the more firmly Ottoman controlled areas to the east and the freer settlements of the western mountains.

With Greek independence in 1827, however, the people of the valley soon turned their attention in other directions. Agios Georgios remained a local center and grew to its present population of 3991. The farmers of the Nemea Valley, however, became even more involved in external economies, producing currants (μαύρη or Κορινθιακή σταφίδα) for export to northern Europe, and also must for wine-making, marketed largely in Argos. The improvement of the Korinth-Argos road, and construction of a railroad in the late nineteenth century, also gave the valley greater access to the growing metropolitan center of Athens. The valley remains a major cash-cropping area today, with wine, currants, grapes, and olives as its major produce.

The active external connections of the Nemea Valley caused a shuffling and reshuffling of its population several times during the modern period. In no sense was this a stable population. Neither was the populating of the valley floor simply the downward move of just one original upland village. The familial histories of the area's inhabitants reveal a more complex situation.

The valley's population has grown almost seven times larger than its 1820 size of 110.[6] While many residents have departed to pursue both marriage and economic advancement in Argos, Korinth, Athens and other destinations, the net flow of migrants into the valley has been even greater. Farmers and shepherds from the westward mountains, as well as from many other regions in Greece, have entered the area throughout the modern period.

Both present-day villages in the valley were formed during these population shifts. Neither existed at the start of the modern period. At that time, there were several small, dispersed clusters of houses scattered along the western ridge of the valley. None of these older settlements has survived. At least two of these settlements, Lekosi and old Koutsoumadi, were small villages of 5-20 families each, a size consistent with general estimates for Peloponnesian villages at that time.[7] Both were listed in Venetian documents for the early 18th century.[8] Several other settlement clusters along the western ridge and other parts of the valley were simply small hamlets or καλύβια belonging to a single patriline, some serving as winter homes for transhumant shepherds who summered in the mountains of Stymphalia. In the early nineteenth century, there were thus no settlements of any size, certainly no villages, on the floor of the Nemea Valley. Indeed, travelers to the central part of the valley describe the area as virtually uninhabited (e.g., Curtius 1851:510; Dodwell 1819:209). With removal of the Ottoman presence after the Greek Revolution, however, various families built new housing clusters scattered across the open lands of the valley bottom and nearby plateaus. Much of this territory fell under the category of National Lands made available to Greek peasants at that time (see McGrew 1985). Some of these clusters were καλύβια, used seasonally by shepherds still connected to the western mountains. Others were year-round hamlets. Virtually all revolved around a single patriline. The smaller original settlement of Lekosi was completely deserted for such other locations within a few decades. After 1876, when the larger hillside village of old Koutsoumadi was devastated by an earthquake, its residents also abandoned that site for other locations. As many as half moved onto the valley floor, producing two primary clusters of houses: one at the present-day village of new Koutsoumadi, the other at the present-day village of Iraklio.

These two new settlements only became villages, however, after other processes had occurred. One of these events was the administrative reorganization of the rural Greek population by the central government at the turn of the century. The older system had emphasized δήμοι (*demoi*), large regions around market towns including many villages and hamlets. The new system reduced the geographical size of the districts included in δήμοι by also establishing κοινότητες, smaller districts, generally organized around villages. The administrative advantages encouraging village formation at this time thus included the ability to control local affairs and to articulate with the national government directly, rather than through nearby towns. Once the new settlements of Iraklio and new Koutsoumadi were able to establish their identity as villages, they were collectively designated as the new κοινότης of Koutsoumadi which broke away from the former δήμος of Agios Georgios in 1912 (Vayiakakos 1974:68).[9]

A second force favoring village formation was the legal distribution of the National Lands to families living upon them toward the end of the nineteenth century. This strengthened the commitment of various family lines to the region. By this time, even most shepherds had switched from pastoralism to cash cropping, and had correspondingly converted their καλύβια into year-round hamlets. As various families intermarried, and land was distributed through dowry and patrimony to the new couples, the fields farmed by any one family became scattered throughout the valley, thus creating an impetus for centrally located residence. The road running east west through the valley, and connecting Agios Georgios to the new railroad depot at Dervenakia to the east, also favored condensation of settlement along this axis.

Elderly residents today recall stories of a conscious effort to form "real villages" in this atmosphere. Some families of both Iraklio and new Koutsoumadi donated land for churches, cemeteries, and squares explicitly to move their settlements toward village status, something which was essentially accomplished by the end of the nineteenth century. By this time, both also had παντοπωλεία (general stores) where some modicum of imported foodstuffs and other items were now offered.

These two villages have remained to the present, both increasing significantly in size up to about 1970, after which both experienced some decrease. The number of people living in scattered hamlets outside the villages has declined, although there are still over a dozen families who do so. Those who moved into the villages most often accomplished this through marriage to a village resident. Only 3.2% of the families entering Iraklio or new Koutsoumadi in the twentieth century did so without a marriage link.

These villages do not, however, exhaust the description of contemporary settlement in the valley. There are still a half dozen patrilineal hamlets, as well as seasonal housing for a few transhumant shepherds. The area is also dotted with καλύβια used as temporary shelters by villagers during seasons of intense agricultural labor in outlying fields. There are seven small churches, still in use at least once a year, scattered among the fields. In an archaeological sense, the landscape thus has many activity areas, and contains a diverse set of field huts, pump houses, boundary stones, chapels, sheepfolds, and familial territories. Even the ruined houses of former hamlets and καλύβια give daily reminders that the patrilinies which used to live in them have a long-standing legitimacy in the valley.

The ways in which local residents describe their settlement patterns is also revealing.[10] They recognize a range of settlement types from the καλύβι (temporary shelter) to the πόλις (*polis*, city). Between these extremes are the κωμόπολις (*komopolis*, market town), the χωριό, and smaller clusters of housing known by a variety of terms and approximating what I have here labeled hamlets. Sometimes these smaller settlements are simply called μερικά σπίτια (several houses) belonging to a particular family. At other times, they combine the family name with an ending such as -εïκα. They may also be referred to as συνοικίες (*sinoikies*, neighborhoods), similar to the neighborhoods within a village or town. Such συνοικίες, whether located in the villages or standing alone, generally revolve around a core patriline which originally settled the area.

From such discussions an important distinction between hamlets and villages emerges. Villages contain a coalition of different patrilinies which united to form the settlement, whereas hamlets represent but a single line. It is particularly telling that those who still live in the valley's outlying hamlets have relatively few kinship ties to the families of its two villages. Hamlets tended to arise at the start of the modern period, as open lands were developed for agriculture. Forces then favored intermarriage and the formation of village coalitions, as agricultural exploitation of these areas stabilized.

The allegiance which villagers feel to either new Koutsoumadi or Iraklio also varies along kinship lines. Consanguineal descendants of the families which historically formed the villages express much attachment to these settlements. They are the most likely to know local history, and the most likely to identify closely with it. Spouses from outside the villages exhibit a lesser degree of allegiance. Those families entering the villages without kinship ties during the last fifty years also identify less with the village. Some members of these families continue to regard themselves as outsiders even though both they and their parents were born in the valley.

The valley's residents also operate as part of a larger settlement system to which they feel additional allegiance. Indeed, in ordinary conversation, inhabitants of Iraklio and new Koutsoumadi are as likely to identify with the nearby κωμόπολις of Agios Georgios as they are with their villages. The medical services, wider range of stores, banks and post office found there are considered as much a part of the local environment as facilities in the two villages. The valley's residents see themselves as part of the entire region around Agios Georgios. This identification with market towns also emerges when villagers relate where their ancestors originated: the name of the κωμόπολις is more commonly given than the specific village.

The region around Agios Georgios is now generally known as Nemea, something which bemuses those scholars of ancient Greece who limit the term more precisely to the valley described in this paper. This usage is, however, consistent with the pattern of regional identification just described. The name Nemea was bureaucratically transferred to Agios Georgios in the early years of the new state when many δῆμοι were given the ancient names of the nearest major archaeological sites. Agios Georgios is now officially known as Nea Nemea to distinguish it from the κοινότης of Archaia Nemea, which contains Iraklio and new Koutsoumadi. In common practice, however, the entire area is referred to as Nemea, and people in the westernmost villages of this area feel at least some identification with people in the easternmost.

Given such demographic variability, local statements concerning villages often use the term χωριό as a simple metaphor for a complex set of social relationships. In ordinary, just as in scholarly, discourse the term village often implies greater permanence than a settlement may actually exhibit. For example, the Stymphalian village of Bouzi is sometimes mentioned as the place from which a number of Irakliote ancestors came. Bouzi is, however, a recent coalescence of families who had formerly lived in dispersed hamlets in that area, and did not yet exist when some of the people from that area moved to Iraklio. Similarly, when other residents of Iraklio and new Koutsoumadi say their villages were simply rebuildings of the hillside village of old Koutsoumadi when it was abandoned after the 1876 earthquake, they gloss over the fact that there were people from many other areas also living in the valley floor by this time. Such reified usages of village names are not intended to deceive. As one Irakliote woman explained it, this is just an easy way of talking about something more complex.

The picture emerging from this analysis of modern settlement in the Nemea Valley is one in which villages are part of a range of settlement types important in rural Greek history. The most stable elements of this range are at the upper end: the κωμόπολις and the πόλις. Villages, hamlets, and καλύβια seem to come and go around these other elements, in response to varying forces of political economy. On whatever basis village coalitions have formed at one point in Greek history, the vicissitudes of Greek life have been such that at a later time they could lose their relevance, and people could be pushed to other locations. Greek villages could thus disappear in one place, while new coalitions formed in another.

This view of villages as coalitions is bolstered by certain historical understandings of rural Greek settlements. At least for the early centuries of the Byzantine Empire, the κοινότης was a recognized coalition of peasants allowed to pay their taxes communally (Charanis 1948; Laiou-Thomadakis 1977; Vacalopoulos 1976:56).[11] Laiou-Thomadakis (1977:101-103) feels that "by the middle of the fourteenth century social and demographic factors had worked in such a way that the solid core of the village consisted of a number of households which had relative stability over time and which were related to each other by consanguinity or affinity." Zakynthos (1976:57-67) believes some forms of communal organization continued in the villages of Ottoman times.

Implications

Some eighteen years ago, Dimen and Friedl (1976) called for greater use of regional•perspectives in the anthropology of modern Greece, echoing a similar call for such studies within anthropology in general (Smith 1976). They rightly saw the need to base village studies on an understanding of the larger systems in which these settlements participate. The regional ethnographic research which has accompanied archaeological surveys in Greece has at least partially answered this call. Few of us realized when we started such studies, however, that we would eventually see not just how villages relate to each other, but also how villages themselves are creations of the give and take of regional relationships.

Such a shift in conception of the village from solid understratum to impermanent coalition carries many implications for the ethnography of modern Greece. Interpretation of local statements about village history and allegiance must consider these as cultural constructions, reflecting at least to some degree how the speaker is related to the core founding families of a village. At the same time, the anthropological maxim that familial loyalty is in some tension with village unity (e.g., Campbell 1964; DuBoulay 1974:41; Friedl 1962; Herzfeld 1985) is given even greater meaning when villages are seen as coalitions which can be dissolved as well as founded. Most certainly the demographic history of a village affects the social relations within it.

This rethinking of the village also has ethnoarchaeological implications. Whether or not comparisons between past and present can be validly undertaken is, as Gould has pointed out (1980), a point worth raising. Those of us who struggle forward and suggest, through a leap of faith, that modern life can at least present some interesting analogies for archaeological interpretation (Renfrew 1984) must, of course, look for the most apt parallels. This task is further complicated in Greece by the idealization of the ancient Greek past in western intellectual life. Both affirmations and denials of continuity between the Greek past and present have carried political, imperialistic and nationalistic agendas that cloud many discussions of Greek history. As we struggle out of this haze, it is important to realize that the most isolated and stable villages may not actually present the best analogies for the Greek past.

Indeed if much of the Greek past was demographically dynamic, static parts of the present would constitute the least likely parallels for many periods. The Greek landscape has witnessed a succession of systems, alternating periods of centralization with periods of more localized control, periods of open trade with periods of retreat from foreign rule. In seeking ethnoarchaeological analogies, assumptions of direct continuity seem less fruitful than the identification of similar forces of political economy for various periods.

In this light, contemporary Greek life presents more to ethnoarchaeology than the occasional maintenance of an archaic technique. The modern period reveals the changes from a period of economic retreat to one of expansion, from an imperial system to a national one, and from a feudal economy to a global, capitalized one. Examining contemporary settlement transformations enables us to make better judgments about similar shifts that appear at various points in the archaeological record. For example, the archaeological survey of the Nemea region has revealed at least one transition during antiquity when a phase of minimal settlement was followed immediately by the sudden appearance of many sites, rather than a gradual increase in settlements. While this seemed puzzling at first, it actually parallels very closely what happened in the modern period as the valley was opened for settlement after a period of sparse habitation. As described above, the Nemea Valley recently went from only slight settlement on the western ridges, to a host of different hamlets scattered over the area, before its eventual reduction to two villages.

Such understandings would not have emerged without a survey of the full range of settlement and land use in the region. By concentrating on distinct villages, much anthropological work has missed the other forms of rural settlement that both precede and accompany villages. The arguments behind a non-site centered approach to the past also support a non-village centered approach to the present. Cultural anthropologists might well adopt the same fluidity in their understanding of villages that survey archaeologists have recently developed in terms of sites.

In converse fashion, we need to think more about how archaeologists might discern the kind of cultural attitudes toward land use that inform this paper. Much more work needs to be done on comparing ethnographic conclusions based on interviews with archaeological conclusions based on material culture. These two kinds of analysis may not, however, be as different as they have sometimes seemed. As Fotiadis (Watson and Fotiadis 1990) has recently argued, both verbal statements and material objects act as signs. The meaning of each is not easy to determine in either case. Regional surveys may indeed be able to assist in this process. By comprehending the full array of activity areas on a landscape, archaeologists can better assess the multiple attachments to place that build a group's identity at a given point in time.

The ethnoarchaeology that is emerging from regional surveys in Greece thus attempts to bring the full power of both ethnography and archaeology to bear on each other. Comparisons are made between systemic descriptions of regions rather than single traits removed from context. Thus, what is ethnoarchaeologically important about seemingly archaic farming techniques is not just whether they carry on ancient traditions, but also the extent to which they are used in economic systems appropriate for comparison to various periods of the past (see Chang, this volume). In contemporary times, industrial and familial systems of production co-exist and even shape each other in many societies, including Greece (Kearney 1986; Nash 1981; Wallerstein 1974; Wolf 1986). The mere continuance of some techniques of great antiquity thus does not mean they are carried out the same way and have the same output as under more isolated economic systems in certain periods of the past. Surely, terrace farming in a period of cash cropping is different from terrace farming in a period of economic retreat.

Just as surely, what is ethnoarchaeologically important about a contemporary village is not how long it has been in existence, but rather whether we want to compare new villages now with new ones in the past, exploratory hamlets now with similar ones in antiquity. Indeed some contemporary villages of great age are more atypical than not. As this paper has attempted to show, Greek villages which come and go are probably more common than those which stay forever.

References Cited

Anoyatis-Pele, D.
   1987 *Connaissance de la population et des productions de la Morée à travers un manuscrit anonyme de la fin du XVIIIe siècle.* Manourtios, Athens.
Antoniadi-Bibicou, H.
   1965 Villages désertés en grèce: un bilan provisoire. In *Villages désertés et histoire économique*, pp. 343-417. École Practique des Hautes Études, Paris.
Aschenbrenner, S.E.
   1986 *Life in a Changing Greek Village.* Publications in Ancient Studies No. 2, University of Minnesota, Minneapolis.
Baxevanis, J.J.

1972 *Economy and Population Movements in the Peloponnesos of Greece.* National Centre of Social Research, Athens.

Beuermann, A.

1954 Kalyviendorfer im Peloponnes. In *Ergebnisse und Probleme Moderner Geographischer Forshung*, pp. 229-238. Walter Dorn, Bremen.

Bialor, P.

1976 The Northwestern Corner of the Peloponnesos: Mavrikion and Its Region. In *Regional Variation in Modern Greece and Cyprus*, edited by M. Dimen and E. Friedl, pp. 222-235. Annals of the New York Academy of Sciences, No. 268. New York.

Burgel, G.

1965 *Pobia.* National Centre of Social Research, Athens.

Campbell, J.K.

1964 *Honour, Family and Patronage.* Oxford University Press, Oxford.

Chang, C.

1981 *The Archaeology of Contemporary Herding Sites in Greece.* Unpublished Ph.D. dissertation, Department of Anthropology, State University of New York at Binghamton.

Charanis, P.

1948 On the Social Structure of the Later Roman Empire. *Byzantion* 17:39-57.

Cherry, J.F., J.L. Davis, and E. Mantzourani (editors)

1991 *Landscape Archaeology as Long-Term History: Northern Keos in the Cycladic Islands.* Monumenta Archaeologica 16, UCLA Institute of Archaeology, Los Angeles.

Clark, M.H.

1976 Gathering in the Argolid: A Subsistence Subsystem in a Greek Agricultural Community. In *Regional Variation in Modern Greece and Cyprus*, edited by M. Dimen and E. Friedl, pp. 251-264. Annals of the New York Academy of Sciences, No. 268. New York.

Crumley, C.L., and W.H. Marquardt (editors)

1987 *Regional Dynamics: Burgundian Landscapes in Historical Perspective.* Academic Press, New York.

Currier, R.L.

1976 Social Interaction and Social Structure in a Greek Island Village. In *Regional Variation in Modern Greece and Cyprus*, edited by M. Dimen and E. Friedl, pp. 308-313. Annals of the New York Academy of Sciences, No. 268. New York.

Curtius, E.
1851 *Peloponnesos.* Justus Perthes, Gotha.

Dimen, M., and E. Friedl (editors)
1976 *Regional Variation in Modern Greece and Cyprus.* Annals of the New York Academy of Sciences, No. 268. New York.

Dodwell, E.
1819 *A Classical and Topographical Tour Through Greece During the Years 1801, 1805, and 1806.* Rodwell and Martin, London.

DuBoulay, J.
1974 *Portrait of a Greek Mountain Village.* Clarendon Press, Oxford.

Evangelinides, M.
1979 Core-Periphery Relations in the Greek Case. In *Underdeveloped Europe: Studies in Core-Periphery Relations,* edited by D.Seers, B. Schaffer and M. Kiljunen, pp. 177-195. Humanities Press, Atlantic Highlands, N.J.

Fallmerayer, J.P.
1965[1830] *Geschichte der halbinsel Morea wahrend des Mittelalters.* G. Olms, Hildesheim.

Forbes, H.A.
1976 "We Have a Little of Everything": The Ecological Basis of Some Agricultural Practices in Methana, Trizinia. In *Regional Variation in Modern Greece and Cyprus,* edited by M. Dimen and E. Friedl, pp. 236-250. Annals of the New York Academy of Sciences, No. 268. New York.

Frangakis, E., and J.M. Wagstaff
1987 Settlement Pattern Change in the Morea (Peloponnisos) c. A.D. 1700-1830. *Byzantine and Modern Greek Studies* 11:163-192.
1992 The Height Zonation of Population in the Morea c. 1830. *Annual of the British School at Athens* 87:439-446.

Friedl, E.
1962 *Vasilika: A Village in Modern Greece.* Holt, Rinehart and Winston, New York.

Gavrielides, N.
1976 The Cultural Ecology of Olive Growing in the Fourni Valley. In *Regional Variation in Modern Greece and Cyprus,* edited by M. Dimen and E. Friedl, pp. 265-274. Annals of the New York Academy of Sciences, No. 268. New York.

Gell, W.
1810 *The Itinerary of Greece.* T. Payne, London.

Gould, R.
  1980 *Living Archaeology.* Cambridge University Press, Cambridge.
Hadjimichalis, C.
  1987 *Uneven Development and Regionalism: State, Territory and Class in Southern Europe.* Croom Helm, London.
Handmann, M.E.
  1981 De la soumission à la dépendance. In *Aspects du changement social dans la campagne Grècque,* edited by S. Damianakos, pp. 221-244. National Center for Social Research, Athens.
Herzfeld, M.
  1982 *Ours Once More: Folklore, Ideology, and the Making of Modern Greece.* University of Texas Press, Austin.
  1985 *The Poetics of Manhood: Contest and Identity in a Cretan Mountain Village.* Princeton University Press, Princeton.
  1991 *A Place in History: Social and Monumental Time in a Cretan Town.* Princeton University Press, Princeton.
Hirschon, R.
  1989 *Heirs of the Greek Catastrophe: The Social Life of Asia Minor Refugees in Piraeus.* Clarendon Press, Oxford.
Houliarakis, M.
  1975 Γεωγραφική, Διοικητική, καί Πληθυσμιακή Εξέλιξις τής Ελλάδος, *1821-1971.* National Centre for Social Research, Athens.
Kayser, B.
  1963 Les Migrations Interieures en Grece. In *Contributions to Mediterranean Sociology,* edited by J.G. Peristiany, pp. 192-200. Mouton, The Hague.
Kearney, M.
  1986 From the Invisible Hand to Visible Feet: Anthropological Studies of Migration and Development. *Annual Review of Anthropology* 15:331-361.
Kenna, M.
  1983 Institutional and Transformational Migration and the Politics of Community. *Archives européenes sociologique* 24:263-287.
Kolodny, E.Y.
  1974 *La Population des Îles de la Grèce.* EDISUD, Aix-en Provence.
Koster, H., and J.B. Koster
  1976 Competition or Symbiosis? Pastoral Adaptive Strategies in the Southern Argolid, Greece. In Dimen and Friedl (1976), pp. 275-

285.
Kremmydas, V.
   1972 *Τό Εμπόριο τής Πελοποννήσου στό 18ο Αιώνα (1715-1792)*. Moschonas, Athens.
Laiou-Thomadakis, A.E.
   1977 *Peasant Society in the Late Byzantine Empire*. Princeton University Press, Princeton.
Lawrence, D.L., and S.M. Low
   1990 The Built Environment and Spatial Form. *Annual Review of Anthropology* 19:453-505.
Lowenthal, D.
   1985 *The Past is a Foreign Country*. Cambridge University Press, Cambridge.
McDonald, W.A., and G.R. Rapp (editors)
   1972 *The Minnesota Messenia Expedition: Reconstructing a Bronze Age Regional Environment*. University of Minnesota Press, Minneapolis.
MacFarlane, A.
   1977 *Reconstructing Historical Communities*. Cambridge University Press, Cambridge.
McGrew, W.W.
   1985 *Land and Revolution in Modern Greece, 1800-1881*. Kent State University Press, Kent, OH.
McNall, S.G.
   1974 *The Greek Peasant*. American Sociological Association, Washington, DC.
McNeill, W.H.
   1978 *The Metamorphosis of Greece Since World War II*. University of Chicago Press, Chicago.
Miliarakis, A.
   1886 *Γεωγραφία Πολητική Νέα καί Αρχαία τού Νομού Αργολίδος καί Κορινθίας*. Estias, Athens.
Moore, R.
   1992 *From Shepherds to Shopkeepers: The Development of Tourism in a Central Greek Town*. Unpublished Ph.D. dissertation, Department of Anthropology, University of California, Berkeley.
Mouzelis, N.P.
   1978 *Modern Greece: Facets of Underdevelopment*. Holmes and Meier, New York.
Nash, J.

1981 Ethnographic Aspects of the World Capitalist System. *Annual Review of Anthropology* 10:393-423.

Panayiotopoulos, V.

1985 Πληθυσμὸς καί Οἰκισμοί τῆς Πελοποννήσου 13os-18os Αιώνας. Commercial Bank of Greece, Athens.

Philippson, A.

1892 *Der Peloponnes*. R. Friedlander, Berlin.

Pouqueville, F.C.H.L.

1826 *Voyage de la Grèce*. Firman Didot, Paris.

Rangavis, I.R.

1853 *Τά Ελληνικά*. K. Antoniados, Athens.

Renfrew, C.

1984 *Approaches to Social Archaeology*. Harvard University Press, Cambridge.

Renfrew, C., and J.M. Wagstaff (editors)

1982 *An Island Polity: The Archaeology of Exploitation in Melos*. Cambridge University Press, Cambridge.

Saint-Vincent, M.B. de

1834-36 *Expédition Scientifique de Moree*. F.G. Levrault, Paris.

Sivignon, M.

1981 Evolution de la societé rurale dans l'ouest du Peloponnese: Methochi (Achaïe). In *Aspects du changement social dans la campagne grècque*, edited by S. Damianakis, pp. 32-41. National Centre for Social Research, Athens.

Smith, C.A. (editor)

1976 *Regional Analysis*. Academic Press, New York.

Spirinodakis, B.G.

1977 *Essays on the Historical Geography of the Greek World in the Balkans During the Turkokratia*. Institute for Balkan Studies, Thessaloniki.

Standing, G.

1984 *Population, Mobility and Productive Relations*. The World Bank Papers No. 695, Washington, DC.

Sutton, S.B.

1978 *Migrant Regional Associations: An Athenian Example and Its Implications*. Unpublished Ph.D. dissertation, Department of Anthropology, University of North Carolina at Chapel Hill.

1983 Rural Urban Migration in Greece. In *Urban Life in Mediterranean Europe*, edited by M. Kenny and D. Kertzer, pp. 225-249. University of Illinois Press, Urbana.

1988 What is a Village in a Nation of Migrants? *Journal of Modern*

Greek Studies 6:187-215.

Vacalopoulos, A.
  1976 *The Greek Nation.* Rutgers University Press, New
  Brunswick.

van Andel, T.H., and C.N. Runnels
  1987 *Beyond the Acropolis: A Rural Greek Past.* Stanford
  University Press, Palo Alto.

van Andel, T.H., and S.B. Sutton
  1987 *Landscape and People of the Franchthi Region.* Excavations
  at Franchthi Cave, Greece, Fascicle 2. Indiana University Press,
  Bloomington.

Vayiakakos, D.
  1974 Γλωσσικαί-Λαογραφικαί-Τοπωνυμικαί Ερευναι περί
  Κορινθίας. Πελοποννησιακά Παράρτημα Πρακτικά 2:47-91.

Vryonis, S. (editor)
  1978 *The "Past" in Medieval and Modern Greek Culture.* Undena,
  Malibu.

Wallerstein, I.
  1974 *The Modern World System.* Academic Press, New York.

Watrous, L.V.
  1982 *Lasithi: A History of Settlement on a Highland Plain in
  Crete.* Hesperia Supplement No. 18, American School of Classical
  Studies at Athens.

Watson, P.J., and M. Fotiadis
  1990 The Razor's Edge: Symbolic-Structuralist Archeology and the
  Expansion of Archeological Inference. *American Anthropologist*
  92:613-620.

Whitelaw, T.M.
  1991 The Ethnoarchaeology of Recent Rural Settlement and Land
  Use in Northwest Keos. In *Landscape Archaeology as Long-Term
  History: Northern Keos in the Cycladic Islands,* edited by J.F.
  Cherry, J.L. Davis, and E. Mantzourani, pp. 403-454.
  Monumenta Archaeologica Vol. 16, Institute of Archaeology,
  University of California, Los Angeles.

Wolf, E.R.
  1986 The Vicissitudes of the Closed Corporate Peasant
  Community. *American Ethnologist* 13:325-329.

Wright, J.C., J.F. Cherry, J.L. Davis, E. Mantzourani, S.B. Sutton,
and R.F. Sutton
  1990 The Nemea Valley Archaeological Project: A Preliminary
  Report. *Hesperia* 59:579-659.

Zakynthos, D.A.

1976 *The Making of Modern Greece: From Byzantium to*
      Independence. Rowman and Littlefield, Totowa, NJ.

Endnotes

1. Panayiotopoulos (1985:212) and Vacalopoulos (1976:225-230) argue con-
   vincingly that the downward movement of the Peloponnesian population
   actually occurred at least a century before the Greek Revolution of the
   1820s. This is consonant with the recent work of economic historians who
   see the rural Greek population as having begun to produce for the
   markets of western European capitalism long before they declared
   independence from the Turks (e.g., Kremmydas 1972; Mouzelis 1978).
   Frangakis and Wagstaff (1987, 1992) also document that certain lowland
   areas were well-populated in the late Turkokratia and early days of the
   Greek state, and go on to question whether there was ever an upland
   concentration. Evidence from other areas would seem to verify that
   indeed there was, but what Frangakis and Wagstaff have identified is that
   not all regions were equally affected, that the lowlands were never totally
   abandoned, and that the downward trend began earlier than some scholars
   have believed.

2. Official administrative classifications of Greek settlements have tended to
   mask these smaller rural settlements. The administrative classifications of
   both δῆμος and κοινότης refer more to districts than to distinct
   settlements. They can each contain several συνοικισμοί, or settlements.
   While official definitions of these terms have varied over time
   (Houliarakis 1975), δῆμος has generally referred to a district with at least
   one large settlement, κοινότης to one with smaller component settlements,
   and συνοικισμός to one of these components. That some census reports
   did not identify component συνοικισμοί of a κοινότης, and separate
   hamlets have sometimes been lumped together as a single συνοικισμός has
   compounded the impression that villages are the only rural settlements.

3. The Southern Argolid Project was overseen by Michael Jameson of Stanford University. See van Andel and Runnels (1987) for an account of the
   survey. Hamish Forbes shared the task of researching the modern period
   with me, and proved an invaluable co-worker. My participation involved
   two field seasons (1982, 1983). The project was funded by major grants
   from the National Endowment for the Humanities and Stanford
   University.

4. The Kea Survey Project was directed by John F. Cherry, Jack L. Davis,
   and Eleni Mantzourani (see Cherry et al. 1991). I am particularly
   indebted to Todd Whitelaw for the many insights he offered through his
   precise study of the scattered rural farmsteads in the northern part of the
   island. The project was funded by a major grant from the Institute for

Aegean Prehistory. My participation in the project consisted of one field season in 1984.

5. The Nemea Valley Archaeological Project was directed by James C. Wright, John F. Cherry, Jack I. Davis, and Eleni Mantzourani (Wright et al. 1990). During this project, I was joined by several remarkable research assistants, including William Alexander and Anastasia Karakasidou. My participation with the project is still on-going and has been carried out in five field seasons since 1985. The project is funded by major grants from the National Endowment for the Humanities, the National Geographic Society, and the Institute for Aegean Prehistory.

6. Population estimates for the Nemea Valley in the 1820s are in some conflict with each other. The figure of 110 people used here is a compromise between the 20 families listed for the area by Pouqueville (1826:14), and the 34 families listed by Saint-Vincent (1834-36:68) and repeated by Houliarakis (1975). Panayiotopoulos (1985:240) also lists a figure of 13 families for the area according to the Venetian census of 1700.

7. Anoyatis-Pele (1987) analyzed French documents of 1790 to conclude that the average Peloponnesian village size fell between 34 and 140 people. Panayiotopoulos (1985:193) concluded from Venetian documents that the modal Peloponnesian village size in 1700 was seven families.

8. Settlements listed as "Lecossi" (Lekosi) and "Cuzzomandi" (Koutsoumadi) appear several times in the Nani Archives, housed in the National Library in Athens. The Grimani census of 1700 (Panayiotopoulos 1985:240), however, lists only a settlement called "Curcumadi" (Koutsoumadi).

9. Vayiakakos (1974:68) notes that there were originally 33 δῆμοι in the Korinthia, including the δῆμος of Nemea centered at Agios Georgios. In 1840, this was reduced to 11, one of which was still Nemea. In 1912, however, the system was reorganized into but three δῆμοι, and 122 κοινότητες in the Korinthia. The old δῆμος of Nemea was broken up into several different κοινότητες, one of which was Koutsoumadi (what was later renamed the κοινότης of Archaia Nemea).

10. Such examination of local attitudes toward settlement has been suggested by Crumley and Marquardt (1987:3) for regional survey work in general.

11. Both Charanis (1948) and Laiou-Thomadakis (1977:44-63) also feel that toward the end of the Byzantine Empire, a feudal land tenure system grew in importance, displacing many of these free κοινότητες. The term χωριό then came to stand for both land and peasants, or the entire productive unit, held by a landlord. Over time, however, χωριό simply became the name for any rural settlement containing a church, a store and other such public facilities.

Chapter 15

Production-Oriented Ethnography: The Cultural Anthropologist's Role in Understanding Long-Term Social Change

Mark T. Shutes

Introduction

The research in cultural anthropology herein described is part of a multi-disciplinary project designed to unravel the complex processes of change that have taken place since the 4th Century A.D. within an area of the Northern Peloponnesos known as the Korinthia. Although this present research will focus predominantly upon a smaller representative part of that area, the current villages and agricultural lands of what is known as Ancient Korinth, other areas within the Korinthia will be similarly examined in future research in order to furnish as complete a record of modern life as possible throughout the entire region.

As is indicated by the title of this work, I am concerned to demonstrate that an analysis of the agricultural production strategies employed by the members of a rural community constitutes a singularly effective way for a cultural anthropologist to contribute to team research with a focus on long-term change, for such an analysis not only produces a data base that is crucial to an understanding of the current direction of change within a community, but also provides an "anchor" in the present from which to assess the various kinds of partial information about past tendencies in land use, production and social organization that may be available through census data, historic records and archaeological excavation.

In what follows I shall: (1) examine the theoretical basis for such a claim; (2) show how such an approach provides an excellent interface between the work of the cultural anthropologist and other members of a multi-disciplinary research team; (3) review the research methods currently being employed in Ancient Korinth; and (4) offer a discussion of the research findings in Ancient Korinth to date.

Production and Change: The Theoretical Basis

Traditional social science theories concerning rural change and development have been recently subject to significant empirical criticism in light of the fact that the various approaches consider the rural agricultural producers to take no active role in the change process; i.e., to be merely the passive recipients of externally-generated change processes. This theoretical assumption has produced, therefore, an artificial dichotomy of possibilities with respect to the outcome of change: (1) either the rural producers totally accept the changes from the outside and initiate a process of transformational value changes; the so-called "Modernization" approach, or (2) they resist the changes in favor of their traditional community values and gradually wither away to extinction; the so-called "Peasant" approach (cf. Breathnach and Cawley 1986; Curtin 1986; Curtin and Wilson 1989; Gibbon 1973; Goodman and Redclift 1982; Hannan 1982; Long et al. 1986; Mouzelis 1978; Popkin 1979; Shutes 1991; Weintraub and Shapira 1975).

The weaknesses of the Peasant approach are twofold. First, they are clearly "passive", in that they portray individuals as being totally determined by a complex of traditional community values that they seem unable to alter, even when it means their own economic demise. Obviously farming has not remained completely traditional in rural areas of the European Community (EC), and many individual farmers must have made significant alterations in their values.

Popkin (1979:2) asserts that students of this approach become convinced that the traditional values of rural communities are fundamentally more moral in their economic outcomes than their modern capitalist counterparts because the traditional value structures provide for the welfare of the entire group. Individual members of such groups are viewed, therefore, as resisting change and innovation in the short run in order to gain the long-term benefits of security for themselves and their families. He further suggests that such convictions are based upon "unsupported or unexamined premises and that crucial parts of their view of peasant institutions are without foundation" (Popkin 1979:3). They lack foundation, he continues, because they attribute more importance to norms than to the individuals that actually create them (Popkin 1979).

Second, the Peasant approach pays inadequate attention to economic measurement. Proponents are so concerned with the identification of community values and their effect upon farming practice that they rarely empirically examine the crucial economic variables that are clearly at work in such communities, namely the impact of the external market upon the farming strategies employed in the local community and the measurement of the actual productivity of those strategies. Seldom do Peasant approaches actually measure variability in local farm productivity.

The problems with the Modernization approach are also twofold. First, the approach also assumes a "passive" role on the part of rural community members. In this case, they are seen to reject automatically any existing community values that are not in keeping with the emerging capitalist and market economy, regardless of whether or not some of the older values may still prove efficacious in the maintenance of certain local relationships. Second, the approach is exclusively economic in its emphasis and pays little or no attention to existing patterns of social interaction at the local level. By assuming a homogeneous transformation to mainstream class-oriented values, it ignores the ways in which capital and market intrusions are modified and negotiated according to local community norms.

Both approaches clearly contain fatal flaws in their attempted analysis of rural change and development. Each approach theoretically ignores a crucial data component, and both approaches fail to consider any active role for the rural producers, either in terms of economic decisions or modifications in their social norms. The analytical dilemma with such communities is that they have a foot in both worlds. Their history over the past one hundred years reflects a transition from predominantly (although *never* exclusively) household subsistence production to commodity production for the national and international marketplace. And yet, until recently, that transition has been sporadic and unpredictable as various forms of capital intruded on their production plans. They have had to adjust their production strategies to these intrusions and come to terms with the inevitable value conflicts that such adjustments entail.

Any reasonable analysis of changes in such communities must, therefore consider all of these factors. Goodman and Redclift (1982) state this case very neatly:

> The family-labour farm...is not the direct product of capital, nor does it depend for its reproduction on the realization of an average rate of profit. Nevertheless, once incorporated into commodity production, its conditions of existence are determined by the capitalist mode of production and the particular forms of capital to which it is subordinated. Consequently... they can be analyzed and compared in terms of their relations with different forms or branches of capital. That is...the dynamics of these household forms of production will be structured by the specific relations established with different capitals. The capitalist transformation of rural petty commodity production accordingly will be a diverse, differentiated process determined by the mix of capitals and their respective modes of expansion in agriculture [1982:94].

Adequate analysis, therefore, must (1) incorporate a history of the various forms of capital and market intrusion into the local rural community, and a complete documentation of the changes in production, and subsequent changes in social relations, that such intrusions produced.

Given the "diverse and differentiated" nature of this process, it is quite likely that any local community will exhibit a mixture of both capitalist and non-capitalist production strategies at any given point in time. Curtin (1986) clearly identifies such a mix for farm communities in his discussion of farming in the West of Ireland, and says the following:

> ...understanding change and development in the West of Ireland can only progress further through a careful analysis of the interrelationships between capitalist and non-capitalist forms of production and by focusing upon what Long has called 'the adaptive strategies developed by rural producers for solving their livelihood problems' (1984). Such an approach allows us the possibility of understanding recent changes in the West of Ireland agriculture in terms of their historical specificity...whilst at the same time avoiding the errors of simplistic 'modernization' or 'peasantization' models [1986:75].

Here Curtin suggests the second important component to the analysis of such communities: the core of the historical analysis must be "strategic", that is, (2) it must focus upon the active role that farmers play in making production decisions, and the economic, political and ecological factors that shape such decisions through time.

In addition, given the mix of production strategies, it is also likely that the existing social relations will reflect such a mix of strategies, an on-going "norms negotiation", if you will. Any appropriate approach must also consider this dynamic interaction. Popkin (1979) speaks directly to this issue:

> By using the concepts of individual choice and decision making, we can discuss how and why individuals decide to adopt some sets of norms while rejecting others. From this perspective, norms become problematic, and questions arise which might otherwise be overlooked. What is an enforceable norm? Under what conditions will individuals consider bending or breaking norms?...Where do these particular rules come from? [1979:18]

Here the third crucial component of the analysis emerges. The approach (3) must allow the investigator to identify the appropriate norms that govern production decisions at any point in time, and the conditions under which such norms are "negotiable".

These three components, then, historical specificity, strategic orientation, and norm negotiation must be incorporated into an analysis of rural change and development in order to avoid the problems inherent in more simplistic approaches. It is this kind of analysis that I refer to as a production-oriented approach to rural ethnography.

Further, and more importantly, when agricultural policy is based upon the "passive" theories that are not sensitive to local and regional differences in production strategies, the desired pattern of "take-off" and development is rarely successful, and can actually destroy successful locally-initiated processes of change (cf. Breathnach and Cawley 1986; Curtin and Wilson 1986; Long et al. 1986). Greece, whose agricultural production is dominated by small family-run farms, has struggled to find an appropriate agricultural policy, and critics of that policy have regularly decried the lack of empirical studies which emphasize the active role of local farmers in the initiation, acceptance, or rejection of alternatives to their present production strategies and the relationship of such decisions to local values (Mouzelis 1978; Weintraub and Shapira 1975). In addition, given the fact that most of the existing protectionist policies offered to small farmers in the EC will be eliminated or phased out beginning in 1993, understanding the relationship between production strategies and social change at the local level takes on even greater significance for EC member states whose agricultural self-sufficiency depends upon such knowledge (cf. Bowler 1985; Clout 1984; Fennell 1979; Hill 1984; Shutes 1993).

The inference from the above is, I believe, quite clear. Ethnographic research within rural agricultural communities must focus upon the production decisions made by local farmers and identify the ecological, social, economic and political factors that affect such decisions if it is to contribute meaningfully to any kind of theoretical dialogue on the processes of modern rural change. Further, when ethnographic accounts at the local level do not emphasize these processes, there can be little hope for the development of regional, national and super-national agricultural policies which are sensitive to the ways in which local production decisions are made, resulting in confusion, hostility and waste on a grand scale.

The present corpus of ethnography for rural Greece certainly suffers from this lack of focus on production and its relationship to social change. Though rich and varied in their presentations of rural village social life, few if any of the accounts quantify the basic aspects of village production, such as margins of profit, costs for labor, costs for materials, price of land, market prices for commodities, availability of markets, and individual local differences in farm size, soil quality and strategy. Rather, they tend to follow the classic Peasant approach, wherein production is presented generally and qualitatively and described within the context of stable and traditional rural values which have only recently come under assault from the outside forces of modernization and change (cf. Campbell 1964; Dimen and Friedl 1976; Friedl 1962; Herzfeld 1985; Lambiri 1965; Sanders 1962).

Sutton (in Wright et al. 1990) has recently criticized scholars interested in Greek antiquity for underutilizing the ethnographic materials on contemporary Greek life, saying that their efforts in this regard reflect an implicit assumption that current Greek villagers are carriers of an unbroken agricultural tradition only recently transformed by the processes of industrialization, urbanization, and tourism. This assumption is only heightened by the tendency of most village studies to emphasize the deleterious effects of recent out-migration, thus giving the mistaken impression that these settlements have long been stable.

I would submit that it is not only the ethnographers' emphasis upon out-migration, but also their distinct lack of emphasis upon the internal dynamics and variability of local production that is responsible for the "mistaken impression" that such communities have remained unchanged and unchanging until relatively recent times. When economic variability at the local level is either ignored, subsumed into a general description of "village farming", and/or portrayed as being totally determined by traditional values, an essential element of the change process is lost, namely, the active role played by local farmers in forging the economic strategies that shape their social futures.

Finally, it should be noted that the concerns of a more traditional value-oriented ethnography are not endangered by an approach which takes production variability and change as its central focus. The extent to which collectively held values and traditions impact upon individual decisions is still a crucial question, and a production-oriented approach only adds a higher level of specificity and empiricism to our answers. Clearly not every individual within a Greek rural village begins and ends life with the exact same social and economic standing. The variability is intrinsic, and ethnographic techniques must reflect that variability in individual choice and circumstance in order to fully understand how such communities change.

Production and History: An Interface

In addition to providing information that is essential for the assessment of future change within a community, a production-oriented ethnography greatly facilitates the interpretation of past changes in a number of significant ways. First, in working with individual farmers and their production strategies, it is usually possible to document directly changes in agricultural production that have taken place over the past 150 years, since such changes are within the living memory of the older farmers within a community. These changes typically include such things as alterations in basic technology, land use, crop selection, marketing strategy, and labor requirements. Where economic census data are also available over a similar period of time, as is the case with Greece, these data can be used both to validate the information gained from local farmers and to evaluate the extent to which the production changes documented at the local level are applicable to the wider region.

Second, the collection of individual social histories from each of the farm units in the local community provides an excellent basis for documenting the patterns of migration that have typified the local community over the past 150 years. The availability of social census data also permits both the validation of the local information and its possible regional extension. Further, social histories yield invaluable information about changes in land tenure and inheritance patterns, labor patterns, and other social concerns which can affect the production strategy of local farmers.

Third, the completion of the above two steps provides a reasonable "anchor" for the evaluation of other historical resources that may in themselves provide only partial and/or incomplete information about the local community or region, such as village and church records, local and regional histories, trade and commercial documents, memoirs, etc. These resources, in combination with the social and economic histories provided by the ethnography can then be used to expand our knowledge of the local community and region well into the past.

Fourth, because production-oriented ethnography is fundamentally concerned with the strategic use of land, capital and labor, and the changes that occur in these factors over time, it becomes possible to identify both long and short-term trends in the use of local land resources, such as settlement patterns and crop preferences, over approximately 150 years. This information, when combined with earlier historic sources on production trends and strategies can be invaluable to archaeologists seeking to understand continuity and change in such processes in the more distant past (cf. Sutton in Wright et al. 1990).

Clearly, production-oriented ethnography can make a significant contribution to team research concerned with long-term change in a region. Finally, although I have herein been concerned with the contribution that ethnography can make to a multi-disciplinary study of change, it should be obvious that the work of the ethnographers' colleagues in history, archaeology and geophysics also provide invaluable sources of information and interpretation for the ethnographer.

Ethnographic Methods in Ancient Korinth

A production-oriented ethnography of the sort discussed above will seek to answer the following questions:

(1) What is the current distribution of land holdings among the rural producers in Ancient Korinth? Recording the number of farms and the distribution of farm parcels according to ownership is a crucial element in such an ethnography. The current cost of land and the strategies employed for obtaining new land must also be recorded. Ownership in particular can be a complex issue in Greece, since the system of inheritance tends to produce an intricate division and separation of land parcels.

(2) What is the current land utilization pattern in Korinth? The ethnographer must also be responsible for recording the current pattern of land use within Ancient Korinth, which involves a description of the type of crops being grown on each parcel of land within the community.

(3) What is the current technological organization in Ancient Korinth? The ethnography must also include a description of the current range of technology that is applied to the various agricultural enterprises and the cost and relative efficiency of such technology.

(4) What is the current labor organization in Ancient Korinth? The labor strategies of community farmers is another crucial dimension of the ethnography. Information concerning the use of hired labor and family labor for the various enterprises must be recorded, including the cost of hired labor.

(5) What is the current marketing strategy in Ancient Korinth? A knowledge of the current marketing strategies used by the local farmers must also be recorded, including the current prices received for the various crops produced, and the mix of crops employed by farmers in order to maximize their income potential.

(6) What are the ecological limits to present levels of production in Ancient Korinth? This category must include information about the current quality and productive capacity of the local soils and the availability of suitable water supplies, given the present and future strategies of local farmers.

(7) What is the current social-demographic breakdown in Ancient Korinth? Information about the age, sex, education, occupation, and inheritance patterns for every member of the farm households must also be recorded.

(8) How have the above factors changed in the past 150 years? The ethnography must continuously seek to link the current aspects listed above with those that have occurred over the past 150 years, approximately. Such information can be accessed through interviews with older farmers, in cases where a certain strategy or technique has totally disappeared, and confirmed through reference to agricultural census data and locally available records.

My short-term goal in this present research is to be able to produce, as accurately as possible, a data base of the present variation in agricultural production strategies within the village of Ancient Korinth, including a description of the present land use and land tenure patterns, labor strategies, marketing strategies, social and demographic distributions and, in association with the geoarchaeologist, the current limits to the use of productive land resources. Once this data base is established, the long-term goals of the project are to examine the patterns of historical changes that have taken place in this current strategy, and to eventually associate these empirical change factors with changes in local community social interaction and values.

Research Findings to Date

As of this present date, a total of twelve weeks has been spent in ethnographic research in Ancient Korinth, including seven weeks during the summer of 1991 and five weeks during the summer of 1992. What follows is a summary of the progress of that research.

(1) A complete set of agricultural and social demographic census material for Ancient Korinth has been transcribed, beginning in 1879 and ending with the 1980 census data. The preliminary analysis of this material is presently underway, and will be summarized at the end of this section.

(2) A complete set of 1987 topographical and parcel distribution maps for the area has been acquired, including a set which identifies the distribution of parcels devoted to vineyards and olive groves. In addition, 1987 aerial photo maps of the area were acquired, which match the scale of the topos exactly. These maps and photos were used as the basis for a land use survey which began in the summer of 1992. To date, 1500 of the approximately 3000 parcels included within the current community boundaries have been mapped and the land use of those parcels recorded, including information about irrigation. This survey should be concluded during the summer of 1994.

(3) Formal interviews with 25 local farmers, the president of the village, the president of the local cooperative, and the owner of the local agricultural hardware store have been carried out and transcribed. These interviews involved local accounts of the changes that had taken place in farming within the community over the past 100 years, local descriptions of the present agricultural strategies employed by the communities farmers, and local expressions of the problems of farming under present EC guidelines. The analysis of this material is just beginning, but some preliminary findings will be discussed at the end of this section.

(4) Informal discussions and interviews with a variety of different community members were also carried out and recorded in a daily field journal, which was kept throughout the twelve week period. These discussions and interviews are with local cafe owners and shopkeepers,

and industrial employees and focus primarily upon the kinds of changes that have taken place in the commercial center of the village over the past 150 years, although information concerning immigration, the EC, and local business competitive strategies are also included.

Although the project is still in its very early stages, sufficient data is now available to offer a brief summary of the current dynamics of change that are taking place within the community of Ancient Korinth. Perhaps the single most important aspect of change in Ancient Korinth is the remarkable increase in population experienced by the community within the past 100 years.

In 1879 there were 606 residents recorded for Ancient Korinth. This had increased to 1,724 by 1980, the last date for which census totals are presently available, and local experts place the number today in excess of 2,000 people. Much of this growth is the result of in-migration from other less prosperous regions within the Peloponnesos as well as an influx of people leaving the over-crowded conditions around Athens, only 80 kilometers to the northeast of Ancient Korinth. The situation has become even more complex as of late with the entrance of both legal and illegal Albanian refugees, who bring few or no resources with them to the community.

Many of the recent migrants have sought employment opportunities on local farms, in the oil refineries located on the Saronic Gulf, or in the numerous new industries and commercial enterprises that have arisen in the burgeoning market town of New Korinth, which is only fifteen minutes by public transport from Ancient Korinth. The net result of all of this has been an increasing competition for land and labor resources within the local community between the farmers, who are still the predominant group and the new migrants who are seeking land for housing and/or other commercial enterprises. These new relationships have yet to work themselves out fully, but clearly such processes have the potential for the transformation of basic social relationships within the community.

The preliminary analysis of community agricultural production also reveals massive changes over the past 100 years, as farmers have moved away from the older pattern involving olives, wheat, grapes and sheep/goat complexes into the more volatile and lucrative markets of oranges, lemons, apricots, tomatoes and other fresh vegetable products. This move has been spurred in part by the entrance of Greece into the European Community, but also by the developing local markets in New Korinth and Athens. Such farming is more risky and involves much more astute knowledge of the local, national and international markets.

It also entails a much higher investment in technology, as is witnessed by the fact that the vast number of parcels which contain such products require continuous irrigation, fertilization, and pest and weed control. Clearly such changes, when combined with the social changes discussed above, indicate that a new set of production rules and strategies is emerging within the community, which also has the potential to transform existing social relationships.

From an historical perspective, there is every indication that such rapid adjustment to changing markets is not new to the farmers of Ancient Korinth, who have always been blessed and cursed by their ideal geographic location for commerce, as is indicated by their 18th Century shift away from currants to table grapes, and the more recent shift from apricots to oranges when market conditions changed. The data thus far reveal little evidence to support the notion that farmers in this community have only recently been forced to abandon their "traditional" farming practices in response to outside market pressures. Rather it supports the idea that farmers have been making market decisions and readjusting their production strategies on a continuous basis.

The first twelve weeks of work have been exceptionally successful, both in terms of the acquisition of data but also in terms of the establishment of a good working relationship with the members of the local community. Both farmers and shopkeepers in the area are now aware of our interests in their community, and have expressed a willingness to help us carry out that research in the future. The establishment of this "rapport" is crucial for the long-term goals of this research project.

Conclusion

I have herein suggested that a production-oriented approach to ethnography, with its emphasis upon historical specificity, strategic orientation, and norm negotiation, can greatly facilitate the analysis of short-term change in rural communities while avoiding the more fundamental errors inherent in "passive" and simplistic peasant or modernization approaches. Further, the multiple analytical requirements of the approach link the ethnographer conceptually and methodologically with other disciplines interested in long-term change, so that, in accomplishing their own research agenda about more recent changes, the ethnographer will necessarily share one or more "research frames" with archaeology, agronomy, ecology, ethnoarchaeology, geology, or history.

These shared frames constitute the essence of successful multidisciplinary research, and certainly the disciplines mentioned above have already proven the value of having common analytical goals in the study of long-term changes in human organization. I believe, with Sutton (this volume), that ethnography can make a major contribution to this collaborative effort, but that it must first refine its theoretical and methodological approach to community change before that contribution can become a reality. The work that we have begun in Ancient Korinth is an initial step toward the attainment of such a goal.

Acknowledgments. The 1991 season of field work was funded by a grant from the Wenner-Gren Foundation for Anthropological Research, and the 1992 investigations by a grant from the Graduate Research Council of Youngstown State University.

References Cited

Breathnach, P., and M. Cawley (editors)
  1986 *Change and Development in Rural Ireland.* Geographical Society of Ireland Special Publication No. 1. Cardinal Press, Maynooth, Ireland.
Bowler, I.R.
  1985 *Agriculture Under the Common Agricultural Policy: A Geography.* Manchester University Press, Manchester.
Campbell, J.K.
  1964 *Honour, Family and Patronage.* Clarendon Press, Oxford.
Clout, H.
  1984 *A Rural Policy for the EEC?* Methuen, London.
Curtin, C.
  1986 The Peasant Family Farm and Commoditization in the West of Ireland. In *The Commoditization Debate: Strategy and Social Network,* edited by N. Long, J. Douwe van der Ploeg, C. Curtin, and L. Box, pp. 58-76. Papers of the Department of Sociology No. 17. Agricultural University Wageningen, The Netherlands.
Curtin, C., and T.M. Wilson (editors)
  1989 *Ireland From Below: Social Change and Local Communities.* Galway University Press, Galway.
Dimen, M., and E. Friedl (editors)
  1976 *Regional Variation in Modern Greece and Cyprus.* Annals of

the New York Academy of Sciences, Vol. 268. New York
Academy of Sciences, New York.

Fennell, R.

1979 *The Common Agricultural Policy of the European Community:
Its Institutions and Administrative Organisation.* Granada, London.

Friedl, E.

1962 *Vasilika.* Holt, Rinehart and Winston, New York.

Goodman, D., and M. Redclift

1982 *From Peasant to Proletarian: Capitalist Development and
Agrarian Transitions.* St. Martin's Press, New York.

Herzfeld, M.

1985 *The Poetics of Manhood.* Princeton University Press,
Princeton.

Hill, B.E.

1984 *The Common Agricultural Policy: Past, Present and Future.*
Methuen, London.

Lambiri, I.

1965 *Social Change in a Greek Country Town.* Monograph No. 13.
Centre of Planning and Economic Research, Athens.

Long, N. (editor)

1984 *Family and Work in Rural Societies: Perspectives on
Non-Wage Labour.* Tavistock, London.

Long, N., J.D. van der Ploeg, C. Curtin, and L. Box

1986 *The Commoditization Debate: Strategy and Social Network.*
Papers of the Department of Sociology No. 17. Agricultural
University Wageningen, The Netherlands.

Mouzelis, N.P.

1978 *Modern Greece: Facets of Underdevelopment.* Holmes and
Meier, New York.

Popkin, S.L.

1979 *The Rational Peasant: the Political Economy of Rural Society
in Vietnam.* University of California Press, Berkeley.

Sanders, I.T.

1962 *Rainbow in the Rock.* Harvard University Press, Cambridge.

Shutes, M.T.

1991 Kerry Farmers and the European Community: Capital
Transitions in a Rural Irish Parish. *Irish Journal of Sociology*:
1:1-17.

1993 Rural Communities Without Family Farms? Family Dairy

Farming in the Post-1993 EC. In *Cultural Change and the New Europe: Perspectives on the European Community*, edited by T.M. Wilson and M.E. Smith, pp. 123-142. Westview Press, Boulder.

Weintraub, D., and M. Shapira

1975 *Rural Reconstruction in Greece: Differential Social Prerequisites and Achievements During the Development Process.* Sage Publications, London.

Wilson, T.M., and M.E. Smith (editors)

1993 *Cultural Change and the New Europe: Perspectives on the European Community.* Westview Press, Boulder.

Wright, J.C., J.F. Cherry, J.L. Davis, E. Mantzourani, S.B. Sutton, and R.F. Sutton

1990 The Nemea Valley Archaeological Project: A Preliminary Report. *Hesperia* 59:579-659.

Chapter 16

Sheep for the Ancestors: Ethnoarchaeology and the Study of Ancient Pastoralism

Claudia Chang

Introduction

By its very nature, pastoralism is a regional phenomenon. Even semi-nomadic forms of animal husbandry require people to move their flocks several times a year. In so doing, they utilize a broader range of the landscape than their sedentary agricultural counterparts. To comprehend such a subsistence pattern one must examine the multiple sites, scattered over the terrain, that pastoralists employ. An ethnoarchaeological examination of pastoralism must not only study the contemporary distribution of sites and the movements of herders among them, but must also address the question of how such systems operated in the past.

How did ancient, prehistoric and historic, herders use the heavily dissected, mountainous and valley regions of Greece? The two models proposed for prehistoric and ancient pastoralism are: (1) long-distance seasonal transhumance divorced from farming systems, where herders traveled between summer pastures in the mountains and winter pastures on bare fallow fields in the lowlands, and (2) mixed farming and herding systems where herders maintained livestock close to village settlements (Cherry 1988; Garnsey 1988; Halstead 1981, 1987, 1990; Hodkinson 1988; Jacobsen 1978, 1984; Jameson 1988; Killen 1985;

Skydsgaard 1988; Whittaker 1988). Both models have been derived from well-known historical and ethnographic examples of pastoral groups in rural Greece (Campbell 1964; Koster 1977; Schein 1974; Sivignon 1968; Wace and Thompson 1914). Ethnographic and historical cases of νομάδες or pastoral transhumants such as the Sarakatsani, Koutsovlach, and other ethnic groups in Greece have served as the "prototypes" for explaining pastoral adaptations from the Neolithic Period through Classical Greece (Cherry 1988). Today, in Greece the majority of goat and sheep flocks belong to sedentary village herders: thus, pastoralism is fully articulated with cereal farming and tree crops (Koster 1977). By applying such models to the reconstruction of pastoral production on the rural landscape of Greece, archaeologists and ancient historians have been able to speculate about the vital role herders may have served in linking village and town, rural hinterland and urban πόλις *(polis*, city-state). Yet much of the discussion remains speculative, reliant upon hypothetical models that have not yet been empirically tested in the archaeological record.

The objective of this paper is two-fold: (1) I will critically evaluate how archaeologists and ancient historians use ethnography and anthropology to understand pastoralism; (2) I will put forth some ideas about how ethnography and ethnoarchaeology might contribute to a more fruitful investigation of ancient pastoralism (cf. Nandris 1985). I will use my own ethnoarchaeological research on village pastoralism in the Peloponnesos and pastoral transhumance in southern Macedonia as an example of how ethnography and anthropology can be used more effectively by prehistorians and ancient historians in their studies of rural economies on the Greek landscape. Furthermore, my arguments will build upon Forbes' (1992) statement that ethnoarchaeology and ethnographic studies on rural economies in Greece provide a comparative framework for reconstructing farming practices in ancient periods: "At the heart of the practice of ethnoarchaeology (as indeed of social/cultural anthropology), is the comparative method: the use of data gathered in one location or theoretical sphere to compare with other data" (Forbes 1992:89). Forbes (1992) then continues his discussion about how the "rules of thumb" used by Methana farmers in olive cultivation may be applied to the study of ancient olive cultivation. He cautions us that Greek farmers' rules of thumb about crop cultivation and scientifically derived facts about soils, plants, and agronomy are not necessarily compatible sets of data. Scientific data on agronomy are usually constructed to convince farmers to try new breeds or to change their practices; ethnographic informants do not necessarily see their practices in terms of quantification or from a scientific perspective. Therefore, Forbes argues that both sets of data must be used. In the same vein, I wish to propose that ethnoarchaeological and ethnographic data on modern Greek pastoralism provides "rules of thumb" for practicing animal husbandry today. Many of the "rules of thumb" derived by Koster (1977) and others on the economic rationality of contemporary pastoral systems are intended to provide comparative material for the study of ancient and prehistoric pastoralism, not to posit direct relationships between present and past. In a similar vein, the research objectives of most ethnoarchaeological research conducted on pastoral sites have been explicitly aimed at drawing analogies between present pastoral adaptations and prehistoric and ancient rural economies based on an animal husbandry component (Blitzer 1990; Chang 1981, 1984, 1992, 1993; Chang and Tourtellotte 1993; Murray and Chang 1981).

The assumption underlying my own ethnoarchaeological research is that past landscapes and rural economies can only be understood by knowing more about functioning rural economies found on the Greek landscape today. However, it is also the case that contemporary Greek herding and farming economies are embedded in larger market structures and that the prehistoric and ancient environments were significantly different from contemporary ones (Halstead 1987a, 1990). My own ethnoarchaeological research asks these questions: (1) Under what ecological, economic, and socio-political conditions do pastoral systems flourish? (2) What should an archaeological survey expect to find as the key material artifacts or architectural features of pastoral encampments, corrals, or animal folds? (3) How "visible" are pastoral sites in the archaeological record? Like Forbes (1992), the ultimate goal of my work has been to provide comparative material from contemporary pastoral systems that can be applied to an archaeological data base. Archaeological surveys often provide important information on settlement patterns and site locations. Settlement patterns and site loci across varied environmental landscapes may be used to reconstruct patterns of prehistoric land use. If pastoral sites can be identified positively, then archaeologists can begin to reconstruct systems of pastoral land use on the rural Greek landscape (Chang and Koster 1986).

Pastoral Land Use in Antiquity: A Brief Summary

Archaeologists posit that the development of mixed farming and herding systems organized at sedentary village communities occurred during the Neolithic and continued into the Bronze Age. The articulation of the two economic strategies of cereal-pulse cultivation and livestock (sheep, goats, pigs, cows) husbandry is the basis for small-scale village organization during the Neolithic Period in the lowlands of Greece, Crete, southern Greece, and the Plains of Thessaly (Halstead 1981:307, 1984; Jarman and Jarman 1968; Payne 1975). The most common assumption is that Neolithic pastoralism was a meat-based economy and that by the Bronze Age, the beginnings of plow agriculture and the use of draft animals resulted in the secondary products revolution in which milk and fibers were exploited, as well as meat (Sherratt 1981, 1983). The zooarchaeological evidence does not definitely prove an evolutionary development from pastoralism based on meat to one based on secondary products (Payne 1975). In a recent article, Halstead (1987b) suggests that in a late Neolithic faunal assemblage from Kastri on Thassos, there is a high kill-off pattern for ovicaprine juveniles in the first year, followed by a smaller peak in the second year--a pattern consistent with a mixed meat-milk production strategy. Other zooarchaeological data, though, show a stronger dependence on meat-based pastoralism during the Neolithic Period. From these data, some archaeologists conclude that animal husbandry activities were confined to mixed farming systems in which flock animals manured fields on a cereal/pulse rotation. Flocks were relatively small (under 50 head) and represented an "intensively" based management system in which animal husbandry articulated directly with cereal/pulse cultivation (Cherry 1988; Halstead 1981, 1984, 1987a). Cherry (1988:21-22) critiques an earlier interpretation made by myself and Koster (Chang and Koster 1986) and suggests that Neolithic animal husbandry could have included a wider range of products and encompassed more strategies than mixed farming and herding. He argues that the severity of environmental conditions during the 6th and 5th millennia B.C. would have limited anything but the very modest introduction of a "package of domesticates" from the Near East into the Balkan Peninsula. Thus he subscribes to Halstead's model by which small flocks of ovicaprines would have been kept near cultivated land where meat, and possibly milk products, would have served as dietary supplements, or "fall-back" resources, when crops failed (Cherry 1988:21).

By the late Bronze Age, the Linear B records show that large numbers of sheep were kept at Knossos (Killen 1964, 1985) and probably provided luxury wool for the palace. The 100,000 head of sheep documented by the Knossos tablets suggest the existence of a palace pastoral economy that managed to control pasture resources throughout central Crete and exercised control and limits on individual flocks owned by peasant herders (Chang and Koster 1986; Cherry 1988). This suggests the existence of a continuum of pastoral strategies in Minoan Crete, ranging from large palace flocks to individually-owned household flocks, where the state attempted to limit and subordinate individually owned flocks to its own pastoral interests. Cherry (1988:25) argues that in Minoan and Mycenaean palace economies, specialized herd economies controlled by the elite could have served as a form of capital intensification and as very effective reserves during periods of crop failure or diminishing returns from cereal cultivation. In fact, one means of minimizing bad year returns in agriculture would be to have a sufficient number of livestock in the form of capital reserves in the Palace economy or on the hoof (Halstead 1989). The single most important issue that emerges from these discussions on the evolution of animal husbandry systems is that animal husbandry must be examined in prehistoric contexts in terms of its economic, social, and political advantages, and not merely as a form of ecological adaptation to the variable landscapes of mountainous and lowland regions of Greece. This emphasis allows archaeological explanations to move far beyond the question of whether classical transhumance existed or not, to more important questions of how specialized pastoral systems might have been features of palace economies and predatory to other socio-political institutions (Chang 1993).

In a series of discussions about whether or not pastoral transhumance occurred in the Greek πόλις, Hodkinson (1988) and Skydsgaard (1988) also suggest, from an examination of ancient texts and histories, that a range of pastoral strategies might have existed, from intensive farming in which small flocks of animals were kept outside of settlements, to localized vertical transhumance. Hodkinson (1988) argues that there is no evidence for pastoral transhumance because: (1) land in the Greek πόλις was limited and intensively farmed by a citizen-peasantry with undeveloped channels of trade necessary for long-distance transhumance, and (2) fierce control of land by each competing πόλις limited a herder's access to land from two different city-states, thus circumscribing any type of long-distance movement. Skydsgaard (1988) takes the opposite view; he suggests that although the bulk of animal husbandry in ancient Greece probably occurred within the confines of a mixed farming system, localized seasonal rounds between the mountains and the lowlands would allow for efficient use of mountain pastures. He also argues that ἐπινομία gave rights for members of different communities to graze on common pasture; thus, he counters Hodkinson's (1988) claim that outsiders would have been refused entry into another territory. The social and economic conditions of ancient Greek pastoralism suggest that there was not a specialized class of herders, but often slaves of large landowners served in this capacity (Hodkinson 1988). The very fact that ancient historians are attempting to reconstruct agricultural practices in light of economic and political conditions of ancient Greece shows an initial step toward grappling with other sources of information and incorporating new approaches for the understanding of ancient agriculture and pastoralism.

How can the ethnoarchaeological study of Greek pastoralism contribute to the study of ancient and prehistoric pastoral systems?

Prehistorians and ancient historians who study animal husbandry systems in Greece agree that pastoralism is an economic form that must be understood in relation to specific social, political, and economic conditions. The only remaining trace of an "evolutionary", as opposed to a historical, discussion of pastoralism is the continuing acceptance of Sherratt's (1981, 1983) model of the secondary products' revolution as an explanation for the change from a meat-based economy to one that exploited animals for milk, traction, and wool, as well as meat. By an "evolutionary" explanation, I explicitly mean that pastoralism is seen as a developmental stage whereby animal husbandry systems become further specialized over time and that this specialization is seen in terms of the development of new pastoral products like milk, fiber, and traction. In my mind, the one way to escape the tyranny of such developmental explanations is to reverse the evolutionary formula: that is to suggest that animal husbandry systems from the very beginning of the Neolithic might have exploited milk, meat, fibers, and animal transport (not traction). If we start with this statement, as wrong-headed and contrary to current thinking as it may seem, we can then consider the idea that herd-animal commodities are not in and of themselves what makes a pastoral system "specialized."

The assumption is usually made that Neolithic pastoralism was meat-based. At Suberde in Anatolia, of the 300,000 bone fragments, only about 5 percent could be identified as to species. About 9,000 were identified as sheep/goat (Redman 1978 citing Perkins and Daly 1968). The assumption is usually made that these sheep/goat remains were used for meat. Using ethnographic data collected on the energetics of cereal and herd animal management practices in the Near East and Africa, Russell (1988) points out that it would be most productive from an energetic standpoint for early Neolithic herders implementing a meat-only strategy of animal husbandry to have kept camels first, cattle second, sheep third, and goats fourth. Since this inverts the actual sequence of animal domestication in the Near East and Africa, he then suggests that we reconsider the possibility of a mixed milk and meat-based pastoral economy at the very outset of animal domestication (Russell 1988:140).[1] If we could actually know what products were used by Neolithic and Bronze Age populations, arguments that rely upon ecological and environmental parameters for discussing pastoral systems would seem less arbitrary because we could discuss much more specifically the labor, herbage, and fodder requirements of pastoralism based on the exploitation of milk, wool, or meat, or on any combination of these products.

In the anthropological literature, specialization is defined by the degree to which a pastoral sector becomes "divorced" from other aspects of the rural economy and pastoral specialists enter into careers which include trading, raiding, smuggling, and other predatory activities that feed off the state. Zagarell (1989) argues that in the Bakhtiari Mountains of Southern Iran, a Chalcolithic highland pastoral economy arose out of a mixed farming and herding economy of the Neolithic Period. This specialized upland economy did not push the lowland communities across the threshold of state-level development (Zagarell 1989:300). In fact, the highland communities were a counterweight to lowland development; it is even likely that highland pastoral confederacies or societies were far more influenced by lowland states than vice versa. For the purposes of my argument, I wish to suggest that pastoral specialization in Greece, if it did entail a "highland" component, was dependent and even predatory upon lowland centers. Pastoral mobility itself allowed for subsidiary career opportunities in activities such as trading, raiding, and smuggling. While not wishing to draw too heavily upon historical and ethnographic examples of Koutsovlach herders, one can certainly describe an historical situation from the 19th century throughout the early 20th century in which such herders living on the fringes of the Ottoman Empire and the emerging Greek nation-state did manage to occupy the political and economic interstices of both political entities (Wace and Thompson 1914).

The other essential issue that needs to be addressed is that of herd demography: how many animals (sheep, goats, pigs, cattle) were kept in village, town, or palace communities during different time periods? The demographic balance between pasture and fodder requirements and the number of animals is always a key element for understanding pastoral land use. In fact, many of the arguments put forth on the nature of pastoral systems in antiquity hinge upon demographic projections of whether the Greek agrarian landscape could have supported large or small flocks of animals. As ethnographers have suggested, it is access to pasture lands, either within the village area or in distant villages, that often drives the contractual and political arrangements made between herders and farmers in modern Greece (Campbell 1964; Schein 1974; Koster 1977; Sivignon 1968). Hodkinson's (1988:54-55) discussions of pastoralism in the ancient city-state specifically concentrate on how large land-owners could gain rights to common pasture lands and the size of pastoral units available to those herdsmen who did engage in periodic mobility. This is, to me, the crux of understanding pastoral production as an economic system, especially as a specialized economic sector that is divorced from cultivation. While labor management at the household, community, or palace level and distribution mechanisms for storing, trading, or marketing herd-animal commodities are also crucial elements of any animal husbandry system, the fundamental relationship among animals, land, and resources still needs to be assessed more rigorously.

The two issues of pastoral land use I focus on specifically are: (1) the use of pasture lands among individual households in mixed village farming systems and in pastoral transhumant systems; and (2) the range of animal husbandry systems extant in the Grevena Province today. In discussing these topics, I also wish to demonstrate how our ethnographic and ethnoarchaeological research has broader applications for regional survey projects in Greece. I offer programmatic suggestions as to how the links between ethnographic, ethnoarchaeological, and archaeological survey research might be made more explicit, thus benefitting more fully from collaborative research. A caveat is in order: these suggestions apply directly to the study of pastoral land use and are not meant to cover the wide range of ethnographic, ethnoarchaeological, and archaeological topics examined by regional survey projects throughout Greece.

The Ethnoarchaeology of Greek Pastoralism in Didyma and Grevena

During 1978 and 1979, I recorded all animal fold sites in the Didyma Basin around the village of Didyma in the southern Argolid. The locations of sheep and goat folds on the maquis zone above the olive groves and fertile farmlands of the basins indicated that two systems of animal husbandry were extant in Didyma: (1) an intensively managed sheep system where small flocks of sheep and goats (under 100 head) were kept by households who also owned agricultural land; and (2) an extensively managed sheep or goat system where large flocks (over 100 head) were kept by households who depended primarily upon animal husbandry as their economic mainstay. The shepherds who ran an "intensively" managed flock situated their folds on the edge or margins of agricultural areas and grazed their animals on maquis, fodder, and fallow; the herders who ran "extensively" managed systems situated their folds on village common lands and grazed their flocks predominantly on maquis. The spatial distribution of these animal folds over the landscape indicated that each animal fold represented a territorial claim to a grazing area. Although the informal grazing territories on the village common lands, usually in the maquis area, were not fenced (i.e., open range) herders openly engaged in conflicts over these territories and defended these territories from invasion by other herders.

Koster (1977; personal communication 1992) noted that Didyma herders actually attempted to maintain the common lands, choosing not to overgraze these areas because they realized the adverse effects of poor rangeland on household milk production (inadequate forage would lead to lessened milk returns). Certainly the ethnoarchaeological record confirmed that herders did evenly space their fold locations in relationship to flock size and informal grazing territories (Chang 1981). In a recent article Halstead (1990) argues that Bronze Age settlements in Thessaly were mixed farming settlements, that population sizes at such communities were relatively low, and that social storage occurred in the form of livestock or stored cereals. The primary difference between the model posited by Halstead (1989) for Bronze Age Thessaly and Didyma herding is that the modern villagers are engaged in mixed farming and herding within a market context while Bronze Age producers depended primarily upon a subsistence economy reliant on some forms of exchange and redistribution by elites.

How then can ethnoarchaeological research contribute directly to archaeological interpretations of Bronze Age mixed farming in Thessaly? First, by focusing on spatial arrangements of specialized, outlying facilities necessary for maintaining village animal husbandry systems, I was able to establish the relationship that exists between animal numbers, fold locations, and intra-site spacing. Such a problem should be partially applicable to the archaeologist studying Bronze Age settlements in lowland or upland areas.

The economic forces that control village pastoralism in contemporary Greece are different from those that controlled Bronze Age mixed farming, yet the ethnoarchaeological data on the spatial arrangements of pastoral facilities across a landscape may be of direct utility to a prehistorian. In Halstead's (1989) model of social storage for Bronze Age settlements in Thessaly could it be possible that outlying pastoral facilities exist at the periphery of Bronze Age settlements? Could the presence of such outlying facilities represent differing patterns of land use by which there were herd management strategies ranging from "intensively" to "extensively" managed animal flocks within an area of village-owned land? We might also ask--what if Mycenaean palaces did control wool flocks? Would this also suggest that, like the Minoan palace economies, there were also individual peasant households which kept their own flocks and were in some ways controlled and limited by pasture resources already designated for the royal flocks? Here the ownership and access to pasture units would be a key issue for determining whether there was control over pasture lands by elites and subordination of independent herdsmen who might have been forced to use more marginal grazing areas. In the absence of written documents, the distribution of pastoral facilities, the spatial arrangements of settlements and outlying features, and other kinds of locational evidence from archaeological landscapes might be the only means of reconstructing land-animal relationships in prehistory.

Koutsovlach herders practice summer transhumance in the upland areas of the Grevena Province on the eastern flanks of the Pindos Mountains. The long-distance movements of Koutsovlach and Sarakatsani pastoral transhumants between the mountain refuge communities (Perivoli, Avdella, Smixi, and Samarina) of Vlachohoria and the plains of Thessaly have often been cited by archaeologists as the "ethnographic analogy" for pastoral transhumance during prehistoric periods and in antiquity (Cherry 1988; Halstead 1987a,

1989, 1990; Hodkinson 1988). In 1988 I initiated an ethnoarchaeological survey of pastoral sites across three environmental zones on the eastern flanks of the Pindos Mountains (Chang 1992, 1993; Chang and Tourtellotte 1993; Koster 1987). The objective of this survey was to outline the ecological and economic factors of sedentary village pastoralism and seasonal long-distance transhumance. The pastoral facilities found in six village areas from the High Pindos Mountains (1300-1500 m), the Lower Pindos Mountains (1000-1300 m), and the Pindos Foothills (800-1000 m) were examined. The spatial distribution of animal corrals and folds in these six village areas was studied to determine whether site locations selected by individual herding households were informal territorial markers of actual grazing areas held by households. The aim here was to test the assumption that there was a demographic balance between numbers of herd animals and the amount of territory claimed formally or informally by the herder. This should be visible in the material patterning of pastoral sites across the landscape.

In other papers (Chang 1993; Chang and Tourtellotte 1993) I have discussed the relatively widely dispersed grazing territories used by transhumant herders (average flock size is 150 animals per herding household) in Zone 1, the High Pindos, the more densely organized grazing territories used by year round village herders (average flock size is 40-50 animals per household) and summer transhumant herders (average flock size is 150 animals per household) in Zone 2, the Lower Pindos, and the very competitive and tightly organized grazing territories of year round village flocks in mixed herding and farming households (average flock size is 60 animals per household) in Zone 3, the Pindos Foothills. Using agricultural statistics from 1986, we have calculated ratios of 5.1 to 7.9 ha. of village area per animal (sheep/goat) for Zone 1; ratios of 2.3 to 6.4 ha. of village area per animal (sheep/goat) for Zone 2; and a ratio of 4.45 ha. of village area per animal (sheep/goat) for Zone 3. The range of ratios of village land to number of sheep and goats suggests a rough correlation between sheep and goat numbers and available pasture land.

Even as a "rule of thumb", the demographic balance between animal numbers and actual grazing land requires far more detailed investigation of all the factors of contemporary land use. For example, in Zone 1, the High Pindos, much of the village area has been re-forested, and little to no agriculture is practiced today, although a small number of orchards and fields were cultivated (Wace and Thompson 1914). The pastoral sites in Zone 1 are not packed tightly across the landscape because herders must range far with large flocks of animals to exploit the seasonal flushes of mountain pasture (Koster 1977). Beef cattle kept in Zone 1 also affect land/animal ratios. In Zone 2, land use has changed dramatically because of village depopulation after the Civil War of 1948-49: large portions of village land that had been planted in orchards, vines, cereals, and fodder were abandoned. Abandoned fields are now being used by year-round village herders or summer pastoral transhumants. Thus, spatial patterning of στάνες (*stanes*, animal corrals) and μάντρες (*mandres*, animal folds) reflects a filling in process whereby pastoralists are using land once cultivated by agriculturalists. Zone 3 represents the more typical mixed herding and farming system, in which flocks of sheep and goats are kept in animal folds in or adjacent to the village settlement. Sheep and goats graze in oak forest areas during the summer before crops have been harvested and in the winter they graze on fallow, fodder, and stubble. Herders must provide winter fodder for flock animals. Ethnoarchaeologically, there are two site types, sometimes seasonally differentiated: (1) the summer strunga (milking pen) and (2) the μάντρα, or year round masonry-laid or concrete animal fold, with an attached fodder barn. The animal folds are part of the village settlement, whereas the summer milking pens may be more distantly spaced close to the oak forests and other grazing territories.

Extrapolating from the Grevena data, I propose the following models of pastoral land use and village settlement that may be examined using archaeological survey data:

(1) *Summer pastoral transhumance*: many archaeologists argue this type of pastoral adaptation may have been present only during the Medieval Period, and not in prehistoric times (Cherry 1988; Halstead 1987a, 1990). The ethnoarchaeological data on summer transhumant sites indicates that the best places to look for such sites would be in upland areas where cultivation is marginal (Chang 1992, 1993; Chang and Tourtellotte 1993). In environmental zones marginal for farming, where natural or man-made deforestation may have taken place, pastoral facilities should appear as ephemeral features, which are evenly distributed across mountain terrain, usually separate from village settlements.

(2) *Winter pastoral transhumance*: in the Thessalian plain today, winter transhumant μάντρες resemble the animal folds used by year-round village pastoralists. The distinguishing characteristic is the use of extensive flock management, so that flocks are large in size (150 head of sheep and goats) and fodder storage is a necessary component. These

animal folds tend to be more distant from the village settlements than the pastoral facilities used by year-round village herders. The ethnoarchaeology of winter pastoral transhumance, not sufficiently studied yet, is fascinating and might suggest to prehistorians like Halstead (1987a, 1989, 1990) that Bronze Age settlements in Thessaly could have engaged in a range of pastoral production strategies. Some of the techniques might not have been "classic seasonal transhumance," but could have engaged an occupational class of herders that did travel long distances between mountains and lowlands with palace flocks, while village herders continued to participate in mixed farming-herding strategies.

(3) *Mixed farming-herding systems*: in Grevena this form is found in most communities located at 800 m or below. Historically, in villages in Zone 2 at the upper elevational limits for farming (900-1100 m), pastoral production consisted of 60-80 percent of the herding households participating in mixed farming-herding production and only 20-40 percent participating in long-distance seasonal transhumance. Archaeologically, this should be the most ubiquitous form of pastoral production, and, therefore, would be typified by pastoral facilities attached to, or in the proximity of, village settlements. The late prehistoric sites of Vitsa (Vokotopoulou 1986) and Karpenisi (Emmanoulidhis 1969, 1971), located at an elevation of 1000 m in the Pindos Mountains, are interpreted by Halstead (1990) as mixed farming-herding communities found at high elevations, rather than as summer pastoral transhumant sites. The historical circumstances following the Greek Civil War in which the eastern Pindos villages in Zone 2 were increasingly taken over by pastoral transhumants after the demise of upland agriculture, would indicate that Halstead's (1990) suggestions are well founded. One way of substantiating the existence of upland mixed farming-herding contexts in prehistoric periods is to conduct full-scale survey in the uplands. In mixed herding-farming situations, the spatial arrangements of the prehistoric human settlement to the outlying pastoral and agricultural facilities should be instructive as to whether the community was a mixed farming-herding community or more typical of summer shepherds' camps.

Conclusions

Future research on ancient pastoral production in rural Greece will benefit from more interdisciplinary efforts between ancient historians, archaeologists, ethnoarchaeologists, and anthropologists. Pastoral production is a poorly understood aspect of the economic history of ancient Greece, historic and prehistoric; too often we are forced to rely upon scant textual references, minimal zooarchaeological data, and archaeological (survey or excavation) remains that frequently are difficult to identify positively as "pastoral features" or "pastoral artifacts." The answers to our questions will never be more than speculative without more substantial data recovered from the archaeological or textual records. What ethnoarchaeology and ethnography can provide for archaeologists and ancient historians is a comparative framework--a way to frame specific questions. While the modern Greek rural economy provides the archaeologist and ancient historian with models and analogies, its own place in history and within a particular cultural setting cannot be ignored. In a similar vein, I hope that prehistorians and ancient historians recognize that they cannot blindly adopt models of rural production derived from the work of anthropologists or ethnoarchaeologists without considering how very different and varied the past is from the present.

Ethnoarchaeology contributes directly to our understanding of a changing landscape in a region over time. Certainly the ethnoarchaeology of pastoralism in Grevena has provided new directions for an examination of how herders and farmers use the natural environment and topography of upland areas in Greece. Chang and Tourtellotte (1993) describe increased visibility of upland Bronze Age and Hellenistic Period sites at contemporary στάνες where animals have churned up the soil and caused surface erosion, thus exposing buried ceramic and lithic materials. The ethnoarchaeological study of contemporary herding sites across three or four environmental zones in the Grevena Region has demonstrated the variation of farming and herding land use strategies across an upland area. The variation of pastoral strategies across this terrain and environmental zones is important; it demonstrates to archaeologists that the study of pastoralism in ancient and contemporary contexts must be conducted in regions and not only in single locations. Many of the ways in which contemporary herders use grazing resources, situate themselves on the margins of agricultural and forest lands, and are integrated into rural village production systems, suggest that herding systems must be examined as part of large-scale land use systems, and not just within single village locations. In this respect we must see herding systems extending beyond single site locations and ranging across the varied and diverse physical topography, as well as socio-political geography, of Neolithic, Bronze Age, and historic ancient landscapes.

Acknowledgments. Research funding for the Grevena ethnoarchaeological survey was obtained from the Wenner-Gren Foundation in 1988 and 1989. Sweet Briar College Faculty Summer grants provided funding for the 1990-1993 seasons. This chapter owes its greatest debts to the few tenacious archaeologists who continue to research the problem of prehistoric pastoralism in the Aegean.

References Cited

Blitzer, H.
   1990 Pastoral Life in the Mountains of Crete: An Ethnoarchaeological Perspective. *Expedition* 32(3):34-41.
Campbell, J.K.
   1964 *Honour, Family, and Patronage: A Study of Institutions and Moral Values in a Greek Mountain Community.* Clarendon Press, Oxford.
Chang, C.
   1981 *The Archaeology of Contemporary Herding Sites in Didyma, Greece.* Unpublished Ph.D. dissertation, Department of Anthropology, State University of New York at Binghamton.
   1984 The Ethnoarchaeology of Herding Sites in Greece. *MASCA Journal* 3(2):44-48.
   1992 Archaeological Landscapes: The Ethnoarchaeology of Pastoral Land Use in the Grevena Province of Greece. In *Space, Time and Archaeological Landscapes,* edited by J. Rossignol and L. Wandsnider, pp. 65-89. Plenum Press, New York.
   1993 Pastoral Transhumance in the Southern Balkans as a Social Ideology: Ethnoarchaeological Research in Northern Greece. *American Anthropologist* 95:687-703.
Chang, C., and H.A. Koster
   1986 Beyond Bones: Toward an Archaeology of Pastoralism. In *Advances in Archaeological Method and Theory, Volume 9,* edited by M.B. Schiffer, pp. 97-148. Academic Press, New York.
Chang, C., and P.A. Tourtellotte
   1993 The Ethnoarchaeological Survey of Pastoral Transhumant Sites in the Grevena Prefecture of Greece. *Journal of Field Archaeology* 20:249-264.
Cherry, J.F.
   1988 Pastoralism and the Role of Animals in the Pre- and Protohistoric Economies of the Aegean. In *Pastoral Economies in Classical Antiquity,* edited by C.R. Whittaker, pp. 6-34.

Cambridge Philological Society Supplementary Volume No. 14, Cambridge.

Emmanoulidhis, G.
1969 Ευρυτανία: μεσοελλαδικά ευρήματα εκ Καρπενησίου. *Athens Annals of Archaeology* 2:358-64.
1971 Ευρυτανία: νέαι ειδήσεις εκ Καρπενησίου. *Athens Annals of Archaeology* 4:196-200.

Forbes, H.
1992 The Ethnoarchaeological Approach to Ancient Greek Agriculture: Olive Cultivation as a Case Study. In *Agriculture in Ancient Greece, Proceedings of the Seventh International Symposium at the Swedish Institute at Athens, 16-17 May, 1990*, edited by Berit Wells, pp. 87-104. Göteborg, Sweden.

Garnsey, P.
1988 Mountain Economies in Southern Europe. Thoughts on the Early History, Continuity and Individuality of Mediterranean Upland Pastoralism. In *Pastoral Economies in Classical Antiquity*, Supplementary Volume No. 14. edited by C.R. Whittaker, pp. 196-209. Cambridge Philological Society, Cambridge.

Halstead, P.
1981 Counting Sheep in Neolithic and Bronze Age Greece. In *Patterns of the Past: Studies in Honour of David Clarke*, edited by I. Hodder, G. Isaac, and N. Hammond, pp. 307-339. Cambridge University Press, Cambridge.
1984 *Strategies for Survival: An Ecological Approach to Social and Economic Change in the Early Farming Communities of Thessaly, Northern Greece.* Unpublished Ph.D. dissertation, University of Cambridge.
1987a Traditional and Ancient Rural Economy in Mediterranean Europe: Plus ça Change. *Journal of Hellenic Studies* 107:77-87.
1987b Man and Other Animals in Later Greek Prehistory. *Annual of the British School at Athens* 82:71-83.
1989 The Economy Has a Normal Surplus: Economic Stability and Social Change among Early Farming Communities of Thessaly, Greece. In *Bad Year Economics*, edited by P. Halstead and J. O'Shea, pp. 68-80. Cambridge University Press, Cambridge.
1990 Present to Past in the Pindhos: Diversification and Specialisation in Mountain Economies. *Revista di Studi Liguri*, A. LVI(1-4):61-80.

Hodkinson, S.

1988 Animal Husbandry in the Greek Polis. In *Pastoral Economies in Classical Antiquity*, edited by C.R. Whittaker, pp. 35-74. Cambridge Philological Society Supplementary Volume No. 14, Cambridge.

Jacobsen, T.W.

1978 Transhumance as a mechanism of exchange in Neolithic Greece. *The Archaeological Institute of America Abstracts* 3:47.

1984 Seasonal Pastoralism in the Neolithic of Southern Greece. A Consideration of the Ecology of Neolithic Urfirnis Pottery. In *Pots and Potters: Current Approaches in Ceramic Archaeology*, edited by P.M. Rice, pp. 27-43. University of California Institute of Archaeology, Los Angeles.

Jameson, M.H.

1988 Sacrifice and Animal Husbandry in Classical Greece. In *Pastoral Economies in Classical Antiquity*, edited by C.R. Whittaker, pp. 87-119. Cambridge Philological Society Supplementary Volume No. 14, Cambridge.

Jarman, M.R., and H.N. Jarman

1968 The Fauna and Economy of Early Neolithic Knossos. *Annual of the British School at Athens* 63:241-64.

Killen, J.T.

1964 The Wool Industry of Crete in the Late Bronze Age. *Annual of the British School at Athens* 59:1-15.

1985 The Linear B Tablets and the Mycenaean Economy. In *Linear B: A 1984 Survey*, edited by A.M. Davies and Y. Dulhoux, pp. 241-305. Louvain University Press, Louvain.

Koster, H.A.

1977 *The Ecology of Pastoralism in Relation to Changing Patterns of Land Use in the Northeast Peloponnese.* Unpublished Ph.D. dissertation, Department of Anthropology, University of Pennsylvania.

1987 Appendix IV: The Ethnography of Herding in the Grevena Area. In *The Grevena Report*. N.C. Wilkie, ed. Manuscript on file at the Department of Anthropology, Carleton College.

Murray, P., and C. Chang

1981 An Ethnoarchaeological Study of a Contemporary Herder's Site. *Journal of Field Archaeology* 8:372-81.

Nandris, J.G.

1985 The Stina and the Katun: Foundations of a Research Design in European Highland Zone Ethnoarchaeology. *World Archaeology* 17(1):256-268.

Payne, S.
   1975 Faunal Change at Franchthi Cave from 20,000 B.C. to 3000
   B.C. In *Archaeozoological Studies: Papers of the
   Archaeozoological Conference 1974*, edited by A.T. Clason, pp.
   120-31. Elsevier, Amsterdam, New York.
Perkins, D., Jr., and Patricia D.
   1968 A Hunter's Village in Neolithic Turkey. *Scientific
   American* 219(5):97-106.
Redman, C.L.
   1978 *The Rise of Civilization: From Early Farmers to Urban
   Society in the Ancient Near East*. W.H. Freeman, San Francisco.
Russell, K.W.
   1988 *After Eden: The Behavioral Ecology of Early Food
   Production in the Near East and North Africa*. BAR International
   Series 391. British Archaeological Reports, Oxford.
Schein, M. (Dimen)
   1974 When is an Ethnic Group? Ecology and Class Structure in
   Northwestern Greece. *Ethnology* 14:83-97.
Sherratt, A.G.
   1981 Plough and Pastoralism: Aspects of the Secondary Products
   Revolution. In *Patterns of the Past: Studies in Honour of David
   Clarke*, edited by I. Hodder, G. Isaac, and N. Hammond, pp.
   261-305. Cambridge University Press, Cambridge.
   1983 The Secondary Exploitation of Animals in the Old World.
   World Archaeology 15:90-104.
Sivignon, M.
   1968 Les Pinde du Pinde Septentrional. *Rue de Geographie de
   Lyon* 43:5-43.
Skydsgaard, J.E.
   1988 Transhumance in Ancient Greece. In *Pastoral Economies
   in Classical Antiquity*, edited by C.R. Whittaker, pp. 75-86.
   Cambridge Philological Society Supplementary Volume No. 14,
   Cambridge.
Vokotopoulou, I.
   1986 *Βίτσα: τά Νεκροταφία μίας Μολοσσικής Κομής:1. Text.*
   Ministry of Culture, Athens.
Wace, A.B., and M.L. Thompson
   1914 *Nomads of the Balkans*. (Reprinted in 1971). Books for
   Library Press, New York.
Whittaker, C.R.
   1988 Introduction. In *Pastoral Economies in Classical Antiquity*,

edited by C.R. Whittaker, pp. 1-5. Cambridge Philological Society Supplementary Volume No. 14, Cambridge.

Zagarell, A.
  1989 Pastoralism and the Early State in Mesopotamia. In *Archaeological Thought in America*, edited by C.C. Lamberg-Karlovsky, pp. 268-279. Cambridge University Press, Cambridge.

Endnotes

1. Russell uses a foraging model to demonstrate the value of mixed cereal and animal husbandry practices. He also discusses at great length why the faunal record is problematic for determining what products were exploited by early Neolithic people in the Near East. His ethnoarchaeological research on animal husbandry practices was conducted in Jordan. By examining the cost-benefit ratios of meat/milk based strategies in areas where dryland cereal cultivation of barley and wheat also occurred, he strongly suggests that mixed meat-milk production strategies were the most efficient form of pastoral exploitation (Russell 1988).

VII.
DOING ARCHAEOLOGY IN GREECE

Chapter 17

Archaeology in Modern Greece: Bureaucracy, Politics, and Science

P. Nick Kardulias

Introduction

In the June 14, 1990 edition of the newspaper *H Καθημερινή* (*The Daily*) reporter Nikos Stathoulis presented an investigative report entitled "*Ο Πολιτισμός μας Λεηλατείται*" (Our Culture Is Being Looted) in which he claimed that the Greek Ministry of Science and Culture and the Greek Archaeological Service were not providing adequate protection for Greece's cultural heritage. One example he cited was a French excavation in the Cyclades that had "destroyed antiquities." This article triggered a rebuttal from the current Director of the French School of Archaeology in Athens, Olivier Picard. In this instance there was evidence of negligence on the part of the French archaeologist. This exchange, however, is symptomatic of a larger problem in which Greek scholars and public officials increasingly view the work of foreign archaeologists with a jaundiced eye. What can and should be a cooperative effort to understand the Hellenic past often bogs down into bureaucratic trench warfare in which looters plunder the no-man's land of archaeological sites largely left vacant or only marginally protected because a systematic, effective policy has evaded discovery or implementation.

As a result of such conditions, the process of archaeological investigation by foreigners in Greece has become entangled in a series of problems. Many of the difficulties foreign scholars experience result from two major sources: (1) the historical context of the archaeological enterprise in the country, and (2) the institutional structure of archaeology in Greece. Below I deal with the first issue briefly to provide a basic background for a fuller discussion of the second issue. I argue that Greek archaeology, because it is deeply embedded in the state, operates frequently to obstruct foreign work. This policy serves no one well and should be revised. There is ample evidence to suggest that archaeology in Greece is subject to political pressures that can distort the scholarly pursuit of knowledge. Thus, the discussion of the second issue will focus on the political aspect of doing archaeology in Greece. The situation will be viewed in terms of a model of political behavior developed by David Easton.

Before I proceed to a discussion of the historical and institutional issues, it will be necessary to define the key concepts mentioned in the subtitle. According to political scientist David Easton (1977:93) politics "...is concerned with understanding how authoritative decisions are made and executed for a society." As a process, politics need not be identified exclusively with particular components in a society. In other words, we can witness the operation of political dynamics not only in and among governmental structures, but also within all sorts of organizations, formal and informal, that have to generate collective decisions. Easton provides a model of political action that defines inputs of such a system as demands and support, and outputs as decisions or policies. Members of a society, and thus participants in a political system, "... act within the framework of an ongoing culture that shapes their general goals, specific objectives, and the procedures that the members feel ought to be used...The culture embodies the standards of value in a society and thereby marks out areas of potential conflict, if the valued things are in short supply relative to demand" (Easton 1977:98). In short, individuals in different organizations determine the avenue to pursue in the effort to acquire, regulate, or dispose of certain resources whose value is determined by relative scarcity. People develop rational strategies to achieve goals, and politics refers to the formulation and implementation of the decisions and the consequences of such behavior. I will argue that archaeological sites and permits for their investigation are such limited commodities.

The German sociologist Max Weber (1946:196-8) provided a classic definition of bureaucracy that has wide applicability. According to

Weber, bureaucracies exhibit six key traits: (1) division of labor, (2) hierarchical statuses, (3) codified norms, (4) disinterested role enactment, (5) technical competence, and (6) formal, written communications. Weber's emphasis was on efficiency in large formal organizations and he stressed the dispassionate performance of duties, a point which is open to debate. I take the first three characteristics as the truly definitive elements. Bureaucratic organizations in all spheres of society are hierarchically organized with specialized positions in a structured setting with formal regulations. Technical competence is subsumed or implied by specialization. The Greek Ministry of Culture and its antiquities branch, the Greek Archaeological Service (GAS), qualify as elaborate bureaucracies. In addition, the foreign archaeological schools in Greece have well-entrenched bureaucratic structures of their own.

Science is an investigative procedure that follows a rigorous method in the effort to examine empirical phenomena. The intent is to add to the body of knowledge by systematic consideration of hypotheses that can be tested against data. The propositions so derived are provisional in the sense that they are open to change in light of new evidence; they must be and are, as many adherents of scientific method suggest, falsifiable statements. One of the concerns of science is to eliminate errors or mistakes and the ability to revise previous thinking is crucial to this task. In addition, many scholars argue that science has as a primary goal the promulgation of general or covering laws that explain the operation of universal processes. Some social scientists argue we can also generate covering laws that deal with human behavior. Such laws would crosscut temporal, spatial, and cultural differences between societies. In archaeology, this perspective is known as the processual approach or the New Archeology (Binford 1989). Although a number of foreign archaeologists, especially Americans and British, working in Greece have adopted the processual approach, it is a perspective that most Greek archaeologists either are not familiar with or reject because of the tradition-bound nature of training in classical archaeology. This difference is one of the underlying causes for some misunderstandings between Greek and foreign scholars of the past. The goals of scientific archaeology also confront obstacles in the form of political considerations and entrenched bureaucrats. I should make clear at this point that many foreign archaeologists are also averse to the tenets of the New Archeology and its stress on science as a hypothetico-deductive method for the examination of cultural phenomena (see

Binford 1989 for a succinct statement concerning the goals of the New Archaeology; Dyson 1993).

A Brief History of Archaeology in Greece

Greece is virtually synonymous with archaeology. Whether one speaks of the Parthenon, Mycenae, Delphi, or Knossos, the image is powerful and reinforces the notion of Greece as the fountainhead of western civilization. Along with this valued legacy goes a much less hallowed one. Of the many westerners who responded to the attraction of sites where the giants of Greek history, philosophy, drama, and science strode, some hoped to return home with a tangible reminder of the visit and that past civilization. Some merely yielded to the antiquarian penchant for beautiful objects and carried off valuable ancient treasures, but fortunately others took a more serious scholarly interest in retrieving elements of the Hellenic past. It was this latter concern that led Heinrich Schliemann, Arthur Evans and many others to spend their professional lives, and in some cases their personal fortunes, seeking to interpret what Bibby (1956) called the testimony of the spade.

The distrust that greets many foreign archaeologists in Greece has its strongest roots, perhaps, in the well-known story of the Elgin Marbles. Thomas Bruce, the Seventh Earl of Elgin, and British Ambassador to the Sublime Porte in the early 19th century, requested and received permission from Turkish officials in 1801 to record, copy, and carry away any antiquities on the Akropolis of Athens. Elgin's subordinates took full advantage of the official firman and removed a host of sculptural and architectural pieces, including one of the Karyatids from the south porch of the Erechtheion, and sculptured metopes, sections of the Ionic frieze, and other pieces from the Parthenon. The pieces eventually ended up in the British Museum (Ceram 1979:45). Some contemporary observers of the Greek scene denounced this act. Lord Byron roundly condemned such systematic looting in *Childe Harold's Pilgrimage* (Canto II):

> Come, then, ye Classic Thanes of each degree,
> Dark Hamilton and sullen Aberdeen,
> Come pilfer all the Pilgrim loves to see.
> All that yet consecrates the fading scene:
> Oh! better were it ye had never been,
> Nor ye, nor Elgin, nor that lesser wight,

The victim sad of vase-collecting spleen,
House-furnisher withal, one Thomas hight,
Than ye should bear one stone from wronged Athena's site.

During the 1980s the effort to return the Elgin Marbles to Greece became a cause celebre. Minister of Culture and Science Melina Mercouri spearheaded this unsuccessful attempt. Few would argue that Greece's claims are not legitimate, but the affair also had a distinct political aspect. A number of Greeks, including members of the government, see this matter as an example of a pernicious foreign influence that systematically demeans Greece. Some refer to a scientific imperialism in which foreign scholars play a role, perhaps unwittingly, in keeping Greece in a secondary or tertiary position by dominating the Greek archaeological scene with their investigations. Attempts to secure the return of antiquities and to limit excavations by foreigners undoubtedly reflect such attitudes to some degree.

There is of course some truth to Greek claims. Beginning shortly after Greece's independence in the 1830s and continuing to the present there has been a consistent Western presence on the Greek archaeological scene. The establishment of foreign schools in Athens assured an institutional base for field and archival research. These schools have, with the consent of the Greek government, established proprietary rights to certain important excavations: The American School in the Athenian Agora and Korinth, the Germans at Olympia and the Athenian Kerameikos, the French in Argos and Delos, the British at Knossos, etc. A mountain of scholarship has emerged from these long-term commitments, but the Schools were also the vehicles for exporting materials for study and exhibit; archaeologists transported some of the objects excavated by the foreign schools to Europe and America to allow scholars to examine the material, and to place some of the finer pieces on display in museums. Such actions, in which acquisitive desires clearly outweighed the desire to accumulate data and refine our knowledge of classical antiquity, can be viewed rightfully as an expropriation and exploitation of the Greek past.

Furthermore, one cannot view archaeology as divorced from the larger intellectual and cultural context. Here I will consider only the political milieu, but clearly one can draw parallels with folklore studies, literary criticism, historiography, and other fields in how they influenced and were affected by the scholarly trends of the time. The great European powers played an important role in the realization of Greek independence in the nineteenth century (Woodhouse 1986), albeit to a large degree as a result of their own strategic concerns, and have maintained an often unwelcome political presence ever since. As Mouzelis (1978:14-29) points out, since independence, the West has incorporated Greece into a world capitalist market, with a dramatic impact on the livelihood of the country's natives. As the degree of incorporation increases, some argue, Greece gets led along certain paths not of its own choosing and not to its benefit. The establishment of the foreign archaeological missions was simply an extension of this phenomenon. Since foreign intervention in Greek internal affairs has often had, or at least been perceived to have, a negative impact on the country, it is perhaps only natural that Greeks should view the archaeological schools as yet another expression of exploitative neo-colonialism. This attitude in turn engenders restrictive policies.

Politics and Bureaucracy in Greek Archaeology

In general, the work of foreign scholars is looked on with favor by Greek academics; there is an active discourse between Western and Greek intellectuals. At times of heightened political tension, however, expressions of Greek nationalism occasionally vent themselves in a xenophobia that encompasses intellectual as well as other activities. The past decade in particular has witnessed the growth of anti-Western, especially anti-American, sentiment that has cast relations between Greece and her traditional allies in a rather negative light. Many of the Greek attitudes have their origin in the tumultuous years of the military junta and the disastrous consequences of the Greek army's attempted assassination of Archbishop Makarios on Cyprus which resulted in the Turkish invasion. The common Greek perception of American culpability in these events has fueled informal and official retaliation on the part of Greece. One must consider the practice of archaeology in Greece in light of these broader political developments. That the larger political realm has an impact on the practice of a seemingly innocuous intellectual discipline is in large part due to the official incorporation of archaeology into the governmental structure. First, I discuss the organizational structure of archaeology in Greece. Then I will examine some specific ways in which archaeology plays a truly political role.

In Greece, as in many European nations, archaeological materials are considered national resources whose regulation is a prerogative of the state. This attitude and the actions that can emanate from it make great practical sense because it is possible to formulate a coherent national policy to deal with archaeological sites and materials. The implementation of such a policy, however, requires the establishment of appropriate political appendages that often blossom into full-blown bureaucracies that may lose sight of archaeology's scientific goals and may indeed impede those goals. To some degree, this is the situation that confronts the foreign archaeologist working in Greece. The administrative machinery set up to assure proper care of antiquities can and does inhibit the performance of important work.

Before I go further, it is necessary to step back and say something about the political arena in which Greek archaeology must operate. In the administrative hierarchy, archaeology falls in the Ministry of Culture and Sciences (Tsatsos 1977). The GAS is the government agency charged with the responsibility of overseeing the performance of fieldwork, archival and museum research, conservation and preservation of sites and material. The GAS also acts as a clearing-house for permits granted to foreign archaeologists. The GAS maintains a central office in Athens and has 25 regional offices, or εφορείες (*eforeias*), of Prehistoric and Classical Antiquities, 13 εφορείες of Byzantine Antiquities, and seven εφορείες of Modern or Recent Monuments throughout the country (Section B, Chapter A, Articles 33-37). The head of each office is a προϊστάμενος (proïstamenos, or director) beneath whom are varying numbers of ὑφιστάμενοι (assistants), guards, and conservators, all state employees whose jobs to some extent depend on political fortunes. These individuals are responsible for excavating and curating materials from planned and emergency (salvage) projects. British archaeologist Anthony Snodgrass (1987:95) notes that Greek antiquity law prohibits the destruction of any ancient remains prior to professional assessment. The manpower assigned to the GAS is inadequate to accomplish such an immense task. As a result, many materials are rapidly removed and inadequately stored, never to be systematically studied because the GAS must move on to the next salvage job. These conditions undermine the scientific endeavor since only a small fraction of the excavated material ever receives proper analysis and reporting. A vast data bank concerning the past lies in the storage section of every Greek museum. All too often, haphazard storage of these materials makes it nearly impossible within a few years to discern key information concerning, for example, provenience, without which the remains are worthless as aids in interpreting the past. To be sure, there are many conscientious employees of the Service who strive to perform high quality work under these trying conditions. There are also those people, unfortunately, whose greatest concern is not with retrieving the record of the past but with bureaucratic infighting. As a result, little systematic field archaeology gets done in many regions. Many GAS employees exhibit bureaucratic paranoia because promotions and even their jobs often hinge on superiors who are in turn subject to shifting political currents. The Minister of Culture and the Director of the GAS are, to a considerable extent, political appointees, so the people in various regional offices feel, rightly or wrongly, that they must cultivate certain connections and constantly protect their flanks against co-workers who do not share their political affiliation. The goals of archaeology can and do too often get lost amidst such bureaucratic jockeying.

The foreign archaeological missions could assist the GAS in its duties, but what should be a natural alliance falls prey to other considerations. By Greek law each foreign school receives a limited number of permits each year. There are, of course, more requests and many archaeologists must wait years for an opening to appear in order to conduct field research. I agree with the need to regulate archaeological investigations. The law is intended to eliminate the massive export of antiquities that virtually denuded many important sites of priceless treasures. With the rapid pace of construction in Greece and the concomitant discovery and destruction of sites, however, the GAS requires significant assistance. But the restrictions on foreign permits and the exigencies of funding dictate that permit requests be limited to significant research problems, not salvage work. Archaeological permits are a limited political resource that the Greek government, through the GAS, dispenses.

Let me elaborate. Although there are justifiable historical reasons for limiting foreign archaeological work, the critical situation, with the regular destruction of sites because of inadequate personnel and funds, requires a substantial response and the current system is simply not up to the task. In an effort to maintain control of archaeological resources, the Greek government established rules to regulate excavation by foreigners. Since 1932 (Public Law 5351, Article 37), each foreign school is limited to three excavation permits, and more recently to three surface locational surveys, per year. The permit restriction applies across the board to large and small missions alike, so that, for example, the British School of Archaeology receives the same number of permits as the Swedish Institute, despite the difference in the number of scholars affiliated with each mission and the resources (financial, technical, etc.) each group can bring to bear on research problems. The bureaucratic tangle is substantial. Consider this statement from a recent circular of the American School:

According to rules adopted by the Managing Committee of the American School of Classical Studies and the policy of the Greek Ministry of Culture (Directive 55647/776/11-10-83), all American scholars who wish to excavate in Greece, or to study, photograph or draw objects in Greek museums and storerooms should request that application for permission be made to the Greek authorities on their behalf by the American School.

The foreign schools submit such permit requests by November 1, but it is not unusual for a researcher to arrive the following May or June prepared to begin work but without any official word about the status of the permit application. The wheels of the archaeological bureaucracy grind exceedingly slowly. Such procedures play havoc with funding and planning for fieldwork. Many American funding agencies do not allow the flexible scheduling that the permit situation in Greece, and many other countries, necessitates. Failure to receive legal permission to begin work as stated in a proposal's timetable may result in cancellation of the agency's funding. Laws and regulations intended to maintain Greek control of a valuable national resource have, thus, unintentionally impeded scholarly work. In addition, Greek governmental policy reinforces the status quo in the foreign schools by requiring that all permit applications go through those institutions, which commit many of their resources to old, established excavations (e. g., the Athenian Agora) supervised by leading figures in the foreign missions.

The preceding discussion deals with archaeology as a political resource that involves a large bureaucracy and levels of decision-making at a rather specific level. In this instance, the issuing of permits can be modeled as a particular political process. The permits are a limited resource whose allocation the government controls. Inputs occur in the form of application procedures that outline prospective research. One attempts to gain a favorable output, i.e. approval of a permit request, by demonstrating serious scholarly intent, rigorous methodology, etc., in presenting the research proposal. Informal support-building techniques are also important. For example, several past Directors of the American School have curried favor with Greek politicians because the latter, especially in the Ministry of Culture, are crucial in gaining permission to work in the country. Final decisions on the granting of permits are made by the Central Archaeological Council of the GAS. The composition of the Council in part reflects the broader political system; adherents of the party in power generally outnumber those tied ideologically to the opposition. Certainly many members of the GAS try to remain apolitical in the performance of their duties, but

political emotions do run high at times. I have witnessed situations of
near paralysis in regional offices when decisions concerning foreign
archaeologists had to be made but no one was willing to expedite the
research because people feared the consequences of any action that
someone higher in the bureaucracy might view with disfavor. The best
strategy in these cases is to do nothing, so the scholar languishes in
research limbo as a result of bureaucratic paranoia. Such conditions
were especially prevalent after the inconclusive June 1989 general
elections; no one wanted to do anything that could be used against them
when a regular government finally came to power. Thus, matters
concerning permits and other issues have as much to do with
bureaucratic in-fighting and strategies for implementing a particular
political agenda as they do with archaeology per se. This situation is
inevitable since archaeology falls under government control. To place
this discussion in a broader context, Herzfeld (1982a), in his analysis
of the etymology of excuses, suggests that εὐθυνοφοβία (*euthinofovia*,
fear of responsibility or blame) results in inertia at any time when the
situation is anomalous, i.e., any action may be seen as inappropriate by
one's superiors and could lead to a reprimand or other punitive
sanction. Although the rhetorical performance itself is a form of action,
from the outsider's viewpoint nothing gets done.

Archaeology also serves broader political goals in Greece. First, it
serves as a means to heighten a sense of national identity. Neil
Silberman (1990) notes that governments in the Mediterranean have
turned archaeology into a tool of national ideology. Various countries,
including Greece, stress those elements of the archaeological record
that serve to make of the past a coherent, unified theme, that begins
with some golden age and continues unbroken to the present;
archaeology is a tool in the effort to maintain the integrity of the ethnos
and its great legacy. As Herzfeld (1982b, 1987:1-27) has demonstrated,
modern Greeks have struggled to reappropriate their past, and to imbue
it with meaning that suits their own goals. When left to the devices of
Western intellectuals, the Greek past became an idealized vision to
which modern Hellenism could not measure up. As foreign
archaeologists uncovered the wonders of Classical Greece, the
accomplishments of its descendants paled to insignificance in the eyes
of many Europeans. This attitude, although on the wane, still holds
sway behind the walls that often separate foreign dighouses and
missions from the surrounding Greek neighborhoods and creates
unnecessary obstacles to good relations; the foreigners often present
themselves as separate enclaves, uninterested in "mingling" except

where and when necessary. For some Greeks, the foreign schools are an intrusive and unwelcome reminder of the paternalistic attitude and exploitative behavior many Europeans have exhibited for decades. As a result, some Greeks are willing to believe that the foreign schools are subtle extensions of neo-colonialism, and even to suggest that the archaeologists therein are spies. Although geared to a different audience and not as extreme, the suggestion by the Greek government in the 1980s that the foreign schools be closed reveals a distinct dissatisfaction with the manner in which those schools have operated.

A second and more explicit use of archaeology in the political process occurred in the June 1989 general election. The socialist party, *ΠΑΣΟΚ* (an acronym, PASOK, for the Panhellenic Socialist Movement), proved particularly adept at incorporating archaeology into its political platform. An election pamphlet on cultural matters reserved a special place for archaeology. The party touted its support for excavations, conservation and restoration projects (including the Parthenon, Mystra, and monuments in Thessaloniki), building new museums, and tripling the personnel in the GAS. This listing of accomplishments is part of the effort to build a support base for elections. The effort also seems well suited to PASOK's ideological agenda. The uniqueness and grandeur of Hellenism revealed through archaeology bolster the Socialists' strong nationalist position, which explicitly argues that Greeks have a distinct sociopolitical persona that does not need to be allied with any particular power in order to gain importance for its own identity.

At yet another level, allusions to Greece's glorious past and its primacy in the development of cultural innovations, as demonstrated by archaeology, help to assuage feelings of inferiority engendered by contemporary geo-political realities; i.e., Greece is relatively insignificant in modern world affairs. If anything, some policies of the Socialist Papandreou government in the 1980s helped to place Greece in an even more marginal status. Some Greek politicians and pundits seem to revel in this peripheral status because it offers the opportunity to tweak the noses of the superpowers, especially the United States, without any real political fallout. Charges of scientific imperialism have little real impact on international relations, but do affect the work of foreign scholars when the bureaucrats translate the ideology into policy guidelines. The resultant constraints have frustrated foreign scholars, some of whom have gone to countries, such as Cyprus, that offer more hospitable research conditions.

Conclusion

It seems clear that certain changes in the way archaeology is done in Greece would ameliorate the present condition for foreign scholars while also providing benefits to the host country. Rather than a synopsis, then, I would like to offer some recommendations. First, the foreign schools must put their own houses in order. Responsible officials should issue explicit statements of professional standards and ethics. Appropriate schedules for the timely publication of results must be established. We must not condone sloppy work simply because the perpetrator is "one of ours." The foreign missions must actively pursue cooperative projects with Greek colleagues. Important strides have been made in this respect but more certainly could be done. For example, the inclusion of more Greek scholars as permanent members of foreign teams is desirable and necessary. Joint training sessions with foreigners and Greeks would help break down some of the barriers and would create a real sense of collegiality.

Zois (1990:48-54), in his review of archaeology in Greece, offers some suggestions to improve relations between the foreign schools and Greek archaeologists which I find appropriate, and in some cases long overdue: (1) The foreign schools should maintain permanent personnel both in Athens and at their major excavations throughout the country to establish and keep up libraries, work areas, and offices to facilitate research. (2) There should always be a certain number of Greek students involved in foreign projects for educational purposes. (3) In addition, there should be present in all foreign projects, from the planning stage to final publication, a permanent group of Greek researchers. (4) Contacts between a foreign project and the εφορεία in that region should become the basis for a substantive scientific collaboration instead of the sporadic interaction now in evidence. (5) The foreign schools should pursue actively collaboration with the Departments of Archaeology in the four major Greek universities (Athens, Thessaloniki, Ioannina, and Crete). I believe the implementation of such a plan would bear immediate fruit for foreign and Greek archaeologists in reduced tension, expanded opportunities, and enhanced quality of the data base available for analysis.

Second, some structural changes in the Greek archaeological community seem to be in order. Manolis Andronikos (1990), the Greek excavator of the Macedonian royal tombs at Vergina, called for greater centralization in the GAS. By reducing the regional offices from 25 to 10-13, he argued the GAS would be able to pool its limited resources and provide a fuller range of services. As he wisely pointed out, excavation is only the beginning of the archaeological enterprise; conservation, restoration, curation, and analysis are all necessary to produce final reports. The current system stretches resources too thin to permit such comprehensive study of data. I would add to Andronikos' assessment that the foreign schools can help fill the gap he discusses, but in order to do so the Greek government must increase the allotment of annual permits to each mission. This does not mean that Greece must give up control of its archaeological resources, but rather that some artificial and unnecessary barriers should be eliminated. Questions of national identity and integrity must be weighed against the imminent and permanent loss of important parts of the Greek heritage. Perhaps the rules could stipulate that any excavation permits above the current limit of three must be for cooperative projects. Whatever the particular formula, Greek archaeologists should not view the changes as an abdication of national principles but as a means to tap the reservoir of foreign scholarly talent and financial as well as technical resources for the resolution of particular problems. Although I do not believe we will ever completely depoliticize archaeology, we can broaden the base from which decisions are made and thus more closely approximate a scientific approach in the discipline.

Acknowledgements. Michael Herzfeld, Michael Toumazou, and Ian Morris read earlier drafts of this paper and made helpful comments. I thank them for their insights without burdening them with the blame for the errors I have made in adopting some of their ideas. The segment of Byron's poem, *Childe Harold's Pilgrimage*, was taken from *Lord Byron. The Complete Poetical Works*, edited by Jerome J. McGann (1980:vol. 2, 48), by permission of Oxford University Press.

References Cited

Andronikos, M.
    1990 Η Αρχαιολογική Υπηρεσία, Ενα Μειζόν Πρόβλημα.
    Η Καθημερινή July 8:B14.
Bibby, G.
    1956 *The Testimony of the Spade.* Knopf, New York.
Binford, L.R.
    1989 The "New Archaeology," Then and Now. In

Archaeological Thought in America, edited by C.C. Lamberg-Karlovsky, pp. 50-62. Cambridge University Press, New York.

Byron, L.
  1980 *The Complete Poetical Works.* Edited by J.J. McGann. Oxford University Press, Oxford.

Ceram, C.W.
  1979 *Gods, Graves and Scholars.* Vintage, New York.

Dyson, S.
  1993 From New To New Age Archaeology: Archaeological Theory and Classical Archaeology--A 1990s Perspective. *American Journal of Archaeology* 97:195-206.

Easton, D.
  1977 The Analysis of Political Systems. In *Comparative Politics: Notes and Readings,* edited by R. Macridis and B. Brown, pp. 93-106. Dorsey Press, Homewood, Illinois.

Herzfeld, M.
  1982a The Etymology of Excuses: Aspects of Rhetorical Performance in Greece. *American Ethnologist* 9:644-663.
  1982b *Ours Once More. Folklore, Ideology, and the Making of Modern Greece.* University of Texas Press, Austin.
  1987 *Anthropology through the Looking-Glass. Critical Ethnography in the Margins of Europe.* Cambridge University Press, New York.

Mouzelis, N.
  1978 *Modern Greece. Facets of Underdevelopment.* Holmes and Meier, New York.

Silberman, N.
  1990 The Politics of the Past: Archaeology and Nationalism in the Eastern Mediterranean. *Mediterranean Quarterly* 1:99-110.

Snodgrass, A.
  1987 *An Archaeology of Greece.* University of California Press, Berkeley.

Stathoulis, N.
  1990 Ο Πολιτισμός μας Λεηλατείται. *Η Καθημερινή* June 17:14.

Tsatsos, K.
  1977 Περί Οργανισμού τού Υπουργείου Πολιτισμού καί Επιστήμων. *Εφημερίς τής Κυβερνήσεως τής Ελληνικής Δημοκρατίας* 1:2975-3004.

Weber, M.
  1946 *From Max Weber: Essays in Sociology.* Edited by H.H.

Gerth and C.W. Mills. Oxford University Press, New York.
Woodhouse, C.M.
   1986 *Modern Greece: A Short History.* Fourth edition. Faber
   and Faber, London.
Zois, A.
   1990 *Η Αρχαιολογία στήν Ελλάδα.* Politipo, Athens.

VIII.
CONCLUSION

Chapter 18

Regional Studies in Greece: A *Vade Mecum*?

Jack L. Davis

Introduction

My remarks in this concluding chapter differ substantially from those that I presented in 1991 in Chicago when many of the papers now published in this volume were first read publicly. The publication of this rich harvest both of old and newly solicited contributions offers me the welcome opportunity to review and revise my thoughts in light of developments in the field of regional studies in Greece that have occurred since 1990.

The ideas expressed in these few pages are hardly intended as a work of refined scholarship; rather they are the result of personal introspection and reflection over the past fifteen years during which I have been involved in conducting regional studies in Greece, and in the twenty years that I have been a member of the American School of Classical Studies at Athens. This paper may contribute, I hope, in some small but tangible way to the growing dialogue concerning the future of Classical archaeology that is currently being fueled by a flood of critical retrospectives of our field published since our symposium by Lake Michigan (e.g., Brown 1993; Dyson 1993; McDonald 1991; Morris 1994). The notable absence that Kardulias noted then in his introductory remarks exists no longer with the addition of these substantial supplements to the few, but significant, evaluations that had been previously published (e.g., Dyson 1981, 1985; McDonald 1985; Snodgrass 1985, 1987; Snodgrass and Chippindale 1988).

The remarks that follow are entirely personal observations; they are intended to promote discussion, not antagonize. And for the most part I mean them to pertain to American archaeology as practiced in Greece. I conclude with proposals which, if adopted, would guide our field in the direction that I would like to see it move. No doubt others will choose not to become my fellow travellers on this journey and will have different perspectives on the goals that we should be setting for ourselves and our students. But whatever the case, it is important for the intellectual development of Classical archaeology that we discuss such matters openly, even if no consensus is possible.

The Status of Classical Archaeology

Classical archaeology is an odd field, odder and more schizoid than many of its critics realize and than many Classical archaeologists may want to admit. Certainly many, or perhaps even most, anthropological archaeologists have little or no idea of its objectives. In the theater of world archaeology, Classical archaeology in recent years has had only the smallest of roles to play and publications by Classical archaeologists have rarely attracted the interest of colleagues working in other parts of the world (cf. Dyson 1985). A review of the pages of the journal *Antiquity* over the past five years makes this point nicely enough: fewer than three percent of published papers are concerned in any way with Graeco-Roman antiquity, despite the fact that *Antiquity* is now widely regarded as the leading non-regionally specific archaeological journal in the world.

Although it remains isolated from world archaeology, probably none of us who practice it would today subscribe to James Deetz's 1967 caricature of Classical archaeology as a kind of archaeology that "is usually taught as art history in university art departments". This was not an entirely fair description of our field even twenty-five years ago when it was written. Most Classical archaeologists today, as then, are not in art departments. Our numbers are more or less evenly split between Classics and art/art history departments, with relatively minor components represented in history, anthropology, and other disciplines (Davis 1994).

The gist of Deetz's remark still rings true, however, and his attitude was understandable, if uninformed. Much, even most, of the formal instruction that traditionally has been offered in American universities by Classical archaeologists *should* be broadly categorized as history of art or architecture. What Deetz's remark does not reflect is the vast gulf that lies between teaching and field practice for a great many Classical archaeologists and their students. Unlike anthropologists, students of Classical archaeology receive for the most part remarkably little training in archaeological methods or theory and are rarely encouraged to think of themselves as members of a wider archaeological community.

In my own case more than twenty years ago, two years into graduate school I asked my advisor when I would learn about field archaeology, to which he replied: "when you get to the field, you will learn by experience from your workmen" (many, but not all, Classical archaeologists [Near Eastern and Mesoamerican archaeologists also] employ local laborers to excavate their sites under the supervision of academic archaeologists who are responsible for record-keeping). And I did learn a great deal about the physical process of excavating from my workmen. What I did not, and could not, gain from them, of course, was any systematic understanding of site formation processes, statistics, cation-ratios, geomorphology, Harris-matrices, or any of the many analytical procedures and conceptual perspectives that were being introduced routinely to the anthropological archaeologist's arsenal during the hey-day of the New Archaeology.

This massive gulf between Classical and other archaeologies indeed widened in the 1970s with the appearance of the New Archaeology, and the decision of most professors of Classical archaeology to reject or ignore its tenets (e.g., Courbin 1988). It is not difficult to comprehend why Classical archaeology did not respond positively to the New Archaeology. Kardulias in his forward to this volume notes quite properly that most Classical archaeology is practiced in the Humanities, not in the Social Sciences. This in itself has positioned it in a state of relative isolation from other archaeologies, and not entirely out of benign neglect. It is impossible to know how many other graduate students of Classical archaeology were discouraged by their professors from studying archaeology in the anthropology departments of their own universities.

Many Classicists view the social sciences as the original home of muddy thinking and the enemy of a traditional rigorous university education, and are loath to fill vacancies in their departments with candidates who explicitly have identified themselves with a social scientific methodology. In turn, most Classical archaeologists have found it necessary to prove their credentials in a subfield of Classics other than archaeology in order to remain in good standing at their institutions. "Can't teach the languages," or "Not art historical enough," are both frequently expressed justifications for slinging applications for new positions in Classics or art history into the rejection heap.

What needs greater emphasis now, however, are the enormous problems that Classical archaeologists face when they attempt to change the course of their own discipline: in our dealings with the federal government, in our professional organizations, and in our colleges. Need for change in each of these arenas demands our consideration and will be considered in turn, but, as they say, the journey of a thousand miles begins at home, in our own departments. For most of us, our professional life there is a lonely existence. Most of us are lucky to have a single archaeologist as a colleague (Davis 1994). As a consequence, we have little control over our own professional reproduction. When the post of a Classical archaeologist in a Classics or art history department becomes vacant, the choice about filling it almost never is the perquisite of archaeologists.

The inability of Classical archaeologists to reproduce themselves is, in my mind, the greatest problem that faces the teaching and practice of Mediterranean archaeology in North America. If Kuhnian paradigm shifts require the "advocacy of a new generation of scientists who have little to lose," Classical archaeology will be left waiting for Godot. Such revolutions in science presume that scholars with new ideas and approaches can at least play *some* part in the system that is to be the object of change. On the other hand, young innovative Classical archaeologists who have dared embrace fashions not acceptable to potential employers are more likely to be found at the fringes of academia than in centrally placed departments and universities--if they are still employed as professional archaeologists.

Anthropology departments have been equally uninterested in providing homes for these academic bag-people. There the Mediterranean world has a very low (nearly non-existent) hiring priority. When anthropologists do decide that they need the services of an archaeologist specializing in the archaeology of complex societies, more often than not they opt for a specialization in the so-called primary civilizations of Mesopotamia, the Near East, or the Far East. Classical archaeology seems to them to have little to offer anthropological archaeology.

Such attitudes toward Classical archaeology on the part of both Classicists and anthropologists are usually founded on an unhealthy

mixture of misunderstanding and misinformation, much of it fostered
because Classical archaeology is so rich in the resources that it offers
the archaeologist; it, unlike many other archaeologies, is large enough
to support considerable internal specialization. One consequence of this
internal specialization is that there exist scholars who are primarily
concerned with aspects of the history of ancient art and consider
themselves to be Classical archaeologists, although they may never or
rarely engage in fieldwork. The research conducted by many of these
scholars has been traditional, in that it follows fairly well-defined
conventions established by renowned predecessors.

Probably the most conspicuous (and, of late, most often criticized;
e.g., Gill 1988; Cherry 1992) practitioners of this brand of Classical
archaeology are the disciples of Sir John Beazley, whose research is
principally employed in studying the stylistic traits of painters (and to
a lesser extent potters) who decorated vases in ancient Athens in the 7th
through 4th centuries B.C. Their goal is "attribution", i.e., the
assignment of a particular vase to a particular artistic hand (Robertson
1963; 1992). Several hundred artistic personalities have been defined
over the past century and their *oeuvres* described and discussed. But the
ultimate goals of such research are often unclear. As sometimes
happens in Classical archaeology, the forest either gets lost for the trees
or practitioners are simply not interested in the forest at all. Whatever
the case, most Classical archaeologists specializing in art historical
studies work inductively without any explicitly formulated set of
research questions; consequently they lack broader disciplinary goals
of the sort that Anthropology provides to its archaeologists.

One can hardly protest the right of such scholars to claim that they
are Classical archaeologists (although some have disclaimed it
themselves; e.g., Robertson 1963), since it is in this kind of meticulous
art historically oriented research that Classical archaeology has its roots
(e.g., Briggs and Calder 1990; Lullies and Schiering 1988). It is
important, however, that both they and we recognize that Classical
archaeology and ancient art history in the later 20th century in North
America are not an identity. And it is equally true that some goals of
Classical archaeology may differ from those of anthropological
archaeology. Such differences can and should be tolerated, but there
can be no retreat or compromise on one point. Since the material
remains of our past are non-renewable resources, all archaeology
(Classical too!) must as a minimum baseline embrace the catholic
perspective on the past that anthropology offers us. Anthropology is a
broader discipline than art history, inasmuch as it has chosen to

examine the material *and* non-material culture of all humankind. On the other hand, too often when art historians turn to archaeological fieldwork, the reconstruction of past societies in their totality is sacrificed in favor of an unjustified concentration on one small aspect of culture--viz., the representational symbolizing activities of ancient elites.

The archaeological establishment in North America also does little to promote positive changes in the practice of Classical archaeology. One of the least logical roadblocks is the division of archaeological funding between the National Science Foundation (NSF) and the National Endowment for the Humanities (NEH), a policy that legitimizes the practice of non-scientific archaeological field research (Office of Management and Budget, n.d.). NEH is intended to support "collaborative research that will have a significant impact on scholarship in the humanities" and includes only "those aspects of the social sciences that employ historical or philosophical approaches." Such separation of funding has perpetuated the myth that certain kinds of archaeologies are special cases, that they can carry on business as usual, no matter that they are out of step with the discipline as a whole.

Furthermore, such conditions serve to encourage Classical archaeologists to favor art historical perspectives. Whereas an archaeologist who works in North America can compete for outright grants of money from NSF, NEH's funds come for the most part in the form of matching dollars. Unlike the successful applicant to NSF, the NEH successful applicant's trials have just begun when s/he receives notice of the award of funding. Not only is valuable research time wasted in supplementary fundraising. In attempts to woo wealthy patrons, a wise Classical archaeologist will choose to emphasize the most visually spectacular aspects of a project and its finds. Such behavior only reinforces the traditional stereotype--Classical archaeologist as hunter of fine art.

Within most of our universities there is a similar illogical discrimination against Classical archaeologists that does not effect anthropological archaeologists so severely: viz., the allocation of space, equipment, and staff support. For a variety of reasons, university administrators seem to assume that social scientists, like natural scientists, need a minimum level of infrastructure in support of their research. Consequently, virtually all anthropological archaeologists whom I know have laboratories, and their institutions also customarily provide research assistants to manage the day-to-day operations of their projects. Quite to the contrary, I am hard-pressed to think of even a handful of Classical archaeologists who control any laboratory space, and poor infrastructure is apparent even in some of our most illustrious programs. College and university administrators alike tend to view Classical archaeology as they imagine the rest of the Humanities to operate--a solitary endeavor conducted by individual scholars in armchairs, book in hand, dog at feet, pipe clenched in teeth.

It is within this sometimes inhospitable and frequently contradictory environment that most of those North American Classical archaeologists who practice regional studies in Greece must operate. As a group we are probably those Classical archaeologists most sympathetic to a social scientific archaeology, yet NSF is essentially closed to us. The fact that our research is less art historical can pose problems for us and our students when we seek employment from Classicists who believe the study of high art is the proper theater of Classical archaeology. Our care and feeding is much more expensive than that of art historically oriented Classical archaeologists since we typically organize large team projects, assemble and curate massive archives, and require high-end programs and equipment such as GIS (Dann and Yerkes, this volume).

Nevertheless, regional studies by Classical archaeologists in the past fifteen years have had an effect on our field out of proportion with the number of practitioners; few Classicists *or* anthropologists seem to comprehend the magnitude of these changes, of which the contributions to this volume are themselves proof-positive. It will be impossible to write any new ancient history of Greece without reference to the regional studies projects that nearly all of the authors here represented have either organized or participated in. This new fieldwork has had at its core the adoption of the techniques of intensive surface survey.

As Kardulias notes in his introduction, archaeological survey has now become a mainstay of Greek archaeology. Although only a relatively small percentage of the country has been intensively surveyed, most provinces have seen at least some action (see maps in Rutter 1993:750; Alcock 1993:34). The wealth of new data produced by such studies has in turn encouraged the establishment of entirely new subfields such as comparative survey, the goal of which is to synthesize evidence from a great many regional studies projects, and then to use this evidence to re-examine traditional pictures of past Greek landscapes based largely on literary sources (see Cherry, this volume). Recent examples of the approach include Cynthia Kosso's *Public Policy and Agricultural Practice: An Archaeological and Literary Study of Late Roman Greece*; and Effie Athanassopoulos' *Intensive Survey and Medieval Rural Settlement: The Case of Nemea.*

Both authors followed Sue Alcock's pioneering lead, first presented in her Cambridge dissertation and now published as *Graecia Capta* (1993). Gregory's paper in this volume makes yet another important contribution to the development of this rapidly evolving subfield, and it is encouraging that such studies appear to be receiving a warm reception from reviewers (e.g., Mattingly 1994).

From one perspective, it is possible to view the New Wave of surveys in Greece as a fairly natural development within the context of a tradition of landscape exploration in Greece that is now nearly 200 years old. In this half-century and in American archaeology alone, we can boast a number of meticulous studies, several now classic, conducted by single individuals or small groups of scholars--e.g., studies of the locations of Athenian demes (Eliot 1962), of settlement distribution in the territory of Korinth (Wiseman 1978), and of military camps of Attica (McCredie 1966). The New Wave of regional studies projects, however, has broken with this earlier tradition of reconnaissance in several important ways:

(1) *Degree of intensity of survey*. Modern surveys consist of teams of archaeologists who inspect entire landscapes in a highly systematic manner; fieldwalkers are usually arrayed in lines and are separated only by a few meters.

(2) *Diachronic focus*. Modern surveys are concerned with every period of the past and every type of site.

(3) *Conceptual basis*. Modern regional studies projects seek to investigate explicitly stated historical or anthropological problems that can only be addressed with data systematically gathered at the regional level.

(4) *Interdisciplinary leadership*. The organization of most modern surveys is interdisciplinary from its inception in that the goals of a project are formulated by a consortium of Classical archaeologists, social scientists, and natural scientists.

(5) *Role of excavation*. Most directors of modern projects have explicitly argued that new excavation is not fundamental to answering the principal questions that guide their research, nor is the discovery of sites to excavate their chief objective.

The New Wave of regional studies in Greece differs in each of these five ways from any of its predecessors, even from the Minnesota Messenia Expedition (Fotiadis 1994). The survey component of this project was conducted in the main by two individuals, William McDonald and Richard Hope Simpson. Locations of sites were in later years predicted on the basis of preconceived models of site location.

The landscape was not systematically examined in its totality. The project was principally interested in prehistoric sites. A principal goal was to find sites to excavate. Conceptual models were drawn from anthropological archaeology, but not from the New Archaeology: the organizers recognized Braidwood, Adams, and Sanders as their intellectual godparents, not Flannery (McDonald and Rapp 1972: 13-17).

It is important to understand that this important conceptual difference exists between the Minnesota project and many or most regional studies projects organized more recently by Americans in Greece. The numerous projects that are stepchildren of the Argolid or Melos projects (including the Keos Survey, The Nemea Valley Archaeological Project, The Pylos Regional Archaeological Project, and The Berbati Survey) all espouse goals that are *sensu lato* those of social science; their interpretive frameworks are grounded in the hypothetico-deductive methodology of the New Archaeology. In fact, most of the archaeologists who have contributed to this volume are intellectually avatars of the 1960s: for them archaeology is not merely scientific, but *social* scientific.

Several natural scientists who have contributed to this volume express frustration and confusion in the dealings with archaeologists in regional studies. The fact that so many Classical archaeologists engaged in regional studies are oriented toward the social sciences may in large part explain this predicament. Classical archaeologists with whom natural scientists may previously have worked on excavations or in extensive surface reconnaissance are likely to have been the type who wants to "populate...accounts with real, known people" (Kardulias). But many Classical archaeologists who "do" regional studies are different. Indeed most of us have framed our research programs so as consciously to direct resources to the exploration of parts of Greece that are not well known from literary sources. It is thus hardly a wonder that communications misconnect so often (see van Andel, this volume). Questions such as the location of the Greek camp at Troy or the morphology of the Thermopylae battlefield at the time of the Persian invasion (see Rapp and Kraft, this volume) have been important issues for some Classical archaeologists, but in the minds of most of the archaeological contributors to this volume, they take a back seat to the reconstruction of regional patterns of settlement and land use.

The root of the problem must lie in the fact that many of the archaeological scientists who practice in Greece have had little or no *formal* training in archaeology. Natural scientists are drafted into archaeological service by friends and colleagues at their home institutions, and then must learn the archaeological side of the business through trial and error. Granted that many or most Classical archaeologists learn natural science in the same haphazard manner, the situation is not ideal in either case. Still, attempts to create a new generation of archaeologists-cum-scientists in America have foundered gravely.

Several factors are to blame. First, there are almost no jobs for archaeological scientists in America, *particularly* for those who specialize in Greece. With virtually all archaeology positions in Classics or art history departments, neither discipline has been inclined to "waste" precious faculty lines on what is viewed as a marginal specialization, especially at a time when many or most university programs face serious financial cuts. On the other hand, in the sciences, where external research dollars have been the name of the game for years, few departments are attracted by the penny-ante enterprises pieced together by Classical archaeologists.

Second, the situation is aggravated when archaeological scientists price themselves out of business by seeking wages for fieldwork commensurate with normal university-scale compensation. All of us are professionals and deserve to be well compensated for our research, but in the current system the plain and simple truth is that few of us *are* or *can* be. Most American Classical archaeologists donate their time to their projects; few are paid for summer research. Our students also generally work for free. And typically we anticipate that those who profit from research by enjoying their name on a by-line will not also profit financially from it.

Third, the successful integration of natural science and Classical archaeology in Greek regional studies has not been expedited by the institutional structure of American research in Greece. Kardulias has discussed in his contribution the so-called "foreign schools" and the role that they do and must play in Greek archaeology, according to the terms of Greek law: all American projects must be conducted under the auspices of the American School of Classical Studies at Athens. But the organization of the American School is often much misunderstood, even by the Greek press and public which have sometimes criticized it as an organ of the American government. The American School is, in fact, a private institution, governed by a council of delegates, who in turn are nominated by member institutions. Nearly all members of the council are from Classics departments and the majority are *not* archaeologists by training or persuasion; some, in fact, have little sympathy with any kind of archaeology, let alone that practiced by social scientists.

The natural scientific component of American archaeology in Greece developed only at the fringe of the school system until recently. It has only been within the past few years that the American School has established an archaeometric laboratory, despite the fact that a similar facility had been established just across the garden at the British School by the mid-70s (Waterhouse 1986). The development of American archaeological science in Greece continues to be discouraged by the extreme conservatism that the current organization of the American School fosters.

Most American archaeologists become members of the American School as graduate students. As members, they participate in the year-long academic program of the school, incorporating extensive travel, on-site seminars, and an archaeological field practicum. The program is authoritative and it ensures that those who complete it have gained a comprehensive knowledge of both the material culture and history of Greece. Unfortunately, however, full membership and most fellowship support for graduate students presupposes an extensive command of ancient Greek language and history--in short, a Classics, not a scientific, background. The system thus discriminates severely against those who are probably most in need of education in Greek history and archaeology, the fledgling archaeological scientists.

There are several structural changes that could greatly improve the way that American Classical archaeology is practiced, and could facilitate the development of regional studies in Greece:

(1) *Whenever possible, Classical archaeologists need to encourage Classicists to re-examine the logic behind their hiring practices.* In America, Classical archaeology is caught in a massive Catch-22: institutions produce and hire art historically oriented Classical archaeologists because they think the job market demands it. No doubt, well-rounded graduate programs in the Classics should furnish their students with a knowledge of Greek and Roman art. But regional studies experts should also be particularly attractive in a Classics environment--after all, Classics by definition is an area studies program. Studies of population dynamics, trade, and patterns of settlement provide a wonderful natural interface between Classical archaeology, ancient history, and ancient cultural studies in general. We need to work harder to convince our colleagues of this.

(2) *Classical archaeologists need to learn to write for multiple audiences*, not just for other Classical archaeologists or the general

public as they have traditionally done, but for a wider community of archaeologists. Greek archaeology has unique contributions to make to a world archaeology. A new Classical archaeology centered on studies of the sort included in this volume does much more than add whistles and bells to the old.

We control the data that is most relevant to the study of the first Paleolithic settlement of Europe (Runnels; van Andel, this volume) and to the origins of agriculture and its initial dispersion from the Near East (Runnels, this volume); we have a wealth of case studies at our disposal that can be used to study the meaning of ethnicity (see Rife and Giesen, this volume), in particular the relationship between human physiognomy and culture; and we have a great deal to say about relationships between specialized archaeological forms such as bath buildings and the rituals conducted in them (see Stys, this volume). The wealth of literary testimonia at our disposal also makes the Aegean an almost ideal setting in which to explore the material consequences of religious action, now that the study of bones by specialists has become routine (see Reese, this volume).

The prospect of the formation of a new alliance between regional archaeology and ethnography is also exciting. Several recent regional studies projects in Greece have chosen to view the modern landscape as one well-documented test case in a series of case studies at the archaeologist's disposal for testing general propositions about the nature of human behavior (e.g., Cherry et al. 1991; Wright et al. 1990). Ethnographers are themselves rupturing the constraints of traditional ethnographic analogies. Images of the tireless peasant (Shutes, this volume) in his "immutable" village are also being discarded (Sutton, this volume). It is not assumed that all agricultural strategies practiced in the past are still in use today (see Hansen, this volume). A particularly healthy sign is the emphasis that ethnographers are now placing on the study of agricultural production strategies and livestock management (Chang, this volume); these activities, of course, have material consequences and help to maintain a lively interface between archaeology and social anthropology.

(3) *Policies of the American School of Classical Studies need to be changed.* An explicit affirmative action program is needed that will encourage more diversity in the student body. Financial support needs to be found to allow non-Classics graduate students (anthropology majors and archaeological science majors) to participate in the regular program of the school (even if this means that a lower level of support is available for Classics students). As an institution that is legally

obligated by Greek law to represent American interests in Greece, the School needs to address its responsibility to the full range of interests and potential interests represented in sponsoring institutions, not just in Classics departments. The Director of the School and its Excavation and Survey Committee should actively solicit and encourage the submission of proposals for field research from archaeologists who are not from backgrounds in the Classics.

(4) *The division of funding for archaeological research between NEH and NSF should be stopped at once.* The traditional rationale for this practice--that Classical archaeologists have more ready access to alternate sources of funding--no longer outweighs the detrimental aspects of the practice. Very few programs in Classical archaeology possess substantial private endowments in support of archaeological research. The effect of federal policy is to inhibit innovation elsewhere and to discourage the development of new centers of excellence (perhaps with different missions) outside the old traditionally dominant institutions.

(5) *Our universities need to be reminded that Classical archaeology has a new face.* We, like our colleagues in anthropology, need infrastructure in America if we are to fulfill the great trust that has been placed in our hands--the publication and interpretation of a great chapter of the past. Without such support, the lasting reputation of a university program in archaeology cannot be assured.

Conclusion

In his introduction to this volume Kardulias speaks optimistically about the development of regional studies in Greece and I indeed share that confidence. In the mid-1990s, however, Classical archaeology in Greece stands at an important juncture. Regional studies formed a vanguard for anthropological archaeology in Greece during the 1970s and 1980s, and the publication of that research is at last beginning to have an effect on mainstream Classics. The course of action we choose to follow in this next decade will determine the nature of Greek archaeology for years to come.

References Cited

Alcock, S.E.
   1993 *Graecia Capta: The Landscapes of Roman Greece.* Cambridge University Press, Cambridge.

Athanassopoulos, E.F.
  1993 *Intensive Survey and Medieval Rural Settlement: The Case of Nemea.* Ph.D. dissertation, University of Pennsylvania, Philadelphia. University Microfilms, Ann Arbor.
Briggs, W.W., and W.M. Calder III
  1990 *Classical Scholarship: A Biographical Encyclopedia.* Garland Publishing, New York.
Boardman, J.
  1988 Classical Archaeology: Whence and Wither? *Antiquity* 62: 795-797.
Brown, S.
  1993 Feminist Research in Archaeology: What Does It Mean? Why Is It Taking So Long? In *Feminist Theory and the Classics*, edited by N.S. Sorkin Rabinowitz and A. Richlin, pp. 238-271. Routledge, New York.
Cherry, J.F.
  1992 Beazley in the Bronze Age? Reflections on Attribution Studies in Aegean Prehistory. In *EIKON. Aegean Bronze Age Iconography: Shaping a Methodology.* 4th International Aegean Conference, University of Tasmania, Hobart, 6-9 April 1992, edited by R. Laffineur and J.L. Crowley, pp. 123-144. Aegaeum 8. Annales d'archéologie égéenne de l'Université de Liège. Histoire de l'art et archéologie de la Grèce antique, Université de Liège, Liège, Belgium.
Cherry, J.F., J.L. Davis, and E. Mantzourani
  1991 *Landscape Archaeology as Long-Term History: Northern Keos in the Cycladic Islands.* UCLA Monumenta Archaeologica 16, UCLA Institute of Archaeology, Los Angeles.
Courbin, P.
  1988 *What Is Archaeology? An Essay on the Nature of Archaeological Research.* University of Chicago Press, Chicago.
Davis, J.L.
  1994 Report from the Committee on the Future of Old World Archaeology. Submitted to the Governing Board of the Archaeological Institute of America, May 1, 1994. Boston.
Deetz, J.
  1967 *Invitation to Archaeology.* The Natural History Press, Garden City, New York.
Dyson, S.L.
  1981 A Classical Archaeologist's Response to the New

Archaeology. *Bulletin of the American Schools of Oriental Research* 242:7-13.

1985 Two Paths to the Past: A Comparative Study of the Last Fifty Years of American Antiquity and the American Journal of Archaeology. *American Antiquity* 50:452-463.

1989 Complacency and Crisis in Late Twentieth Century Classical Archaeology. In *Classics: A Discipline and Profession in Crisis*, edited by P. Culham and L. Edmunds, pp. 211-220. University Press of America, Lanham, Maryland.

1993 From New to New Age Archaeology: Archaeological Theory and Classical Archaeology--A 1990s Perspective. *American Journal of Archaeology* 97:195-206.

Eliot, C.W.J.

1962 *Coastal Demes of Attika: A Study of the Policy of Kleisthenes.* University of Toronto Press, Toronto.

Fotiadis, M.

1994 Modernity and the Past-Still-Present: Politics of Time in the Birth of Regional Archaeological Projects, Greece, 1960s. *American Journal of Archaeology*, in press.

Gill, D.

1988 Expressions of Wealth: Greek Art and Society. *Antiquity* 62: 735-743.

Kosso, C.K.

1993 *Public Policy and Agricultural Practice: An Archaeological and Literary Study of Late Roman Greece.* Ph.D. dissertation, University of Illinois at Chicago, Chicago. University Microfilms, Ann Arbor.

Lullies, R., W. and Schiering

1988 *Archäologenbildnisse.* Von Zabern, Mainz.

McCredie, J.R.

1966 *Fortified Military Camps in Attica.* Hesperia Supplement 11. American School of Classical Studies at Athens, Princeton.

McDonald, W.A.

1985 Preface. In *Contributions to Aegean Archaeology : Studies in Honor of William A. McDonald*, edited by Nancy C. Wilkie and W.D.E. Coulson, pp. xiv-xvii. Center for Ancient Studies, University of Minnesota, Minneapolis.

1991 Archaeology in the 21st Century. *Antiquity* 65:829-839.

McDonald, W.A., and G.R. Rapp, Jr.

1972 *The Minnesota Messenia Expedition: Reconstructing a Bronze*

Age Regional Environment. University of Minnesota Press, Minneapolis.

Mattingly, D.J.
    1994 The Archaeology of Imperialism. *Antiquity* 68:162-165.

Morris, I.
    1994 Archaeologies of Greece. In *Ancient Histories and Modern Archaeologies*, edited by I. Morris, pp. 8-47. Cambridge University Press, Cambridge.

Office of Management and Budget
    1993 National Endowment for the Humanities. Division of Research Programs. Interpretive Research. Collaborative Projects. Archaeology Projects. Humanities, Science, and Technology. Guidelines and Application Forms.

Robertson, M.
    1963 *Between Archaeology and Art History: An Inaugural Lecture Delivered Before the University of Oxford on 15 November, 1962.* The Clarendon Press, Oxford.
    1992 *The Art of Vase-Painting in Classical Athens*. Cambridge University Press, Cambridge.

Rutter, J.B.
    1993 Review of Aegean Prehistory II: The Prepalatial Bronze Age of the Southern Greek Mainland. *American Journal of Archaeology* 97: 745-797.

Snodgrass, A.M.
    1985 The New Archaeology and the Classical Archaeologist. *American Journal of Archaeology* 89:31-37.
    1987 *An Archaeology of Greece*. University of California Press, Berkeley.

Snodgrass, A.M., and C. Chippindale
    1988 Introduction [to Special Section: Classical Matters]. *Antiquity* 62:724-725.

Traill, J.S.
    1986 *Demos and Trittys: Epigraphical and Topographical Studies in the Organization of Attica.* Athenians, Victoria College, Toronto.

Waterhouse, H.
    1986 *The British School at Athens: The First Hundred Years.* British School at Athens Supplementary Volume 19. Thames and Hudson, London.

Wiseman, J.
    1978 *The Land of the Ancient Corinthians*. Studies in Mediterranean

Archaeology 50. Paul Åströms Förlag, Göteborg.
Wright, J. C., J.F. Cherry, J.L. Davis, E. Mantzourani, S.B. Sutton, and R.F. Sutton
   1990 The Nemea Valley Archaeological Project: A Preliminary
   Report. *Hesperia* 59:579-659.

Index

About the Editor

P. Nick Kardulias received a B.A. in Anthropology and History from Youngstown State University, a M.A. in History from the same institution, a M.A. in Anthropology from the State University of New York at Binghamton, and a Ph.D. in Anthropology from The Ohio State University. He has participated in and directed archaeological and ethnoarchaeological field work in Ohio, Pennsylvania, Illinois, Greece, and Cyprus. With interests in lithic analysis, exchange systems, evolutionary theory, and world systems analysis, he has published articles and reviews in *American Antiquity, American Journal of Archaeology, Historical Archaeology, American Indian Culture and Research Journal, Current Anthropology, Journal of Archaeological Research, Journal of Field Archaeology, Journal of Anthropology, Midcontinental Journal of Archaeology, Ohio History, The Old Northwest*, and *Old World Archaeology Newsletter*. Currently he is Visiting Assistant Professor of Anthropology at Kenyon College in Gambier, Ohio.